Frontiers of Historical Imagination

Narrating the European Conquest of Native America, 1890–1990

Kerwin Lee Klein

UNIVERSITY OF CALIFORNIA PRESS

Berkeley / Los Angeles / London

University of California Press
Berkeley and Los Angeles, California

University of California Press
London, England

First Paperback Printing 1999

Portions of this book have been previously published in somewhat different form:

"In Search of Narrative Mastery: Postmodernism and the Peoples without History," *History and Theory* 34:4 (1995), pp. 275–298. © Wesleyan University.

"Reclaiming the 'F' Word, or Being and Becoming Postwestern," *Pacific Historical Review* 65:2 (May 1996), pp. 179–215.

Library of Congress Cataloging-in-Publication Data

Klein, Kerwin Lee, 1961–
    Frontiers of historical imagination : narrating the European conquest of native America, 1890–1990 / Kerwin Lee Klein.
        p.   cm.
    Based on the author's thesis.
    Includes bibliographical references and index.
    ISBN 0-520-22166-4 (pbk. : alk. paper)
        1. United States—Territorial expansion—Historiography.
    2. Frontier and pioneer life—United States—Historiography.
    3. West (U.S.)—Historiography.   4. Frontier thesis.   5. Indians, Treatment of—North America—Historiography.   6. Indians of North America—First contact with Europeans—Historiography.
    7. Historiography—United States—History—20th century.
    I. Title.
E179.5K53   1997
978'.03—dc21   96-35475

Printed in the United States of America

08   07   06   05   04   03   02   01   00   99
10   9   8   7   6   5   4   3   2   1

The paper used in this publication meets the minimum requirements of ANSI/NISO Z39.48-1992 (R 1997) (*Permanence of Paper*). ∞

Language is the archive of history.
—Ralph Waldo Emerson

Language is story.
—Leslie Silko

Contents

Preface

A few years ago I was trying to write a dissertation on the history of anthropology weaving the voices of Native American informants into an account of how interethnic conversations and conflicts had transformed American historical imagination. But as I did my research I found that even before facing the dangers of mixing scholarly and nonscholarly discourse, I needed a book that explained to me how different academic disciplines had defined history in modern America. Unfortunately, no one had written such a book, and so I kept pushing my "background" reading further and further. I told my adviser, Norris Hundley jr., that I needed a book discussing the changes in historical discourse in twentieth-century American philosophy, anthropology, and literary criticism. "Well," said Norris in his deceptively casual fashion, "why don't you write *that* book?" So I did, and here it is.

We can learn a lot about "History" by exploring its edges and mapping its contraries, complements, and cognates. More than one colleague has remarked that "intellectual western history" is an oxymoronic phrase, but frontiers and the West are logical starting points for a conceptual history of "History" in America, since the basic story of western history, the tale of Europe's occupation of Native America, has traditionally encoded a collision between historical and non-, anti-, or prehistorical peoples and places. This book wanders those boundaries, along with the rather different borders of "history" and "theory." History and theory are often imagined as antonyms, but we will interweave them. Forms of argument and forms of emplotment have histories of their own, and we will historicize theories as we theorize history and imaginatively reconstruct a series of conversations about the ways and means of history in modern America.

Since this study traverses a range of disciplinary traditions, I have combined close readings of key textual events with more summary sweeps of intellectual history. I have tried to avoid jargon and keep the notes under control. And I have dispensed with some of the conventions of postmodern scholarly writing. It has become fashionable of late to decorate one's prose with a host of disclaimers professing one's own special situation, the inevitable partiality of any narrative, and the solemn desire to avoid totalizing forms of discourse. Such caveats have served a vital function for historians coming to terms with postcolonial politics, but I fear that the fashion threatens to become an empty ritual. There is some danger that our new discursive modesty reproduces the less admirable scholarly tradition of hedging every argumentative bet. If I do not repeatedly wave flags at the reader ("We are being postmodern now"), it is not because I have reached the final summit of historiography. It is just that I think Mark Twain's famous introductory frame "I was young and ignorant . . . " suffices nicely.

I was young and ignorant when I began this work, and now I am somewhat older. If I am anything else, it is because of the amazing intellectual support and inspiration I have drawn from friends, acquaintances, and colleagues. Norris Hundley has certainly lived up to his legendary reputation as adviser and editor. Robert V. Hine, my undergraduate adviser, first convinced me that I could read both Jacques Derrida and Leslie Silko without leaving history behind, and he is still one of my most helpful readers and critics. The members of my dissertation committee, Melissa Meyer, Peter Reill, Paul Kroskrity, and Vincent Pecora, went far beyond the call of duty in their repeated readings. Stanley Holwitz has been all I could ever hope for in an editor. Although I have chosen to cite only published sources in this manuscript, I am grateful to Peter Blodgett and the staff of the Huntington Library for their assistance and for giving me access to the Frederick Jackson Turner papers. And Blake Allmendinger, Joyce Appleby, Stephen Aron, Robert F. Berkhofer Jr., Claudio Fogu, Dorothee Kocks, Heather Parker, Charles Romney, Doug Weiner, and Liz Westerfield have read and commented on significant portions of the manuscript.

I presented a part of this work at the American Dreams, Western Images conference hosted by the UCLA Center for Seventeenth- and Eighteenth-Century Studies and the William Andrews Clark Memorial

Library. Thanks go to the organizers and attendees. And some of the writing was funded by grants from the Pauley and Carey McWilliams Foundations at UCLA. Thanks to both.

William Wargo and Michelle Moravec deserve no end of praise for suffering so much of this project. Unfortunately, I am too poor to pay them, and so they will have to rest content with these prefatory thanks.

I owe special debts to Katie Streeter.

Kerwin Lee Klein
Los Angeles, 1996

Introduction

History, Narrative, West

The twentieth century has transfigured American historical imagination in dramatic but poorly understood ways. One of the most visible is the growing willingness to imagine America's past as tragic conflict. Once upon a time historians celebrated the making of democracy. Nowadays many imagine that democracy founded on a Native American holocaust. And a suspicion of historical knowledge has accompanied these diverging interpretations.

Can histories tell the truth about the past?

Such questions have proliferated in recent years, with "yeses," "no's," and "maybe's" ringing back in answer. Some of the more provocative responses have come from historiographers like Hayden White who have told us that since historians write narratives, and since no event is narrative in form, histories cannot correspond to their objects. One of the most resounding affirmations of historical knowledge has come from historians Joyce Appleby, Lynn Hunt, and Margaret Jacob, who believe that we may, although imperfectly, know that past which is the object of scholarly inquiry. Yet even they concede that "historical narratives are actually a literary form without any logical connection to the seamless flow of events that constitute living."[1]

We often imagine such disputes as conflicts over whether history can be "objective." Peter Novick's magisterial social history of the discipline, *That Noble Dream*, narrates a history of contention between those who believed history was an objective science and those who believed it was not.[2] But characterizing the difference between White and critics like Appleby, Hunt, and Jacob in "subjectivist" and "objectivist" terms is potentially confusing, since they all share a basic belief that narrative and figurative language are the weak links in historical knowledge. The antagonisms of "narrative" and "literary form," on the one hand, and "logical connection" and "events," on the other, stand on intellectual traditions that are almost immeasurably deep.

The unhappy dichotomy of narrative and knowledge has inspired a series of linguistic purges as historians try to cast out "soft" poetic and rhetorical forms. Some believe we have escaped the old-fashioned narrative history of Great Men, wars, and elections and now can write "analytic" or "structural" histories of culture and society. The more polemical accounts represent the new history as a higher intellectual pursuit and place it at the summit of a lengthy evolution out of narrative evil.[3] American history's creation tale, into which young historians are socialized, has institutionalized the suspicion of historical figures, and it goes something like this:

In the beginning the Romantic Historians told pretty stories but did not rise to empirical analysis. They were followed by the Scientific Historians, who professionalized history but remained too focused on political facts. The Progressive Historians turned attention to social conflict, although their deterministic rhetoric now looks dated. The Consensus Historians wrote intellectual histories whose quiescent narratives harmonized with conservative postwar politics. Finally, the analytic language of the New Social Historians (New Western Historians, etc.) restored conflict and commoners to their proper, privileged places.

One can tell a historian's political allegiances by where he or she places the narrative summit. Does "New Western History" represent the rise of the New Left heroes or does it threaten a hellish future of fragmentation and nihilism? Morals vary, but the basic story—a "march of science" narrative—dominates our professional image. As told by New Western historians like Patricia Limerick and Donald Worster, the story implies that we have advanced from the literary priestcraft of patriarchs like Frederick Jackson Turner to the rigorous scholarship of New Western History: History has (or will) heroically overcome its enslavement by metaphor and rhetoric. Since recent criticism demonstrates that literary forms remain a crucial part of historical discourse, the general plot has become suspect.[4]

Such march-of-science narratives can also reproduce some unhappy politics. Modern science has traditionally legitimated its often brilliant instrumental success by contrasting its factual and logical language with "other" figurative languages. It has associated "soft," "poetic" forms with savages (myths), women (old wives' tales), and children (fairy tales). Science has held out the objectification of a feminized nature as its ideal, and thinkers from Plato to Bacon have employed metaphors of rape and violence to describe rational inquiry. As Evelyn Fox Keller's *Reflections on Gender and Science* (1984) glossed current usage, "When we dub the objective sciences 'hard' as opposed to the softer (that is, more subjective) branches of knowledge, we implicitly invoke a sexual metaphor, in which 'hard' is of course masculine and 'soft' feminine. Quite generally, facts are 'hard,' feelings are 'soft.' " If we carry this basic insight into our discussion, we learn that here too androcentric language structures current debates. Historiographers have feminized figurative language to contrast it with more rational masculine forms. When a New Western historian like Donald Worster denounces the dominion of "myth," "romance," "dreams," "idealization," and "impulses" over the prose of older generations and contends that "detached observers" now use "cool, rational analysis" and "hard evidence" to become "masters of ideology" and let the "truth" come "breaking in," such old codes find new life. Ironically, many of those historians devoted to fighting oppression write their own historiographies in racialized and gendered languages. That such coding is usually tacit rather than intentional has not much weakened the common understanding that the measure of the discipline's maturity is the degree to which it has successfully mastered its effeminate metaphors.[5]

Even in more specialized corners of historiography, the antipathy of narration and knowledge has been affirmed and applauded, racialized and gendered, forgotten and revised. Critical philosophy of history has traditionally divided along specialty and topic. Analytic philosophers like Carl Hempel and Morton White have studied epistemological questions largely to the exclusion of other topics, and the preferred mode of epistemology in Anglo-American philosophy is the logic of "ordinary language" emptied of aesthetic and emotional baggage. Such analyses have had mixed results, but the literature has generally described an array of logically valid forms of historical explanation rather than a single algorithm of knowledge. Scholars approaching history from literary theory, Hayden White the most notorious, have focused on aesthetic forms: modes of emplotment, figures of speech, and so on. White and others have skillfully demonstrated that while historians often employ the apparatus of scientific discourse ("test," "findings," "generalization"), their monographs rely heavily on artistic conventions.

The division of critical labor into logical analysis and literary criticism echoes the common belief that scientific and imaginative or factual and figurative languages are essentially different. Since history has some claim to being "scientific," opposing facts and figures has severe consequences. If histories must be strictly logical to be scientific, then their reliance on narrative and metaphor deals a devastating blow to historical knowledge. As a result, the division of philosophy of history into logical analysis and literary criticism has led to varieties of skepticism. If all we have are "stories" about the past and if we cannot match them to any single "true" story, then we have no epistemic basis for judging one history superior to another. As White puts it, events are not "intrinsically" tragic or comic, so if one historian narrates a tragic account of the European occupation of Native America and another tells a happy story of the "same" events, then any choice between them depends on aesthetic and moral tastes rather than verifiable scientific knowledge. We might say that White sees a claim like "Europeans killed Indians" as a testable, factual statement. We need not doubt whether the "event" took place. But a claim like "The European killing of Indians was a tragedy" is not testable because it moves from a neutral observation language to a language of aesthetic and moral judgment. "Tragedy" carries us from simply observing a historical fact to opining about its value.

Historiographers like White have helped to persuade many historians that even structural histories cannot escape narration, but the old divorce of masculine fact and feminine figure continues to shape the ways we think about history. Even authors who do not tell march-of-science stories of our escape from Turnerian romance indulge in accounts of historical practice which radically separate sentences and stories. In 1987 James Axtell in "History as Imagination" told readers that all histories have a "story line that connects the value-free facts of the past into an intelligible pattern of meaning," adding that "since most historical sequences or collections of facts about past events can be 'emplotted' in a number of different ways so as to provide different interpretations, the historian makes an *aesthetic* choice based on the perceived fit between the facts as he [*sic*] knows them and a number of pre-coded plots." While Axtell seemed to believe that this conclusion affirmed the doctrine of free will, he did not explain how one might adjudicate competing aesthetic choices. In 1992 William Cronon's prize-winning essay "A Place for Stories: Nature, History, and Narrative" deployed the dichotomies of fact and figure to explain interpretive conflict in the nation's origin story. Emplotment, Cronon argued, goes "beyond nature into the intensely human world of values." Like White, Cronon believed that historians can verify individual descriptions, or "facts," but that we subsequently impose the "human artifice" of narrative onto those neutral observations: "Nature and the universe do not tell stories; we do." Aside from the unhappy implication that humans are not part of nature and the universe, Cronon's construction leaves the impression that "nature" and the "universe" *do* speak in observation sentences.[6]

Divorcing fact and figure, sentence and story, analysis and narration, will not help us to understand narrative traditions in historical discourse. As John Dewey told us years ago and as a host of works in the philosophy and history of science has shown, the old, hard-and-fast cleavages between neutral observation language (fact, sentence) and theoretical language (value, story) cannot be so simply upheld. As philosophers of science like to say, all observations are "theory-laden." So far as histories go, we might say that factual descriptions are always "narrative-laden" and that "aesthetic" and "moral" meanings color the most banal historical facts. In other words, the statement "Europeans killed Indians" is neither neutral nor purely descriptive but depends for its meaning on the reader interweaving it with lots of other words, sentences, and stories that, although they may not appear adjacent on the printed page, are necessary for the statement to be anything more than a mess of inky chicken scratches. Such a sentence is saturated with narrative long before any historian fits it into a monograph. And while even monographic narratives are emplotted much like novels and plays, so long as we share understandings of what sorts of situations count as tragic or comic, those patterns are also subject to our messy public practices of authentication. The process of reaching agreement on which narratives are plausible and which are not does not differ in kind from the process of reaching agreement on which statements of historical fact are plausible. There is no magical essence in story or metaphor that lifts either out of the realms of cognition and science.

Narratives are not something we choose or reject at will, nor are they linguistic artifacts we measure against a nonnarrative universe. Stories are what we live in, and in them we find both our worlds and our selves. We differentiate among them, we call some fairy tales and others true stories, and we tend to believe that our favorite tale is the one everyone else should adopt. But we do this from within narrative traditions we can interweave with others but never entirely escape. As our traditions change, so do our histories; as our histories change, so do our worlds;

as our worlds change, so do our traditions. Saying that we live inside narrative traditions is not the same thing as saying that any story is as good as another. It does not mean that we cannot make good instrumental arguments for favoring some histories over others—we do this every day. It *does* mean that we ought to accept the ultimate contingency of those arguments. Such an acceptance is crucial in a pluralist democratic society, for it should encourage us to take seriously the radically different histories of others. It makes real conversation possible. Adopting this attitude means, to use one of Richard Rorty's well-turned phrases, that an inquiry into historical knowledge can only be a "sociohistorical account of how various people have tried to reach agreement on what to believe."[7]

Frontiers of Historical Imagination traces a critical genealogy of the narrative traditions through which historians, philosophers, anthropologists, and literary critics have understood the European occupation of Native America, and it explores how those understandings shaped and were shaped by changing conceptions of history. Either topic could justify a monograph, but each illuminates the other. Historical imagination is typically embodied in some study, attitude, or topic, and while philosophies of history abstract from concrete subjects, like American history, this critical process is parasitic on specific histories. Specific histories, in contrast, often seem independent of what theorists have to say about them, but each specific history presupposes or projects a philosophy of history, however sophisticated or naive. So I will interweave these themes, using philosophy of history to understand histories, histories to understand conceptions of history.

A brief glance at earlier beginnings will help to frame our topic. Frontier history has often been called the history of the American West, and "West" has a history all its own. As Loren Baritz has shown, from Virgil to Thoreau, the West has been a region of truth, beauty, and hope toward which Hellenic (later European) cultures should move. "Western Civilization" and "The West" remain key words of popular and scholarly discourse, and as Edward Said's *Orientalism* (1978) demonstrated, "West" has historically defined itself through exclusion. West is always west *of* something. Traditionally, the "Orient" has defined all that the West is not, giving it an alterego, a sort of absent content that determines the semantic paths "West" can follow.[8]

In his *Lectures on the Philosophy of World History* (1822–1830) Georg W. F. Hegel declared that history had rolled from East to West in great dialectical waves of consciousness and the story of that journey was a story of liberation. The ancient East, he said, knew only that one is free. The Greeks and Romans knew that some are free. Modern Europe knows that all are free. His telling reconciled secular and divine meanings for history and gave it form, content, and purpose. Its form was written history. Its content was the ethical relations embodied in the modern state. And its purpose was the self-realization of spirit. History thus belonged to certain peoples but not to others. The indigenous inhabitants of the Americas and Africa were peoples without history lost to a "voiceless past." Today we think of Hegel as a reactionary metaphysician. And we often imagine Europe's devastation of other cultures and places as a thoroughly tragic affair. We believe we have escaped Hegel, but his collision between people with and without history still structures public memory.[9]

The American West was once the frontier space where migrating European cultures collided with Native America. In the West the historic civilizations of the Old World met the nonhistorical wilds of the New. Today, many New Western historians try to limit the word "West" to the geographic region west of the Mississippi River Valley. In both uses of the word, though, Americans have imagined the West to have a special relation to American history. West, even as a particular arid region of the United States, always also harks back to "The West" as a cultural tradition from ancient Greece to modern Europe. And since Americans have frequently claimed for themselves a privileged place in the course of history, the West is crucial to understanding history in the abstract. The frontier was not just the place where civilization and wilderness made American democracy, it was the ragged edge of history itself, where historical and nonhistorical defied and defined each other. That historical metaphysics still shapes our pasts and futures. We remain obscurely entangled in philosophies of history we no longer profess, and the very idea of "America" balances on history's shifting frontiers.

Our story divides into four books.

Book One: The Language of History. Modernist philosophy and history tried to rationalize language, and we will begin our journey by tracing the efforts of historians and philosophers to escape myth, metaphor, and emotion. Attempts to formalize historical explanations (in this instance, Frederick Jackson Turner's thesis that frontier expansion created American democracy) will lead us into disputes over the ways and means of scientific method. Philosophy's move away from historicism toward the logic of hard science was part of a larger change in form and focus popularized as the "Linguistic Turn." An increasing number of philosophers followed the lead of logicians like Rudolf Carnap, proponent of what came to be known as logical positivism. The new "analytic" philosophy imagined itself as a metascience devoted to delineating the underlying grounds of truth claims made by all scientific disciplines. Analytic philosophy of history forsook old questions about the meaning of history in favor of searching out the timeless logical order of historical discourse. By the 1950s it looked as if the scientific elements of histories were precisely those which were *not* historical. Histories explained only as far as they constructed testable propositions cast as timeless or predictive formulae, as in a "frontier thesis" or "Turner hypothesis." But the project of rationalizing historical discourse did not work out so well as many had hoped, and scholars like Thomas Kuhn eventually described even hard science as messier, more artistic—more historical—than theorists had imagined, and the problems of science and history again converged.

While scholars failed to codify historical explanation, they estranged the languages of science and poesy, and the analytic turns paved the way for more radical linguistic turns deriving from continental hermeneutics, structural linguistics, and a congeries of trends collectively known as poststructuralism. So the postmodern rediscovery of the poetic aspects of historical discourse unleashed dire warnings of relativism *and* inspired calls for the transformation or even abolition of historical imagination. For many thinkers the new turns cast suspicion on the very idea of history. History under any logical description was a final vestige of faith in God's divine plan.

Book Two: From Spirit to System. We can deepen our understanding of these shifts by studying the frontier thesis as part of changing narrative traditions. Turner emplotted the European occupation of Native America as the building of a modern democracy from wild nature. He grounded his project in nineteenth-century idealism and saw the frontier dialectic as part of a cosmic drama of the developing self-consciousness of humanity. In America that universal history manifested itself in a Dantean comedy in which conflicting forces lifted each other up into higher pluralistic resolutions, rejuvenating an evolving democracy along the way. Writers, readers, and researchers institutionalized simple versions of this story, and by 1930 this narrative dominated American history as no other tale ever has. A competing tradition built itself on darker readings as intellectuals like John Dewey blamed many of the nation's social ills on frontier excess. But both traditions focused on a dramatic conflict of nature and history and imagined the story's hero as white, middle class, and male. This dramatic code deflected attention from interethnic conflict by imagining the defining American moment as an encounter with pristine nature rather than a collision of cultural worlds. For decades stories centered on wilderness and civilization predominated in textbooks, although new scientistic vocabularies gradually replaced Victorian poetics.

While Turner sought to transfigure folk memory into historical consciousness, Dewey's more rigorous historicism speaks to our current debates. Unlike most period philosophers, he did not break language or experience into aesthetic, epistemic, and moral splinters but sought a pragmatic philosophy of history that we may adapt for our own purposes. As he saw it, even the most "neutral" empirical descriptions were always embedded in some larger story and aimed at some particular problem or end that shaped their possible meanings. His telling of frontier history exemplified his narrativist conception of history and countered the upbeat Turnerian tellings. By midcentury, though, Turnerian and Deweyan historicisms had been scientized, as we will see, in the work of Merle Curti, a historian who saw himself as intellectual heir to both men. Curti's frontier history epitomized the analytic turns even as it carried forward the notion that American democracy was a product of American wilderness. Much as analytic philosophers abjured metaphysics, Curti and his peers believed that social scientists should recant the fuzzy ideology of story and metaphor which had burdened the work of their predecessors.

Book Three: Time Immemorial. Meanwhile, across the quad, anthropologists were telling different tales. While Turner had stressed the creative power of wild nature, he had acknowledged the part played by Native America. Victorian ethnographers told a grand story of social evolution which described Native Americans as representatives of an earlier stage of human experience through which Europeans had already passed. For a time such accounts harmonized with those told by historians like Turner. But by the 1920s anthropologists like Franz Boas had installed "culture" as the organizing concept of their discipline, and that one word broke American history into halves. Describing the encounter of European and Native American as a conflict between incommensurable cultures opened up a national memory divided by ethnicity and plot: however happy history may have been for white Americans, for the natives it was ruthlessly tragic. Tragedy dominated anthropology for the first half of the twentieth century, and when in the 1950s the new specialty of "ethnohistory" emerged, its practitioners commonly incorporated the ethnographic tragedy into their own works. By the 1960s even nearsighted scientists could see that Native Americans had not disappeared. Driven partly by American Indian scholars like Vine Deloria Jr., a new story emerged in which Native American cultures heroically survived and even overcame Euro-American oppression. In today's cultural studies, metaphors of holocaust, democracy, history, and culture circulate side by side.

Ethnographic tragedy also enabled more radical turns. By the late 1920s the culture concept tended to be cast in language that was at best ahistorical. Some works, Ruth Benedict's *Patterns of Culture* (1934) one of the most important, went even further and associated history with European experience and rejected it in favor of alternative modes of discourse. Benedict held out Nietzschean mythopoesis as an alternative to historical consciousness. For many other anthropologists the ahistorical vocabularies of functionalism and structuralism offered more "scientific" languages. In anthropology history looked like an antiquarian devotion to the dead hand of the past. "History may lead to anything," said the famous structuralist Claude Lévi-Strauss in his *The Savage Mind* (1962), "so long as you get out of it." Despite their antipathies, the mythopoesy of Benedict and the scientism of Lévi-Strauss shared both a suspicion of history and a romantic enthusiasm for radically "other," nonmodern, non-Western ways of being. In the end, the culture concept threatened to dispense with history altogether.

Book Four: Histories of Language. In the second half of the twentieth century American historians drifted away from the frontier narrative, but literary critics in American Studies found it central to American culture. Scholars like Perry Miller and Henry Nash Smith declared the nation's relation with nature the key to its sense of selfhood. Many felt the popular belief in a mythic frontier past encouraged political oppression at home and overseas. Again scholars contended that America suffered from narrative traditions saturated with emotion and poesy, and they proposed to replace those mythologies with rational analysis. Some assailed the working language of American studies and argued that the bad old ethno- and androcentric myths were still alive and well in modern literary criticism. Critics like Smith found themselves pressed hard by arguments that if the new analytical languages were to be taken seriously, the traditional justifications for studying high literature were just so much mysticism. At the same time students of race and gender attacked the supposition that works written mostly by Anglo males about other works written mostly by Anglo males could represent some larger "culture" that subsumed the experience of others.

Ironically, while a scholar like Merle Curti saw scientism and democracy as natural allies, in American studies the various crusades to divest language of metaphysics also undermined the search for an American mind or culture. Competing empirical accounts of American experience suggested that it could be subdivided almost infinitely. This discovery accompanied a growing awareness that the rationalization of language had failed to produce its ideal object, the single language of human cognition. From this combination of events two strangely interwoven developments have emerged. In one a flood of "new historicisms" stress the historicity of all discourse, including the sort of literature that had long been thought of as timeless. But a second development has turned away from historicism altogether as some literary scholars follow other social scientists to identify historical imagination with theology and metaphysics. While many applaud the return of history to literary and ethnographic criticism, that return is bound up with antihistorical linguistic traditions.

There are at least two readings of our story. One reading is a happy tale about history's escape from constricted horizons into more open dialogue. Turner saw his own work as a heroic attempt to broaden history to include the common man, the white male frontiersman absent from the Great Man histories that he had grown up reading. A few decades later Walter Prescott Webb contended that the true subalterns were those white middle-class males who lived in the "real" west beyond the hundredth meridian. But even this effort left Euro-American women, Native Americans, Chicanos and Chicanas, African-Americans—all the "others"—outside of the heroic horizon. By the sixties the Turnerian custom of placing new subaltern heroes at the center of the story had produced a widening array of tales and morals. Today we rightly tell happy Whiggish stories of how we have improved our conversation to include voices Hegel and Turner could not hear. Turnerian social history, the interest in local documents, the reconstruction of the everyday lives of common people from statistical data, and the culture concept have all expanded our horizons. Our new histories have unmasked previously hidden forms of oppression, now measured by race, class, gender, sexual orientation, and even species. We celebrate new subaltern heroes, and this is, it seems to me, a happy development. Read this way, our tale is a Dantean comedy of the progress of understanding. It is a narrative of liberation.

But there is a very different reading. Here the story is an unhappy one. We have abandoned much that was good in older historical traditions. We have lost our willingness to tell the big story and to see history as literary and moral event. We have enlarged our circle, but we have also committed ourselves to a depressingly fragmented and hyperspecialized world. What remains is existential arithmetic and visions of division, categories, and counting as ends in themselves. We have given ourselves over to a darkly bureaucratic existence, and the mark of our despair is our willingness to imagine even oppression as a calculus. The Turnerian custom of cheering for the underdog threatens to devolve into subaltern one-upmanship: My hero is more subaltern than yours; my hero suffers from two oppressions rather than one, or three oppressions rather than two; we have multiple, finite heroes and oppressions that can only be joined arithmetically. Read this way, the tale is a tragic narrative of decline, of the fragmentation of understanding. It is a narrative of enslavement.

The twist is that we must tell both stories, for each calls forth the other. There is a Turnerian connection between Emerson's cry for a poem of America that could transpose our barbarous folk symbols into an allegory of democracy, and our current valorization of our new histories as politically correct literary forms. There is a complex affinity between the democratization and the bureaucratization of American history. The analytic turns of our century have opened a world in which we can imagine history as many broadening circles of experience, but they have also given us a world in which history seems to be something we can cast off at will. But these tales have written us, as we have written them, and so we cannot simply willfully replace science with literature or irony with metaphor or comedy with tragedy or democracy with holocaust. We are all these equations, this is what dialogue is, and we will find our new selves—as our precursors found theirs—in these shifting frontiers.

BOOK ONE

The Language of History

What Was the Frontier Thesis?

The tale has been told so many times that it has been ritualized into one of the origin stories of American history: In 1893 Frederick Jackson Turner stood before the annual meeting of the American Historical Association to read a brief essay, "The Significance of the Frontier in American History," and articulated a set of ideas that reshaped historiography. Euro-America's frontier expansion into "free land" explained the development of American democracy. This claim, later called the Turner or frontier hypothesis, placed Turner at the center of his profession, made the West a respectable field of study, and described the European and Euro-American occupation of North America as the central topic in United States history. Historiographers differ on whether Turner's early success enriched or impoverished the discipline, but most see it as a crucial event in the evolution of historical scholarship from Victorian belles lettres into a modern, state-certified social science. For decades Turnerian history dominated the profession as no other field ever has. And Turner's "frontier thesis" became a testing ground for attempts to formalize historical discourse.[1]

Frederick Jackson Turner introduced a new vocabulary into history by using old words in new ways, borrowing terms from other disciplines, and mixing these elements with familiar themes and idioms. His eclecticism is legendary, and researchers have traced his notes, musings, and marginalia back to unlikely origins. Some of his disciples devoted lifetimes to determining what the master intended. But most historians took a more pragmatic view. Even before his death in 1932, the primary questions arising from the frontier thesis focused not on what Turner intended it to mean but on how it might be understood. Did the frontier thesis have anything useful to offer historical understanding? And was it true?[2]

If we wish to isolate a "frontier thesis," we might begin with the very first paragraph of the 1893 essay.

In a recent bulletin of the superintendent of the census for 1890 appear these significant words: "Up to and including 1880 the country had a frontier of settlement, but at the present the unsettled area has been so broken into by isolated bodies of settlement that there can hardly be said to be a frontier line. In the discussion of its extent, its westward movement, etc., it cannot, therefore, any longer have a place in the census reports." This brief official statement marks the closing of a great historic movement. Up to our own day American history has been in a large degree the history of the colonization of the Great West. The existence of an area of free land, its continuous recession, and the advance of American settlement westward explain American development.

The proposition most often identified as the frontier hypothesis appears in the last sentence: "The existence of an area of free land, its continuous recession, and the advance of American settlement westward explain American development." The sentence contains neither "frontier" nor "hypothesis," but many historians liked the label. The essay opened with the United States census bulletin's description of the disappearance of the "frontier line," and the connotations of "hypothesis" pointed toward the sort of empirical inquiry that scholars imagined themselves doing: testing hypothetical explanations of past phenomena.[3]

Turner's thesis describes an effect in need of explanation (American development) and a cause (the frontier). Before connecting cause and effect, we need to define them. The quote from the census report describes the frontier line as a dividing boundary. On one side of the line (Euro-American) population density measures two or more persons per square mile; on the other side it falls below that figure. This measurement anticipates the "advance of settlement westward" into "free land," defining both free land and settlement in terms of population densities while describing the frontier as the place where the two converge. But the essay layers other meanings onto this one. Only a few paragraphs after the introduction, still another side of "frontier" comes into view: "The frontier," said Turner, is "the meeting point of savagery and civilization." One sentence later he returned again to the question:

What is the frontier? It is not the European frontier—a fortified boundary running through dense populations. The most significant thing about it is that it lies at the hither edge of free land. In the census reports it is treated as the margin of that settlement which has a density of two or more to the square mile. The term is an elastic one, and for our purpose does not need sharp definition. We shall consider the whole frontier belt, including the Indian country and the outer margin of the "settled area" of the census reports.[4]

Less than halfway through the piece, semantics threaten to careen out of control. The opposition of "savagery" and "civilization" alone deserves (and has received) entire monographs. In 1893 the terms were current in sociology, economics, and anthropology as "value-neutral" labels referring to specific stages of social evolution. The meeting point of savagery and civilization suggested not just an intersection of Euro-American and Native American societies but the convergence of two cleanly differentiated chunks of history, a face-to-face encounter, in the present, of the past and future of humankind. But the relation of savagery and civilization to free land and settlement is not a simple analogy. Savagism may align with the free-land side of the frontier line or it may take in that area where Euro-American settlers mingle with the wilderness, including Euro-Americans as well as Indians.

The insistence on uniquely American meanings also stands out: the American frontier "is *not* the European frontier." Turner later revised this sentence: "The American frontier is sharply distinguished from the European frontier—a fortified boundary running through dense populations. The most significant thing about the American frontier is that it lies at the hither edge of free land." And for an 1894 entry in *Johnson's Universal Cyclopedia,* he reworked the statement yet again: "In the U.S. the frontier is not a fortified boundary-line separating populous states, but by common usage implies the outskirts of civilization, the regions but partially reclaimed from savagery by the pioneer. In the reports of the U.S. census the frontier-line has been defined as the inland line limiting the area which has an average, county by county, of two or more inhabitants to the square mile." Free and settled, savage and civilized blur noticeably in these lines, but parallel constructions distinguish American and European usage, contrasting the dense population and fortified landscapes of Europe with the free lands of America awaiting reclamation.[5]

Despite Turner's professed disinterest in precise definition, few historians have spent so much energy and ink on a single term. By the time his first book, *The Frontier in American History,* anthologized his essays in 1920, meanings and synonyms for "frontier" had multiplied remarkably. The frontier was "the West," "the hither edge of free land," "the line of the most effective and rapid Americanization," "the graphic line which records the expanding energies of the people behind it," "a migrating region," "the mere edge of settlement," "the belt of territory occupied" by frontiersmen, and "a form of society rather than an area." In letters and conversations Turner professed his interest in "the movement of population into unsettled geographic provinces." And in a major professional address he qualified his earlier implication that any single force could explain American development. "In truth," said Turner in advocacy of multiple causation, "there is no single key to American history. In history, as in science, we are learning that a complex result is the outcome of the interplay of many forces." This may suggest causes *in addition to* the frontier, but given the sweep of Turner's usage, we could easily read the frontier *as* an "interplay of many forces," subsuming a multiplicity of causal agents.[6]

The repeated appeal to the United States Bureau of the Census offered a handle for historians to grab. The census definition (the convergence of regions with fewer than two and with two or more persons per square mile) opens the essay, just ahead of "free" and "settled" lands, keeping those terms temporarily anchored. If no other authority could guarantee the exchange value of the historian's language, the federal government presumably could. If Turner used frontier in highly elastic ways, the Census Bureau had fixed, as only bureaucracies can, its own specific meaning for the term, and historians all over the world could explore that tremendous resource with some reasonable expectation that their raw data, if not their conclusions, would correspond to those of their colleagues. And although Turner's frontier could not be reduced to this single definition, by welding the concept to a specific and standardized body of research materials he contributed a great deal to the viability of the frontier thesis in the academic jungle.

Though historians eager to dive into the archives might roughly agree on the meaning of "free" and "settled" land, "American development" posed its own problems. Again, Turner supplied a grocery list of items that might be hung on the phrase, but most interpreters fastened on those sections of his essay subtitled "Growth of Democracy" and "Intellectual Traits." The first begins with this important paragraph.

But the most important effect of the frontier has been the promotion of democracy here and in Europe. As has been pointed out, the frontier is productive of individualism. Complex society is precipitated by the wilderness into a kind of primitive organization based on the family. The tendency is anti-social. It produces antipathy to control, and particularly to any direct control. . . . The frontier individualism has from the beginning promoted democracy.[7]

Development means democracy. And democracy evolves out of individualism based on the family unit. The frontier reduces complex European society to its primitive constituent elements, the family unit associated with a particular individual, the frontiersman. American society gradually integrates these units into a more complex aggregate, but the whole, democracy, retains those primitivist traditions of antipathy to direct control which prevent egalitarian America from reproducing autocratic Europe.

Turner's construction nonetheless leaves democracy indefinite. The section "Intellectual Traits" provides another much-quoted passage describing the sort of frontier traits that produced a specifically American democracy.

The result is that to the frontier the American intellect owes its striking characteristics. That coarseness and strength combined with acuteness and inquisitiveness, that practical inventive turn of mind, quick to find expedients, that masterful grasp of material things, lacking in the artistic but powerful to effect great ends, that restless, nervous energy, that dominant individualism, working for good and for evil, and withal that buoyancy and exuberance which comes with freedom, these are the traits of the frontier, or traits called out elsewhere because of the existence of the frontier.[8]

If all of these various frontier traits are components of American democracy, then American development is very complex indeed. Encompassing place, process, population, and period, the frontier and democracy sweep through the past holding in combination a mixture of warring elements: migration and colonization, town building and warfare, competitive individualism and cooperative community.

If historians took these two keywords, Turner's cause and effect, and placed them in columns with just a few of their component parts, the resulting chart would look like this:

frontier	*democracy*
free land/settlement	individualism
savagery/civilization	practicality
margin of civilization	coarseness
political border	egalitarianism
community building	economic mobility

Even this cursory list gives at least twenty-five different possible causal equations as we mix and match particular causes, in the left-hand column, with effects from the right-hand column. Since readers might extend either column to much greater length and since we have not yet added in the connotations of these words, the complexity of combination is clearly staggering. Add verb phrases to connect the columns (explains, causes, contributes to, produces, evolves into, and so on) and the proposition becomes chaotic indeed.

Even if historians legislated one specific label for each term, one specific verb phrase, and one set of connotations for each part of the equation, we still cannot ensure that all readers understand the resulting sentence in exactly the same way. We can make this point with one of Turner's most explicit claims: "The frontier was responsible for the development of democracy." Compare these different formulations:

> The *frontier* was responsible for the development of democracy in America.

> The frontier was responsible for the *development* of democracy in America.

> The frontier was responsible for the development of *democracy* in America.

> The frontier was responsible for the development of democracy in *America*.

This critic's parlor trick suggests some of the challenges posed by what initially looks like a reasonably straightforward historical proposition. Since we might similarly treat any series of sentences or even any connotations that do not appear on the printed page, possible readings proliferate.

We ought to resist the inclination to blame Turner or his terms and reflect instead on the general problem. What words could bear comparable scrutiny? How might historians, working in what philosophers call ordinary language rather than mathematical logics designed for specific uses, keep meanings from rocketing off in unwanted directions? Of course, one might concede the impossibility of fixing meaning by scholarly fiat and still believe that Turner made things worse by voluntarily bringing so many uses into a single place—it is bad enough that meanings will pile up uninvited, but why go out of your way to tempt fate?

Jumping ahead a bit, we might carve out an intellectual clearing by pointing to yet another word, what philosopher W. H. Walsh has called colligation. Colligatory concepts, as described by Walsh in his lucid *Introduction to the Philosophy of History* (1951), draw together seemingly disparate processes, ideas, and items under a single "appropriate conception." "Frontier," like other colligatory terms (Enlightenment, romanticism, reform), synthesizes a variety of elements into an overarching unity. Walsh argued that colligation extends beyond simple classification to a form of historical explanation, a way of making particulars intelligible as parts of some coherent whole. And like romanticism or Enlightenment, the American frontier subsumes those things which a historian might reasonably persuade his or her audience are intrinsically related. So this is part of what historians do: They generate new ways of describing past experience, and one of the ways in which they do this is through colligation.[9]

Turner attracted both criticism and acclaim for his particular spin on this language game. With the hindsight of a century, the critic may immediately note the ethnocentrism of Turner's prose, since numerous indigenous peoples occupied the "free lands" of North America. In 1962 ethnohistorian Jack D. Forbes declared that Turner had erred in distinguishing the American frontier from the European frontier: "In its narrowest and most non-ambiguous usage then, frontier refers to a boundary or border region—a place where two groups confront each other." By Forbes's definition frontier describes an interethnic or international situation, and Turner's smooth conflation of Indian and Hispano peoples with wilderness and free lands effectively legitimated Euro-American imperialism. And in the late 1980s Patricia Limerick began campaigning to have the word erased entirely from the vocabulary of working historians. "Frontier," said Limerick in her important study *Legacy of Conquest: The Unbroken Past of the American West* (1987), "is an unsubtle concept in a subtle world."[10]

In 1966 intellectual historian John T. Juricek charted the genealogy of the contested term. He traced it back to medieval Latin and then forward through several centuries of semantic change. Frontier apparently worked its way into Western Europe as a term for the outer militarized border region of a single political entity. By the nineteenth century, European frontiers usually referred to a political boundary between two or more nation-states. Fifty years before Turner's essays appeared in print, American usage basically conformed to that in Europe: "Until about the mid-nineteenth century most Americans would have agreed that the United States, like the English colonies before it, did not border on emptiness in the West. Rather, like European nations, it bordered on other countries—Indian countries." In Juricek's telling, after the war between the United States and Mexico, the Kansas-Nebraska Act of 1854, and the Gold Rush, it became impossible to describe a single, clear, north-south boundary separating Indian country from American territory. In 1882 the Census Bureau more or less arbitrarily fixed a line of Euro-American population density "beyond which the country must be considered as unsettled." By the end of the century frontier had cycled back to its original conception as the outer border of a geographic area occupied by a single political entity, albeit with a multitude of new connotations. Much of what was new came from Turner's stylistic innovations, particularly those which emphasized the distinctively American nature of the frontier, such as westward movement, community building, and "free" land.[11]

Juricek did not hazard a guess as to how much of this linguistic history Turner knew, but he ventured this assessment: "Turner achieved a sudden dominance over the writing of American history largely because no one perceived how new and original his ideas actually were." Turner reworked historical language into a form that harmonized well with the tacit beliefs of his readers, notably their faith in American exceptionalism. The frontier thesis brought together into one place the disparate qualities and processes that Euro-Americans felt to be unique about the United States. But if Turner's colligation exemplifies the way that historians create concepts by drawing together "intrinsically related" objects under a single term, this nevertheless postpones rather than resolves our difficulties. "Intrinsic" and "relations" are no more transparent or reliable than democracy or frontier, and we will have to return to these issues again and again. For the moment, however, Walsh's word magic provides us with a useful way of beginning. And Turner's refiguration of historical language, for all its vagaries and ethnocentrism, remains quite stunning in its breadth and originality.[12]

Few could accuse the 1893 essay of incompleteness. From a definitive proposition Turner chased his terms and claims through four centuries, restating, redefining, and reframing his lexicon first from one perspective and then another, suggesting source materials (Census Bureau data and the local archives of the West), an overarching research topic (the frontier), and a periodization (the four-hundred-year frontier era of American history). What more could a historian offer the profession? Not much, according to the most enthusiastic of Turner devotees. These at first were few, and it took a decade for the frontier thesis to work its way into the mainstream of professional and public consciousness. Enthusiasts included his former professor Woodrow Wilson and sometime western historian Theodore Roosevelt, and it certainly helps, as many have observed, to have a couple of presidents in your corner if you hope to take the country by storm. But when searching for crucial factors in the rise of Turnerian history, we might more reasonably invoke the breadth of the frontier thesis, its ideological resonance with the nation's middle classes, and the importance of a unifying problematic for an academic discipline interested in upward intellectual mobility. And rise it did.[13]

By 1932 the frontier thesis dominated synthetic understandings of the American past. Looking back, in "A Generation of the Frontier Hypothesis" in 1933, Frederic Paxson observed: "As rapidly as the frontier hypothesis was recognized it was accepted. Its author was acclaimed as prophet and lawgiver. . . . It is almost without precedent that a fundamental new philosophy should be substituted for an old one, or for none at all, without resistance." Paxson, author of the first book-length synthesis of frontier history, left little doubt that in 1933 he himself found Turner's vision still valid, but he nonetheless recognized that the profession had adopted Turner's claims with a good deal of haste and almost no critical testing of the notion: "The appraiser of the Turner hypothesis finds little help in print. There has been little convincing cross-examination of any of its major points."[14]

In Turner's lifetime comparatively few critiques of the hypothesis appeared in print and those few offered little systematic analysis. One common complaint echoed Paxson's remarks: Turnerians had adopted the hypothesis as gospel without putting it to the empirical test. A second critique assailed the notion that any single causal force could explain American development. In Charles Beard's words, the "agrarian thesis" was "inadequate" to explain the course of American history. A third, and perhaps the most inventive criticism, accepted the importance of the frontier while inverting Turner's optimism. The frontier did explain American development, and the nation was bigoted, selfishly individualistic, and backward-looking. For John Dewey the legacy of the frontier was narrow-mindedness, anti-intellectualism, and intolerance; for John Almack the entire notion was a "hangover from Puritanism." (It is significant that these commentators did not note what now appears so blatant—Turner's ethnocentrism.) This critique slid vaguely into a fourth, an implication that the frontier thesis was a conservative myth obscuring historical reality. Charles Beard suspected that the overweening emphasis on East-West conflict hid more important divisions in American society, blinding historians and their readers to the conflict between "the capitalist and organized labor. . . . On this point our orthodox historians are silent. The tabu is almost perfect. The American Historical Association officially is as regular as Louis XVI's court scribes." (This was the harshest note printed before Turner's death.) But most critics raced through their critiques en route to introducing alternative causes, with immigration, urbanization, class conflict, and slavery being the most notable.

When we look back, these early attacks appear both limited and suggestive. The limits are strategic ones, as these efforts devoted relatively little time and space to analytic criticism. But the dissenters' preference for advancing explanations of their own should tell us something about both historical practice and the respect that Turner personally commanded within the discipline, since advancing a competing theory usually appears less confrontational than directly trashing someone else's position. These criticisms also largely prefigure the themes of years to come, and although questions and assaults began to accumulate during the depression era, they filled out rather than expanded these five general approaches. So keeping our story line in view, we need to jump ahead to the 1940s, a decade in which submerged assumptions about historical language and practice surfaced with a vengeance.[15]

Histories and Hypotheses

Yale historian George W. Pierson gives us a focal point for looking at serious efforts to formalize and test Turner's claims. In two articles, "The Frontier and the Frontiersmen of Turner's Essays" (1940) and "The Frontier and American Institutions: A Criticism of the Turner Theory" (1942), he advanced the most systematic critique of the Turnerians thus far. Turner's statements were provincial, "emotional," and "positively illogical," riddled with "confusion" and "contradiction" and grounded on the "vaguest of poetic concepts." Pierson keyed on "frontier," chasing, as we did above, through Turner's endlessly radiating circles of associations. Colligation, had Pierson known the word, held no attraction for the social scientist. He offered a lengthy account of the failings of the frontier explanation.

To a people noted for their materialism, their romantic sentiment, their cultural timorousness, and their isolationist patriotism, he offered the epic and soothing legend of the Great "Frontier." . . . [H]e was inclined to exploit a whole congeries of explanations, shifting the burden of proof as circumstances seemed to warrant. . . . [H]e intruded into his definition of "frontier"—and so into his whole hypothesis—certain moral or social meanings.

... [T]he word "frontier" has been, and will be found again, a Pandora's box of trouble to historians. . . .

To alchemy, symbolism, poetics, emotion, nationalism, romance, epic, myth, and legend, Pierson applied the acid of logic. Not only was the frontier a vague, poetic notion but its effects, individualism and democracy, looked equally vaporous. "In the first place," said Pierson, "let it be observed that Turner nowhere defines his two master words. Accordingly, each reader is forced to make his own translation." The failure led to interpretive anarchy, and confusion would be ended only if some enterprising scientist cast ambiguous terms into a semantic "cyclotron."[16]

Despite complaints that Turner failed to offer precise definitions, the problem is really the opposite: Turner advanced altogether too many. Pierson's view suggests that in order to produce commensurable results, scientists need to speak the same language, measure the same phenomena. Their terms must be standardized, not idiosyncratic. Historical propositions must impose a single meaning on all readers rather than fostering a state of interpretive anarchy where each reader is free to make his or her own translation. It is significant that the only Turnerian usage for which Pierson demonstrated any sympathy was the Census Bureau's numerical denotation. Frontier, democracy, and individualism seem susceptible to multiple readings, and this, for Pierson, explained both their logical inadequacy and their attractiveness to the profession. The concepts fairly dripped with nationalism and emotionalism, appealing to the base instincts of historians, to affect and not intellect, to hearts and not heads.

In 1941 Pierson surveyed his colleagues' opinions of both Turnerian frontier history and its challengers. He sent questionnaires (a favorite tool of period social science) to more than two hundred leading academics; more than half responded, and most of these included established scholars. The questionnaire had three parts: "The Contents of the Hypothesis"; "Attacks on the Frontier Hypothesis"; and "Defense." Each of these parts was then subdivided. The first section asked, "What was the frontier and what were its results?" Here Pierson offered respondents eighteen frontiers and eight results, allowing multiple responses as well as written comments. In the second section, "Attacks," readers chose from among nineteen specific criticisms. And in the third section, "Defense," the questionnaire offered twelve different responses as to why Turner's critics might be "misguided." The bottom line for most readers was whether historians still regarded the hypothesis as true. The tally suggested they did: "The champions and believers still clearly outnumber the critics . . . [and] a pronounced majority seem a long way from abandoning certain central propositions." Nonetheless, Pierson warned, written comments and ambiguous votes suggested that despite the superficial consensus the guild was far from united: "In large part, no doubt, because of our lack of an authoritative frontier canon, disputes outnumber agreements, and American historians seem to be scattered throughout a whole series of ideological positions."[17]

Pierson believed that "emotional prejudice" and semantic confusion stood between historians and a dispassionate reappraisal of the hypothesis. He lamented the impossibility of discussion on a "purely disinterested, theoretical level; rather, reference is sooner or later (and usually sooner) made to the master. And the result is heat. Minds tend to close, opinions to harden." Despite the professionalization of the discipline, personal loyalties still held sway over rational inquiry, and scholarly community depended as much on affective emotional bonds as on shared scientific practices. A related difficulty was that "many of us are reluctant to define what the frontier theory was." Indeed, the most popular criticisms revealed by the survey were that the frontier explanation was too simple and the term too vague. On the one hand, many historians believed with Pierson that no single causal force could explain American development, and therefore the frontier thesis was simplistic. But, paradoxically, many also felt that a significant problem with the frontier was that it subsumed a multiplicity of causal forces, and therefore the frontier thesis was too complex. There seemed little hope of fixing definitions through electoral solidarity, for votes on the content of the term "frontier" spread out through all eighteen possible categories, and Pierson noted that even this list could be extended.[18]

Even more intriguing was the uneasiness with the very idea of a hypothesis or theory. Although three out of four respondents believed that there was some recognizable frontier theory that could be "discussed, argued, *and voted on* in detail," doubts crept in. Some mistrusted the survey format, one anonymous scholar saying, "I don't much like this type of jury investigation. It's a good deal like trying to establish the validity of a scientific finding by a vote of Congress." And Pierson noted that a sizable number of respondents, mostly Turner defenders, "go to the point of questioning whether there is, or ever was, a hypothesis in the first place." To his dismay, many Turnerians actually defended the poetic elements of the essays, describing the thesis as an interpretive device rather than a theory. Said one, "There has been much talk of a more or less loose nature about the 'Turner theory' or the 'Turner hypothesis.' Frankly, I do not believe that there is any such thing." Others declared the "real Turner" absent from the questionnaire and invoked the importance of his seminars as well as his writings. Pierson sighed that "the reader will begin to understand why it is that fifty years after its formulation historians are still not agreed on either the contents or the validity of the celebrated frontier interpretation. Feelings have been too personal and too warm; the hypothesis has been too vaguely and too variously understood; theorizing and logical analysis have alike been deprecated in our profession." Summarizing the results, Pierson concluded that "we seem to be discovering that we know less than we had supposed about historical causation."[19]

Now our story opens onto broader questions about historical practice. What is a historical "hypothesis"? Most early twentieth-century methods texts did not even ask this question. Most did not index the term or discuss hypothesis construction and testing. Most followed the traditional, vulgar Baconian format outlined in Charles V. Langlois and Charles Seignobos, *Introduction to the Study of History*, which became available in English translation in 1898. In this view historians compiled a bibliography on a general subject, certified the authenticity of their archival sources, subjected them to various critical methods for determining what in them was factual, and then allowed the facts to form patterns that the historian simply reported. This was the style of the German school of "Scientific History," as popularized in the United States by Turner's mentor, Herbert Baxter Adams. For strict traditionalists "hypotheses" were to be avoided like the plague, since they generated prejudices and expectations that could bias the historian's interpretation of the bare facts.[20]

More sophisticated notions of scientific method gradually drifted into the mainstream of the history profession. Anyone familiar with the way that physical scientists worked in 1900 understood the importance of hypotheses. But historiographers seemed unsure of how hypotheses worked. Homer Hockett's *Introduction to Research in American History* (1931) was the first popular methods text to address this topic. Hockett suggested that hypotheses were "tentative conclusions" derived from a preliminary investigation of evidence which then are tested and reformulated as research progresses. The formulation agrees with George Pierson's usage. But Hockett surfaced in Pierson's survey as a defender of Turnerian history, arguing that critics should "allow for overstatements and understatements" and recognize a "deep

harmony" that Turner sensed but "never worked out in a formal statement." If a hypothesis is simply a set of tentative, preliminary conclusions, then any number of sentences from Turner's 1893 essay could be
read as hypotheses, but Hockett and many others refused to reduce the
Turner thesis to a single "formal statement."[21]

If historians could not find a careful treatment of "hypothesis" in
methods texts, they might have turned to the Social Science Research
Council, an interdisciplinary group bringing together noted humanists
and social scientists. In 1946 the SSRC's committee on historiography
published the bulletin *Theory and Practice in Historical Study*. Merle
Curti, a Turner student, described one of the committee's baseline assumptions: "Advances in any given field of knowledge are made by devising hypotheses for further appraisal, exploration, testing, correction,
and generalization." But the chapter on precision in historical terminology, by historian Charles Beard and philosopher Sidney Hook, does
not include "hypothesis" in its glossary. To find the word in use, we
need to read chapter 1, "Controlling Assumptions in American Historiography," where authors John Herman Randall and George Haines
used the term enthusiastically and often. They called Turner's frontier
proposition a "hypothesis," a "heuristic principle," a "functional principle," a "principle of selection," and a "central theme." Indeed, in their
view Turner was "clear upon the role of interpretive hypotheses in historical investigation" and revolutionized history by daring "to advance
explicitly not only a new principle of selection, but also a full-fledged
hypothesis to guide the investigation and interpretation of historical
facts. . . . For those who grasped Turner the battle was over. Principles
of interpretation were fruitful, and they were most fruitful when related
to continuing problems." The significance of Turner's thesis lay not in
its content, its deep harmony with an intuitively sensed past, but in its
carefully fashioned and innovative formal statement.[22]

A more obscure work from the same period, the *Guide to Historical
Method* (1946) by Gilbert J. Garraghan, S.J., and Jean Delanglez, S.J.,
offers a brief but suggestive discussion. This text distinguishes two
types of hypothesis: "the *explanatory*, the purpose of which is to account for a phenomenon, to ascertain its cause or causes; and the *descriptive*, which aims to supply a framework for the orderly grouping
and presentation of data." But is the frontier hypothesis explanatory or
descriptive? Claiming that the interaction of free land and settlement
explains American development would seem, as Pierson argues, to class
the thesis as explanatory. But Garraghan and Delanglez's gloss of de-

scriptive hypothesis ("a framework or center of reference for scattered data, thereby giving them a coherence and a meaning which otherwise they would not possess") also strikes a familiar chord with readers of the 1893 essay (while also perhaps reminding us of Walsh's colligatory concepts), and although these authors included the frontier thesis as an example of a historical hypothesis, they did not say whether it was descriptive or explanatory.[23]

To illustrate these different understandings, we can compare and contrast the distinctive views of two scholars who agreed that the frontier thesis was a genuine hypothesis while disagreeing on what that meant. Paxson, in his 1933 essay, claimed that Turner

offered a new hypothesis to a group of colleagues who, as a whole, had generally been content to deal with facts as facts. He induced them to shift from the work of the antiquarian or pamphleteer, and to seek, if not for "Law in History," at least for evidence that would tend to make plausible the connection of cause and consequence. Historical causation, in general, cannot be proved. What we can most often do is to indicate a degree of probability. . . . His hypothesis is now a generation old. It has not been proved and cannot be.

In this view hypotheses serve as "frameworks" or "matrices" for otherwise insignificant and isolated facts. They are interpretive devices rather than verifiable propositions. Their causal connections might be demonstrated plausible or even probable but never definitively proven. Paxson did not spell out what alternative criteria might be used to evaluate hypotheses, but the essay suggests that his own judgment rested simply on efficacy: How useful a device is the frontier thesis? Compare this with George Pierson's contention that "the fact that the hypothesis has been widely accepted, has exercised great influence, and has not yet been upset, seems to most of us (as undoubtedly it would have seemed to Turner) quite insufficient proof of its validity." Here a hypothesis is a preliminary step toward a true explanatory statement about the past. Historians should generate propositions so logical and transparent that they can be conclusively verified or disproven by empirical test.[24]

Hypotheses in history are proving as elusive as Turner's frontier, the semantics of historical method as incorrigible as those of the 1893 essay. If representing the past is problematic, representing historical practice poses its own problems. May we abstract a frontier hypothesis from Turner's work? Three out of four respondents in 1941 said yes. Is there then some general agreement on what the term hypothesis means? Apparently not. We cannot blame discord on the deficiencies of Turner's vocabulary or the zeal of his supporters. At issue were (and still are) poorly articulated but divergent methods and aims. Hypothesis, at least in the usage of midcentury American historians, seems to have been one of Walsh's colligatory terms. And the situation is going to get worse before it gets better, for right at this point the historians' debate shades into another more technical argument over scientific explanation that winds its way through philosophical journals and monographs. To our two understandings of hypothesis—as a preliminary step toward true theories or as an interpretive strategy for limiting empirical scope—we will have to add yet a third, the description of hypotheses as "falsifiable" rather than verifiable propositions.

Empiricists from Francis Bacon to George W. Pierson have held that scientists gather data and then arrive at generalizations inductively by drawing inferences from those data. Science progresses by replacing provisional hypotheses with "true," verified, theories. The philosopher of science Karl Popper believed this view mistaken. Declaring that the "problem always comes first," he argued that empiricists reversed the real order of scientific inquiry. To collect or even define data, one has to have some problem or hypothesis already in view. The whole point is to formulate a problem, specify some hypothetical proposition, and then attempt to *falsify* it. Hypotheses thus never lose their hypothetical nature but remain forever tentative and provisional. Furthermore, the entire process follows a series of deductive (rather than inductive) logical steps. The first step begins with a general law. The second step specifies a particular case in which the scientist is interested. From these two premises, general law and specific case, the scientist *deduces* a conclusion. Scientists advance and then attempt to falsify hypothetical causal explanations, devising, revising, and discarding, but never arriving at any verifiable resting place. The best one can hope for is a hypothesis that doggedly resists efforts to prove it false.[25]

What Popper's account meant for history was not immediately clear. Even if physicists worked in this way, did historians already follow such deductive procedures? And if not, should they? Popper's 1935 book, *The Logic of Scientific Discovery,* did not appear in English until 1959, and these questions work their way into our story via logical positivist Carl G. Hempel's 1942 article "The Function of General Laws in History." Despite its unglamorous numbered paragraphs and obscure illustrations, the piece opened a dynamic conversation in the philosophy of history and the social sciences that continued for more than two decades. Debate over historical method and theory, hitherto scattered across a variety of journals, disciplines, and topics, suddenly converged on Hempel's account of explanation.[26]

Hempel claimed a central place in historical practice for Popper's notion of falsification and declared that "general laws have quite analogous functions in history and the natural sciences." His "unity of method" thesis holds that scientific historical research replicates or at least approximates the method described by Popper. Since most period historians did not publish their accounts as syllogisms, the argument required some development. In Hempel's view historians do rely on deductive arguments, although these might not surface in the text. Instead, they remain unconscious steps in hypothesis construction. Since the laws involved are typically part of everyday commonsense assumptions about the way human behavior works "they are tacitly taken for granted." And these tacit assumptions may be so far buried beneath the historian's terms ("hence," "consequently," "because") that the philosopher must reconstruct them via an elaborate textual analysis. Since historians seldom explicitly articulate their explanations, Hempel suggested that they most frequently offer "explanation sketches" relying on "probability hypotheses" rather than general "deterministic" laws. Thus the qualifier: General laws have *analogous* but not necessarily identical functions in natural and human sciences. Hempel did not, however, deny that historians might eventually arrive at genuine explanations. If not yet a true science, history was at least a protoscience bound by the same logical rules as physics or chemistry. Under the label "covering law model," this notion worked its way into scholarly conversation.[27]

Covering law theorists faced the indifference and hostility of most historians. Although in 1954 the SSRC committee on historiography published a bulletin calling for the construction of falsifiable hypotheses and followed this in 1962 with still another report on generalization in history, historians were even less united on this front than on Turnerian history.[28] The works of Popper, Hempel, and other analytic philosophers filled out the bibliographies of the methods texts and bulletins, but they almost never appeared in the actual essays written by historians. As one philosopher remarked, the 1962 SSRC bulletin contained only one index entry for Popper and none for Hempel, and the entire work held but one passing reference to the philosophers' debate. Volume editor Louis Gottschalk noted that "the historian willy-nilly uses generalizations at different levels and of different kinds." But if, as Pierson said and methods texts demonstrate, historians knew less about causation than they liked to admit, the philosophers' abstract exchanges did not seem very helpful. Sensitive to such complaints, Carl Hempel searched various historical monographs for illustrations, and in a 1962 article he examined Turner's seminal essay.[29]

In Hempel's close readings the logician played literary critic, burrowing under surface syntax, working backward from explicit conclusions to particular conditions, and finally uncovering the "tacit" universal law. His reading of Turner examined three different passages, including that which draws the consequences of the frontier process for American culture.

Examining the various consequences of this moving-frontier history, Turner states that "the most important effect of the frontier has been in the promotion of democracy here and in Europe," and he begins his elaboration of this theme with the remark that "the frontier is productive of individualism. . . . This tendency is anti-social. It produces antipathy to control, and particularly to any direct control"; and this is, of course, a sociological generalization in a nutshell.

Turner's thesis originates with a presupposed but unstated universal law: Frontiers produce individualism and antipathy to social control, and individualism and antipathy to social control promote democracy. The thesis then moves to a specific case: America had a frontier. From these initial conditions, or cause, the historian deduces a prognosis or effect: America became democratic. The frontier metaphor hides a syllogism, and the analytic philosopher deciphered a rational scientific method in even Turner's poetic prose.[30]

Hempel's conclusions layer another understanding of hypothesis onto our discussion, giving us at least four imaginable theoretical views of Turnerian history.

1. There is no frontier hypothesis. It is impossible to abstract a single, testable, formal statement or hypothesis from the whole of Turner's work.

2. There is a frontier hypothesis, but it is only a useful heuristic for understanding the past and cannot be definitively proved or disproved.

3. There is a frontier hypothesis, but the goal of historical practice is verification, and the Turner hypothesis must be proved true or else abandoned.

4. There is a frontier hypothesis, but it is a generalization that can never be proved but only falsified.

Once we add to this list the semantic possibilities of "frontier" and "democracy," potential readings of Turner multiply exponentially. Little wonder that George Pierson suspected Turnerian consensus.[31]

Explaining History

The covering law model did not sweep historians off their theoretical feet. Although it seemed increasingly unlikely that such propositions as the frontier hypothesis could be definitively verified, falsification did not colonize methods texts. The analytic tastes of the philosophers did find some influence in the "New Economic History," which in the 1960s began to adopt the cliometric models and computerized data analysis of mainstream economics, but few social or intellectual historians embraced Hempel's vision. This reluctance partly reflected ignorance. Few historians subscribed to the *Journal of Philosophy*, and even fewer had any significant expertise in propositional calculus. But even if they had, the readings produced by the covering law theorists tended to be wildly uncompelling. No one could point to any useful general historical laws. Hempel's own analyses seemed unlikely to persuade an audience of historians. His reading of Turner, although imaginative, elegant, and economical, tells us little because historians did not claim that the frontier was a generalizable concept. Both Beard and Pierson had observed that other countries with frontiers did not enjoy democracy, and as we have seen (and as Hempel would have discovered had he read the 1893 essay more carefully), Turner observed that other places and times had experienced frontiers, but "in the case of the United States, we have a different phenomenon." Did this falsify the frontier hypothesis or disqualify it as an explanation-sketch? At least one reader, Morton White, thought not, and he attempted to develop a more credible account of the logic of history.[32]

White, professor of philosophy at Harvard and author of several important intellectual histories, brought an impressive breadth of experience to the discussion in 1965 with his *Foundations of Historical Knowledge*. He found Hempel's understanding of covering laws simplistic. In fact, historians frequently and justifiably advance explanatory statements which imply the existence of some law but which do not, even unconsciously, assert covering laws of the sort Hempel demanded. Hempel's readings, argued White, usually produce implausible laws precisely because of the *complexity* of explanation. He noted that "simple-minded" covering law theorists attack Turner's thesis by observing that many notoriously undemocratic countries have had frontiers. But Turner and the other historians who have been criticized in like fashion "must have realized that the generalizations underlying their singular causal statements were more complex" than those suggested by Hempel. "They must have realized, for example, that the presence of the frontier is not in general a sufficient condition for the rise of democracy and held, rather, that the presence of a frontier along with other features of American life at the time constituted such a sufficient condition even though [they] did not mention these other features in their singular causal statements." Since covering laws are so complex, historians do not completely and explicitly articulate them but instead *infer* that such laws exist and support their explanations.[33]

According to White, the key to historical explanation is not regularity, as when Hempel's model suggests that democracy regularly follows the development of a frontier, but uniqueness or "abnormalism." When explaining events, historians seize on unusual or abnormal factors as causal agents: "We try to explain a given train wreck because trains are not usually wrecked. . . . And given the fact that a train wreck is unusual, we can see at once, it is argued, why the fact cited as the cause cannot be a normal or usual feature of the operation of trains or of some particular train." White did not use Turner to illustrate this argument, but if he had, the result might have looked like this. Given that the appearance of democracy in eighteenth-century America is an unusual event and given the uniqueness of American democracy vis-à-vis democracy elsewhere, we have a historical abnormality, an effect or consequence that invites causal explanation. In Turner's view the abnormal antecedent of this intriguing effect was the American frontier, something distinguished from other frontiers by its mobility and free lands. And the general law relating cause to effect is quite complex: Frontiers of a certain type, in the presence of other conditions, produce democracy; America had a frontier and the additional conditions of the required sort; therefore, America became democratic.[34]

By the time White finished his analysis of how historians construct causal chains, the problem looked depressingly difficult. Once one has chosen an effect for explanation, such as American democracy, one has to settle on a cause. Historians look for some unusual antecedent. Turner selected the frontier, which appeared prior to and then overlapped the development of democracy. The problem is that we have no algorithm for determining whether the frontier or some other cause should be viewed as the *true* abnormal cause of American democracy. Other historians might emphasize different possible causes in place at the same time, perhaps the English common law tradition, or the emergence of American capitalism, or the ideological tendencies of European immigrants. Difficulties mount when we realize that the historian may push a causal chain further into the past. Why stop with the North American frontier as the cause of American democracy? What caused that frontier? One could as easily propose European geographic expansionism, or mercantilism, or even the ideological climate of the Renaissance as the cause of North American frontiers and hence democracy. And the historian could regress still further, to the European agricultural surpluses of the fifteenth century, or the compact theory of government, or into the depths to some unmoved First Mover—Genesis or the Big Bang. The selection of a particular causal chain and the decision as to where to break in and begin a historical account depend on the perspective of the individual historian.

How would one then test Turner's thesis? How does one justify a causal explanation?

White hedged his answers to such questions. As he saw it, historians make warranted factual statements. To integrate these factual statements into causal explanations they rely on very complex laws. But to justify selecting one particular cause, one sequence of factual statements rather than another, requires an appeal to extrahistorical factors:

In short, what the historian regards as the abnormal antecedent, and hence as the cause, may depend on the manner in which he looks at the subject under investigation. . . . [B]ut there is no "criterion" that I know of for deciding that one point of view reveals *the true* cause. Moreover, there does not even seem to be a point of view which is *normally* taken by historians when the facts, so to speak, present them with a choice of view. And historical language is in this respect like the ordinary man's language. Within history one finds the same possibility of variety as one finds in ordinary language.

Here values edge into historical discourse. Deciding which cause is decisive, which event deserves explanation, and which facts are relevant requires decisions by the historian which cannot be found in some logical rulebook.[35]

At least one reviewer, philosopher Rudolph H. Weingartner, found White's view distressingly relativistic. By admitting individual judgment into scholarship, White threatened to reduce historical knowledge to historical opinion. Knowledge, said Weingartner, is a public matter, and although tastes for certain kinds of history may be culturally conditioned and different scientific theories may produce different causal claims, these are social variables and not the idiosyncrasies of individuals. Values do enter into the construction of histories, but not primarily in the selection of abnormal causes. The historian's interests determine "not the *answer* he gives to a question, but the *question* he asks in the first place." The selection of a cause depends on the historical problem one hopes to address, and this in turn depends on the way in which the historian conceives his or her central subject. The real level at which contingency enters the construction of history is individuation, the creation of a historical subject (the frontier, American development) about which one may ask questions or make claims.[36]

In other words, the problem is not simply how will the historian relate two distinct terms, such as predemocratic America and democratic America, but how does the historian distinguish them in the first place? How does the historian single out individual items from the booming, buzzing confusion of sense data? The way in which he or she defines predemocratic and democratic America determines the ways in which they can be connected. Switching metaphors, we might say that the historian confronts not a chain or even chains made of individual links but a torrent of muddy water. Weingartner believed that Morton White had oversimplified by implying that the past offers itself up in chain-link-shaped chunks and the individual historian's task is to decide which pieces go together. The situation is both better and worse than this. It is worse because the historian has to *create* rather than simply discover pieces or links or objects. But it is better in that the decisions about how to do this are not a matter of free individual choice but are conditioned by the tradition and theoretical framework in which the historian works.

The first reservation, that contingency enters history in the way that historians constitute their subjects, takes us back to Turner's vocabulary and W. H. Walsh's notion of colligation. George Pierson's intuition that in order to make causal explanations one first had to define cause and effect was quite sound. It is not, however, quite strong enough as it stands. To create a subject such as American development or the frontier is to draw a series of events into relation or at least prefigure the sort of relations that can be drawn. Definition is not an incidental step prior to causal analysis; it is part of it. As Morris Cohen observed in 1946 (albeit in service of a different thesis), "The task of identifying the connections between an event and its causes is not essentially different from the task of identifying the event in the first place. . . . The problem of causation is thus merely an aspect of the wider problem of individuation."[37]

The second reservation, about "subjectivism," applies less to the work of Morton White than to the entire genre of analytic philosophy of history. White brought social factors into his account by pointing out that historical explanations require reference to *custom:* "It should be noticed that because custom may lead us to call some laws explanatory and others not, we need to know the way in which custom works— in other words, why it dignifies some laws by calling them explanatory. Moreover, if it is custom that decides, custom may decide differently in different cultures." This conclusion may admit a certain relativism, but it does not look much like anarchy. We can understand Weingartner's anxiety, though, if we note that White, like most analytic philosophers, focused on individual items, whether texts, sentences, or historians. The sentences in history monographs thus look like a result of arbitrary decisions by individual authors. But we are not likely to learn much about custom by focusing on a single individual, let alone a single sentence. So the constraints of method undercut White's interest in social process. And the dynamics of historical communities created additional difficulties. Although White spoke of custom's constraints on decision making (one may not fabricate any cause one likes), as he observed, the norms of historical practice are quite plastic. Not only are there no *universal* laws for privileging some cause or sequence of facts over another, historical practice lacks even a consistent *normative* rule for such judgments.[38]

If the analytic philosopher's love of individual propositions did not look like the fast track to understanding how and why custom blessed certain explanations and rejected others, the attempts of historians to describe the process did not look much more convincing. More than twenty years after George Pierson and the Social Science Research Council called for careful discussion of historical method, the ways and means of historians still looked chaotic. One of the great books in American historiography, Richard Hofstadter's *The Progressive Historians: Turner, Beard, Parrington* (1968), illustrated the confusion. Hofstadter enjoyed the benefit of two decades of methodological debate by historians and philosophers, and he spent a lot of time rubbing elbows with such famous sociologists as Seymour Lipset and Daniel Bell. He had also been an early critic of the frontier thesis. In articles and books he had denounced Turnerian history as an agrarian mythology and described the frontier as a source of parochial chauvinism. A leading intellectual historian, he seemed ideally positioned to bring together all the voices that had hitherto talked past one another. But in *The Progressive Historians* Turner emerged as the most important historian of his age and Hofstadter declared the frontier thesis to have an indisputable "core of merit." He concluded that "among all the historians of the United States it was Turner alone of whom we can now say with certainty that he opened a controversy that was large enough to command the attention of his peers for four generations." Describing the Turnerian legacy in these generally favorable terms, though, did not keep Hofstadter from offering his own criticisms.[39]

Hofstadter described Turner's work as schizophrenic. On one side lie the romantic metaphors denounced by the critics. On the other lie sociological statements based on fact. Turnerian criticism thus becomes a "fine exercise in discrimination," discarding poetic form while retaining analytic content. Although Hofstadter recognized the historical climate that produced Turner's belletristic prose, he deplored the master's footloose figures. The central problem remained the term "frontier," where romance overwhelmed reason. Of Turner's use of the Census Bureau's definition, he remarked that this "stroke of hyperclarity only underscores the general confusion." Warding off charges of nitpicking, Hofstadter assured readers that intellectual rigor demanded rigorous language, quoting literary critic Henry Nash Smith: "Turner's metaphors threaten to become themselves a means of cognition and to supplant discursive reasoning." Of course, one must not veer too far in the other direction and slide into naive positivism. The trick is to strike a reasonable balance. Said Hofstadter in summary judgment, "History is neither philosophy nor science, but it is rational discourse that has to proceed in accordance with certain rules." What those rules might be, what a rulebook of rational historical discourse might look like, how discursive reasoning without metaphors might proceed, Hofstadter did not explain. But he doubted that historians would ever agree on any single causal force as dominant in the American past.[40]

Historical explanation remained murky. Although denying that history might be a science, Hofstadter insisted on reworking Turner's formulations into a rational, rule-ordered discourse. But if history cannot be a science, how does one justify such attempts to delimit historical language? And if a rational, rule-ordered discourse is not a science, what is? And if historians cannot construct testable explanations, singling out decisive causal forces, why submit Turner's hyperbole to the tender mercies of rationalistic discursive rules (whatever they might be)?

These and other questions occurred to one of the book's reviewers, Morton White. The philosopher lauded its biographical reconstruction but questioned its theoretical rigor and imprecise language: "The question that any student of Beard and Turner must face is that of analyzing what they meant, or could have meant, by saying that economics or the frontier was central or decisive. On this question Hofstadter is not very helpful." Hofstadter in fact declared such questions to be matters of opinion so contested that historians could never resolve them. But if this is true, said White, then all of Hofstadter's demythologizing and brave talk of rational discourse goes out the window.

If Hofstadter cannot weigh the importance of one contributing factor as against another, on what ground can he say that the Turner factor or the Beard factor is *not* central or, for that matter, that anything is not central? That historians should not be able to arrive at a "final consensus" on which factor is central is not surprising, but that they should not have any clear conception of centrality seems to me depressing so long as they keep making assertions about what is or is not central.

White agreed that singling out causes ultimately rests on social values, but he condemned Hofstadter's inconsistency. Hofstadter first asserted that we cannot assess the truth of causal explanations and then declared Turner's thesis, in its original poetic form, untrue. And after conceding the impossibility of consensual evaluations of competing causal claims, he labeled history a rationalistic discourse governed by (unspecified) rules. If Morton White's *Foundations of Historical Knowledge* left unresolved the question of how to judge one explanation better than another, Hofstadter questioned the possibility of making any causal explanations whatever. Almost three-quarters of a century after Turner formulated it, the "frontier problem" remained unresolved, testimony to the intractability of the question of historical explanation.[41]

Systems and Paradigms

By the time Hofstadter wrote his landmark book, the philosophers' debate over historical explanation had stretched along a continuum with clearly defined poles.[42] At one extreme stood the hard-core devotees of Hempel's covering law model. A bit farther along stood Morton White and other defenders of a modified covering law theory. At the other extreme Hempel's hard-core critics invoked idealist philosopher R. G. Collingwood, whose posthumously published work *The Idea of History* (1946) argued that the historian's task is the reenactment of past experience, that one explains past events by imagining oneself into the mind-sets of historical actors. It was in this context that W. H. Walsh produced his account of colligation. William H. Dray, one of Walsh's students, reworked the accounts of Collingwood and Walsh in order to address the covering law theorists head-on.[43] In Dray's view historians produced explanations by imagining, reconstructing, and describing the reasons historical agents had for acting in a certain way. When answering such questions as "Why was Louis XIV unpopular?" or "How could it be that Louis XIV was unpopular?" historians sought to re-create the circumstances, emotions, and rationale of those individuals responsible for making poor Louis a social pariah. This "rationalist" account (Dray called it "libertarian") appealed to those uncomfortable with the deterministic implications of Hempel's model, which depicted individuals as atoms at the mercy of the inexorable processes of nature.

Unfortunately, theory lagged behind practice. We have seen the difficulties the covering law model ran into when faced with actual histories, and the salvage efforts did not look promising. Dray, in contrast, assumed that histories recounted past events whose central characters were rational human actors, whether kings, queens, or criminals. But by the late 1950s the rise of social or structural history had produced subjects like "the Mediterranean" and "Feudalism" rather than individual persons. The Annales historians, from Lucien Febvre to Fernand Braudel in France, and many of Turner's students in the United States, dealt with topics not amenable to rationalist explanations. Some of these historians categorically denied any interest in the mainstays of traditional history: individuals, events, and narratives.[44] Like their counterparts in sociology, economics, and anthropology, they spoke less of mechanical causation of the sort where cause A mechanically and clearly produces effect B and more of the "functional relations" of different parts—variables, functions, inputs, outputs, structures—of integrated social systems. History thus undermined both poles of the philosopher's debate. Turning away from individuals and toward social structure, it did not always appeal to rational agency. And by invoking systems whose components were reciprocally or functionally, rather than mechanically, related, history eased away from the sort of connections that had interested such philosophers as Morton White.[45]

In the early 1970s Murray G. Murphey declared the philosophers out of touch with contemporary historical scholarship. He believed that recent developments in the social sciences could help historians avoid the limitations of both the strict covering law and rationalist theories. The chief problem with the covering law model was that no one had located any historical laws true for all times and places. As a result, the imaginative reconstructions by philosophers produced laws so "general as to be trivial or so specific as to admit but one case." In *Our Knowledge of the Historical Past* (1973) Murphey claimed to solve this problem by substituting probability equations for universal laws. Such "causes" as the frontier were associated with such "effects" as American development by correlations that could be quantitatively measured. If historical laws did not predictably apply in all places and times, one might at least say that some relations were empirically stronger than others.[46]

At the same time, Murphey avoided Dray's dependence on the intentions of individuals by discussing culture and social structure. Bringing his knowledge of contemporary social science into play, he argued that many cultural customs were so systematic or "law-like" that they could serve as the objects of historical explanations. Individuals were not the free, autonomous, rational actors of classical liberalism but the products of social forces, conditioned by the roles, structures, institutions, and expectations of the societies they inhabited. Insofar as societies were systematically organized, their features might be reconstructed and measured by the social sciences, history included.

Customary patterns are often sufficiently strong to yield very high levels of probability and they are, therefore, particularly good examples of law-like social patterns. Where the sort of structural supports which enforce custom are lacking, regularities in behavior are often much less marked. The literature of the social sciences is filled with findings of "significant" relations among variables, meaning associations too strong to be due to chance only, but that yield quite low probabilities of prediction. Nevertheless, even in these cases, we are dealing with genuine associations which reflect an underlying structure of causal relations governing behavior.

Historians and social scientists uncover law-like cultural patterns that can be ranked by their degrees of reliability. In this view historians draw on three levels of generalizations: "those which are true of the members of a given society at a given time, those which are true of the members of all societies of a given type, and those which are true for the members of all societies." All of these could produce valid explanations, but most historians relied on the first level, reconstructing the customary rules and patterns that governed some particular society at a specific time in the past.[47]

Murphey effectively integrated two methods of explanation. The first replaced universal laws with probabilistic or statistical generalizations. And the second replaced a strictly causal or mechanical explanation with a "functional" explanation. Some event or process is explained in terms of its function or role in some larger historical or cultural system. Historical laws do exist, but they are specific to particular societies and times. Producing such laws is part of understanding the past on its own terms, defining the sociohistorical system or context to which an event or individual belongs and penetrating beneath its surface to discover the underlying, rule-ordered structure. He suggested that the frontier thesis exemplified this process.

It is always the problem of the historian to discover that system of thought and action which gives significance to the events he is studying, and the great historian is one who is particularly successful in doing this. . . . [T]he incredible hold of Turner's frontier thesis has been due to the fact that it provided a set of generalizations which appeared to explain a great many otherwise unexplained phenomena.

Turner's thesis was one of those generalizations true only of a given society at a given time. Hempel had tried to cast the frontier hypothesis as a generalization true of all societies. Morton White's gloss, although more sophisticated than Hempel's, made the same mistake. Although Murphey did not discuss the frontier thesis at length, he seemed to view it as a probabilistic hypothesis about the social structures of frontier America.[48]

Murphey's account reflected the growing importance of systems theory, a heterogeneous intellectual movement bound by a shared notion of society or culture as system. More specifically, his examples draw from structuralism. For structuralists, beneath the confusing social surface of contingency and chaos lay structural mechanisms of necessity and order. Not all these theorists agreed on what structure looked like, and such respected figures as psychologist Jean Piaget, linguist Noam Chomsky, and sociologist Robert Merton offered very different approaches. For French anthropologist Claude Lévi-Strauss language and linguistics offered the best way into any description of society, and he described method in these terms:

First, structural linguistics shifts from the study of *conscious* linguistic phenomena to study of their *unconscious* infrastructure; second, it does not treat *terms* as independent entities, taking instead as its basis of analysis the *relations* between terms; third, it introduces the concept of *system* . . . [F]inally, structural linguistics aims at discovering *general laws.*

The affinities with Murphey's account stand out. Drawing causal relations is a matter of reading individual elements as parts of a larger system. This system comprises not the collection of individuals but their network of interrelations. How this all worked out differed from system to system and theorist to theorist. If we follow Murphey's reading to its implied end, we see Frederick Jackson Turner as a protostructuralist and the frontier thesis as a testable proposition about the interrelations of various social structures.[49]

Murphey did not directly map his model onto the Turner thesis, but philosopher Elazar Weinryb did. His 1975 article "The Justification of a Causal Thesis: An Analysis of the Controversies over the Theses of Pirenne, Turner, and Weber" described a causal thesis as consisting of three parts: description of cause (Turner's frontier); description of effects (American democracy); and justification of the causal statement (argument and evidence). Different investigators typically extend the life of a thesis by revising these elements, and Turner's stretchable terminology facilitates this sort of redescription. As Weinryb pointed out, criticisms may strike at particular elements of the frontier while leaving others intact. And his ultimately sympathetic assessment of Turner's thesis rested on Stanley Elkins and Eric McKitrick's 1954 community study, "A New Meaning for Turner's Frontier," which recast all three Turnerian elements of cause, effects, and justification within systems theory.[50]

A careful look at the work of Elkins and McKitrick can help us to understand what Murray Murphey meant by probabilistic functional explanations. As social historians, Elkins and McKitrick approached the frontier thesis with a certain critical enthusiasm. They deplored Turner's rhetoric but believed that "a host of problems may be examined with fresh interest if we put in testable terms facts which [Turner] knew by instinct." The problem was to strip poetics from logic. To this end they replaced Turner's Victorian figures with the vocabularies of systems theory. Inspired by the community studies of sociologist Robert K. Merton, they redescribed Turnerian cause and effect. From Turner's cause, the frontier, they drew the single element of community building and defined its "variables" as "a period of problem-solving and a homogenous population whose key factor is the lack of a structure of leadership." They similarly sharpened Turner's effect, American development, into political democracy. As a working definition they proposed "a manipulative attitude toward government, shared by large numbers of people. Let it be thought of as a wide participation in public affairs, a diffusion of leadership, a widespread sense of personal competence to make a difference." Having redescribed their component elements, they then connected them, relying on Merton's structural-functionalist framework. For Merton social systems consisted of social roles, structures, statuses, and their functional relations, and the social scientist describes some particular event or process in terms of its function in the larger system.[51]

Elkins and McKitrick described two stages in community life. In the first, frontier conditions impose a "typical pattern" of widespread participation and political awareness: "What we exhibit here are the elements of a simple syllogism; the first settlers anywhere, no matter who they were or how scanty their prior experience, were the men who had to be the first officeholders." (Here, ten years after Carl Hempel's seminal article, we finally find a syllogism in historical prose.) In other words, each new community demanded an entire set of political roles and statuses, and since members were relatively few, a high percentage of them participated in these structures. From this egalitarian distribution of political roles emerged an enduring social pattern: "An egalitarian tone was set, and ceremonial observances by which the experience was reinvoked and reshaped made their way into the social habits of the people." This tradition passed over into the second stage, that of town life, as a result of the "organic connection" between urban capitalism and political democracy. What ensured democracy, beyond the social pattern reproduced in public ritual, "was dependence on the favor of large numbers of people in market communities where manipulation was a daily habit, dependence on a favor which must be continually renewed. . . . Under such conditions a prior structure of leadership, a self-perpetuating planter oligarchy, an aristocracy of money and birth, would simply have melted away." Frontier and town societies show a systematic set of interconnections between various social structures. The process of community building ensured a high degree of political engagement; this produced a democratic cultural pattern that was in turn reinforced by the market economy; and the whole reproduced itself through social rituals in which these patterns were publicly affirmed and re-created.[52]

What sort of a justificatory procedure is this? It redescribes Turner's original thesis and vocabulary, bringing specific elements of them together into a single systematic phenomenon. Elkins and McKitrick effectively singled out items of Turner's frontier and democracy and then recombined them in a theory of social systems adopted from sociology. We have seen this method before, although not under the rubric of causal explanation. As Elazar Weinryb observed, this is W. H. Walsh's colligation—the integration of a variety of intrinsically related elements into a single term or process. And in Weinryb's view, it is a valid scientific method of causal explanation: "The work of Elkins and McKitrick . . . consists of redescriptions of the cause-phenomenon and the effect-phenomenon in a theoretical vocabulary that belongs to a specific theory which seems to be well-tested."[53]

Rudolph Weingartner's point about the importance of the ways in which historians constitute their subjects thus reenters our discussion: definitions are not incidental to causal relations but are part of them. The historian individuates certain subjects or events (community building and political democracy) from the flux of experience and then colligates them under a single term (the frontier process or social system). By redescribing cause and effect, one redescribes the ways in which they may be connected and that connection justified. The theory itself, in this case structural-functionalism, sets the boundaries on objects, events, and their relations. Theory, rather than whimsy, determines what is relevant, essential, and intrinsically related. But this means that connections hold true only *within* a particular theoretical language. Some alternative scheme, say a Marxist structuralism, might colligate its subjects differently and provide a radically different (but potentially quite well justified) account of the same data. As Elkins and McKitrick replaced Turner's organic systems with Merton's structural-functionalism, so Merton's model might be replaced in turn. The question then becomes, Why this theoretical language rather than some other? The query returns us to Morton White's assessment of the importance of the cultural tradition in which historians work, the ways in which custom determines what counts as an effective explanation.[54]

Questions have multiplied since we first postponed our discussion of colligation. Before we can address them, we need to come up for air and look at the historical view in 1975. More than thirty years had passed since George Pierson's survey revealed the dominance of Turnerian history. Now, after three decades of debate and research, we have at least four analysts—Hempel, White, Murphey, and Weinryb—contending from their different perspectives that the frontier thesis is a valid scientific causal explanation; we have heard Hofstadter, one of America's foremost historians and Turnerian critics, concede the general reasonableness of Turner's thesis; and we have seen a number of works invoked as verifications or at least corroborations of the frontier hypothesis. Turnerian history should be thriving. But we cannot quantify the popularity of the thesis in the 1970s, for no one repeated Pierson's survey. Indeed, no one would have thought it necessary, for most historians probably thought of the Turner thesis, if they thought of it at all, as a historical relic.[55]

Frontier history had slipped from dominance into obscurity. Why, if the frontier hypothesis still had not been definitively formulated, let alone conclusively verified or falsified, did historians abandon it? According to a number of prominent historians, we ought to think of the change as a paradigmatic shift, a revolution in historical practice analogous to those described by Thomas Kuhn in his landmark book, *The Structure of Scientific Revolutions* (1962). According to Patricia Limerick, "by the late 1970s, the pressures had built up on the fault lines of the old paradigm and something had to give." Limerick's label is more suggestive than systematic; these days "paradigm" weaves in and out of popular discourse, decorating bumper stickers and T-shirts as well as monographs, and most historians use the word without any deep theoretical intent. The immediate implication, though, is that "paradigm" might offer us some insight into the ways in which historians and other social scientists move from one theoretical framework, such as structural-functionalism, to another.[56]

Before we wander any farther down this path, we need to gloss Kuhn's study. Kuhn claimed that science does not proceed in a linear, cumulative fashion. Scientists do not simply substitute true(r) hypotheses for those which have proven incompatible with empirical data. Rather, scientists form interpretive communities that operate within a horizon of shared models, goals, and values. These "paradigms" dictate what counts as observable data and restrict the questions scientists can formulate, thus ensuring a high degree of community consensus. Such "normal science" is conformist, tightly organized, and almost irrationally resistant to competing ways of organizing inquiry. Since no single hypothesis ever accounts for all empirical data, simple falsification cannot overthrow a given paradigm. Instead, scientists spend most of their time puzzle-solving, attempting to account for anomalous data within a prescribed framework. Anomalies eventually pile up, competing frameworks appear, and the community finds itself in crisis. Inquiry thus moves in sporadic revolutions or shifts in which scientists abruptly abandon one entire theoretical system for another. In this view, "falsification, although it surely occurs . . . might equally well be called verification since it consists in the triumph of a new paradigm over the old one." And because different paradigms define and structure data in competing ways, in some vague sense "the proponents of competing paradigms practice their trades in different worlds." Neither the routines of normal science nor the triumph of one paradigm over another can be accounted for by some general logic of explanation. Kuhn thus offered an account of the customs of science invoked by both Morton White and Rudolph Weingartner.[57]

An entire body of scholarship crystallized around Kuhn's account, and we will not be able to assess its merits in the following pages. It figures in our conversation in two ways. First, the debate in philosophy of science highlights the improbability of shaping history into the highly idealized, rationalistic discourse imagined by so many analytic philosophers and historians. Once subjected to close scrutiny, science looked messier and more historical than had long been assumed. And if even the "hard" sciences could not reduce their procedures to a single explanatory logic, a universal algorithm, what hope or need could historians have of codifying their language?[58] Second, some historians and historiographers have suggested that Kuhn's vision of scientific inquiry accurately describes historical scholarship.[59] The claim should spark our interest. If it seems unlikely that we can abstract a single testable proposition, a central frontier hypothesis, from the jungles of Turnerian history, perhaps we might still describe it as a paradigmatic structure. To our four theoretical positions on frontier history (there is no frontier hypothesis; there is a frontier hypothesis but it is an unprovable heuristic; there is a frontier hypothesis and it must be verified or abandoned; there is a frontier hypothesis but it can only be falsified) we need to add a fifth: There is a paradigm of frontier history.

First, we need to determine what a paradigm looks and acts like. This is no simple task, for *The Structure of Scientific Revolutions* colligated a variety of items under the single term "paradigm." Margaret Masterman, a sympathetic critic, found twenty-two distinct uses of the word in Kuhn's text, making Turner's semantics look threadbare by comparison. Kuhn himself later suggested replacing the term with the phrase "disciplinary matrix." Such matrices bind together scientific communities, and Kuhn singled out four elements as the supporting walls of the building that houses an interpretive community. The first, symbolic generalizations, consists of formal statements that all group members accept as givens, such as force equals mass times acceleration, f = ma. The second is shared belief in particular models, which might range from simple heuristics to complex ontologies. The third, shared values, becomes most important during revolutionary or crisis periods in science, providing the grounds for choosing among incompatible practices. The fourth consists of an accepted canon of "exemplars." By this Kuhn meant the concrete, textbook problem solutions that students master as they are socialized into their discipline. Schrödinger's equation or Keplerian orbits serve would-be scientists as exemplars of how to practice physics.[60]

If we hope to import "paradigm" into history, at least in anything more than a colloquial sense, Kuhn's list raises many problems. To begin with, even the most specialized historians seem not to work inside all four walls of a disciplinary matrix. Certain groups of historians may share heuristic models, such as the frontier thesis; some may even share notions of what historians ought to do; but Kuhn's first and fourth elements, shared symbolic generalizations and exemplars, are not found in historical practice, at least not in the way in which they are found in, say, theoretical physics. Not only do historians communicate almost exclusively in ordinary language but training in history, as Kuhn pointed out, proceeds very differently from that in most physical sciences. There, graduate students spend years working their way arduously through textbook after textbook, mastering exemplar after exemplar, all in the same ways and forms, before ever going on to their own research. This discovery should lead us to suspect that historian David Hollinger was on the mark when he suggested that while Kuhn's work illustrates the tremendous potential of historicist understandings of science, its normative implications for history are extremely limited.[61]

If Turner's thesis dominated early twentieth-century American history in a way that no other has ever done, it ought to be the best possible candidate for description as a Kuhnian paradigm or disciplinary matrix. Although we might describe Turnerian frontier history as a shared heuristic model, thus providing a rickety first wall for a disciplinary matrix, even the Turnerians could not agree on any particular symbolic generalization. This demolishes the second supporting wall. Part of the reason historians could not arrive at some final consensus on devising and testing a frontier hypothesis is that historians did not agree on what a hypothesis was or should be (or even if they needed one). As the White-Hofstadter collision demonstrates, the historical community lacked a normative rule for assessing causal claims. This deficiency undermines wall number three, shared aims and understanding of the goals of inquiry. It also points out the apparent absence of the fourth wall, an accepted canon of exemplars of valid causal explanation. So the walls come tumbling down, and if we extend Kuhn's metaphor into historical practice, we find warring scholars huddled around the single wall of heuristic models, hurling bricks at one another.[62]

Moreover, even if we use paradigm to describe such things as structural-functionalism,[63] we still do not have a plausible description of frontier history. Turner's frontier thesis mixed Victorian idealism and social evolutionism; Elkins and McKitrick reframed it within structural-functionalism. Even if we call Turner's social evolutionism and Elkins and McKitrick's structural functionalism "paradigms," they are operating inside some larger structure of frontier history amenable to incorporating different theoretical models. We are looking for something more encompassing and less constrictive than Kuhn's disciplinary matrices. Reading the decline of Turnerian history as a paradigmatic shift does not take us very far. Indeed, viewing history in Kuhnian terms as a "proto-science" leaves us in much the same place as if we adopted Hempel's model: History is a discipline without a home, without true explanations, without a true paradigm.

Narrative Explanations

Like the debate in philosophy of science, conversation in philosophy of history scattered to the four winds in the 1960s. The rise of narrative theory displaced the quarter century of polarized exchange over Hempel's covering law model. The "narrative theorists," related simply by the fact that they all wrote on narrative and history in the 1960s and early 1970s, comprised philosophers W. B. Gallie, Louis Mink, Arthur Danto, and historian Hayden White. Their work suggested that the covering law dispute had reached an impasse because its terms kept philosophers from seeing what was obvious once one actually spent a little time reading history books: historians told stories. All the technical attempts to adapt covering law or functionalist models to history were so much intellectual gymnastics and largely tangential to the daily practice of most working historians.

Louis O. Mink, philosopher at Wesleyan University and author of a subtle history of R. G. Collingwood's thought, set off in his own distinctive direction in a 1965 article entitled "The Autonomy of Historical Understanding." Mink observed that neither falsification nor verification theories accounted for the ways historians work. Here was a serious deficiency, since the ultimate test of any potential scientific explanation is that it account for available evidence. But neither verificationist nor falsificationist theories could explain the persistence of the frontier hypothesis. In fact and in practice, said Mink, "even generalized hypotheses are not abandoned by historians when disconfirmed, nor can the survival be dismissed as unfortunately ideological." To illustrate the point, he turned to the frontier hypothesis. He did not cite Turner directly, preferring instead to quote Turnerian Ray Allen Billington, framing the citation with prose evoking the coarseness and strength of Turner's frontiersman.

Historians are often rough-and-ready in their use of terms. A leading defender of Frederick Jackson Turner's "frontier hypothesis," for example, observes of Turner's critics that they refused to recognize "that Turner was advancing an hypothesis rather than attempting to prove a theory." To a logician this is puzzling: a theory *is* a set of hypotheses, and it is logically impossible to entertain an hypothesis except in connection with a theory to be proved or disproved.

Yet such a curious usage may reveal that historians mean something quite different by the term "hypothesis" or that hypotheses function quite differently in historical inquiry than in scientific inquiry—including social science. It may not be a logical gaffe but a significant symptom that Turner's "frontier hypothesis" has never been precisely formulated and yet has been a supremely fertile source of suggestions of specific inquiries to be undertaken.

Mink saw the debate surrounding the frontier hypothesis as evidence that histories were "interpretive narratives" rather than scientific reports and that historians told stories rather than verifying or falsifying hypotheses. Since he hoped to build an epistemological foundation for history which distinguished it from physical science, this conclusion suggested to him that the historian's use of narrative differentiated historical and scientific discourse. In subsequent articles Mink compared fiction and history and entertained the idea of narrative as a cognitive instrument.[64]

For the moment, though, we need to remain at the sentence level in order to work out just what implications these claims might have for the frontier hypothesis. To do this, we need to turn to the work of

Arthur C. Danto, an analytic philosopher at Columbia University. More than any other single individual actually engaged in this debate, Danto effectively dissolved the claim that historical explanations ought to be reduced to individual, falsifiable propositions. After several initial articles that struggled with the significance of story for historical language, he gradually worked toward a description of narrative as a reputable form of scientific explanation.[65]

Danto's first really original contribution to the discussion appeared in 1962 with his article "Narrative Sentences." Narrative sentences are propositions whose "most general characteristic is that they refer to at least two time-separated events though they only *describe* (are only *about*) the earliest event to which they refer." In other words, they create a meaning for an event by relating it to some later event. Danto offered the example, "The Thirty Years' War began in 1618." Lacking clairvoyance, no one could have said this in 1618. Such claims are always retrospective, and historians create meaning by relating one happening to a later one: "A particular thing or occurrence acquires historical *significance* in virtue of its relations to some other thing or occurrence in which we happen to have special interest, or to which we attach importance, for whatever reason. Narrative sentences are then frequently used to justify the *mention,* in a narrative, of some thing or event whose significance might otherwise escape a reader." This seemingly innocent statement holds the radical implication that no past event has a fixed meaning; since the future is contingent, as it changes, so does the potential significance of past events. And as Morton White's historian might link any number of different causal statements depending on his or her individual interests, so Danto saw no sure bounds on the ways that different events might be associated. In this passage the historian employing narrative sentences seems to depend on what White had called abnormalism, where a historian retrospectively singles out a specific event or factor as unusual and thus invests it with significance.[66]

Danto's differences from White emerged in 1965, however, when "Narrative Sentences" appeared as a chapter in his magisterial work, *The Analytical Philosophy of History.* Where White had tried to salvage a central place for general laws in historical explanation, Danto subordinated the covering law model to storytelling.[67] Popper's and Hempel's deductive hypotheses described "not simply an event—something that happens—but a *change* . . . An explanation then consists in filling in the middle between the temporal end-points of a change." In other words, historical explanations seek to explain a change over time in some central subject, and they do this through stories. To illustrate the point, we might employ Turner's assessment of the effects of the frontier.

> But the most important effect of the frontier has been the promotion of democracy here and in Europe. As has been pointed out, the frontier is productive of individualism. Complex society is precipitated by the wilderness into a kind of primitive organization based on the family. The tendency is anti-social. It produces antipathy to social control, and particularly to any direct control. . . . The frontier individualism has from the beginning promoted democracy.

Carl Hempel believed this passage hid a syllogism based on a general law. Morton White thought that while Turner had implied the existence of some general law, it must be vastly more complex than the naive one that Hempel imagined. Hofstadter argued that if we hang on to the scientific content while jettisoning its poetic form, the passage offers a reasonably well-verified proposition. Murphey seems to have believed that it rests on an underlying probability statement about the functions of a frontier social system. Weinryb thought that when redescribed and colligated under a theoretical framework, it was a justified causal statement.[68]

Danto's argument suggests that although we might refigure Turner's argument in these ways, we need not, for it is a complete explanation as it stands. The statement "The frontier individualism has from the beginning promoted democracy" is a narrative sentence describing two time-separated events, the existence of predemocratic society and the rise of democracy, while implicitly explaining their relation, the emergence and force of frontier individualism. This sentence, by drawing the reader's attention to items of unusual historical significance, presupposes that democracy represents a change. Euro-American society begins nondemocratic and becomes democratic as a result of the frontier. The construction follows the classic narrative order and minimal plot structure of beginning, middle, and end, and although with enough imagination we might read a general law into the passage, we do not have to. And given the notorious scarcity of such laws, we are well off without the effort.[69]

Danto did not claim to have reduced histories to collections of narrative sentences. His argument dovetailed with Louis Mink's observation that historians do not produce conclusions detachable from their work as a whole but "must read one another's books instead of merely noting their results." In Turner's work, for instance, while a number of his claims take the form of individual narrative sentences, we cannot locate their full meaning in such isolated fragments. Historical explanations, whether phrased as hypotheses or definitive causal claims, never stand alone but refer to a larger narrative structure. As Mink had said, the statement that " 'the frontier was responsible for the development of democracy in America' is clearly not the conclusion of Turner's argument nor a part of it, but a slogan or mnemonic for some main features of the story of that development." We have, in the frontier thesis as in most other historical hypotheses, not simply a falsifiable or verifiable proposition bound by universal or probabilistic laws but a micronarrative and a mnemonic, a capsule summary of a narrative explanation of history.[70]

Danto's description of narrative sentences placed narration at the heart of historical imagination. After his work historiography's common distinctions between narrative and analysis, form and content, description and explanation, came to look less telling. All historical narratives analyze and explain, though some may be less self-consciously thoughtful or critical than others, and the most systematic histories narrate. We should not infer that historians *cannot* attempt to create falsifiable explanations based on lawlike generalizations, for it is clear that at least some of them do. Nor should we conclude that historians never construct testable propositions for which they adduce as much evidence as they can get their hands on. Again, most historians endeavor to do just that. Danto's narrativism implied simply that historical inquiry cannot be reduced to such procedures. Individual historical explanations, whether they appear as syllogisms, probabilistic equations, teleological arguments, theoretical constructs, or narrative sentences, are interwoven, however sketchily, into a story or stories.[71]

Danto did not see narration as a mark of analytic deficiency. Looking back in 1984, he pointed out that his *Analytical Philosophy of History* had contended that "narrative structures penetrate our consciousness of events in ways parallel to those in which . . . theories penetrate observations in science. . . . Narration exemplifies one of the basic ways in which we represent the world, and the language of beginnings and endings, of turning points and crises and climaxes, is coimplicated with this mode of representation to so great a degree that our image of our own lives must be deeply narrational." Louis Mink had also linked narration and cognition, though with considerably less confidence. In a 1970 article, "History and Fiction as Modes of Comprehension," he described narrative as a cognitive form. Specifically, narrative belonged to what he called the "configurational" mode of comprehension, a way of bringing multiple objects together as elements in a single and concrete complex of relationships. Mink implied that narrative subsumed, if it was not synonymous with, colligation.[72]

Mink's association of narration and colligation returns us to our opening discussion of what historians do. What is colligation? A cognitive and linguistic act drawing a variety of disparate items into some larger whole. How does it explain? By individuating an event out of the historical flux. To do this, historians create a plot: they describe two time-separated happenings as part of a single process whose significance may be comprehended by describing it in terms of its antecedents and consequences. What is the frontier? A concatenation of different places and processes, from ethnic interaction to migration to community building, which historians abstract from the chaos of sense data and synthesize into an individual concept. How does the frontier explain? By bringing together its antecedents and consequences: it provides the middle in a narrative whose beginning point is nondemocratic European society and whose endpoint is twentieth-century American democracy. So we have at least two levels of colligation. The first individuates words or terms, such as the frontier. The second individuates events through narratives.

While the work of Danto and Mink sheds light on the previously mysterious operations of colligation, it threatened to make the concept unfashionable. Their descriptions of historical narrative effectively replaced colligation with emplotment. And at the level of individual words and sentences, we will find other schemes proposed for describing the ways that historians bring terms together. This sort of gathering is done with figures of speech, or tropes, and these carry names long associated with poetics rather than logic: metaphor, metonymy, and so on. Another problem remains that of justifying claims that the items of any particular "colligation" are, as Walsh put it, "intrinsically related." If narrative explanation involves singling out an "event" from the flux of experience, how do historians decide where to draw those boundaries? What are the minimal elements of an event?[73]

For Mink, to say that narrative was a cognitive as well as an artistic form was not to say that it was verifiable or fully scientific. Recognizing that historians employ hypotheses as tentative narrative explanations of some historical event or process does allow historians to review the record with some problem in view and assess just how plausible an account the hypothesis outlines. But Mink believed that the function of hypothetical narratives in history differed from the role played by hypotheses in such hard sciences as theoretical physics: "The crucial difference is that the narrative combination of relations is simply not subject to confirmation or disconfirmation, as any one of them taken separately might be." In other words, some isolated descriptive statements, such as "In 1890 the United States Census Bureau declared the frontier closed," may be tested for their coherence with the documentary record. But to explain the meaning of such statements, to say why they are important, historians draw them into a narrative whole by attaching them to other sentences, such as "The existence of an area of free land, its continuous recession, and the advance of American settlement westward, explain American development." And while historians may *warrant* individual descriptions by appealing to historical evidence, the ways in which those descriptions are combined appear not to be definitively warrantable. One could warrant historical facts, Mink concluded, but one could not warrant histories.[74]

The skeptical implications of narrativism grew clearer in 1973 when historian Hayden White published *Metahistory*. White barely mentioned covering law, rationalist, and functionalist descriptions of historiography. All the previous debate had missed the point, he declared, because it had erroneously tried to isolate the "scientific" elements in historical discourse. In fact, history was ineluctably imaginative and literary. Where philosophers focused on individual sentences, White delivered some four hundred pages of close readings of entire books. His theses were bold: Each history depends on some speculative philosophy of history; these rest on poetic rather than cognitive bases; and since there are no sound epistemological grounds for favoring any particular poetic vision, the best reasons for choosing one history rather than another are moral or aesthetic rather than epistemic. Accordingly, his book looked like an elaborate schematic exercise in literary criticism rather than a treatise on the logic of historical discourse. Indeed, for White knowledge and narrative served as antonyms.[75]

White followed the lead of formalist literary critics Northrop Frye and Kenneth Burke, arguing that a limited number of plot forms and tropes characterized historical narratives. Frye had devoted much of his career in myth criticism to analyzing and compiling what he regarded as an exhaustive discussion of the archetypal plot modes, or *mythoi*, common to Western civilization: the romance, the tragedy, the comedy, and the satire, each of which could be further subdivided into numerous categories and combinations. Burke, a Renaissance man whose career had taken him into regions seldom traversed by literary critics (he wrote on everything from St. Thomas Aquinas to Adolf Hitler), had argued that all humans understood history through some form of literary genre. Karl Marx, he said, wrote in the key of high comedy, a plot mode that Burke found especially useful for encouraging productive attitudes toward history and community. White imported these discussions into *Metahistory* and classified the works of Michelet, Tocqueville, Burckhardt, and Marx by plot type, arguing that each literary form, when used to narrate some particular series of historical events, had a political or ideological content. In White's hands emplotment became a sort of historical explanation, and since experience did not offer itself up in ready-made stories, historians imposed one plot form or another on their data, unconsciously drawing off the stock of narrative forms that characterized Western culture.[76]

Historians also explained by employing figures of speech. In place of Walsh's colligation, White offered a typology of rhetorical figures or tropes. Again following Burke, he described four master tropes governing the operation of language: metaphor, metonymy, synecdoche, and irony. Metaphor was the trope of resemblance and object-object relations: My love is a rose, or the history of America is the history of the colonization of the Great West. Metonymy was the trope of contiguity and part-part relations, a figure of speech where a single item stood for an entire series of contiguous items, as one of the links in Morton White's causal chains might stand for the entire series of events. Synecdoche was the trope of integration and part-whole relations, where a part symbolized some quality presumed to inhere in the whole, as when Elkins and McKitrick drew out the nature of frontier community building as a means of elaborating the workings of an entire social system. Irony, the trope of negation, undercut and disrupted the functions of the other three tropes, perhaps even going so far as to undermine the reader's faith in the ability of language to represent something outside itself.[77]

These figures were not simple decoration. As Walsh had seen colligation as an important means of cognition and explanation, White saw the master tropes as basic elements of historical discourse. In one of his murkiest and most provocative arguments, White contended that the tropes were also "deep structures of consciousness," ways of ordering human experience and the world, shaping the way that historians and their publics imagined history to work, delimiting what could count as explanation and evidence. There was thus no way to avoid tropes in favor of nonfigurative forms, no hope of the historian escaping from affective language. Each age and every historian favored one trope at the expense of the others, and this decision, like the choice of some particular plot form, created a historical significance for events that they did not "intrinsically" possess. White held poesy and logic as far apart as Carl Hempel ever had, but he urged historians to recognize the absurd demands of their discipline and commit themselves to heroic existential leaps into the sublime.[78]

Metahistory fractured the debate over historical explanation much as Kuhn's *Structure of Scientific Revolutions* had splintered discussions of explanation in science. Many critics seized on White's apparent skepticism, his claim that historians imposed narratives on their materials rather than the other way around. Others assailed his schematic approach, which assumed the existence of a more or less static grid of literary and linguistic forms and then filed histories under appropriate labels. Still others accused the work of being naively ahistorical. Where did plot forms come from? Why did some tropes dominate certain ages? What parts did readers, institutions, and interpretive communities play? The book was adulated and abominated, and building on the work of Danto and Mink, it marked a turning point in historiographic debate as journals like *History and Theory* devoted ever more space to narrative theory and literary criticism. By 1980 the old battle lines, with covering law theorists on one side and rationalists on the other, had been scribbled over with alternative vocabularies.[79]

White's work shocked historians, but it was in many ways quite conservative. His tastes for myth criticism and existentialist exhortation were anomalous in the early seventies when the "cutting edge" scholars in English and comparative literature were discovering structuralism.[80] Moreover, *Metahistory* effectively answered that ancient (Danto had called it "tedious") question: Clio—Muse or Science? White declared for art, asserting that historical discourse stood radically apart from the sort of scientific knowledge that made airplanes fly. History was "*not* a science" but was "at best" a "proto-science" "indentured" to "fiction-making." The constructions placed White at the end of that idealist tradition marked out by Collingwood, Walsh, Dray, and Mink in their battles with unity-of-method theorists. He also faced a flood of new work in the philosophy of science contending that "science" was more artistic and historical than the positivists and their critics had realized and that the sharp boundaries between understanding and knowing that had grounded the art versus science debates had blurred. In 1970, for instance, W. V. O. Quine's philosophy textbook *The Web of Belief* had described scientific hypotheses as "plausible stories," and philosopher Mary Hesse had explored, at monograph length, the role of metaphor in covering laws. By the time *Metahistory* appeared, its stark contrasts of literary and scientific language were already suspect, and other scholars rushed into the field opened up by White's narratological readings of nonfiction to decode narrative forms in even the mathematical formulae of economics and the differential equations of theoretical physics.[81]

The narrativist debates of the sixties and seventies left a million questions hanging. What did it mean to say that historians told stories? Danto argued that narratives could be legitimate explanations and that human lives were basically narrational. For Mink narrative was a mode of comprehension, but he did not believe that the world structured itself into any particular story line. One could not match historical narratives with history itself since stories, plots, outcomes, and morals differed wildly from historian to historian, place to place, and age to age. White, at his most skeptical, implied that by forcing the chaotic atomism of real experience into artistically coherent story lines historians abandoned any hope of representing the past as it really was. Each of these theorists agreed that historical meaning was contingent on historical form and that historical form was a product of factors and forces not to be found in either a bare evidentiary record or some single logic of inquiry.

These different descriptions of historical narrative moved Morton White's and Rudolph Weingartner's concerns about custom and values to the fore of historiography. Even the covering law model requires some reference to "extrarational" factors when deciding which effects to explain and where to begin a causal chain. As Weingartner observed, such decisions turn on the central subject and questions the historian has in mind. And the choosing or making of subjects and questions are matters of historical habits and interests rather than timeless axioms. But after the deductive process is rolling, with a subject constructed and questions asked, explanations follow a certain logical order. In the covering law model, arguments always move from universal to particular, conclusions may not contain elements not already introduced in the premises, and so on. Once we read histories as narratives, however, even this minimum of predictability disappears. How do we integrate sentences into stories? Where does a story begin and end and why? What plot should the historian adopt? From whose point of view will the story be told? As we will see in the pages to come, we cannot strictly reduce these questions to nonnarrative matters of "fact," "evidence," or "logic."

Where the logical calculus of the covering law theorists did not and could not engage such queries, narrative understandings placed them at the center of criticism. Imagining the dispute over the Turner thesis as a conflict between competing narrative explanations of American history explains how a Homer Hockett could endorse the Turner thesis while refusing to reduce it to a single sentence. Such an approach illuminates the depths of disagreement among historians over whether the thesis had been or could be conclusively verified or disconfirmed. And it will give us a way of looking at historiographic debate that does not describe history as an underdeveloped discipline. How do custom and values work their way into historical discourse? Through language. What do historians do? They tell stories. Having made these observations, Louis Mink went on to claim that "narrative form in history, as in fiction, is an artifice, the product of individual imagination," much as Hayden White argued that historians, consciously or not, chose their explanatory menus from a smorgasbord of literary forms.[82]

Where Mink and White described narration as a private rather than public affair and where they radically differentiated fact and figure, science and history, our story blurs these categories. Narrative explanations extend into natural sciences (biology, geology, and astronomy spring readily to mind) and theory works its way into histories, this one included.[83] Figuration and fiction are not synonyms. Plot forms are not Platonic essences. And the ways and means of narration are not matters of personal taste. Historians are not isolated individual consumers in a free market of narrative forms. We should give up the old-fashioned descriptions of monographs as self-contained artifacts and imagine them instead as textual events, their meanings constructed by readers as well as authors, their forms determined less by private choices than by narrative traditions. If we are to learn how and why "custom" blessed some stories by calling them plausible explanations and discarded others, we will need to explore the historicity of historical language. And we will find the boundaries of interpretive communities in history drawn by the pasts we profess and the worlds we make in the tales that tell us.

BOOK TWO

From Spirit to System

An American Dante: Frederick Jackson Turner

To understand Turner's frontier history, we need to understand his emplotment of *history*. What is history? How to tell it? Early in his career Turner pursued these questions. Most of his commentators have not dealt at length with these theoretical ruminations, preferring to concentrate on the frontier thesis or its presentiments. Most have described his philosophy of history as a simple materialism or denied that he had one at all. As a result, we imagine him as an environmental or economic determinist.[1] The issue edges into a larger set of questions, and prominent among them is the query: Did German historicism take hold in the American historical imagination? One of the leading students of the topic, Dorothy Ross, has argued that it did not, at least not until the Gilded Age, and that Victorians relied on counterhistoricist understandings of national identity. This counterhistoricism took two distinct forms. In "republican" interpretations recurring contact with nature along an expanding frontier preserved civic virtue and so removed the nation from the contingency of history. In "millennial" understandings the nation's covenant with God predetermined its salvation. Each implied that the nation had escaped from history and its threat of social decay into the timeless spaces of nature or grace. Turner's work has been invoked in suppport of these readings of American historical imagination. Whether millenarian or republican, the resulting Turner is, in David Noble's phrase, a historian against history.[2]

Such a millennial or republican understanding of Turner, like its materialist counterpart, is incorrect or at least dangerously simplified. Turner's contemporaries may have read his essays in various ways, but his writing introduced historicism to American academia two decades before the appearance of the "New History" and four decades before one of his students, Carl Becker, delivered the famous "Everyman His Own Historian." Turner's essays took up traditions in idealism and universal history that gave his frontier tales a coherent plotline, an ambitious philosophical frame, and a place in a larger story of history. In German historicism Turner found the materials for an Emersonian project transfiguring folk memory into historical consciousness. To explain his efforts, we should begin a bit earlier than 1893, the year of his most famous essay.

In the spring of 1889 Turner left Johns Hopkins University, a survivor of the institution's new "German system" of graduate training. That fall he was teaching at the University of Wisconsin, Madison. Within a year he had completed his dissertation and received his Ph.D. In August 1891 the twenty-nine-year-old stood up in a Madison lecture hall filled with secondary schoolteachers and read his first major paper as a professional historian, an essay with the modest title, "The Significance of History."[3] He gave his listeners a metaphor: History is a dialectic. In this complex trope American transcendentalism and German historicism converged. And its homemade idealism grew into one of historiography's most famous narrative traditions. That tradition rests on two root metaphors that explain the antinomies of past and present, freedom and determinism, nature and history, good and evil, as elements of a higher unity. The first metaphor, history is a dialectic, imagines history as a narrative in which dramatic conflicts between moral forces resolve into higher, transcendent syntheses without ever fully vanishing. We might call it a literary metaphor, in the strong sense that history *is* a cosmic story we read, write, and live. But this simple gloss barely touches the surface, so we need to spend some time plumbing its depths. And from out of this figure came the second, more famous, trope, Turner's claim that American history is the history of the colonization of the Great West.

A polished exercise in Victorian oratory, "The Significance of History" surveys the variety of histories, narrates an historical account of how this diversity developed, and concludes with an assessment of what it all means. The very first sentence discloses a virtually boundless pluralism. What is history? It depends on whom you ask, for "the conceptions of history have been almost as numerous as the men who have written it." In illustration Turner listed the partisanship of Hume and the hero worship of Carlyle; the picturesque romances of Scott and Seeley; the political monographs of Freeman; and the new social and economic history pioneered by Thorold Rogers. As consumers in the free market of knowledge, historians "may choose from among many ideals." Freedom, though, has its limits, and if we search for cosmic order in apparent chaos, we find intelligible patterns. "In each age a different ideal of history has prevailed," and each of these approaches finds its meaning in the conditions of its age. By way of explanation Turner offered his audience a story of the dialectical development of historical consciousness. That tale anticipates the plot of every other narrative he wrote, explaining how the tension between past and present creates the changing forms of history.[4]

In "The Significance of History" historical consciousness migrates through a series of epochs, each of which transcends without effacing its precursors. The story begins with the savage for whom "history is the painted scalp." In primitive societies history is a cosmic unity explicable by reference to gods and legends, judgment and imagination are inseparably fused, and history is presented as religion. From here we move on to the ancient Greeks, who, according to Turner, first began to separate historical judgment from imagination. In the narratives of Herodotus and Thucydides we find history orchestrated by God-like heroes and presented as literature. From the classics we leap, with scarcely a glance at medieval chroniclers, directly to the German romantics who serve as legitimating authority for the notion of history that Turner hoped to impress on his listeners. Friedrich Schelling appears secondhand as glossed by Lord Acton: "The state is not in reality governed by laws of man's devising, but is a part of the moral order of the universe, ruled by cosmic forces from above." Johann Gottfried Herder appears as the precursor of institutional history. From his discussions of language and myths as historical products, scholars moved on to the careful critical examination of historical texts. In Turner's narrative idealists like Schelling and Herder cleared the way for empiricists like Barthold Niebuhr and Leopold von Ranke who made source criticism the base of historical practice. In America a secularized version of Ranke's empiricism was known as scientific history, and Turner's own mentor, Herbert Baxter Adams, was one of its leading proponents, holding seminars in a room emblazoned with the legend "History is past politics."[5]

Each of these stages of historical understanding reflects the larger spirit of the age. Savage traditions embody the central place of kinship, tribe, and religion in primitive human societies. The classical historians reveal their culture's belief that only citizenship in the polis can bring human beings into history and that the Gods intervene directly in human affairs through the actions of superhuman heroes. Schelling and Herder manifest their age's concern with nationalism and the state, while Ranke embodies his epoch's fascination with science and law. The 1890s, by Turner's account, are the "age of socialistic inquiry," an epoch dominated by economic and social questions and whose histories must reflect this. To address these very broad issues, historians must take up all these previous conceptions and styles, from savagism to romanticism and its empiricist critics, from religion to politics to economics, subject them to scholarly scrutiny, and synthesize them into the plural unity of modern history: "Our conclusion, therefore, is that there is much truth in all these conceptions of history: history is past literature, it is past politics, it is past religion, it is past economics."[6]

Clearly, said Turner, we know more than our predecessors, but we ought not to read our genealogy as a facile progression from superstition to certainty. History does not end with us and can never be finalized. Indeed, "the first lesson the student of history has to learn is to discard his conception that there are standard ultimate histories." Each age takes up the elements of past ages, but this transcendence does not lift any period, even our own, out of history and into a place where we can stand back and declare understanding fully realized. In a carefully italicized and much quoted line, Turner historicized his own profession: "*Each age writes the history of the past anew with reference to the conditions uppermost in its own time.*" This pronouncement quickly builds into something greater than the trivial claim that each age has different interests and so writes about different events. Historical meaning is in constant flux as the very significance of particular events changes.

History, both objective and subjective, is ever *becoming,* never completed. . . . [T]he significance of events develops with time, because today is so much a product of yesterday that yesterday can only be understood as it is explained by today. The aim of history, then, is to know the elements of the present by understanding what came into the present from the past. For the present is simply the developing past, the past the undeveloped present.

Objectivity and subjectivity, today and yesterday, past and present, all are the developing products of a constantly changing history. This was heady stuff for a young assistant professor at a small land-grant college, distant from the nation's cultural power centers. This passage, and the larger thrust of the essay, lifted his work out of the hyperempirical universe mapped in the professional but pedestrian discussions of historical practice by his mentor, Herbert Baxter Adams.[7]

Even a cursory reading places "The Significance of History" within a well-developed Victorian discourse about temporality and human existence. Words like growth, evolution, and development suggest biologist Charles Darwin, whose texts so effectively brought nature into history that they underscored the centrality of historical change in human affairs. (If even nature ran with the historical flow, how fluid must human life be?) This is a cliché both of Victorian thought and its historiographers, but we should not see Turner's story as a straightforward application of biological theory. Developmental conceptions of history were centuries old when Darwin adapted them, and both his and Turner's stories are intimately related to the ancient Judeo-Christian figuring of history as a sequence of ascending ages. Even in Turner's youth major historians like George Bancroft emplotted American history as the evolutionary realization of providential design. So we cannot simply blame Turner's progressive metaphors on *The Origin of Species*. But an increasingly secular tone and the technical connotations of terms like "evolution" *were* new, and they eventually displaced the historical vocabulary of Judeo-Christian tradition, even as they reproduced its basic plotline. We can see this displacement in "The Significance of History." It makes no explicit appeals to God, and while the story ascends, Turner denies that it is predetermined. Here is a history on the border shared by two very different discursive fields, its developmental plot the common link joining Christian and secular modernist historiographic traditions.[8]

"The Significance of History" took up still another venerable topos, the casting of interpretive problems in dualistic equations or antitheses: past and present, body and soul, subject and object. Turner's story does not narrate a simple unfolding of a homogeneous entity called "history." It relates a dramatic struggle between opposed but interdependent forces, the past and the present. In his hands antithesis became interpretive principle and narrative device. This approach was partly a matter of the forms he had inherited, since whether one was a devout Catholic or a committed naturalist the Victorian world turned on such equations. It was also partly deliberate. A prize-winning orator whose first academic appointment was as in rhetoric, Turner worked long and hard on style. He devoted notebook after notebook to the polishing of antithetical constructions: history and nature, savagery and civilization, East and West, good and evil. These often appeared in lengthy, parallel sets of dependent clauses, a device known as parataxis: "That coarseness and strength . . . that practical inventive turn of mind . . . that masterful grasp . . . that restless, nervous energy . . . " Antithesis and parataxis were favorite devices of the period, encouraged by example in the work of popular orators and expounded at length in textbooks. As rhetorician Ronald Carpenter has observed, this technique was not simply an ornament imposed in after-the-fact polishing but a way of experiencing the world.[9]

For Turner history ran this course. "The Significance of History" combines development and antithesis in a single plot. Tensions between conflicting forces, such as past and present or nature and history, work themselves out in a continuous narrative stream, each conflict resolving into higher stages that contain new tensions, and so on. If we think about the essay in this way, we can be more specific about its debts. Here, in rough outline, is Hegel's dialectic. For Hegel history was the story of the developing self-consciousness of what he called absolute spirit, a narrative that overcame the static oppositions of traditional metaphysics without appeal to mysticism or revelation. Opposed forces lifted each other up into higher syntheses, new stages in which both original agonists were simultaneously preserved and transcended and which became the starting point for a new agon. Commentators like Albion Small, one of Turner's professors at Johns Hopkins, frequently reduced dialectic to a rigid logical scheme: Thesis + Antithesis = Synthesis. But in Hegel's *The Phenomenology of Spirit* and *Lectures on the Philosophy of World History* dialectic looks more like a very complex story of the development of human consciousness than a "ritualistic three-step" of logical method. One of Turner's contemporaries, philosopher Josiah Royce, caught the sense of it when he called Hegel's dialectic a *Bildungsroman* of history, and this is the way we should imagine Turner's dialectic.[10]

Turner was no metaphysician, and we may well doubt that he was familiar with the technical details of Hegelian philosophy. He approached these problems simply as an interested intellectual, orator, and storyteller. But in dialectic he found a story line sufficiently compelling to narrate the growth of historical consciousness. Dialectic lifted the homeliest of materials from the dingiest local archive into the broad sweep of cosmic history. It promised to overcome the vulgar dichotomies separating humans from nature and present from past. It could accommodate the popular Darwinian metaphors of growth, succession, and organic inheritance. And it was flexible enough to incorporate the more mechanical schemes of social evolutionists like Herbert Spencer, Lewis Henry Morgan, and Richard Ely, who saw human societies evolving in distinct stages from savagism and barbarism toward civilization.

Turner did not use these schemes in a systematic way—he preferred collage to architectonics—but the plot of dialectic drives his accounts of historical practice and of how America came to be what it is.

So where did he learn it?

We do not know for certain, but Hegel's influential lectures *The Philosophy of History,* the work of American Hegelians in midwestern cities like St. Louis, Cincinnati, and Milwaukee, the studies in German historicism on reading lists at universities like Johns Hopkins, and the textual legacy of transcendentalists like Emerson and Whitman were all potential sources. It is not clear if Turner read Hegel, although as historiographer W. Stull Holt has noted, it seems more likely than not.[11] But Turner inhabited a literary world receptive to Hegel's plot, and he certainly knew it secondhand. In "The Significance of History" the direct link is Johann G. Droysen, one of Hegel's intellectual heirs, one of Herbert Baxter Adams's professors, and an outspoken critic of narrowly scientific history. Having briefly narrated the growth of historical consciousness, Turner drew the moral for his schoolteacher audience with the words of Droysen's *Outline of the Principles of History:* "History is the 'Know Thyself' of humanity—the self-consciousness of mankind."[12]

Turner invoked Droysen repeatedly throughout his career, reiterating this Delphian phrase in essays, letters, lectures, seminars, and orations. In the *Outline* Droysen explained the aphorism and made his debt to Hegel explicit.

All movement in the historical world goes on in this way: Thought, which is the ideal counterpart of things as they really exist, develops itself as things ought to be; and characters, filled with the thought, bring the things to its standard. . . . Thoughts constitute the criticism of that which is and yet is not as it should be. Inasmuch as they may bring conditions to their level, then broaden out and harden themselves into accord with custom, conservatism, and obstinacy, new criticism is demanded, and thus on and on. The continuity of this censorship of thought—"those who hold the torch passing it from one to another"—is what Hegel in his *Philosophy of History* calls "the Dialectic of History."

However fair to Hegel, this is Turner's "Significance of History" in a nutshell. Specific pasts and presents interact to create specific historical forms: the cosmologies of savagism, the epics of the Greeks, the romance of Herder, the monographs of Ranke and Adams. From age to age consciousness develops through dialectical stages, each epoch passing down the historical torch, the higher elements always preserved in ever more complex syntheses, until in 1890s America all these previous moments—religion, literature, politics, economics—are taken up in the modern conception of history. The story is not completed but only becoming, and future presents will find in it new meanings. For Droysen as for Turner this deepening of experience is what history *is*: "History is humanity becoming and being conscious concerning itself."[13]

This premise and conclusion, that history is the developing self-consciousness of humankind, constitutes the first article of Turnerian faith, history is dialectic. It is the closest thing to a unifying principle in Turner's writings and it shaped even his monographs. Like the frontier thesis, the claim that history is the self-consciousness of humanity is a grand metaphor, a claim that history is something else. It is also a mnemonic, a single-sentence summary of an entire story about how history works. And it is the hinge upon which "Significance of History" turns. Once we accept this notion, "all the rest follows." First, history comprises all spheres of human activity, and we cannot separate politics from economics from literature from religion without intellectual violence, for no one department of life can be understood in isolation. Each of these divisions finds its meaning in relation to the others. Next, we see that "history is not shut up in a book," for history changes with each age and revision. Since it is developmental, there can be no ultimate histories, no last words, no timeless natural order. Finally, history reveals both unity and continuity. "Strictly speaking," history cannot be atomized into isolated periods, places, or processes. ("Evil cleaves to the finite spirit," said Droysen.) Differences, divisions, and dramatic conflicts find their meanings in the overarching unity of the story line, what Turner later called, in a wonderful bit of mystic hyperbole, "The One-ness of the thing."[14]

The crux is the romantic faith in holism. Varieties of holism undergirded nineteenth-century social philosophies from Hegel to Comte. Turner fearlessly invoked both idealist and positivist visions, and in his lines unity is both temporal and spiritual. In the temporal sphere the present is the product of the past, all those traditions that have made it what it is. The past too, though, is a product of the present, revised by the conditions, questions, and stories of each age. The relation is dialectical. Past and present are reciprocally and mutually determining, neither fully separate nor fused into a single, undifferentiated moment but held together by their intimacy in history. They find meaning in their relationship to each other. In this way time works as a continuous stream, differentiated and pluralistic, but nonetheless whole.

Spirit comprises the matrix of moral relations that make up human existence, all the bonds of kin, custom, and country that structure human life. Like temporality, spirit too demonstrates an underlying unity and continuity. Here Turner's holism is fairly complex. We have horizontal continuity, in which each nation and society are bound up with all the others into the integrated human universe. Local history is global history, and vice versa. But we also have vertical continuity, for the past works into the present as each national spirit flows into the others, each epoch preserving within it the elements passed down by the previous ages and societies. By reading the social traces of the past off our present-day surroundings, we find support for our belief in temporal connection. "Even here in young America," said Turner, "old Rome still lives." In the Senate chamber, in the code of Louisiana, in the traditions of the Roman Catholic Church, "There is Rome!"[15]

The illustration serves a larger philosophical point. Dialectic shapes history as written and history as lived. As it structures the universe, it also structures the psychology and poesy of historical practice.

Each nation has bequeathed something to its successor; no age has suffered the highest content of the past to be lost entirely. By unconscious inheritance, and by conscious striving after the past as part of the present, history has acquired continuity. . . . So it is true in fact, as we should assume a priori, that in history there are only artificial divisions.

By choosing one style of history rather than another or by revising the forms of our predecessors, we freely hammer the past into the shape we find most plausible and useful. Turner called that process the "subjective" side of history, the way historians narrate memory into order by consciously "striving after" some particular vision. But dialectic also engages the "objective" side of history, both the actual happening of events and the meanings they accumulate. These traditions make up the community's "unconscious inheritance" within which the historian works and which determines the available literary forms and historical modes. Our inheritance constitutes the conditions of possibility within which we revise the past. To that extent historians are destined to wander paths opened by past generations. Yet within these horizons, we reform the past into shapes congruent with the spirit of the age and, since we are products of that history, by rewriting it we remake ourselves.[16]

These were deep and treacherous waters. At issue was the relative significance of necessity and freedom in human life. The general thrust of dialectic was that individuals were the changing historical products of evolving moral forces or powers; Droysen spoke of "partnerships" or "potencies" and suggested that these became concrete in social institutions like the family, the tribe, the state, and religion. Individuals were in some way abstractions from these manifestations of spirit. One might infer that history shapes us far more than we shape it. But the inference undercut Victorian America's liberal political axioms and devout capitalism, which imagined the individual as free moral agent, a rational, autonomous, and typically masculine social actor making his way in the world. Turner's resolution, that the individual historian is the product of tradition but still, in some mediate fashion, able to revise that inheritance, slipped the horns of this dilemma with a bland confidence.

The resolution parallels that explored by Droysen's *Outline*. For the German theorist, the unity of past and present could be warranted by historical investigation. We can read the past in the present as "faded traces and surpassed gleams," like the spirit of ancient Rome bleeding through the law code of Louisiana into the present of Turner's America. These traces make up the inherited familial, political, and social relations that define both national spirit and individual ways of being. Each person thus owes his or her very existence to the past, and even the "I" of the historian is "historically mediated," something to be read off these indistinct signs and then negotiated and rewritten. Here too dialectic shapes existence, as the individual finds himself or herself in the larger order, willfully acting within the patterns determined by past experience. In this way, Droysen believed, we overcome the "false alternative" between freedom and necessity. Turner found the idea persuasive, as far as he understood it, but many others did not. The British historian Lord Acton, for instance, whose writings Turner quoted freely, claimed that Droysen and others of his school had nothing to offer Anglophone tradition. And even in Germany some liberals saw Droysen's historicism as authoritarian.[17] What then made this tradition attractive to Turner and his readers?

We do not know how historicism played to Turner's audience, but even those educators who had never heard of Droysen or Hegel probably found its language reasonably familiar if not altogether accessible. They had grown up listening to variations on these themes, and in two of Turner's favorite writers, Walt Whitman and Ralph Waldo Emerson, German idealism blended with distinctively American forms. In the 1870s Whitman had brashly declared Hegel the only philosopher suited for the New World: "Only Hegel is fit for America—is large enough and free enough. . . . The varieties, contradictions, and paradoxes of the world and of life, and even good and evil, so baffling to the observer, and so often leading to despair, sullenness or infidelity, become a series of infinite radiations and waves of the one sea-like universe of divine action and progress, never stopping, never hasting." Typically enough, Whitman seems to have known Hegel only through secondary accounts but found in these glosses a sense of the "One-ness of the thing" to overcome the vulgar dualisms of Enlightenment and Christian orthodoxy.[18]

Whitman saw himself as Emerson's poet of the future, destined to give voice to American spirit and repair a world torn asunder into nature and history, good and evil, the one and the many. His own projects carefully balanced American newness against the imperatives of heritage. Consider, for instance, his 1868 "Passage to India." Like many period writings, Turner's essays included, the poem begins in the present, moves into the past, and then returns. It opens with one of the wonders of the modern world, the Suez Canal, and then quickly dives toward the voyage of Columbus, exploring the narrative depths that shaped the surface of the nineteenth century.

> The Past—the dark unfathom'd retrospect!
> The teeming gulf—the sleepers and the shadows!
> The past—the infinite greatness of the past!
> For what is the present after all but a growth out of the past?
> (As a projectile form'd, impell'd, passing a certain line,
>   still keeps on,
> So the present, utterly form'd, impell'd by the past.)

Determinism and freedom, past and present, mystically accommodate each other. We might be utterly formed and impelled by the past, but in Whitman's happy chanting we hear no doubt as to the ultimate compatibility of free will and history, self and society, capitalism and democracy, religion and science. These are subject alike to that transcendent "Thou" shadowing every line of *Leaves of Grass,* another set of the infinite radiations of divine progress. Critic Kenneth Burke called this attitude toward history a "comic frame of acceptance," an American theodicy in which good confronts evil with boundless optimism. And in such Emersonian lyrics serious young readers like Frederick Jackson Turner found substitutes for the more orthodox religiosity that had inspired their parents.[19]

Of the many figures involved in the transfiguration of American spirituality, we should single out Ralph Waldo Emerson. The New England minister, orator, and apostle of culture fathered Turner's own writings, and the young historian, like Whitman, was especially taken with the language of Emerson's "The Poet." "Treat things poetically," commanded the prophet, and in this text, which first appeared in the *Essays: Second Series* (1844), Emerson called for a visionary to join together the raw, chaotic fragments of American experience. Dante's *Divine Comedy* had done this literary service for Europe; now America needed an allegory of its own.

Dante's praise is that he dared write his autobiography in colossal cipher, or into universality. We have yet no genius in America, with tyrannous eye, which knew the value of our incomparable materials, and saw, in the barbarism and materialism of the times, another carnival of the same gods whose picture he so admires in Homer. . . . Our log-rolling, our stumps and their politics, our Negroes and Indians, our boasts and their repudiations, the wrath of rogues and the pusillanimity of honest men, the northern trader, the southern planting, the western clearing, Oregon and Texas, are yet unsung. Yet America is a poem in our eyes; its ample geography dazzles the imagination, and it will not wait long for metres.

Antithesis and parataxis dominate Emersonian form: Negroes and Indians, boasts and repudiations, wrath and pusillanimity, rogues and honest men. And form serves content. In Emerson's metaphysics polarities rule the world, but only as the constitutive elements of that transcendent energy he variously called Nature, spirit, soul, the Over-Soul, or simply the "eternal ONE." So in cataloging the country's disunities, the desired end is not chaotic pluralism but the poem of America, the larger self that these antinomies make possible, the spirit that requires the tyrannous imagination of the strong poet to give it voice. Spirit demands expression, but expression demands a Dante, an individual creativity sufficiently self-reliant that it not drown in the overwhelming diversity of experience. And the appeal to Dante engaged artistic politics, for *The Divine Comedy* had elevated Italian vernacular, the form of popular culture, to the status of legitimate art, much as Emerson hoped to see done for the language of America.[20]

Emerson saw no need to travel to Europe for romance. Properly performed, the most menial labor achieved artistry. Romance was a matter of attitude, of careful reading, of finding lyric in unexpected places and epic in actions considered crude and vulgar by European convention. Instead of building a fortified frontier between materialism and idealism, we should turn one into the other, converting America's barbarisms and material wealth into a spiritual currency on a par with that of Europe. The badges and banners of political brawling, the flags and colors of village parades, the homely icons and indices of daily life, all contained entire volumes of meaning, all were symbols available to the creative imagination. "America is a poem in our eyes," stretching out across the continent like so many Homeric stanzas waiting to be transposed into a democratic cadence. In this project the one-time Unitarian minister found his calling. Few American poets denied his influence, even fewer students escaped reading his essays, and virtually no rhetoricians avoided the careful study of his style.[21]

In a prize-winning undergraduate oration of 1883, "The Poet of the Future," young Turner shamelessly rehashed Emerson's "The Poet." In the undergraduate's reworking, Homer and Dante haunt the stacks of the Great Library of the universe in anticipation of the coming American genius: "He will unite the logic of the present and the dream of the past, and his words will ring in the ears of generations yet unborn. . . . As surely as our age transcends all others, so surely will his song rise above all the singers of the past." To this artistry even Dante will bow, witness to "the divinity of man and nature." The Wisconsinite hailed Emerson directly, echoing his rhetorical rhythms, dropping his favorite names, and exploring the relation of the individual and spirit.

All the arts are but different manifestations of this same spirit of genius. The chivalry of the middle ages has now become poetry; for it was poetry then, for there is a poetry of action. "Life," says Emerson, "may be lyric or epic." Here then is the key to our times. That spirit, which in the past has found expression in an epic, such as Homer's, or a drama, such as Shakespeare's, now turned into a new channel, again waits poetic utterance.

The phrasing is Emersonian, the theme is transcendental, the metaphors are literary, but the conception of history is Turner's own. All arts and ages partake of spirit, but it manifests itself in different historical figures and forms. The finding that life may be lyric or epic was key for both Emerson and Turner, but where Emerson's text implies that this discovery attests to the pluralism of experience, Turner reads it as evidence of historical process. Life is not lyric or epic at random. These forms are stages in a story. History moves from epic to lyric to drama, from Homer to Dante to Shakespeare, and while each form preserves traces of its ancestors, there is no pure reversal of succession. Nor is historical form a matter of taking up whichever style strikes our fancy;

those not suited to the place and period will fail. This age has its peculiar poetry of action, its literary form of worldly experience which its histories must reproduce, and only authentic expressions of genius will survive.[22]

Turner delivered "The Poet of the Future" in 1883, one year after Emerson's death. In its style and conception, we can see how his early education prepared him for the historicists he read in graduate school. Transcendentalism's balancing of polar opposites in a higher unity, the fascination with a metaphysics strong enough to replace a strict Christianity yet sympathetic to scholarly inquiry, the sense of the universe as profoundly moral, all these themes readied Turner for the descriptions of historical practice he found in thinkers like J. G. Droysen, Rudolf Rocholl, and Ottokar Lorenz, whose works grace the Eurocentric bibliography of "The Significance of History." "The Poet of the Future" suggests Turner's debt to the transcendentalists, but it also hints at a vision of process and progress more orderly than that articulated in either Emerson or Whitman, a willingness to imagine history as the telling of a grand tale in which cosmic unity expressed itself in an evolutionary fashion. Order resides not in stasis but in story. In 1891 Turner cannibalized the "The Poet of the Future" for "The Significance of History," and Emerson's dictum, Treat things poetically, joined the historicist's, Treat things historically.

The blend looked smooth enough, provided one did not demand too much of it. Emerson, like Whitman, was at least nominally connected to Hegelian tradition, if only as an auxiliary member of the Hegelian St. Louis Philosophical Society. Of course, he was also tangentially related to virtually every famous strand of period thought and culture we could name, and most of these connections are fairly ambiguous. We can safely say only that Emerson was systematically Emersonian, but for a reader trained in his writings, as Turner and most members of his audience were, Hegel's and Droysen's accounts of the growth of historical consciousness must have looked familiar. Consider this passage from Emerson's 1841 essay "History": "A man is the whole encyclopedia of facts. The creation of a thousand forests is in one acorn, and Egypt, Greece, Rome, Gaul, Britain, America, lie enfolded in the first man. Epoch after epoch, camp, kingdom, empire, republic, democracy, are merely the application of his manifold spirit to the manifold world." Beside this stand Hegel's *Phenomenology of Spirit* and *Philosophy of History*. In these texts, standard works in professor George Sylvester Morris's introductory philosophy courses at Johns Hopkins, no history ever is lost, everything of historical value survives in spirit's journey to self-consciousness, and "those moments which the spirit appears to have outgrown still belong to it in the depths of its present."[23]

The limited relation of Emerson and Hegel is one of homology more than genetic influence. Emerson's self-reliant ego is distant from Hegel's notion of selfhood, he viewed history ("the vanishing allegory") with some suspicion, and the mature Hegel would never have signed on to Emerson's throw-away line, "The hint of the dialectic is more valuable than the dialectic itself." But in each of their works readers could imagine ways in which all the apparent contradictions, conflicts, and chaos of experience worked into more satisfying harmonies without melting into homogeneity. Here is the "Know Thyself" that Turner read as the *summa* of historical understanding and that made up the discursive world in which he moved. History is the self-consciousness of the organism we call society, and the historian's role as storyteller is to articulate that self-consciousness, to give voice to spirit and the moments and stages it has traversed in dialectical passage toward its present existence. It is the distinctively American version of spirit that we must attend.[24]

Emerson's spirit moved in mysterious and manifold ways. In his early writings "Nature" speaks of Spirit, the absolute, an ineffable essence more sublime than the scholarly cosmos of traditional idealism. In this construction his more orthodox critics found not the meters of democracy but the mark of the beast, and they described it as devilish pantheism. But if not acceptably Christian, it remained devoutly metaphysical. In the second series of essays nature became a deep power binding all the parts, particles, divisions, and successions of experience into that energetic repose called the Over-Soul. What role history played, a burning question for young historians in the 1880s, remained obscure. In "Nature" history looked like one of those artifices standing between us and an original relation to the universe, a division to be torn down. And even in "The Poet" Emerson held out a pure source outside of history: "For poetry was all written before time was" and every attempt to recapture that lyric is doomed to failure. The historian can never reconstruct the original text. The present impinges, we substitute meanings of our own, and thus "miswrite the poem." One doubts that young Turner found the construction entirely satisfying; his sense of history ran far too deep.[25]

German historicism offered alternatives more easily adapted to the needs of a working historian. Although Hegel's dialectic did not march to the mechanical drumbeat alternately vilified and valorized by his popularizers, it displayed a discipline foreign to Emerson. In Hegel's works national spirit sets a community apart from others while placing it in intimate relation to the movement of spirit or history in the abstract. This spirit of a nation is the accumulated sum of its motion, its narrated identity in time. Nations *are* their history. And the identity of a truly historical nation exemplifies a stage in the larger spirit of history, a moment in spirit's never-ending journey toward freedom. As national spirit is the sum of its deeds, for Hegel spirit in the abstract is the historical summation of all its stages, taken up into one great narrative. Moreover, that universal history develops in space as well as time, marching from the east toward the west, a notion that must have appealed to amateur philosophers on the western edge of American "civilization," the place Hegel called the "land of the future."[26]

For Turner "spirit" did not hold all the technical meanings that it had for Hegel. But his forthrightly positive assessment of historical process finally falls closer to the Hegelians than to Emerson. In his search for historical consciousness, we find no nostalgia for an Ur-text or ahistorical nature. Darwin had brought nature into history so effectively as to change forever the way readers related to Emerson's early essays. Nature evolves, spirit develops, the poetry of action progresses, and this is all well and good. And the concrete poetry of American institutions, customs, events, and transactions held Turner's attention. "The Significance of History" lists the requirements for a successful narration of America. The story must actualize the sort of communal self-consciousness to which both transcendentalists and historicists appeal. It must relate the intimacy of past and present. It must locate a uniquely American history in a global setting. It must imagine the country's inhabitants as historical products. And it must write itself as the evolving synthesis of moral forces interacting with each other and with nature. This understanding, lamented Turner, we do not yet own, for while America may have found its poet in Whitman, it has not found its historian: "The story of the peopling of America has not yet been written. We do not understand ourselves." Turner's peroration left an opening into which a historian of the future might heroically leap, but it also threatened to wander off into very dark corners.[27]

The claim that the meaning of historical events changed with time raised the specter of nihilism. If events had no intrinsic significance, what could stop some historian from willfully perverting the national memory? If Americans did not understand themselves, what possible claims could they make on history? Turner ended his essay by trying to cordon off these vistas, and he did so by appealing to social loyalty. As a narrative of the developing consciousness of spirit, history was above all the story of moral evolution. The whole thrust, purpose, aim, and meaning of history found itself in ethical and moral relations. "Ethics and History are co-ordinates," said Droysen, and Turner affirmed that while the study of history had some use as a "mental discipline," its real value was pragmatic: "Its most practical utility to us, as public school teachers, is its service in fostering good citizenship," and this is the "end for which public schools exist." The teacher of history had his or her own destiny as "apostle of higher culture to the community." Given conscientious, devoted teachers and a systematic effort to popularize historical and scientific knowledge, we could "work a revolution in our towns and villages. . . . [W]e would have an intellectual regeneration of the state."[28]

Beyond such immediate political ends, historian-apostles bore an additional burden. In exchange for self-conscious existence, they and their audiences assumed an intellectual debt, an obligation to the past to reshape it in empirically and morally responsible ways. One could never escape unconscious inheritance, one could never fully raise to rational view all those forces conditioning one's understanding, but deliberate cynical manipulation by the storyteller was beyond the pale. "Of one thing beware. Avoid as the very unpardonable sin any one-sidedness, any partisan, any partial treatment of history. Do not misrepresent the past for the sake of the present. The man who enters the temple of history must respond devoutly to that invocation of the church, *Sursum corda,* lift up your hearts."

Turner was at most a lukewarm Unitarian, but this much loyalty to the older, millennial visions of history remained in his vocabulary. Having opened with a relativized pluralism, he closed with a sacralized injunction to respect the unity of existence, a metaquote of Droysen revising the words of John the Baptist: "History is not the truth and the light; but a striving for it, a sermon on it, a consecration to it." To our jaded ears, such language is marvelously heroic stuff—history as mystery religion, historian as apostle—and this is a measure of our distance. It is hard to imagine the resonance of this sermon in a Madison lecture hall, young Turner in the pulpit at the head of the room, expounding the gospel of the past to his schoolteacher flock, winning souls for history, he and his listeners brought together in the spoken word. But we would be wrong to imagine it as "mere" rhetoric or as a verbal sugarcoating for a harder empirical core. We have no reason to doubt the sincerity of Turner and his listeners. And the movement from the opening salute to historical pluralism to the closing invocation to unity follows its own poetic logic.[29]

Seeing history as dialectic meant seeing it as moral event. The notion is somewhat more subtle than the vision that characterized the work of romantic historians like George Bancroft. Turner did not hold forth a Mosaic law or ethical code. He did not invoke the natural rights of man to which Thomas Jefferson and Thomas Paine had appealed in their rebellion against the state and which many Americans supposed to be their greatest inheritance. Since history developed and changed, there could be no timeless ethical or legal prescriptions. Historical method was grounded only on the customs of each age and society, but these were, broadly speaking, moral relations, for only in them did history, community, and individuals find their existence. Only in them could human life have any value. Only in them could individuals aspire to freedom. And, like Droysen, Turner emplotted the customs and values of his own age and community as a moral norm. What he saw as American freedom of thought and action encouraged the cultivation of a historical consciousness and helped to maintain that continuing process of self-criticism which gave history meaning and direction in the absence of Christian teleology.

A didactic element did remain in "The Significance of History," even though Turner did not hold up the lives of historical figures, a Caesar or a Washington, as models of how to behave. He presented no morality by historical example in this sense, although his schoolteacher listeners must have known and practiced such techniques. Turner was much more present-minded: It is the individual historian who must exemplify virtue for the community and lead it to a self-critical understanding of its own ways. The historian must be the apostle of higher culture. This was the mission of one and all, both Turner and his flock. He reserved his highest praise for those historians, and here he named George Bancroft, Lord Acton, and Droysen, who actively involved themselves in community life. Historians must teach by action, reaching out to politicians and reformers, speaking with broad publics in textbooks and popular journals, and above all encouraging the growth and development of public institutions: elementary schools, high schools, state universities, and college extension courses. Education is not a profession but a calling, and to teach history is to testify to the developing spirit of the moral universe. Through pedagogical and scholarly acts, history advanced, national consciousness matured, and the virtue of the republic could be, not preserved, but *developed*.

"The Significance of History" was a statement of youth but it was hardly wild. It broke with Turner's mentors in scientific history and called for revolution in the towns and villages, but its immediate political tone was relentlessly conservative. Continuity, obligation, debt, responsibility, regeneration, and loyalty to the state suggest bourgeois maturity rather than radical adolescence. Turner appropriated romantic and transcendentalist themes as much as he anticipated Progressivism. He rejected Herbert Baxter Adams's notion of history as the strictly empirical study of past politics, but he moved past this father figure by appealing to another: Adams's own mentor, J. G. Droysen. And he framed this appeal to German historicism in Emersonian language. The historian would replace Whitman as the poet of the future, defining the national spirit and narrating the developing self-consciousness of humanity, all in the service of America's limited democracy.

Turner's statism was conservative, but his historicism threatened a radical break. If each age rewrites history, if history changes with time, what assures us that history, as such, exists? If history is one thing for the savage and another for us, how can we say that we are even talking about the same subject? For Hegel the unchanging essence of spirit in the abstract kept historicism from sliding into relativism. Spirit varied in its particulars from time to time and place to place, but its inner logic followed a determinate pattern, something he first attempted to work out in his *Phenomenology of Spirit* and expanded in his later works on logic. But Turner's homemade historicism sets no clear bounds on the ways history remakes itself. It does not enlist Hegel's abstract and complicated arguments for the dialectical logic of consciousness (which Turner most likely did not know). Nor does it reproduce the timeless essence of Emerson's Over-Soul. In Turner's story Gods and nature dominated the savage consciousness, politics and science shaped the Prussian world, while economic and social questions control his own. But the only grounds for privileging one or another idea of history are the conditions and values of each community. And these shift from age to age and place to place, held together only by the continuity of time and the historian's obligation to act in morally and empirically responsible ways, ultimately measured by evolving instrumental standards. *Sursum corda*, lift up your hearts!

We cannot fairly describe "The Significance of History" as philosophically rigorous. Turner was no philosopher, and he was never terribly systematic. His essays leap breathlessly from passage to passage, theme to theme, and school to school. The optimistic sense that all will cohere seems touchingly hopeful if not truly naive. But we can fairly say that he anticipated twentieth-century historiography by abandoning Hegel's metaphysics in favor of a pragmatic (Hegel would have said utilitarian) understanding. Why choose one history over another, why declare one story of national spirit superior to others? Turner's only answer to these very difficult questions was that a history ought to be judged by its contribution to the moral fabric, for its critical and intelligent loyalty to community. Loyalty included a certain allegiance to the methods of critical scholarship and empiricism, since his age had inherited them and taken them up, but loyalty was only a means to a larger end and not a ground of historical knowledge.

We should also be wary of reading in Turner a simple triumph of idealism over science, not only because he was more poetic than systematic but also because he saw no irreducible conflict between the two. He drew freely on positivists as distinct as Comte and Lamprecht and idealists as different as Schelling and Droysen. Dialectic held these apparent antitheses in harmony: "All arts are but different manifestations of this same spirit." As a result, the methodological dualisms of the late nineteenth century, idealism and materialism, positivism and empiricism, historical understanding and scientific knowledge, looked as transcendable as any of the other categorical divisions scholars might contrive, and the question of whether history was a science or an art looked equally avoidable. Art, science, literature, all came together in history. And since history offers up no graspable unchanging essence—beyond temporal holism—the real core of continuity lies not in history itself but in the making of it, the becoming of it, the endlessly reenacted moral event of writing human community into existence. Such relativistic pragmatism, for 1891 America, *was* fairly radical, although in Turner's own career it remained tightly leashed to a calm content with his own present.[30]

Dialectic circulated through academic discourse in the 1890s, and Harvard still boasted one "Hegelian" philosopher in Californian Josiah Royce, but these traditions were on their last legs in American academic philosophy, assailed by new naturalistic vocabularies: the pragmatism of William James, the psychology of G. Stanley Hall, and, soon, the logic of C. I. Lewis. And yet Turner made dialectic and universal history both form and content of the story of the American past. "The Significance of History" prefigured key themes in his later work, and the frontier dialectic was one of these: "Our history is only to be understood as a growth from European history under the new conditions of the New World." Here we see the kernel of Turner's narrative of the growth of American consciousness. The antagonism between inherited European history and the new conditions of North America produced American democracy, a higher synthesis that preserves traces of both its ancestral agonists and holds in balance a complex of antithetical elements. A year later Turner's "Problems in American History" said it this way: "American history needs a connected and unified account of the progress of civilization across this continent, with the attendant results. Until such a work is finished, we shall have no real national self-consciousness; when it is done, the significance of the discovery made by Columbus will begin to appear." That labor had been Whitman's, but the year of this essay, 1892, was the year of his death. So a new son of the middle border heroically took up the torch, raiding the archives for the raw stuff of American spirit and scanning the historical meters of national identity. The figures of these early essays anticipate Turner's greatest trope: the history of the United States is the history of the colonization of the great West.[31]

Frontier Dialectics

As idealism à la Royce and Morris came under siege in philosophy, it wandered across the quad, and a story line adapted from Hegelian universal history recast historical scholarship. Turner's *The Frontier in American History* (1920) gathered many of the essays he wrote during the quarter-century following 1891's "The Significance of History," and their dialectics reprise that earlier sermon. The struggle between free land and settlement, wilderness and civilization, provides the central drama as nature and history interweave to create the changing forms of American democracy. And just as history holds the traces of the evolving relations of past and present, democracy carries the various antagonisms that contributed to its formation. Although a historical democracy might move in unhappy directions, Turner and most of his readers imagined the story as a happy one, and together they built a tradition of frontier comedy.

Turner's American democracy arose from the frontier dialectic of North American environment and European spirit. In 1893 "The Significance of the Frontier in American History" described the historian's task: "In the settlement of America we have to observe how European life entered the continent, and how America modified and developed that life and reacted on Europe." American Anglo-Saxon institutions did not spring up in transplanted Germanic purity from the earth of the Atlantic seaboard, as Turner's mentor Herbert Baxter Adams believed, but reshaped themselves in dialectical struggle with nature.

The wilderness masters the colonist. . . . In short, at the frontier the environment is at first too strong for the man. He must accept the conditions which it furnishes or perish, and so he fits himself into the Indian clearings and follows the Indian trails. Little by little he transforms the wilderness, but the outcome is not old Europe, not simply the development of Germanic germs, any more than the first phenomenon was a case of reversion to the Germanic mark. The fact is, that here is a new product that is American.

The interaction of free land and settlement, of wilderness and European colonist, produced the higher synthesis of American democracy, a complex spirit holding the traces of all its previous moments together in an evolving matrix.[32]

Turner's frontier dialectic reproduced the great philosophical questions of the day. The single word, frontier, encoded the story's central struggle, commonly expressed in the antitheses of free land and settlement or wilderness and civilization. And these reproduced the abstract divisions of contemporary intellectual life in Western Europe and America, the interaction and interdependence of nature and history, what idealists from Fichte to Droysen saw as the most fundamental of analytic categories. And the estrangement of natural and moral worlds cut to the quick of transcendentalist longing, "this separate Nature so unnatural," and evoked Whitman's dream, "The new society at last, proportionate to Nature." Once again Turner's patrimony enforced a narrative that reconciled, without collapsing, the polarities of nature and history.[33]

In *Frontier*, as in "The Significance of History," dialectic soars and leaps. The story spreads out across the North American continent and may be read off the map from right to left, the synthesis of nature and history becoming more American and less European with each mile and decade traversed. Plot rolls from east to west, from the past to the present, from the Columbian voyages to the urban cityscape of San Francisco's Gilded Age. It can also be read from west to east as universal history impressed in American soil. Turner quoted Italian economist Achille Loria:

"America," he says, "has the key to the historical enigma which Europe has sought for centuries in vain, and this land which has no history reveals luminously the course of universal history." There is much truth in this. The United States lies like a huge page in the history of society. Line by line as we read this continental page from West to East we find the record of social evolution. . . . Particularly in the eastern states this page is a palimpsest.

In the free lands on the western side of the continent, one found peoples living in a state of savagery. Moving east (and upward), one encountered in geographic progression all the developmental steps of social order, from hunting and trapping, to haphazard dirt-farming, to intensive agriculture, to urban industrialism. In America, the development of historical consciousness imprinted the landscape.[34]

At each stop of the frontier's continental march, society evolved from savagery to civilization in the space of a few decades. Along the interface of nature and history, environment broke through the patina of European tradition and elevated the faded traces of past ages to dominance, rejuvenating the barbaric tendencies latent in civilization. As the frontier swept on, each place it had touched retained the imprint of these older forms. But this was not linear devolution. As civilization contained traces of barbarism, the backcountry bore the marks of its civilized antithesis. One could not render such complexity with the linear chronologies of what Turner called "narrative history of the older type," and in his text past and present weave in and out in formal illustration of his faith in temporal continuity. He told the story first from the perspective of one character and region, then retold it from another. In one passage the frontier experience is related in the present tense, in the next we drop back into the past. And this constant collision of past and present, savage and civilized, nature and history, rejuvenated American political institutions by driving them back to the conditions of their deep ancestral past only to mature once more, as nature simultaneously destroyed, preserved, and remade American spiritual existence.[35]

So the tale's dramatic tensions connected with larger conversations defining the relations of human and natural worlds. We have already discussed Turner's concept of history. History is the mutual revision of past and present in a cosmic narrative of moral evolution, a story in which spirit manifests itself in changing customs, habits, and institutions. What, though, is Turnerian Nature? Wilderness, free land, abundance, barrier, nurturer, a spur to profligacy, the sphere in which morality develops; nature is all of these. As a result, the relation between nature and history becomes every bit as mobile as the words themselves. Factor in the resonance of this discussion for Turner's readers, imagine the diversity of expectation they brought to the text, and dialectic grows complex and not entirely predictable. Look first at this example:

European men, institutions, and ideas were lodged in the American wilderness, and this great American West took them to her bosom, taught them a new way of looking upon the destiny of the common man, trained them in adaptation to the conditions of the New World, to the creation of new institutions to meet new needs. . . . [S]he opened new provinces, and dowered new democracies in her most impoverished domains with her material treasures and with the ennobling influence that the fierce love of freedom, the strength that came from hewing out a home, making a school and a church, and creating a higher future for his family, furnished to the pioneer.

Here the story describes the harmonious blending of civilization with its wilderness complement. Nature is republican mother embodying half of white middle-class America's imagined female essence: woman as teacher, as nurturer, as keeper of civic virtue for a masculine community imperiled by the vices of history. Nature teaches, opens, nurtures, and dowers history with gifts. History creates, adapts, and incorporates the natural dowry in a positive dialectic that lifts the spiritual sphere up into a higher future.[36]

A few paragraphs farther along, though, we find the conflict developed quite differently.

The first ideal of the pioneer was that of conquest. It was his task to fight with nature for the chance to exist. Not as in older countries did this contest take place in a mythical past, told in folk lore and epic. It has been continuous to our own day. Facing each generation of colonists was the unmastered continent. Vast forests blocked the way; mountainous ramparts interposed; desolate, grass-clad prairies, barren oceans of rolling plains, arid deserts, and a fierce race of savages, all had to be met and defeated.

This second excerpt narrates a contest whose outcome can only be the annihilation of one or both agonists. The allusion to epic and folklore suggests the masculine contests of battle and adventure, the Homeric quest and Norse epic of invasion, conquest, and slaughter. Both agonists are male, but only one will survive the collision. This is the classic kernel of romance, its outcome the elevation of transcendent hero over vanquished foe. Juxtapose its heroic tone against the first quote, and we might imagine an even darker reading in which nature, despite its associations with masculine tales of camp and trail, is gendered as female in a story of plunder, exploitation, and destruction, giving us a second dominant image of the female in Victorian America, woman as sexual being, either despoiled virgin or fallen seductress. Masculine history negates and transcends feminine nature.[37]

We might complicate the reading by pointing out the technical connotations for Victorian economists of phrases like "free land" or sketching the various ways that Social Darwinists might have read Turner's account of social development, but these examples should suffice to make the point that this story, like all stories, is not an aesthetic monad. Emplotment is more a matter of which connections readers make, of which passages we emphasize, than of formal essence. As in "The Significance of History," dialectic is story. History is the narrative of humanity's developing self-consciousness, and North American history is a chapter in that grand tale. The drama wrote itself into the landscape, and, given dedication and empirical rigor, one could read it off the continental page. But here too the story has multiple meanings, and neither Turner nor his readers could hold it to a single, unified course. Thrown into the tangled text of daily life, the tale shifted with each new reading as different interests manifested themselves in different literary forms. This variation was true not only of the story's kernel, as nature and history shifted from line to line, but of plot mode as well. To get a better sense of this, we need to return to Turner's early explorations of art, literature, and history.[38]

In 1883 "The Poet of the Future" had invoked Emerson's notion that life may be either epic or lyric. Turner added that it might also be drama, as it had been for Shakespeare. But what dramatic form should history take? A year later another undergraduate oration, "Architecture through Oppression," followed Emersonian paths toward a possible answer. To the American traveling in Europe, said Turner, the Old World's cityscapes look ancient, impressive, and aesthetically superior to the "plebeian" styles of American architecture. For the tourist marveling at Notre Dame or the casual reader of *Ivanhoe*, history looks like a straightforward romance, a happy story of the adventures of the few. But the historian could tease a deeper story out of these sources. Beneath the glossy surface of Europe's romance lay the unread but compelling tragedy of the many. The experience of Europe's laboring masses, all those strong-backed workers whose lifeblood had gone into the building of the pyramids, castles, and cathedrals of the Old World, had been a tragic one: "The history of humanity has been a romance and a tragedy! In it we read the brilliant annals of the few who seemed born to reap the fruits of the earth. . . . But the tragedy of humanity! Millions groaning that one might laugh." And the moral? Rejoice in the plain frame buildings and modest cities of the United States, for their homely shapes encode the progressive story of freedom.[39]

German historicism gave Turner a clearer sense of universal history, but it did not change his classification of literary form. Romance served the upper classes, tragedy, the lower. "The Significance of History" cannibalized "The Poet of the Future":

History has been a romance and a tragedy. In it we read the brilliant annals of the few. The intrigues of courts, knightly valor, palaces and pyramids, the loves of ladies, the songs of minstrels, and the chants from cathedrals pass like a pageant or linger like a strain of music as we turn the pages. But history has its tragedy as well, which tells of the degraded tillers of the soil, toiling that others might dream, the slavery that rendered possible "the Glory that was Greece," the serfdom into which decayed the "grandeur that was Rome"—these as well demand their annals.

Turner collapsed form into content, literature into history, art into science: History *is* a dialectical story, the American continent is a page in universal history, the landscape-page is a palimpsest, the colonization of the Ohio River Valley wrote a chapter in that tale, the wilderness was a fair, blank page on which Europeans inscribed a new future, the past is a book we live, write, and read. And European history exemplifies the double plot. It is a romance for those God-like heroes who inhabited the worlds created by the Greeks and the romantic historians like Sir Walter Scott or Francis Parkman but a tragedy for the oppressed commoners whose exploits do not appear in histories of Great Men and novels of character.[40]

For Turner the implication seemed to be that the new social or economic histories of the "common man" would be tragedies. But "Architecture through Oppression" had called for a new future in which life's tragedy did not clash with life's romance, in which these conflicts too could be transcended, swept up in the "wave of democratic utilitarianism" cresting in the New World. And Turner's optimism did not encompass a tragic destiny for his own community. The tragedy of the Greek slaves, the feudal serfs, and the unpropertied classes in the sweatshops of Europe could not articulate American consciousness. Tragedy had two features that worked against reading it into the American landscape. First, the classic tragedies ended with the fall of the hero, while Turner saw his story as a brighter movement toward a complex but nonetheless optimistically open resolution. Moreover, classic tragedies stripped human actors of volition and free will, painting them as so many grains of sand driven before the winds of history. The torment of Oedipus could not generate a productive social bond in Turner's America; however useful an illumination of the lifeways of classical Greece, it could not easily reinforce the liberal philosophy and capitalist economy of the United States.[41]

Romance posed its own problems. In this area the Euro-American literary tradition already was quite rich and its conventions reasonably clear. The histories of Francis Parkman and his contemporaries visibly shared literary features with the romances of the age. As historiographer David Levin has pointed out, these histories paralleled the great novels of character in their vision of history as the deeds of great men. Heroes are aristocratic, from the blue-blood leaders of the French and British military, Montcalm and Wolfe, to the noble savagery of Pontiac, and Parkman's most famous works, *Montcalm and Wolfe* and *The Conspiracy of Pontiac*, emplot a comparatively simple conflict between those forces carrying the course of history and those not so favored. History and its noble hero usually triumph. Conflicts are stark, outcomes happy, the prose picturesque, the heroes noble, and the ideological implications predominantly reactionary, in line with Parkman's assessment of the evils of female suffrage, the rural mind-set, and middle-class political leadership. Little wonder that even in American stories Turner might suspect that elitism lurked behind romance.[42]

Turner could not easily write American history as romance. His rejection of the Great Man conception of history militated against a plot in which individual heroes drove the action, and his allegiance to a limited, middle-class, male-dominated democracy worked against any celebration of natural aristocracy. A subaltern romance, in contrast, with a "realistic" and plebeian protagonist, had little in the way of precedent to recommend it. The story of the frontiersman, the tale that Turner saw as *the* history of America, did not offer a conventional romance hero. This was true not only of Parkman's histories but also of the stories of Turner's great literary predecessor, James Fenimore Cooper. In Cooper's famous Leatherstocking series, Natty Bumppo, the backwoodsman, appears in the early books as a supporting character. The true heroes are genteel and aristocratic. Not until the final work in the series, *The Deerslayer*, does Natty Bumppo come into his own as protagonist, locked in heroic struggle with an evil tribal chieftain. Even here, Cooper ended his tale with the rescue of Leatherstocking by the British army and its aristocratic generals.[43]

Still, a hint of subaltern romance, a story in which the rural white male commoner wins out through superhuman effort, glimmers through certain passages in Turner's work. We have already introduced one of these, Turner's invocation of the pioneer's "task to fight with nature for the chance to exist." The struggle in such moments is starkly antithetical. The frontiersman is larger than life, stronger and more successful than the effete, decadent heroes of European history who, Turner constantly reminds us, ultimately failed to reduce America to their imperial sway. This current of romance flows through Turner's prose, winning out here and there, called up by an opportune juxtaposition, some special emphasis, or a particularly situated reading. Even in the most monographic of his works, *The Rise of the New West,* readers predisposed to romance could read the plot off pivots such as this one: "And on the frontier of the northwest, the young Lincoln sank his axe deep in the opposing forest." No one, least of all Turner, could enforce a specific understanding on any single reader. At its simplest the text projects a romance of the white male frontiersman, a theme seized on by critical social scientists and jingoistic politicians.[44]

Few of us now find such a reading plausible, and it seems unlikely that Turner believed he had appropriated the romance of the few for the middle-class masses. In the late nineteenth century, romance had become the genre of the picturesque, best suited for epic and folkloric re-creations of a mythical past, the whipping boy of literary realism and publicly disdained by writers from Henry Adams to Mark Twain. Romance was what Turner's mentors had tried to overcome, and its naive celebration of the Great Man one of the ideals against which Turner's historicism rebelled. His heroes are social, psychological, and economic types rather than living personalities, more important for their narrative functions than their personal qualities. "The frontiersman," "the pioneer," "the Indian trader," "this dirt farmer," "the capitalist," all the faceless, nameless heroes of the third estate find their roles in the dialectical flow rather than in conscientious, detailed character development. Even the occasional names (Daniel Boone, Andrew Jackson, Abraham Lincoln) are synecdoches of some particular aspect of the American frontier spirit. As with so many great works in American naturalism and modernism, Frank Norris's *The Octopus* an obvious example, Turner's text deals in plot rather than character. His history is all epic sweep and uplift as social actors rewrite their own destinies in the face of grand forces of space and time.[45]

A passage from a 1901 essay, "The Middle West," illustrates the temporal sweep of Turner's history as it ranges back into the past and then forward into an imagined future that is, by implication, our present. The historian projects himself and his readers into the hero's point of view, reenacting, in R. G. Collingwood's term, the thought of a historical agent.

While his horizon was still bounded by the clearing that his ax had made, the pioneer dreamed of continental conquests. The vastness of the wilderness kindled his imagination. His vision saw beyond the dank swamp at the edge of the great lake to the lofty buildings and the jostling multitudes of a mighty city; beyond the rank, grass-clad prairie to the seas of golden grain; beyond the harsh life of the log hut and the sod house to the home of his children, where should dwell comfort and the higher things of life, though they might not be for him.

Spatially, we move from the local to the global, from backwoods clearing to continental conquest, from isolated homestead to bustling metropolis. Morally, Turner's heroes move upward in dialectical waves. The American spirit and its pioneer atoms reach beyond material survival for finer things and greater destinies, seizing on the frontier "the chance to break the bondage of social rank, and to rise to a higher plane of existence." This is no tragedy, but neither is it romance. What we want, Turner had said in 1884, was a future in which we have transcended the conflict of romance and tragedy. There did exist a formal tradition that claimed to do just that, a tradition he knew well.[46]

High comedy had long been the mode of reconciliation, integration, and transcendence. Optimistic but not necessarily humorous, comedy moves from a lower to an upper plane, integrating its agonists into a higher social existence. One of Turner's favorite works, Dante's *Divine Comedy,* offers some useful parallels, both in its progressive motion and in its elevation of the vernacular to a respectable intellectual form. In the *Comedy* Dante progresses from the depths of the Inferno through a liminal Purgatory to a reconciliation with his beloved Beatrice in Paradise. The tale ascends past threatening complications to a happy summit in accord with Northrop Frye's description of the "archetypal" comic plot. Dante, in his "Letter to Can Grande," said that "to understand the title, it must be known that comedy is derived from *cosmos,* 'a village,' and from *oda,* 'a song,' so that comedy is, so to speak, 'a rustic song.' Comedy, then, is a certain genre of poetic narrative different from all others. . . . [I]t introduces a situation of adversity, but ends its matter in prosperity." Comedy, said Frye centuries later, moves from "a society controlled by habit, ritual bondage, arbitrary law and the older characters to a society controlled by youth and pragmatic freedom," a society framed as a moral norm.[47]

Turner's frontier narrative moves away from the Old World where elite romance and subaltern tragedy fought for control of human consciousness and into American democracy where conflict resolves into the balanced harmony of high comedy. His story incorporates all the key continental conflicts and struggles into one plotline.[48] Its concluding democratic synthesis evades the dangerous antinomies of romance and tragedy, elite and proletariat. As the frontier offered a "gate of escape from the bondage of the past," the "higher social plane" of American democracy melds diverse European stocks—German, French, British, Scots-Irish—into a national spirit forged in the "frontier crucible." Turner's summation integrates without erasing these diverse actors: "In the outcome, in spite of slowness of assimilation where different groups were compact and isolated from the others, and a certain persistence of inherited *morale,* there was the creation of a new type, which was neither the sum of all its elements, nor a complete fusion in a melting pot." Neither the arithmetic sum of its parts nor a monolithic whole, here is Northrop Frye's prototypical comedic outcome, a new society, breaking from the ritual and bondage of the old, joining its agonists together in a pluralistic harmony.[49]

America's page in history abstracts the grand story of history's development from barbarism to civilization, the uplift of ages and forces into higher syntheses and more complex combinations, a gathering in the West of all those historical traditions that gave Turner and his readers their civic identities as members of the American Republic, morally transcendent in its "elevation of the plain people." Turner could have claimed more historical subtlety than Dante. Dante's outcome, the reconciliation in Paradise, negates rather than incorporates the experiences of the Inferno and Purgatory. Paradise is all the Inferno is not, the very summit of the star-filled sky to which Dante raises grateful eyes after escaping the netherworld. Turner's final moment holds in dialectical suspension the recombining elements of its predecessors, from New World savagism to Old World civilization. There is no naive reversal of European decadence, natural simplicity, or savage primitivism. Instead, all of these are joined into a world of maximum consciousness, a history that carries multiple meanings inside itself without being directly subsumed into the narrative horizons of Christianity.[50]

Turner's dialectic produces a story of immense complexity, not only in philosophical conception, as past and present remake each other, or in conflict, as the encounter of North American nature and European history creates American democracy, or in plot mode, as romance works with and against high comedy, but also on semantic and social levels. At the semantic level readers cannot avoid plumbing the bottomless depth of Turner's key words, frontier and democracy, without flattening out the story. As the past dwells in the depths of the present, each word, sentence, and story carries more possible meanings, places, and times than the historian can ever fully expound. Each is the narrative sum of its history. Democracy is the story's summit, and the word's historic depth gives it meaning. In a 1918 address to the Minnesota State Historical Society, "Middle Western Pioneer Democracy," Turner appealed again to Whitman to illustrate the point:

> Sail, sail thy best, ship of Democracy,
> Of value is thy freight, 'tis not the Present only,
> The Past is also stored in Thee.
> With thee Time voyages in trust, the antecedent nations sink or
> swim with thee.

Turner's democracy embarked with Whitman's. In like fashion, it contains all the moments of its making, all the great migrations, ideas, and institutions of prior ages as well as those grandiloquent strings of antitheses that so tormented critics from George Pierson to Patricia Limerick: good and evil, selfishness and selflessness, profligacy and practicality, individualism and communalism. None of these terms fully negated the others. Turner read them not as mutually exclusive, either/or possibilities but as the constitutive elements of a higher synthesis, the "Pioneer Democracy" in which he claimed membership. Restricting "democracy" to a homogeneous, unidimensional denotation, a directionless hull emptied of all traces of its development—reducing it, in other words, to what a reader like Pierson would have regarded as a reliable scientific term—would be not only an empirical mistake but also an abrogation of the historian's moral responsibility to past and future.[51]

The Folly of Comedy

Although Turner's frontier comedy resonated favorably with the nation's political ideology, his homemade historicism did not.

If values are the products of specific times and places, then individual rights, democratic institutions, and free choice have no value beyond that assigned them by the community. They are not permanent, timeless, or natural. Liberal historicism looked like a contradiction in terms, and Hegelian philosophy offered little help. Hegel had harshly criticized classical liberalism. He likewise rejected the comic vision that infuses Turnerian history, as evinced in this highly visual passage wherein even Turner might have recognized his own backwoods communities.

The general basis of comedy is . . . a world in which man has made himself, in his conscious activity, complete master of all that otherwise passes as the essential content of his knowledge and achievement; a world whose ends are consequently thrown awry on account of their own lack of substance. A democratic folk, with egotistic citizens, litigiousness, frivolous, conceited, without faith or knowledge, always intent on gossip, boasting, and vanity—such a folk is past praying for; it can only dissolve in its folly.

Hegel would have described frontier comedy as a transient moment within a greater tragic pattern. And even Droysen had denounced the idiocy of "vulgar liberalism" and spoken out against a written constitution. Turner's dialectic would not easily reconcile such traditions with American sensibilities.[52]

Originally, Turner's faith in historical practice as moral event had addressed the tensions between historicism and liberalism, but by the 1920s his solution looked quite fragile. Optimism came harder after a world war. At issue was the delicate balance of holism and individualism. If the spirit of a people is greater than the sum of their persons, if the community to which individuals owe loyalty is greater than their own selves, individuals find identity and rights in the community, and the positive freedoms of the state outweigh the negative liberties of the individual. World War I gave such notions new meanings. Many blamed world war on the excesses of German philosophy. (As early as 1884 Lord Acton had denounced Droysen as the historian of imperialism.) And Turner firmly and publicly condemned Prussian militarism even as he continued his historicist exploration of the relations between individual and collective selves.[53]

Still another problem shadowed Turner's American history. If the frontier had produced American democracy, how would it endure now that the frontier was gone? Turner's dialectic held that the highest content of past epochs was never entirely lost. To the extent that historians could revise the past by choosing those elements best suited to carrying the nation forward into a bright future, democratic spirit could thrive. But the unconscious inheritance, that material weight of the past that limited the historian's creative freedom, was not so easily controlled. The form of democracy would remain, but its narrative content might change for the worse: "If . . . we consider the underlying conditions and forces that create the democratic type of government, and at times contradict the external forms to which the name democracy is applied, we shall find that under this name there have appeared a multitude of political types radically unalike in fact." Some readers avoided the dilemma by rejecting historicism in favor of older millennial or republican visions. In millennialism American political development realized divine providence. In republicanism it harmonized with natural law. Either way, the new nation transcended history.[54]

We have already seen a Turnerian sense of history too strong to collapse into nature. Dialectic carries the force of moral norm, but it does not pretend to the regularity of natural law, nor does it ever reach a final summit. Turner's work certainly grew more naturalistic as he aged (by 1910 he was using the sort of scientist metaphors that Droysen had so mistrusted), but nature was no longer the static mechanical object of Enlightenment fantasy. Even nature was historical, and contingency, flux, and freedom dominate history where "all was motion and change." We cannot easily describe Turner's democracy as an escape from history. Whitman's more optimistic moments may have hinted at such an outcome, but the Turnerian essays flatly deny any final resolution. There can be no prime mover, no last word, no ultimate histories. True, the material forces of free land had directed the four-hundred-year period of American history, but these now were gone, and the forthcoming age would find its defining conflicts in different arenas. Environmental determinism had been specific to that period in North America and was not a general force operative in all places and times. In the twentieth century Americans must deliberately develop the national consciousness.[55]

Twenty years after he had first presented his story, Turner was ready to revise it. During the late nineteenth and early twentieth centuries urban and industrial landscapes transformed the country. Smokestacks and railroads replaced log cabins. And pioneer house raisings and rugged individualism gave way before the concentration of wealth and a growing "self-consciousness of labor" to reveal new contradictions in the democratic synthesis. In 1914 Turner declared that to those Americans living in the frontier period "democracy and capitalistic development did not seem antagonistic. . . . [But] with the passing of the frontier, Western social and political ideals took new form. Capital began to consolidate in even greater masses, and increasingly attempted to reduce to system and control the processes of industrial development. Labor with equal step organized its forces to destroy the old competitive system." The collision of capitalism and democracy was the new contest of postfrontier America, and Turner saw its emergence as the virtual "birth of a new nation."[56]

The development of modern America provided an opportunity to illustrate his claim that historical meaning changed over time, for the new antithesis could now be read back into American history where it had not been legible in 1893. The tension between pioneer democracy and corporate capitalism flowed out of the frontier experience and had grown up inside the American spirit. Turner placed three liberal ideals—discovery, democracy, and individualism—at the heart of that spirit. First was the ideal of discovery, a key premise for an expanding capitalist economy. The second was democracy, a community of "free self-directing people" amenable to electing and following effective political leadership. The third was individualism, the willful exercise of free choice and suspicion of governmental limits on that exercise. During the frontier era natural abundance provided fields for discovery and balanced the two key pioneer ideals, unbounded individualism and democratic restraint. But "time has revealed that these two ideals of pioneer democracy had elements of mutual hostility and contained the seeds of its dissolution." With hindsight one could rewrite frontier history and "trace the contest between the capitalist and the democratic pioneer from the earliest colonial days."[57]

Turner wove a new subplot into the dialectic of history and nature, but he did not substantially retreat from a historicized liberalism. Indeed, the revision recalled his demand that the historian serve as apostle of culture by shifting discovery from a material to a spiritual plane: "As we turn from the task of the first rough conquest of the continent there lies before us a whole wealth of unexploited resources in the realm of the spirit. . . . The Western spirit must be invoked for new and nobler achievements." At the base one still found individualism and democracy, neither of which could survive without the other. One could not maintain liberal ideals of freedom, liberty, and choice if one substituted class rule for representative government. Yet democracy could not survive the selfishness that often lurked behind appeals to individualism and free markets. The notion of a communal past held in trust for the future offered the best hope of transcending this new agon. Though the frontier was gone, the future was open, and by mature exercise of creative freedom Americans could reshape both memory and destiny. In a letter to publisher Max Farrand, Turner made the point explicit: "Effective building must proceed from the *general consciousness of the American people* as well as from foundations suddenly created out-of-hand by the exceptional man. And this consciousness is, in part at least, *to be created*." Americans must write their history with comic optimism so that it "may not become the lost and tragic story of a futile dream."[58]

When imagining Turner's legacy, we should keep his compromised historicism in view. The midwesterner revised the work of his mentor by reading history as the dialectical product of conflicting impulses rather than an insular, homogeneous unfolding of biological germs. He transfigured the aristocratic frontier romances of Francis Parkman and James Fenimore Cooper into heroic anthems of the people. He hammered historical narrative into a shape more complex than the linear chronologies handed down by both romantic and scientific historians. And he remade American history in the process, changing the possibilities of realism and public memory. All these levels shaped and were shaped by the social action of the text, by history as meaningful moral event. On this social level responsibilities loomed large. Though Turnerian creation was less self-reliant than the acts of will we find in Emerson or Whitman, it was more egoistic than that of Hegel and Droysen. Could Americans willfully banish tragedy from the national consciousness? Was spirit so easily fabricated? Would the democratic synthesis continue successfully to rewrite its heritage, or would it, as Hegel predicted, dissolve in its comic folly, betrayed by the hubris of believing that one could make one's history, one's future, and one's self?

Provincial Politics

Turner's resolution of the tension between historicism and democracy stood on the circular relation of stories and selves. For him histories rested on the changing customs and values of the community. And communal identities were defined, their customs and values charted, and their selfhood constructed in historical narratives. Communities *were* their histories. So the ways that historians wrote American spirit into existence became much more than a simple antiquarian matter of reporting what one had happened to stumble across in the archives. The questions were, who would get to define American identity, and whose customs and values would set the standards for historical practice? Turnerians generally agreed that westerners told the best stories, even though they did not always agree on the boundaries of the true West. The first several decades of the century were an age of appeals to regional consciousness, and the development of specifically western visions of American history served this trend, as western, middle-class male academics remade America in their own image. But that image was in flux. By 1920 America was a very different place from what it had been in 1890, and Turner faced serious challenges to his beliefs that history is dialectic and that American history is the story of the colonization of the Great West.

Turner's solution to the interpretive challenges offered by the new urban, industrial America lay not only in the moral force of dialectic but also in the particulars of western history. Regionalism could overcome the destructive conflict between selves and state while also explaining how frontier history continued to shape a frontierless society. To prevent devotion to the nation from becoming so abstract that it overwhelmed individual identity, as it had in Prussia, historians needed to develop local attachments to mediate selves and state. For Droysen the key intermediaries had been family, tribe, and religious community. Karl Marx had privileged economic class. Turner did not deny the importance of these structures, but he was searching for a specifically *American* manifestation of spirit. In a series of essays including "Sections and Nation" (1922) and "The Significance of the Section in American History" (1925), later the core of *The Significance of Sections in American History* (1932), Turner invoked Josiah Royce and *region*.[59]

History was a contract not just between the national memory and the historian but between an entire range of local identities as well. These local identities were a product of the frontier. As history had swept across the continent, it did not encounter a monotonously uniform nature. Rather, the American people

were entering successive different geographic provinces; they were pouring their plastic pioneer life into geographic molds. They would modify these molds, they would have progressive revelations of the capacities of the geographic provinces which they won and settled and developed; but even the task of dealing constructively with the different regions would work its effects on their traits. . . . The outcome would be a combination of the two factors, land and people, the creation of different societies in the different sections.

The frontier had left its impress on each section, and that imprint remained long after the wilderness had passed. As in John Locke's dictum, "In the beginning, all the world was America," in Turner's story, in the beginning, all America was the West. Each section had once been the West, each had experienced its frontier phase, each shared a dynamic past with the others, and this bound the country despite increasing regional self-consciousness: "Underneath all there is a common historical inheritance, a common set of institutions, a common law, and a common language. There is an American spirit. There are American ideals. We are members of one body, though it is a varied body." America's different sections were analogous to the different nations of Europe, but where Europeans resolved conflict through war and diplomatic voodoo, America's sectional interests joined peacefully in common legislative action. Their antithetical disputes resolved into the overarching unity of the nation and frontier dialectic carried over into the new age.[60]

Just as sectional consciousness was the best line of defense against jingoism, national spirit was the best bulwark against faction and must be cultivated else regionalism grow parochial. The risk was that each section might develop its self-consciousness to the point of substituting its own narrative identity for the nation's.

There is always the danger that the province or section shall think of itself naively as the nation, that New England shall think that America is merely New England writ large, or the Middle West shall think that America is merely the Middle West writ large, and then proceed to denounce the sections that do not perceive the accuracy of this view as wicked or ignorant and un-American. This kind of nationalism is a sectional mirage, but it is common, and has been common to all the sections in their unconscious attitude if not in clear expression. It involves the assumption of a superiority of culture, of *Kultur,* to which good morals require that the nation as a whole must yield.

We do not know if Turner aimed these criticisms at his own practice, but the irony would scarcely be blunted had he written in confessional mode. In his story the West is creator and guardian of American spirit. This suggests that those sections most recently and truly West, those in which the origins of pioneer democracy remain most legible, more nearly embody that spirit. All sections are American, but some are more American than others.[61]

Turner's regional jealousies surfaced repeatedly. If each historian wrote from the perspective of his or her own region (and as part of a distinct sectional consciousness no historian could do otherwise), how

land region found on the Great Plains many novelties, many new experiences. Thus it appears that we have had in America two types, as well as two epochs, of pioneering; first of the forest and last of the plain; and as we look back on these two contrasting adventures, the Plains experience seems the more remote and unusual; softened by the glamour that diffuses and sometimes makes grotesque our view of distant things. In ordinary parlance, we say that, of the two experiences, the one on the Plains is the more romantic.

Midwestern Turnerians, of course, did *not* say that. Their heroes wore coonskin caps, not cowboy hats. Webb's "we" spoke to a delimited group, and later works, notably *Divided We Stand,* sharpened his regional focus. The South and the arid West shared a common heritage. They had been dominated and exploited by the Yankees in the urban centers of the North and East, from Madison to Boston. If Turnerians wanted an authentically subaltern hero, the "true" regional perspective on American history, they needed to look southwest.[68]

And every page of Webb's text fairly screamed "Texas!" *The Great Plains,* with its maps, climatic statistics, tables, patent office illustrations, and great slabs of quotation, looks less like a scholarly monograph than a collage of the contents of one of the one-room Texas schoolhouses in which both Webb and his father had labored as educators. Juxtaposed against Turner's more polished texts, two differences stand out. First, the frontier experiences of *The Great Plains* are highly particular and "transient" rather than repetitive. Turnerian spirit dissolves like a mirage in the desert heat. The present stands radically apart from the past: history is disturbingly distant, and we are but "vicarious adventurers" in that strange land. (Webb later described a historical seminar as an "exploring party" and likened the historian to the *conquistador.*) Spatially, too, regionalism sunders rather than binds. Geography divides America into two epochal regions, forest and plain, and two peoples, Yankees and everyone else. On this dry ground Webb took his stand, staking out a loyalty to place distinct from that of the midwesterners but offering yet another elevation of the western, white, male subaltern to hero.[69]

So Turnerians of all stripes reached for what philosopher Josiah Royce called a "higher provincialism," a sense of shared regional destiny that could anchor community in the bedrock of a familiar space and a common past while shoring up a liberal future. For westerners from Wisconsin to Waco, this was a subversive act, an attempt to break New England's cultural stranglehold and rewrite the national consciousness in their own image. For Turner it looked like the best means

might Americans fairly arbitrate among competing histories? What was the basis for choosing, say, Turner's frontier history over Parkman's? "The Significance of History" had suggested evaluating histories by the values of the community to which the historian owed loyalty. And communities were situated not only in time (and here Turner could claim an advantage) but also in space. If his own tale had any single moral, it was that the West was, in a phrase borrowed from Lord James Bryce, "the most American part of America." Since spirit ran strongest in the direction of the setting sun, the native westerner (Turner had one in mind) could claim a privileged relation to American spirit: "Parkman, in whose golden pages is written the epic of the American wilderness, found his hero in the wandering Frenchman. Perhaps because he was a New Englander he missed a great opportunity and neglected to portray the formation and advance of the great backwoods society which was finally to erase the traces of French control in the interior of North America." New Englander and Boston Brahmin, the patrician Parkman had thrown his gaze back to the lost past of European dominance rather than forward to frontier America rising.[62]

American self-consciousness had suffered from the eastern domination of politics and publishing. The classics of American history and literature had been studies in New England provincialism: " 'I love thy rocks and rills, thy woods and templed hills,' runs our American anthem. It was written by a New Englander and its scene is that of New England, not of the snow-capped mountains, the far stretches of the Great Plains, or arid America." Regional chauvinism and elitism had written Turner's subaltern hero out of the great American histories. The rural, backwoods Mississippi River Valley had not had its heroic due. A 1909 address before the Mississippi Valley Historical Association swept relativism offstage: The perspective of the Mississippi Valley is the "true perspective" on American history, and the "social destiny of this valley will be the social destiny, and mark the place in history, of the United States." This place, this people, these heroes, this spirit, this story, these were Turner's own.[63]

Turner replaced Whitman as Emerson's American Dante and wrote himself into the national imagination, inscribing his own identity on the public memory in letters centuries high. He made his autobiography the story of the nation, projecting his own community, place, and personality into the American self. By 1925 Turner, now holder of a prestigious chair at Harvard, was such a local icon that the *Wisconsin Magazine of History* published a full-page photograph of the local hero on the facing page of his scholarly article, "The Significance of Sections in American History." Here was self-construction with a vengeance, a protagonist visibly risen to a higher future and whose tale traced a comic trajectory from frontier backwoods to the civilized eastern summit of academia. And the world revealed in Turner's story was no less personal, no less local. For all its debt to tradition, America owed its democratic freedoms not to Athens, Rome, or medieval tuns, but to the piney sand country and clapboard skyline of Portage, Wisconsin. No strong poet, as critic Harold Bloom has remarked, truly chooses his or her precursors. Turner did not choose his West: It chose him, and we find Turner as he found Parkman, awash in histories. The midwesterner, less naive than some, faced the prospect calmly: "I think the ideas underlying my 'Significance of the Frontier' would have been expressed in some form or other in any case. They were part of the growing American consciousness of itself." Turner's calm was born partly of a pragmatic conviction that faith in liberalism and moral value was a fine and true thing to profess, and partly of poetic hubris, the artist's belief that the cosmic spirit pulsed through each line of his text, that Frederick Jackson Turner was the chosen instrument of a righteous destiny.[64]

In new professional associations like the Wisconsin State Historical Society and the Mississippi Valley Historical Society, in new journals like the *Mississippi Valley Historical Review* and *Agricultural History,* and in the state colleges and land-grant institutions of the West and the South, the spirit if not always the letter of Turnerian history opened up new worlds for those sympathetic readers who might claim for their own lives the historical significance previously monopolized by the great men of the eastern seaboard. Turner's cosmic story of spirit gave local archives a glamour and scholarly legitimacy, his teaching placed disciples in departments of history all over the country, and popular textbooks inducted schoolchildren by the thousands into the frontier comedy. H. Hale Bellot, looking backward in 1950, declared the resulting community of memory a distinctively "Midwestern school" of history, a loosely knit group of scholars, students, librarians, archivists, editors, and readers networked throughout the Midwest and, after Turner's elevation to a Harvard professorship in 1910, ensconced in the heart of Brahmin territory, bound by a shared belief that their story was America's story.[65]

By the 1930s, however, the network was coming apart. Turner had been a western historian because he was an *American* historian who saw the West as the key to American history. He had not been a specialist.

But increasing numbers of historians were specialists, and m specialized in the history of the West. And to specialize in tory, that topic had to be smaller than American history. I perience needed to be divided into regional experiences. H all be brought back together again, lacking the vision of hi lectic, the faith in the cosmic story, was another question. R Turner's brake on a runaway national consciousness, prove of the more powerful wedges driving apart the One-ness o As we have seen in Turner's own swipes at New Englanders, ism could sunder as well as join.[66]

Sectional jealousy inspired Walter Prescott Webb's *The* (1932). As a devout Texan, Webb did not believe the Missi Valley defined American spirit. In his rough and readabl tossed off an alternative frontier history in which the trans West played the dominant part. In this true West Euro-Am up against new, harsher, tougher frontiers. Arid, treeless, and sunbaked, these "Great Plains" (which in Webb's idiosy age included virtually all of the United States west of the nir meridian) forced radical changes in law, social organization nology. Barbed wire, the windmill, and legal doctrines more to irrigation agriculture and ranching, all resulted from the of Euro-American pioneers and arid West. The upshot was th West rather than the humid Midwest represented Americ ence.[67]

Webb did not share Turner's enthusiasm for historicist His 1955 presidential address to the Mississippi Valley Histo ciation declared of Droysen and the Prussian school (who flated with the empiricism of Ranke—they were all Germans that "what they taught . . . we learned in 1914 and rehearse And the view that emerged from Webb's texts, less dialec Turner's, fractured frontier history even as it shared in th comic vision. Here is *The Great Plains* in one of its closest Turner.

In a given region the frontier has a brief and transient existenc experiences in that region are not repeated or even approxima generations that follow. For this reason a certain glamour difi around the frontier, and the people look back upon its hardship ferings with a feeling of vicarious adventure. The frontier expe the Great Plains were *not,* moreover, a repetition of frontier exp the region from which the settlers came. A frontiersman from

of staving off the ironic turn from comedy to tragedy. But Turner's essays and Webb's history demonstrated the potentially divisive and parochial tendencies of regionalism, even within the uncertain bounds of the "West." This politics of identity was a politics of exclusion. One was a westerner or a midwesterner by virtue of what one was not: not an easterner, not a European, not a foreigner. And even these boundaries could be divided, for Webb's westerner was most emphatically not a midwesterner. Ultimately, the lines of identity cut across region as well. The frontiersman was not a woman, not a black, not a Mexican, not an Asian, not an Indian.

These were the interpretive horizons of scholarly frontier history. The story might be read and emplotted as romance or as comedy, the past might be more or less distant from the here and now, the different regional chapters in that story might squabble among themselves over pride of place, but all those admitted to the historian's circle agreed on both the race and gender of the narrative hero. By midcentury this was virtually all that remained of Turner's sense of the One-ness of the thing: the tacit agreement that middle-class white males had been the driving force of frontier history, a faith that the story was basically happy, and the corollary sense that historians could find a moral high ground in cheering for the underdog. These were widely shared but seldom articulated beliefs. Once driven into the bright light of debate where they needed to be justified against criticism, they became more a source of conflict than a ground of consensus.

John Dewey and the Frontier Tragedy

Not everyone loves a happy ending. In the fourth century B.C. Aristotle described comedy as an inferior form and devoted the lion's portion of his *Poetics* to tragedy. Modern philosophers from Hegel to Nietzsche took up the topic, and by the middle twentieth century a theory of tragedy seemed requisite for a major social philosophy. So we should not be surprised when we find that as enthusiastic Turnerians shared in frontier comedy, other Americans gathered around more tragic readings. Many of these thinkers were eastern intellectuals associated with journals like the *New Republic,* the *Freeman,* and the *Dial.* In 1964 cultural historian Warren Susman, in "The Frontier Thesis and the American Intellectual," ably explored the dynamics of their search for a usable past and their unhappiness with the atomism, philistinism, and obscurantism of modern times. In their works Freudian psychology collided with Turnerian history, and as Susman put it, "the frontier became the scapegoat for all that was wrong with contemporary America." In books like Van Wyck Brooks's *The Ordeal of Mark Twain,* Lewis Mumford's *The Golden Day,* and Walter Weyl's *The New Democracy,* the frontier West became the locus of all the violent, red-necked, dirt-eating squalor that the urban imagination could conjure.[70]

An exemplary frontier tragedy appeared in *The New Republic* in 1922 in the form of "The American Intellectual Frontier," a short essay by John Dewey, one of the country's leading philosophers. Dewey, like Turner, grew up in a middle-class, Protestant, semirural environment. He studied at Johns Hopkins University, where his youthful Emersonian enthusiasms met German idealism, and he completed his minor field under the direction of Turner's mentor, Herbert Baxter Adams. In 1891, the year Turner (at Wisconsin) delivered "The Significance of History," Dewey (at Michigan) published his last systematic defense of Hegelian philosophy. By World War I he too was grappling with the problematic relation between German historicism and militarism and resolved the difficulty by divorcing himself from the absolutist tendencies of German thought and culture while remaining a radical historicist. And again like Turner, though with greater sophistication, he devoted hundreds of pages to the relation of history and democracy. History for Dewey was not text but tool, a lever, in his metaphor, with which we attempt to lift ourselves into better worlds.[71]

Dewey's frontier history hoped to lift American culture out of the period warfare between religion and science. "The American Intellectual Frontier" opens in the present of 1922, looking out on William Jennings Bryan's campaign against the teaching of evolution in the public schools. Bryan's success in stirring evangelical Christians to exclude Darwinian biology from American education "raises fundamental questions about the quality of our democracy. . . . For Mr. Bryan is a typical democratic figure." Bryan is not that mythical creature, the Great Man imposing his heroic will on a passive world, but a typical historical product of the middle-class, Protestant Midwest. The frontier migrations in the border, southern, and western states produced the Second Great Awakening and an obscurantist tradition in which the pioneer's antipathy to privilege extended itself "to fear of the highly educated and expert." Andrew Jackson's democratic republic celebrated populist ideals but turned its back on the cosmopolitanism of a Jefferson or a Franklin.[72]

Dewey's democracy, like Turner's, synthesizes antithetical impulses, for westward expansion generated both liberalism and illiberalism, tolerance and intolerance, community and parochialism. And like Turner's frontier, this one too continues its spiritual work even after its carnal demise: "As the frontier ceased to be a menace to orderly life, it persisted as a limit beyond which it was dangerous and unrespectable for thought to travel." In this mediated fashion, the past works into the present and Jacksonian democracy weaves into Bryan's evangelism. Bryan "does not represent the frontier democracy of Andrew Jackson's day. But he represents it toned down and cultivated as it exists in fairly prosperous villages and small towns that have inherited the fear of whatever threatens the security and order of a precariously attained civilization along with pioneer impulses to neighborliness and decency." The irrational elements of America's unconscious inheritance threaten to displace the liberal tradition as healthy aversion to privilege becomes kneejerk reaction. Some historical explanation is needed, and the narrative we need to amend is Turner's account of America's frontier heritage, freshly packaged in his new collection of old essays, *The Frontier in American History.*[73]

Dewey did not simply invert Turner's celebratory frontier history. Looking ahead to Bryan's resurgent evangelism, the pragmatist mapped out a new telling that sought to reject religious obscurantism without descending to vulgar polemics about the idiocy of rural life. The religious crusade against modern science in public discourse was not a simple social pathology. It had historically been interwoven with much that was good and sensible in American thought and culture.

We are evangelical because of our fear of ourselves and of our latent frontier disorderliness. The depressing effect upon the free life of inquiry and criticism is the greater because of the element of soundness in frontier fear, and because of the impulses of goodwill and social aspiration which have become entangled with its creeds. The forces which are embodied in the present crusade would not be so dangerous were they not bound up with so much that is necessary and good. We have been so taught to respect the beliefs of our neighbors that few will respect the beliefs of a neighbor when they depart from forms which have become associated with aspiration for a decent neighborly life. This is the illiberalism which is deep-rooted in our liberalism.

The contradiction at the core of the democratic synthesis developed along the frontier, where fear of anarchic individualism produced the good of community loyalty. This community loyalty now threatens to efface the good of critical individualism, and America's frontier heritage threatens American democracy.[74]

Dewey was not a professional historian, and he wrote "American Intellectual Frontier" for a popular market. But in a way the essay's methodological modesty makes it more engaging, for Dewey did not argue that new evidence forced us to rethink frontier history. He was not criticizing Turner's *Frontier in American History* for faulty collation of data or failure to open up the right archives. So far as events were concerned, Dewey made few descriptions he could not have supported by citing Turner's own work. What was at issue was the significance, the meaning and the moral, of frontier history. He invoked all those antitheses of American development that Turner had pointed out but found in them a very different narrative resolution. Before taking his tale apart, we need to detour through a few corners of Dewey's writings, for he returned time and again to these topics.

Over a decade later Dewey's *Liberalism and Social Action* (1935) distilled three defining elements from American liberalism: liberty, individualism, and free intelligence. Where Turner saw the balance of liberty and individualism threatened by the disappearance of the frontier, Dewey seized on the popular belief that rights existed in nature. Americans still held an absolutist view of natural rights, one well suited to revolt against monarchy but ill suited for dealing with modern problems: "If the early liberals had put forth their special interpretation of liberty as something subject to historical relativity they would not have frozen it into a doctrine to be applied at all times under all social circumstances." Blindness to the historicity of natural rights philosophy led Americans into dogmatism and condemned them to lives of regimentation and oppression. Dewey thus reconciled liberalism and historicism. Liberty was not an abstract essence found in nature but a relation: It was always liberty *from* some harm, or liberty *for* someone, or liberty to *do* some particular thing. Since relations changed with historic conditions, so did liberty. The tragic lack of an effective historical consciousness generated the present crises of American liberalism, the conflicts between religion and science, industrialism and democracy.[75]

Dewey's historicism did more than Turner's to undo historical epistemology. In his 1938 study *Logic* Dewey assailed the old antinomy of historical facts and historical interpretations. He derided the old view of history as a collection of neutral descriptions of historical facts which the historian transforms into a narrative or else links through explanatory laws. There exist no purely descriptive or purely narrational state-

might Americans fairly arbitrate among competing histories? What was the basis for choosing, say, Turner's frontier history over Parkman's? "The Significance of History" had suggested evaluating histories by the values of the community to which the historian owed loyalty. And communities were situated not only in time (and here Turner could claim an advantage) but also in space. If his own tale had any single moral, it was that the West was, in a phrase borrowed from Lord James Bryce, "the most American part of America." Since spirit ran strongest in the direction of the setting sun, the native westerner (Turner had one in mind) could claim a privileged relation to American spirit: "Parkman, in whose golden pages is written the epic of the American wilderness, found his hero in the wandering Frenchman. Perhaps because he was a New Englander he missed a great opportunity and neglected to portray the formation and advance of the great backwoods society which was finally to erase the traces of French control in the interior of North America." New Englander and Boston Brahmin, the patrician Parkman had thrown his gaze back to the lost past of European dominance rather than forward to frontier America rising.[62]

American self-consciousness had suffered from the eastern domination of politics and publishing. The classics of American history and literature had been studies in New England provincialism: " 'I love thy rocks and rills, thy woods and templed hills,' runs our American anthem. It was written by a New Englander and its scene is that of New England, not of the snow-capped mountains, the far stretches of the Great Plains, or arid America." Regional chauvinism and elitism had written Turner's subaltern hero out of the great American histories. The rural, backwoods Mississippi River Valley had not had its heroic due. A 1909 address before the Mississippi Valley Historical Association swept relativism offstage: The perspective of the Mississippi Valley is the "true perspective" on American history, and the "social destiny of this valley will be the social destiny, and mark the place in history, of the United States." This place, this people, these heroes, this spirit, this story, these were Turner's own.[63]

Turner replaced Whitman as Emerson's American Dante and wrote himself into the national imagination, inscribing his own identity on the public memory in letters centuries high. He made his autobiography the story of the nation, projecting his own community, place, and personality into the American self. By 1925 Turner, now holder of a prestigious chair at Harvard, was such a local icon that the *Wisconsin Magazine of History* published a full-page photograph of the local hero on the facing page of his scholarly article, "The Significance of Sections in American History." Here was self-construction with a vengeance, a protagonist visibly risen to a higher future and whose tale traced a comic trajectory from frontier backwoods to the civilized eastern summit of academia. And the world revealed in Turner's story was no less personal, no less local. For all its debt to tradition, America owed its democratic freedoms not to Athens, Rome, or medieval tuns, but to the piney sand country and clapboard skyline of Portage, Wisconsin. No strong poet, as critic Harold Bloom has remarked, truly chooses his or her precursors. Turner did not choose his West: It chose him, and we find Turner as he found Parkman, awash in histories. The midwesterner, less naive than some, faced the prospect calmly: "I think the ideas underlying my 'Significance of the Frontier' would have been expressed in some form or other in any case. They were part of the growing American consciousness of itself." Turner's calm was born partly of a pragmatic conviction that faith in liberalism and moral value was a fine and true thing to profess, and partly of poetic hubris, the artist's belief that the cosmic spirit pulsed through each line of his text, that Frederick Jackson Turner was the chosen instrument of a righteous destiny.[64]

In new professional associations like the Wisconsin State Historical Society and the Mississippi Valley Historical Society, in new journals like the *Mississippi Valley Historical Review* and *Agricultural History*, and in the state colleges and land-grant institutions of the West and the South, the spirit if not always the letter of Turnerian history opened up new worlds for those sympathetic readers who might claim for their own lives the historical significance previously monopolized by the great men of the eastern seaboard. Turner's cosmic story of spirit gave local archives a glamour and scholarly legitimacy, his teaching placed disciples in departments of history all over the country, and popular textbooks inducted schoolchildren by the thousands into the frontier comedy. H. Hale Bellot, looking backward in 1950, declared the resulting community of memory a distinctively "Midwestern school" of history, a loosely knit group of scholars, students, librarians, archivists, editors, and readers networked throughout the Midwest and, after Turner's elevation to a Harvard professorship in 1910, ensconced in the heart of Brahmin territory, bound by a shared belief that their story was America's story.[65]

By the 1930s, however, the network was coming apart. Turner had been a western historian because he was an *American* historian who saw the West as the key to American history. He had not been a specialist.

But increasing numbers of historians were specialists, and many of them specialized in the history of the West. And to specialize in western history, that topic had to be smaller than American history. National experience needed to be divided into regional experiences. How it would all be brought back together again, lacking the vision of history as dialectic, the faith in the cosmic story, was another question. Regionalism, Turner's brake on a runaway national consciousness, proved to be one of the more powerful wedges driving apart the One-ness of the thing. As we have seen in Turner's own swipes at New Englanders, provincialism could sunder as well as join.[66]

Sectional jealousy inspired Walter Prescott Webb's *The Great Plains* (1932). As a devout Texan, Webb did not believe the Mississippi River Valley defined American spirit. In his rough and readable prose, he tossed off an alternative frontier history in which the trans-Mississippi West played the dominant part. In this true West Euro-Americans ran up against new, harsher, tougher frontiers. Arid, treeless, windswept, and sunbaked, these "Great Plains" (which in Webb's idiosyncratic usage included virtually all of the United States west of the ninety-eighth meridian) forced radical changes in law, social organization, and technology. Barbed wire, the windmill, and legal doctrines more congenial to irrigation agriculture and ranching, all resulted from the interaction of Euro-American pioneers and arid West. The upshot was that the arid West rather than the humid Midwest represented American experience.[67]

Webb did not share Turner's enthusiasm for historicist philosophy. His 1955 presidential address to the Mississippi Valley Historical Association declared of Droysen and the Prussian school (whom he conflated with the empiricism of Ranke—they were all Germans, after all!) that "what they taught . . . we learned in 1914 and rehearsed in 1941." And the view that emerged from Webb's texts, less dialectical than Turner's, fractured frontier history even as it shared in the broadly comic vision. Here is *The Great Plains* in one of its closest passes to Turner.

In a given region the frontier has a brief and transient existence, and the experiences in that region are not repeated or even approximated by the generations that follow. For this reason a certain glamour diffuses itself around the frontier, and the people look back upon its hardships and sufferings with a feeling of vicarious adventure. The frontier experiences on the Great Plains were *not*, moreover, a repetition of frontier experiences in the region from which the settlers came. A frontiersman from the woodland region found on the Great Plains many novelties, many new experiences. Thus it appears that we have had in America two types, as well as two epochs, of pioneering; first of the forest and last of the plain; and as we look back on these two contrasting adventures, the Plains experience seems the more remote and unusual; softened by the glamour that diffuses and sometimes makes grotesque our view of distant things. In ordinary parlance, we say that, of the two experiences, the one on the Plains is the more romantic.

Midwestern Turnerians, of course, did *not* say that. Their heroes wore coonskin caps, not cowboy hats. Webb's "we" spoke to a delimited group, and later works, notably *Divided We Stand,* sharpened his regional focus. The South and the arid West shared a common heritage. They had been dominated and exploited by the Yankees in the urban centers of the North and East, from Madison to Boston. If Turnerians wanted an authentically subaltern hero, the "true" regional perspective on American history, they needed to look southwest.[68]

And every page of Webb's text fairly screamed "Texas!" *The Great Plains,* with its maps, climatic statistics, tables, patent office illustrations, and great slabs of quotation, looks less like a scholarly monograph than a collage of the contents of one of the one-room Texas schoolhouses in which both Webb and his father had labored as educators. Juxtaposed against Turner's more polished texts, two differences stand out. First, the frontier experiences of *The Great Plains* are highly particular and "transient" rather than repetitive. Turnerian spirit dissolves like a mirage in the desert heat. The present stands radically apart from the past: history is disturbingly distant, and we are but "vicarious adventurers" in that strange land. (Webb later described a historical seminar as an "exploring party" and likened the historian to the *conquistador.*) Spatially, too, regionalism sunders rather than binds. Geography divides America into two epochal regions, forest and plain, and two peoples, Yankees and everyone else. On this dry ground Webb took his stand, staking out a loyalty to place distinct from that of the midwesterners but offering yet another elevation of the western, white, male subaltern to hero.[69]

So Turnerians of all stripes reached for what philosopher Josiah Royce called a "higher provincialism," a sense of shared regional destiny that could anchor community in the bedrock of a familiar space and a common past while shoring up a liberal future. For westerners from Wisconsin to Waco, this was a subversive act, an attempt to break New England's cultural stranglehold and rewrite the national consciousness in their own image. For Turner it looked like the best means of staving off the ironic turn from comedy to tragedy. But Turner's essays and Webb's history demonstrated the potentially divisive and parochial tendencies of regionalism, even within the uncertain bounds of the "West." This politics of identity was a politics of exclusion. One was a westerner or a midwesterner by virtue of what one was not: not an easterner, not a European, not a foreigner. And even these boundaries could be divided, for Webb's westerner was most emphatically not a midwesterner. Ultimately, the lines of identity cut across region as well. The frontiersman was not a woman, not a black, not a Mexican, not an Asian, not an Indian.

These were the interpretive horizons of scholarly frontier history. The story might be read and emplotted as romance or as comedy, the past might be more or less distant from the here and now, the different regional chapters in that story might squabble among themselves over pride of place, but all those admitted to the historian's circle agreed on both the race and gender of the narrative hero. By midcentury this was virtually all that remained of Turner's sense of the One-ness of the thing: the tacit agreement that middle-class white males had been the driving force of frontier history, a faith that the story was basically happy, and the corollary sense that historians could find a moral high ground in cheering for the underdog. These were widely shared but seldom articulated beliefs. Once driven into the bright light of debate where they needed to be justified against criticism, they became more a source of conflict than a ground of consensus.

John Dewey and the Frontier Tragedy

Not everyone loves a happy ending. In the fourth century B.C. Aristotle described comedy as an inferior form and devoted the lion's portion of his *Poetics* to tragedy. Modern philosophers from Hegel to Nietzsche took up the topic, and by the middle twentieth century a theory of tragedy seemed requisite for a major social philosophy. So we should not be surprised when we find that as enthusiastic Turnerians shared in frontier comedy, other Americans gathered around more tragic readings. Many of these thinkers were eastern intellectuals associated with journals like the *New Republic,* the *Freeman,* and the *Dial.* In 1964 cultural historian Warren Susman, in "The Frontier Thesis and the American Intellectual," ably explored the dynamics of their search for a usable past and their unhappiness with the atomism, philistinism, and obscurantism of modern times. In their works Freudian psychology collided with Turnerian history, and as Susman put it, "the frontier became the scapegoat for all that was wrong with contemporary America." In books like Van Wyck Brooks's *The Ordeal of Mark Twain*, Lewis Mumford's *The Golden Day*, and Walter Weyl's *The New Democracy*, the frontier West became the locus of all the violent, red-necked, dirt-eating squalor that the urban imagination could conjure.[70]

An exemplary frontier tragedy appeared in *The New Republic* in 1922 in the form of "The American Intellectual Frontier," a short essay by John Dewey, one of the country's leading philosophers. Dewey, like Turner, grew up in a middle-class, Protestant, semirural environment. He studied at Johns Hopkins University, where his youthful Emersonian enthusiasms met German idealism, and he completed his minor field under the direction of Turner's mentor, Herbert Baxter Adams. In 1891, the year Turner (at Wisconsin) delivered "The Significance of History," Dewey (at Michigan) published his last systematic defense of Hegelian philosophy. By World War I he too was grappling with the problematic relation between German historicism and militarism and resolved the difficulty by divorcing himself from the absolutist tendencies of German thought and culture while remaining a radical historicist. And again like Turner, though with greater sophistication, he devoted hundreds of pages to the relation of history and democracy. History for Dewey was not text but tool, a lever, in his metaphor, with which we attempt to lift ourselves into better worlds.[71]

Dewey's frontier history hoped to lift American culture out of the period warfare between religion and science. "The American Intellectual Frontier" opens in the present of 1922, looking out on William Jennings Bryan's campaign against the teaching of evolution in the public schools. Bryan's success in stirring evangelical Christians to exclude Darwinian biology from American education "raises fundamental questions about the quality of our democracy. . . . For Mr. Bryan is a typical democratic figure." Bryan is not that mythical creature, the Great Man imposing his heroic will on a passive world, but a typical historical product of the middle-class, Protestant Midwest. The frontier migrations in the border, southern, and western states produced the Second Great Awakening and an obscurantist tradition in which the pioneer's antipathy to privilege extended itself "to fear of the highly educated and expert." Andrew Jackson's democratic republic celebrated populist ideals but turned its back on the cosmopolitanism of a Jefferson or a Franklin.[72]

Dewey's democracy, like Turner's, synthesizes antithetical impulses, for westward expansion generated both liberalism and illiberalism, tolerance and intolerance, community and parochialism. And like Turner's frontier, this one too continues its spiritual work even after its carnal demise: "As the frontier ceased to be a menace to orderly life, it persisted as a limit beyond which it was dangerous and unrespectable for thought to travel." In this mediated fashion, the past works into the present and Jacksonian democracy weaves into Bryan's evangelism. Bryan "does not represent the frontier democracy of Andrew Jackson's day. But he represents it toned down and cultivated as it exists in fairly prosperous villages and small towns that have inherited the fear of whatever threatens the security and order of a precariously attained civilization along with pioneer impulses to neighborliness and decency." The irrational elements of America's unconscious inheritance threaten to displace the liberal tradition as healthy aversion to privilege becomes kneejerk reaction. Some historical explanation is needed, and the narrative we need to amend is Turner's account of America's frontier heritage, freshly packaged in his new collection of old essays, *The Frontier in American History*.[73]

Dewey did not simply invert Turner's celebratory frontier history. Looking ahead to Bryan's resurgent evangelism, the pragmatist mapped out a new telling that sought to reject religious obscurantism without descending to vulgar polemics about the idiocy of rural life. The religious crusade against modern science in public discourse was not a simple social pathology. It had historically been interwoven with much that was good and sensible in American thought and culture.

We are evangelical because of our fear of ourselves and of our latent frontier disorderliness. The depressing effect upon the free life of inquiry and criticism is the greater because of the element of soundness in frontier fear, and because of the impulses of goodwill and social aspiration which have become entangled with its creeds. The forces which are embodied in the present crusade would not be so dangerous were they not bound up with so much that is necessary and good. We have been so taught to respect the beliefs of our neighbors that few will respect the beliefs of a neighbor when they depart from forms which have become associated with aspiration for a decent neighborly life. This is the illiberalism which is deep-rooted in our liberalism.

The contradiction at the core of the democratic synthesis developed along the frontier, where fear of anarchic individualism produced the good of community loyalty. This community loyalty now threatens to efface the good of critical individualism, and America's frontier heritage threatens American democracy.[74]

Dewey was not a professional historian, and he wrote "American Intellectual Frontier" for a popular market. But in a way the essay's methodological modesty makes it more engaging, for Dewey did not argue that new evidence forced us to rethink frontier history. He was not criticizing Turner's *Frontier in American History* for faulty collation of data or failure to open up the right archives. So far as events were concerned, Dewey made few descriptions he could not have supported by citing Turner's own work. What was at issue was the significance, the meaning and the moral, of frontier history. He invoked all those antitheses of American development that Turner had pointed out but found in them a very different narrative resolution. Before taking his tale apart, we need to detour through a few corners of Dewey's writings, for he returned time and again to these topics.

Over a decade later Dewey's *Liberalism and Social Action* (1935) distilled three defining elements from American liberalism: liberty, individualism, and free intelligence. Where Turner saw the balance of liberty and individualism threatened by the disappearance of the frontier, Dewey seized on the popular belief that rights existed in nature. Americans still held an absolutist view of natural rights, one well suited to revolt against monarchy but ill suited for dealing with modern problems: "If the early liberals had put forth their special interpretation of liberty as something subject to historical relativity they would not have frozen it into a doctrine to be applied at all times under all social circumstances." Blindness to the historicity of natural rights philosophy led Americans into dogmatism and condemned them to lives of regimentation and oppression. Dewey thus reconciled liberalism and historicism. Liberty was not an abstract essence found in nature but a relation: It was always liberty *from* some harm, or liberty *for* someone, or liberty to *do* some particular thing. Since relations changed with historic conditions, so did liberty. The tragic lack of an effective historical consciousness generated the present crises of American liberalism, the conflicts between religion and science, industrialism and democracy.[75]

Dewey's historicism did more than Turner's to undo historical epistemology. In his 1938 study *Logic* Dewey assailed the old antinomy of historical facts and historical interpretations. He derided the old view of history as a collection of neutral descriptions of historical facts which the historian transforms into a narrative or else links through explanatory laws. There exist no purely descriptive or purely narrational statements. One could not comprehend any description without some sense of temporality against which to read it; one could not comprehend any narrative without an implicit background description. We do sometimes abstract descriptions from narratives, and vice versa, but that is a matter of convenience. Unlike later theorists from William Dray to Hayden White, Dewey did not see the world as a collection of facts to be joined by acts of scientific or artistic will. "Were the facts as isolated and independent in existence as they appear to be in a sentence when the latter is separated from context," they would be as incomprehensible as if "uttered by a parrot." Determined to impress on readers the need for thinking of description and narration together, Dewey awkwardly joined them with a hyphen: narrative-description. The insistence on the "coexistence" of narrative and description reflected his sense that history was an elemental mode of existence rather than a fixed object.[76]

Dewey's most explicit thematization of history appeared in his discussion of narrative and existence in *Logic*. This work is notoriously difficult, and we will not tie up all of its loose prosaic ends. But several points speak directly to our story, beginning with Dewey's elevation of narrative to an ontological principle. In his account of how we should imagine existence as a process, he argued that all existence is narrational. The account dissolved the old dualisms of subjects and objects, organisms and environments, historians and history: "An organism does not live *in* an environment; it lives by means of an environment. . . . The processes of living are enacted by the environment as truly as by the organism; for they *are* an integration." One might object that this defies common sense. We do not talk about birdair or fishwater or historianhistory. Birds live in the air, fish live in water, and historians write history. Dewey quickly elaborated: "The difference is not just that a fish lives *in* the water and a bird *in* the air, but that the characteristic functions of these animals are what they are because of the special way in which water and air enter into their respective activities." Birds and fish (and historians) are what they are by virtue of what they *do;* they are defined by their respective activities; and they act only by means of their environments. Acts determine identities, not vice versa.[77]

The relation of organisms and environment is reciprocal. Birds, fish, and historians act by means of their environments, change those environments in the process, and thus change yet again the possible ways in which they can act. And since they are their actions, they change themselves. This interaction takes the narrative form of a historical series:

Each particular activity prepares the way for the activity that follows. These form not a succession but a series. . . . When the balance within a given activity is disturbed—when there is a proportionate excess or deficit in some factor—then there is exhibited need, search, and fulfillment (or satisfaction) in the objective meaning of these terms. . . . Indeed, living may be regarded as a continual rhythm of disequilibrations and recoveries of equilibrium.

Each activity begins from a starting point, disrupts equilibrium, and concludes in a restored equilibrium that begins a new cycle. This motion is continuous and developmental. Each action changes both environment and actors and creates a new set of conditions of existence. As organisms grow more complex, so do actions, disruptions, and reintegrations. But all existence is historical, and there is no sharp, qualitative border to be drawn between nature and humanity: reflexes, instincts, habits, customs, cultures, aesthetic preferences, emplotment, and the logic of inquiry all grow out of what Dewey called the "existential matrix."[78]

Existence consists of tripartite story lines of beginning, middle, and end, or situation, conflict, and resolution. We begin in a state of repose or dynamic equilibrium. Actions disturb that equilibrium, and the disturbance generates a sense of "need." Need produces an action toward recovery or reintegration in a new equilibrium, and the story ends with "fulfillment or satisfaction." The basic plot encompasses everything from the amoebic search for energy to the writing of Hegel's *Phenomenology of Spirit* to sexual intercourse. And since each resolution creates a new set of conditions and identities, each solution or equilibrium creates new conflicts, resolutions, and stories ad infinitum. Dewey's prose, however, created difficulties. In particular, he used the word "experience" to denote the interactive relationships that made up the existential matrix. Most readers, though especially philosophers, thought of experience as something that happened to active subjects. Subjects go out and experience the world, historians go out and experience history in the form of archival evidence. But Dewey sought to prevent that sort of division of the world into thinking subject and experienced object.

Dewey warned against reading experience as the simple interaction of an autonomous organism with an independent environment. The distinction between environment and organism is only a "practical and temporal one." We do not have a given organism (historians, for instance), on the one hand, and a given environment (such as the past), on the other, which then engage in a third element called "interaction." Interaction is the preeminent force, and organism and environment are abstractions from it: "Integration is more fundamental than is the distinction designated by interaction of organism *and* environment. The latter is indicative of a partial disintegration of a prior integration, but one which is of such a dynamic nature that it moves along (as long as life continues) toward reintegration." Distinct organisms do not collide with environments to make narrative experience. Narratives make organisms and environments. Organisms and environments (subjects and objects, historians and pasts) are defined through stories, differentiated from each other by the middle, conflictual stages of interaction, before being brought back together in the story's resolution (this much of Hegel's dialectic remains in Dewey's mature prose). And since the organisms and environments we describe are narrative products, each story in some way remakes both organisms and environments.[79]

To make the point concrete, we might say that civilization, wilderness, frontier, and democracy are all narrative products. But in contrast with such later narrativists as Louis Mink and Hayden White, Dewey did not believe that the historian stood in a chaotic field of facts and events upon which he or she imposed narrative order. Nor did he or Turner simply report the ways pre-existing objects interact. Instead, they abstracted objects and agonists—wilderness and civilization, frontier and democracy—from the stories in which they lived. These historical actors found purpose, meaning, and existence in the tales through which they were defined and constituted as active agents. Of course neither Dewey nor Turner made up their wildernesses and democracies from scratch. They grew up into worlds of stories and descriptions which they adapted to their own contemporary needs. From these stories they abstracted descriptions associated with particular labels, like frontier and democracy, which they then read back into the original narrative, and so on, in an ongoing and dialectical process of refinement. And since each story or reading remakes its subjects and objects, Dewey's and Turner's frontiers and democracies cannot be said to be strictly identical. Each narrative redefines its characters. For Dewey this narrative pluralism was not, as White and Mink believed, an epistemological problem. It is simply the way inquiry works. Authentication of a narrative-description was a matter of probability and persuasion rather than absolute certainty.[80]

Dewey was not talking only about stories in books. Historians and pasts, like all other subjects and objects, also are abstractions from storied existence. So while we might accurately say that as historians we tell stories, this equation is reversible: stories tell us. Like all other objects, selves are "events with meanings." Here linger traces of Dewey's early idealism. The notion that subject and object are defined by their role in some larger synthetic unity, that existence is historical, that nature and history are joined together in this flow, and that identities are basically narrative in both content and form, all these are part of Hegel's legacy. Unlike Hegel, though, Dewey did not see history as grounded by any eternal values, logic, purposes, or meanings. Stories are plural, we can tell only one at a time, and they cannot all be added up into a single universal history. Their compatibility derives from a sort of existential narrative logic more mechanical than what we have seen thus far in Turner (or, for that matter, in Hegel). Dewey projected an optimistic sense that all stories move in stages toward conclusions, however provisional these end points may be. Needs are fulfilled, conflicts reconciled, problems solved. His thematization of history was much more rigorous than Turner's but shared its idealist origins, cosmic optimism, and social commitments.[81]

Dewey did not fear interpretive chaos. Like Turner, he saw inquiry as a social contract: "That the requalifications that are made from time to time are subject to the conditions that all authentic inquiry has to meet goes without saying." Authentic inquiry is that which solves problems, and its necessary conditions are simply those which facilitate problem solving. The *Logic* claimed to be an empirical account of scholarly problem solving rather than a Mosaic injunction as to how it ought to proceed. What counts as a problem or solution is provisional. Problems, said Dewey, must grow out of actual situations, social tensions, and public needs. Their boundaries are determined by the material means of inquiry and by anticipated consequences: they must project a resolution, an end-in-view whose status is and must remain hypothetical and revisable. In physical inquiry we arbitrate problems and ends with comparative ease. But social inquiry is trickier, for here the verification of results depends more heavily on shared belief in the efficacy of some particular problem-solution: "Any hypothesis as to a social end must include as part of itself the idea of organized association among those who are to execute the operations it formulates and directs. . . . The evils in current social judgments of ends and policies arise, as has been said, from importations of value from outside of inquiry." The danger lies in fixing ends according to some timeless *ethos*, such as rights in nature or Christian conceptions of sin and redemption. Dewey believed that we may test and revise even those values that condition the way we select problems and solutions.[82]

Dewey's retelling of frontier history, though written more than a decade before the *Logic,* illustrates the latter's claims. In "American Intellectual Frontier" we have a contemporary problem: the tension between inherited religious ideals and scientific practice working its way through public institutions and disrupting social equilibrium. We also have a social need: to resolve this problem in the most efficacious manner. The situation grew from a past that must be understood in order to move us to a future in which the conflict no longer threatens social solidarity. So Dewey told his readers exactly how and why Bryan's evangelism had come to shape American existence. Such religiosity was a frontier product, and the same forces that made America democratic created a loyalty to absolutist ideals—natural rights and original sin— which threatened to make America undemocratic.

"The American Intellectual Frontier" is a historicist parable of the dangers of fixed values and systems of belief. Only an effective historical consciousness can save American democracy. Only historicism allows us to resolve such disputes without physical violence, only historicism can open a future in which liberalism survives as anything other than a semantic form emptied of its social content. By Dewey's lights, histories are judged by the degree of community assent they can mobilize, by their efficacy in achieving desirable social consequences, and by their productivity in creating a future into which inquiry may be carried forward. Bryan's Christianity is dangerous because it threatens to mandate a story in which beginnings, middles, and ends are always the same. It thus freezes, once and for all, the definitions of what counts as "neighborliness" and "community" and thereby closes off all the ranges of imaginable communities, pasts, and futures—the choices— that Dewey's liberalism celebrates. If we accept Bryan's vision, inquiry will become propaganda, a trivial, ritualistic affirmation of what everyone already believes to be true. The story's problem and moral are quite lucid. America's frontier experience produced conflicting necessitarian and pragmatic philosophies of history, and we should opt for pragmatism in order to ensure a free future.[83]

By context, by implication, and by Dewey's own use of the word, this *particular* story is a frontier tragedy. The North American dialectic of civilization and wilderness fractured the American self, generating a deep fear of wilderness disorder and anarchic individualism. The result is repression, the elevation of an absolutist sense of community, and the constraint of individual expression and scientific inquiry. This ironically undercuts the democratic synthesis that was supposed to be the frontier's legacy to the twentieth century. Dewey's frontier tale does not affect the inevitability projected by paradigmatic tragedies like *Oedipus Rex,* but it does share the classical desire to locate the tragic flaw, or *hamartia,* in hubris. In Dewey's tale America's tragic flaw lies in its self-rightous belief that natural rights or Christianity lie beyond history. In this attitude lies "the tragedy of liberalism," the pride in natural rights philosophy anticipating America's fall into industrial capitalism. This looks much less mechanical than the tripartite narrative scheme proposed by the *Logic.* But what looks like a problematic separation of the logic of inquiry from the aesthetics of emplotment blurs if we move further into Dewey's work.

Pragmatism's Conception of Emplotment

In Dewey's pragmatism the objects we call tragedies and comedies are as real and factual as tables and chairs. In the early twenties, when Dewey was writing "American Intellectual Frontier," he was also reading Aristotle and working on his Paul Carus lectures, which he delivered in 1922 and later published under the title *Experience and Nature.* This major venture into metaphysics anticipated his later discussions of the logic of inquiry. It also offers some insight into the ways that Dewey related poetics and logic and hints at the sort of claims he might have made for the efficacy of his frontier tragedy.[84]

For Dewey dramatic emplotment was a matter of relations rather than artistic essence. Recall Turner's invocation of Emerson: "Life may be either epic or lyric." To this Turner added the provison that life may also be dramatic. Dewey reworked the idea yet again, arguing that existence is always drama. Life is never, as lyric claims to be, a solipsistic revery of self-reliant ego apart from the world. Consciousness requires other selves, for "meanings do not come into being without language, and language implies two selves involved in a conjoint or shared undertaking." We achieve meaning only with such a "community of action." Here lies pragmatism's trinity: two interactive and relational selves brought together in the temporal flow of language. Even soliloquy is the "product and reflex of converse with others" and takes the form we call drama: "Imagination is primarily dramatic, rather than lyric, whether it takes the form of the play enacted on the stage, of the told story or silent soliloquy. . . . Through speech a person dramatically identifies himself with potential acts and deeds; he plays many roles, not in successive stages of life but in a contemporaneously enacted drama." This dramatic narrative makes up both individual and collective selves. One might infer that we manipulate narratives to realize some separate end called community identity, that we tell stories in order to bring about common ends. But Dewey went further: "Communication is not only a means to common ends but *is* the sense of community, communion realized." Communities are their histories, individuals are their dramas.[85]

Drama took many forms. Traditionally, critics had divided the genre into tragedies, comedies, and (sometimes) a third, mysterious form called tragicomedy. Dewey's metaphysics described these forms as factual objects of particular stories with methods, ends, and a place in some community of action rather than impositions on the raw stuff of an independent world: "Empirically, things are poignant, tragic, beautiful, humorous, settled, disturbed, comfortable, annoying, barren, harsh, consoling, splendid, fearful; are such immediately and in their own right and behalf." The notion that the world is chaos and that plot forms are glassy essences or artifacts of unnatural human thought came from the traditional but, Dewey believed, contrived separation of existence into thinking subject and known object. But plot forms are genuine things, structures of lived experience, the outcomes of narrative interactions, each carrying, just like any other object-name, a past history and a projected future.[86]

So how do we choose among competing narrations of the "same" event?

In "American Intellectual Frontier" Dewey demonstrated his preference for tragedy, and brief passages sprinkled throughout *Experience and Nature* hinted at its origins. He did not claim a timeless foundation for his choice: "Comedy is as genuine as tragedy. But it is traditional that comedy strikes a more superficial note than tragedy." The canon, from Aristotle forward, had privileged the tragic over the comic, describing the former as more elevated, as more spiritual, as less earthbound. Tragedy had a certain classist appeal; intellectuals exalted tragedy whereas the broad public lost themselves in comedy. Dewey vaguely seconded Aristotle: "Popular fiction and drama shows the bias of human nature in favor of happy endings, but by being fiction and drama they show with even greater assurance that unhappy endings are natural events." Uncritical love of comedy is a bias, and bias is a problem to be solved. Beneath the happy stories enjoyed by the masses lie their tragic countertexts, the darker and equally genuine tales that have customarily attracted intellectuals like Dewey. Although comedy and tragedy are existential equals, the intimation that tragedy requires a more rigorous inquiry or more refined sensibilities gives it a shiny appeal that Turner (and his audiences) would not have approved.[87]

Only the changing contrasts of tragedy and comedy made both meaningful. The philosopher imagined this sort of critical counterpoint, the reading of Deweyan tragedy against Turnerian comedy, as the real basis of a community of action. "Poets who have sung of despair in the midst of prosperity, and of hope amid the darkest gloom," said Dewey, "have been the true metaphysicians of nature. The glory of the moment and its tragedy will surely pass." Tragedy is no more real than comedy. But poets who sing of despair amidst prosperity or who narrate the tragic in a comic world elevate experience, driving us toward a more open future by confronting us with the contingency of our stories, selves, and worlds. It is no accident that Dewey's frontier tragedy appeared in a popular journal in 1922, hard on the heels of Turner's own *Frontier in American History* and at the peak of public faith in a happy past.[88]

One of Dewey's keenest students, Sidney Hook, later spoke of the "tragic sense of life" at the heart of Deweyan pragmatism. Hook admitted that the description swam against the critical current, which typically stressed pragmatism's optimistic beliefs in the openness of the future, the degree to which humans made their worlds, and the social action of ideas. All these notions, which both Hook and Dewey shared, did work against the necessitarian tragedies one found in, say, Sophocles. But in Hook's view Deweyan history was tragic in a uniquely American manner. Much as Turner had revised the comedy of a Dante or a Shakespeare, Dewey had revised tragedy.

I mean by the tragic sense a very simple thing which is rooted in the very nature of the moral experience and the phenomenon of moral choice. Every genuine experience of moral doubt and perplexity in which we ask "What should I do?" takes place in a situation where good conflicts with good. If we already know what is evil, the moral inquiry is over, or it never really begins. . . . All the serious perplexities of life come back to the genuine difficulty of forming a judgment as to the values of a situation: they come back to a conflict of goods. . . . Where the choice is between goods that are complex in structure and consequential for the future, the tragic quality of the moral dilemma emerges more clearly.

We should recognize several Deweyan themes in Hook's prose. Historical judgments rest on future consequences rather than past objects. Inquiry and social freedom depend on a refusal of absolutes. Existence is pluralistic, "requalified," in Dewey's word, with each new narrative description and thus joyously complex.[89]

Hook's gloss illuminates Dewey's "American Intellectual Frontier." That story's agon of science and religion is not a stark conflict between reaction and progress. The forces driving Bryan's crusade, Dewey warned, "would not be so dangerous were they not bound up with so much that is necessary and good." The quest for a community of faith preaches a solidarity that is necessary and potentially productive; its injunction to schools and educators to respect the deeply rooted religious convictions of local populations is a serious one deserving of attention, and we should have sufficient respect for the beliefs of our neighbors that we can accommodate their spiritual commitments, especially when those are the basic threads weaving individuals into community. The tragedy is that while a liberal Deweyan society is founded on freedom of expression allowing groups and individuals to redescribe the world, not all of these different stories are compatible; they will not resolve themselves peaceably into an overarching Hegelian unity. Only one narrative will be reproduced in the state educational system, and we must choose that story which best ensures a future of choice and social action.

Hook favorably contrasted Dewey's pragmatism with Christianity and with what he described as the twentieth-century incarnations of Hegelian political philosophy, communism and fascism. As Hook saw it, only the Deweyan quest for creative intelligence could productively reform a modern world structured by physical, political, and emotional violence. The saving grace of pragmatism was its renunciation of hubris, of any naive claims to absolute truth and certainty: "It [pragmatism] is an attempt to make it possible for men to live in a world of inescapable tragedy—a tragedy that flows from the conflict of moral ideals—without lamentation, defiance, or make-believe." Classical tragedy and Christian redemption belonged to a lost world. Their epochs lay in the European past, not in the American future.[90]

For some, pragmatism raised the question of what counted as an authentically tragic vision. If tragedy had been so far revised that many of its defining conventions no longer struck readers as "realistic," then the pragmatic understanding of history had passed from tragedy into satire. The drama critic for the *Nation*, Columbia University professor Joseph Wood Krutch, made the point most effectively in his provocative 1929 polemic, *The Modern Temper*. Tragedy, said Krutch, is the cultural product of specific historical periods, and those periods are now behind us. God and nature have dwindled to mere manipulable, analytical concepts in a darkened universe. The modern spirit is enfeebled. For tragedy to achieve realism, one needs a premodern conception of human dignity, the grandness of passion, and the amplitude of life: "Tragedies, in that only sense of the word which has any distinctive meaning, are no longer written in either the dramatic or any other form, and the fact is not to be accounted for in any merely literary terms." The universe has shifted, realism has devolved, and we have lost faith in our ability to find a desirable meaning in existence.[91]

Hook's pragmatic tragic sense of life is not, by Krutch's lights, truly tragic. It has nothing of that sense of the innate nobility of humanity that elevated Shakespeare's *Hamlet* to artistic and metaphysical heights. In the plays of Ibsen, the aphorisms of Nietzsche, and the naturalized ethics of Dewey, we cannot find the faith in moral purpose that underwrites a tragic understanding. Real tragedy belonged to earlier ages of humanity. "A too sophisticated society," such as our own, "has neither fairy tales to assure it that all is always right in the end nor tragedies to make it believe that it rises superior in soul to the outward calamities which befall it." In Krutch's telling, Hook's Deweyan world, with its refusal of lamentation and make-believe, is depressingly satirical, its actors adrift in an amoral, ironic conception of the universe from which they cannot escape. Appeals to tragedy and comedy are simply empty contrivances. Literature might ape the formal conventions of tragedy, but these forms no longer command an intelligent loyalty. We mark the bounds of realism by contrasting it, as Hook did, with both the naive and hopeless "defiance" that refuses the findings of the laboratory and the "make-believe" of the genuine tragedy that ennobled Sophocles, Shakespeare, Hegel, and their audiences.[92]

Dewey did not read his own story as satire. He carefully separated his pragmatism from skepticism and reaffirmed the dignity found in responsible revisions of social existence. But Krutch's anxiety is understandable if not inescapable. If critics believed pragmatism emptied the world of meaning, Dewey's own prose is partly to blame, for he repeatedly conflated ethical absolutism with "morality" as such. In "American Intellectual Frontier," for instance, he cautioned against "movements which embody moral emotions rather than the insight and policy of intelligence." Such passages opposed morality and inquiry, emotion and intelligence, hearts and heads, in a way that most readers probably did not spend much critical energy contemplating. Juxtapose such antitheses with Dewey's warning, in the *Logic,* of the "evils" of "importing" values into inquiry, and we can imagine a reading in which the utility of scientific inquiry lies in its very denial of aesthetics and ethics and which associates amoral scholarship with social reform. This was not Dewey's intent, but it was the ideal of countless scientists and administrators, the fear of at least one drama critic, and a reading many historians qua social scientists were prepared to enact.[93]

Merle Curti's Corporate Frontier

The Turnerian heritage we have reconstructed did not dominate the consciousness of Turner's immediate successors. History joined other spheres of American society in rolling toward a more technocratic existence, and frontier historians rolled with it. Few thought of Turner as a "narrative historian," a label they associated with Bancroft's and Parkman's romances of Great Men. More often they spoke of his "analytic" turn, Carl Becker, for instance, noting that "if in all his writing there are more than five pages of pure narrative, I do not know where to find them." These were the seasons of George W. Pierson's discontent, and the faithful rallied to the defense of the master's scientific reputation. Historians like Stanley Elkins, Eric McKitrick, Ray Allen Billington, and Merle Curti all emphasized Turner's scientism. This social science reading conserved his credibility with suburban professionals uncomfortable with words like "spirit." Those historians whose enthusiasm for happy stories survived totalitarianism and the A-bomb believed that modern scientific vocabularies would bring frontier history into closer alignment with reality. These new Turnerians read idealism and poesy out of history even as they extended Turner's famous metaphor: frontier comedy is the story of America.[94]

Today, strict social science readings of Turner look quite implausible. The scholarly apparatus that has since grown up around history monographs did not characterize Turner's published work. "The Significance of History" did not offer any footnotes, only a brief bibliography of esoteric works (mostly German) in philosophy of history. "The Significance of the Frontier in American History" decorated its pages with fifty-four footnotes, citing a mix of monographs and primary sources. But despite its conspicuous reference to the vast data base compiled by the Bureau of the Census, the article barely scratched the surface of these materials. In 1925 "The Significance of Sections in American His-

tory" (which Turner called "monographic") boasted only two footnotes, and one of these cited his earlier essay, "Sections and Nation."
The article did mention an entire series of maps that correlated soil
types, climatic regions, literacy, farm values, and election returns. "I
have had the photographer superimpose these maps one upon the
other," declared Turner, but readers had to take this on faith, for he did
not append the maps to the article. The extensive research that typified
his graduate seminars did not appear on many published pages, partly
because he wrote only one book-length monograph and partly because
of logistics. In a noncomputerized era the manipulation of statistical
data was an almost unbelievably daunting task, and Turner himself lamented that it was a job for not one historian but many.[95]

The studies most often invoked as rigorous tests of the frontier thesis
appeared in the 1950s and listed multiple authors on their title pages:
Stanley Elkins and Eric McKitrick's "A New Meaning for Turner's
Frontier" (1954) and Merle Curti's ("with the assistance of Robert
Daniel, Shaw Livermore Jr., Joseph Van Hise, and Margaret W. Curti")
*The Making of an American Community: A Case Study of Democracy
in a Frontier County* (1959). Of the two studies the second is by far the
more imposing, involving as it did a small army of researchers over a
period of many years. Styled after social science monographs, using the
technical language of structural-functionalism, and featuring computerized research techniques, the book opened up a narrative world
very different from the one Turner inhabited. Yet the book reads like
an extended dialogue with the absent midwesterner, as each chapter
struggles to pull Turner into the age of the "Organization Man" and
create a modern historical form still connected to historiographic custom.[96]

Curti's influential early work framed the study. A Turner student,
successor to the Frederick Jackson Turner chair at the University of Wisconsin, and participant in the Social Science Research Council's report
on history and theory, he re-created Turner as prototypical social scientist. In the 1931 SSRC *Methods in Social Science: A Case Book,* Curti's
contribution, "Analysis 23: The Section and the Frontier in American
History: The Methodological Concepts of Frederick Jackson Turner,"
opens with this sentence: "Frederick Jackson Turner has never definitely
formulated a philosophy of history, nor set forth in organized form his
conception of historical method." As Curti read him, though, he had
demonstrated a consistent social evolutionist approach concerned with
generalization while abjuring universal historical laws. His methodology resembled that of natural science in its acceptance of multiple, pro-

visional hypotheses. In a memorial essay, "Frederick Jackson Turner, 1861–1932," Curti credited Turner with having brought history out of the humanist darkness and into the bright "sphere of the social sciences." As for the frontier thesis itself, all the results were not yet in.[97]

Curti was no dialectician. His Pulitzer prize–winning intellectual history of 1943, *The Growth of American Thought* (later voted the best work of its period by the members of the American Historical Association), concludes a sketch of Hegelianism in America with the brutal sentence, "Hegel had taught in effect that whatever is, is right." Some years later intellectual historian Robert Skotheim described *The Growth of American Thought* as a Manichaean "conflict between reform ideas which looked forward in history and antireform ideas which looked backward." Curti placed all his heroes in this simple story. He saw Turner as a Darwinian proponent of the "so-called scientific or objective school of history." Turner was history's answer to John Dewey, whose early Hegelianism Curti similarly passed over in silence, and both he and Dewey find their historical significance as exemplars of naturalism who introduced empiricism to American science and ended the bad old days of idealist abstraction and religious reaction.[98]

Curti's romance of reason over priestcraft appealed to many readers in an age of team science, computer pioneering, and multiversities. By the sixties "The Professionals" and "The Wild Bunch" had replaced the lone cowboy hero, the computer was replacing the Underwood, and the historical cognoscenti heralded the "New Social History" as the cutting edge of scholarship. Curti rode all these waves, and he caught them early. In 1940 he contributed to an anthology edited by another Turner student, Caroline F. Ware. *The New Cultural Approach to History* (1940) spoke of the need for historians to adopt social science models to reconstruct the histories of common people by attending to the "patterns of culture" and the "functionally interrelated" "structures" of past societies. Social science used methods different from the source criticism professionalized by older generations. In his 1952 presidential address to the American Historical Association, "Democratic Themes in Historical Literature," Curti announced that he was using quantitative analysis to "test the validity of Turner's contention. . . . In this study we are asking questions of highly qualified authorities—of authorities so highly qualified as to inspire at least me with awe. We are asking these questions of International Business Machines!" By 1959 the returns were in, and it looked like a triumph for science, Wisconsin, and democracy.[99]

The Making of an American Community exemplifies a number of changes that set the literary forms of "structural," "analytic," or "New Social" history apart from earlier historical narratives. While not the most influential of such works, it typified their formal structure. The first paragraph of chapter I warned readers to expect something new. The authors might have written a traditional and complete history of Trempeleau county, but they did not. They regretted omitting so much "vivid and picturesque material," but they had set their sights on bigger game in the form of two major historical controversies: Can history be truly objective, and is Turner's frontier thesis valid? The authors joined both battles: "We decided to apply objective tests to the Turner thesis about democracy." Curti brought a wide range of reading to this problem, for in "Democratic Themes in Historical Literature" he had surveyed the topic and concluded that historians could not claim a consensus on the meaning of "democracy." To keep their study within manageable bounds, he and his coauthors appealed to Turner's intentions: "In our opinion it is fair to summarize his views by saying that to him American democracy involved widespread participation in the making of decisions affecting the common life, the development of initiative and self-reliance, and equality of economic and cultural opportunity. It thus also involved Americanization of the immigrant." The point was not to analyze Turner's writing but to derive specific propositions, apply them to historical data, and assess their validity.[100]

Many new social histories resembled the "reports" of science journals, and the new format encouraged an opportunistic, if not mercenary approach to reading. Over thirty years later the form still looks familiar. The monograph typically opens with a concise statement of the problem, the research tradition, and the test design. Brief and utilitarian (*Making*'s first chapter runs ten pages of prose including notes), such chapters are remarkably well suited to skimming. The work then proceeds, as this one does for fourteen chapters, to a detailed account of the research program or test. And such reports conclude with a summary of test results or "findings" (*Making*'s "Conclusion" is seven pages long). For the harried social scientist frantically running to keep abreast of the widening flood of monographs, the format makes life livable. One can read introduction and conclusion, skim the most interesting middle chapters, glance at a few charts, and then trust other specialists to judge the integrity of research detail. Lacking even that modicum of time or interest, readers could flip through the back pages of the major journals, which devoted an increasing space to synoptic book reviews, and consume the entire volume in a bite-sized abstract provided by a specialist reviewer. *The Making of an American Community* and similar works not only refigured historical writing; they also enforced new regimes of historical reading.[101]

Curti et al. attempted to derive and test a series of predictive hypotheses from Turner's frontier thesis, and while Carl Hempel's name appears nowhere in the book, the covering law debate haunts every chapter, most of which reproduce the book's tripartite form: problem-tradition-design, test, findings. Most chapters also adapt that pattern to Turnerian tradition by asking what sort of numbers we should expect to find in census data if Turner's thesis is valid. They then tell how the authors set about testing that expectation and conclude by assessing whether the data confirm Turnerian expectations. Merely outlining a single chapter would demand more pages than we can spare, but a brief reading of chapter 8, "Fortunes of the New Farmers," will demonstrate just how systematic an effort informed *The Making of an American Community.*

The first paragraphs defined the problem, whether pioneer faith in frontier opportunity matched up with social reality. Earlier chapters had found non-English-speaking nativity groups "consistently inferior to other groups in value of property." If that inferiority persisted through several decades, it would be evidence against Turner's thesis. The authors proposed a test.

What expectations or hypotheses concerning the fortunes of farm operators are valid or implied in the Turner thesis? If our interpretation of the thesis is valid, we should in the first place find that, among the groups of farm operators who came into the country in the 1850's and the 1860's, the groups from very poor countries would *on the whole* be able to get as much land as those with more advantages. In the 1880 census, with land more scarce and conditions changing, our hypothesis would be that there would be less "equality" between these groups . . . One important test of basic frontier theory is, then, to find out whether there was or was not substantial equality between leading nativity groups in amount of acreage obtained *in the early decades* of the county, *among new farmers.*

If Turner's frontier thesis is valid, then we should find a substantial equality in farm acreage among new farmers of all nativity groups in the early decades of settlement. This is what Carl Hempel called an inductive-statistical hypothesis or what Murray G. Murphey described as a probabilistic generalization specific to a particular time and place—the frontier Midwest in the period 1860–1880.[102]

To test the hypothesis, the authors examined the agriculture schedules of the census and graphed the results. The graphs chart median farm size by decade and nativity group. In the 1860 census median farm size for the cohort "U.S., native-born" was 135 acres; for "English-speaking, foreign born," 123; for "non-English-speaking, foreign born," 112: "These 1860 curves are eloquent testimony to the ability of the common man to get Trempeleau farm land. . . . The general form of the curves for all three groups is strikingly similar." By the 1870 census those numbers had risen, with the median acreage of foreign-born cohorts actually leading the native U.S., 166 to 162. By 1880 much of the best "free land" had already been settled in Trempeleau county and medians declined slightly, although the authors assured readers that "the county was still a land of opportunity." They summarized their findings:

Had he been present in Trempeleau County in the year 1870, Turner would have certainly seen abundant evidence that many poor immigrants at least thought they had reached the promised land. The bustle, the talk, the boasting, the coming and going, the general confidence and optimism that are reflected in contemporary accounts and newspaper notices—these manifestations of the pioneer spirit are shown by our curves and tables to rest on a solid basis of accomplishment.

As Curti knew, Turner had not lived in Trempeleau, but he had lived only a handful of counties to the south, in a very similar corner of Wisconsin. He may have had relations in Trempeleau, he likely went to school with relatives of those pioneers enumerated in the census tables, and in Portage he would have witnessed kindred changes and experiences.[103]

So the sifting of census data from Trempeleau not only tested the frontier thesis, it also reconstructed the social environment within which that thesis took shape. Read "literally," *The Making of an American Community* is about three decades in Trempeleau. Read allegorically, it is about the making of a historian, a thesis, and a scholarly interpretive community. And it "vindicates" Turner's powers of scientific observation. As he inhabited a social milieu like the one depicted in these graphic measurements of social progress, he must have been led by observation, as much as by artistic intuition, to his assessment of the results of the interaction of wilderness and settlement. His more poetic essays drew on newspaper accounts, diaries, and the self-understandings of pioneers, but Curti et al. believed they had demonstrated that "spirit" rested on a rational, material foundation.

Having completed one set of tests, Curti and his collaborators mapped out another set of predictions: "If Turner's general theory is sound, there should be rapid improvement in economic position over the years for all groups getting a start in years when farm land was still cheap and plentiful." They broke down this proposition into a series of hypotheses aimed at specific bodies of data to measure the value of farms, property, produce, implements, and livestock differentiated by decade and nativity group. Test results confirmed Curti et al.'s Turnerian expectations:

That land-hungry small farmers from the poorer countries of Europe could do so well in Trempeleau in less than ten year's time must have made a great difference in their feelings. We have direct words from very few of them, but not much imagination is required to realize that an experience like theirs would be found to affect their outlook on life, to nourish pride, and to stimulate hope. Even those who did not do as well as their neighbors must have been influenced toward a positive attitude by the success of others.

This passage employed yet another convention of the new history, the use of statistical data to imaginatively reconstruct the "feelings," "outlook," and "attitude" (other historians might say "spirit," "mentalité," or "ideology") of people who left no written records. For histories of the élite the historian may turn to books, diaries, letters, newspaper accounts, and all those literary traces of the lives of great men that lay behind the multivolume productions of George Bancroft and Francis Parkman. But the masses leave no direct record of their voice, and the historian must speak for them by reading their speech off the impress they have made on the bureaucratic structure of the state.[104]

To adequately re-create the experiences of the common people, Curti et al. hinted, we need to press cautiously beyond enumeration and into empathy. The self-consciously "objective" rigor of social science generalization is good as far as it goes, but in order to determine how structural change shaped popular sentiment, we need to follow R. G. Collingwood's description of historical inquiry: We must imaginatively project ourselves into their experiences. Assuming that these people were rational human beings (assuming, in other words, that they thought, felt, and acted much as Curti et al. would have in like circumstances), they must have responded positively, optimistically, and hopefully to their environment. Their success, measured in acreage and property values, must have kindled in them pride and faith in democratic institutions, and the sometimes greater success of their neighbors must have inspired them to new heights of capitalist achievement.

The passage illustrates the materialism in *The Making of an American*

Community. First, material things, what the authors called "economic" and "social structure," determine ideology, not the other way around. Material conditions, as measured by property accumulation, mediately determine thoughts, feelings, and attitudes. The very un-Deweyan assumption that causality flows upward from material base to dependent superstructure allows the historian to read the thoughts of common people from their statistical remains. Second, progress, equality, and democracy (or, alternatively, decay, oppression, and authoritarianism) can be measured, itemized, and compared. Here the data limit freedom of intellectual movement, for if this is not the case, there is little conceivable reason for pursuing this elaborate analysis. Finally, since material structure determines culture, it must ground literary and historical forms. This being the case, since Frederick Jackson Turner lived in this environment, those material conditions both inspired and legitimated his understanding of American history. This is the ultimate vindication of the frontier thesis, that Turner's comic optimism had a material basis.

If we were philosophers of history writing in the year 1975, we could draw a variety of morals from our discussion. Although the text appeals to no absolute general laws, it does use an adapted version of the covering law model. We expect to find a probabilistic correlation between frontier conditions, especially the availability of free land, and the development of factors associated with democracy, such as egalitarian patterns of property ownership. But we could also appeal to *Making* in support of the functionalist or theoretical explanations discussed by Murray G. Murphey and Elazar Weinryb. The historians explain the frontier process of land development by placing it within a theoretical model, structural-functionalism. There is a measurable relation between land availability and democracy in frontier societies, and that relation is a function of a theoretically postulated system. And as we have seen, Curti et al. also used R. G. Collingwood's explanation by reenactment. Having determined that Trempeleau evinced a comparatively egalitarian pattern of property distribution and having described the social function of that pattern, they attempted to imaginatively reconstruct the mind-set of all those individual actors in Trempeleau. Hand the book over to three different analytic philosophers, and we stand a good chance of receiving three different accounts of the logic of historical explanation.

So what holds all of these explanations together?

The frontier story. We can imagine *The Making of an American Community* surviving the loss of any, perhaps even all, of these logical models and still remaining frontier history, but we cannot imagine it without the basic narrative structure handed down by Turnerian tradition.

Curti would not have considered his collaborative product a "narrative history." Unlike narratives, *Making*'s conclusions were "findings," not literary constructions, and its story was a true one, not a "frontier myth" of the sort associated with vivid and picturesque prose. It is significant that the one section of the work that the authors explicitly described as narrative in form is chapter 15, "Leadership," with its biographical portraits of Trempeleau county's great political men. Here lies another convention of the new social history, its self-conscious differentiation from "narrative" history. Curti and many other social historians associated narrative with biography, soft rhetoric, myth, and social elites. They identified social history with analysis, scientific method, and the common people. The construction allegorized storytelling by distinguishing it from and subordinating it to "analysis." The oppositions are both consistent and crude.

The Making of an American Community and similar works revised rather than escaped narrative, and that revision both extended and broke with Turnerian tradition. The book's affinity for older, comic emplotments of frontier history is most evident in the book's synoptic passages, as in this excerpt from chapter 2:

To sum up, the first settlement in Trempeleau County reflected the easygoing and versatile activities of a remarkable Kentucky-born soldier, trader, and farmer of sorts, whose patriarchal sway over his numerous family connections embraced nonetheless a sense of fellowship with Whites and Indians alike. The next step in the creation of the community was democratic in a different sense. It was taken by a handful of aggressive and ambitious Yankees. They had glorious dreams of a community better than any they had known in the older part of the country—better for themselves and everyone else. . . . [These] promoters can be said to have filled a democratic function in translating into actuality the potential equality of opportunity for anyone with a little cash to acquire land. In so doing, they of course advanced their own interests! But even the exceptional newcomers who did not succeed in turning to much account the potential advantage of early presence on the scene could share in the feeling that they too were helping to build a new community in which everyone was to be judged by his contributions to the common enterprise.

The first frontiersman was a veritable "Daniel Boone," holding both Indian and white worlds in harmonious balance. This stage was succeeded by aggressive capitalists whose private greed frontier abundance

turns to public benefit, as self-centered materialism realizes its "democratic function" in the building of community. The resulting society, in
its elevation to a higher democratic existence, in its integration of both
successful and less successful into a harmonious mix, and in its "Americanization" of diverse Old World stocks, rested on a comic summit that
resembles Turner's, at least in outline. The plot parallels Turner's also
in its central conflict, the interaction of "wilderness and settlement."
It begins with the arrival of Euro-Americans and ends in the late 1880s,
with the development of the last of the county's "free land." Turner's
developing wilderness, "a fair, blank page" upon which white middle-
class males inscribed their destiny, finds graphic form in a series of maps
Curti and his collaborators appended to their volume, charting the
transformation of Trempeleau county from an original blank, Edenic
purity to a social slate filled with the lines of population density and
political borders.[105]

The Making of an American Community did not simply impose Turnerian narrative on nonnarrative descriptions of historical fact. The historians did not assemble their story after collecting their data. Before
this project could ever have been proposed, its authors needed, first, a
sense that history was a progressive, linear series of interrelated events
that could be differentiated and then rejoined and, second, a more
specific vision of *frontier* history. Turner's frontier story makes it possible to imagine the census statistics as historical data. Lacking that
narrative expectation, the census data remain unreadable. Only by virtue of their relation to a historical narrative can we speak of the census
schedules as evidence of historical facts. And in this case we can identify
the general tale from which those factual descriptions have been abstracted. In expectation and findings, in kernel and in plot, *The Making
of an American Community* committed itself to Turnerian tradition.

Elsewhere *Making* stood apart, for Curti et al. replaced Turner's
"spirit" with Robert Merton and Talcott Parsons's "system." Like
Elkins and McKitrick's more modest effort, *The Making of an American
Community* finds social unity in "economic structure," "property structure," "social relations" and "interrelations," and the systemic "functions" of "roles," "institutions," and individuals. The new vocabulary
described society in mechanistic terms as a functional, integrated system. Its various relations and functions interacted in observable and
reasonably predictable ways, ways that could for the most part be reliably
captured in the statistical compilations of the state.

Along the road from Turner to Curti, historical understanding metamorphosed from poetics to engineering. For Curti method held the keys to transcending the conflict between selfish individualism and social solidarity. Spirit must be counted, democratic ideals must be objectified, and historians "may still choose what aspects of the past" to carry into the future. Curti later hinted that his negation of Turnerian and Deweyan historicism was deliberate: "I think it is possible to choose whether one wants to express what I have been saying in the symbols of the Christian vision of man's weakness and of his ability to progress toward redemption; or whether he wants to put it in the humanistic and naturalistic terms that American thought about human nature and social values also includes." Curti's analytic turn sought to expel the last vestiges of metaphysics from historical understanding. American thought should be empirical rather than theoretical, experimental rather than speculative, and scientific rather than metaphysical, or else it risked devolution into the internecine conflicts that devastated twentieth-century Europe. To use the words of Daniel Bell's famous 1959 book, history must enforce the end of ideology.[106]

The shifting complexity of Turnerian semantics fell by the wayside, and with it went the shades of gray on gray which Turner's best passages achieved. Analytic thought had no patience with dialectical poesy. A thing was either p or not p, and there was no room for Hegel's nonsense about "difference within identity," or Whitman's chaotic selfhood— "Do I contradict myself? Very well, then, I contradict myself / I am large. I contain multitudes"—or for that matter, Turner's pluralistic spirit, with its multifarious elements at once distinctive and unified, its developing democracy both good and evil, selfish and selfless. Spirit and system built two very different worlds. We can map that border in "community," a word easily as treacherous as democracy or frontier. Both Curti and Turner held out the obligation of historical science to contribute to communal self-understanding, but Curti's work illuminates some of the tension in that ideal. Community could be local, sectional, national, or universal. Turner bounded up and down this ladder, urging development of each level as a means of preventing any one threatening the others. To that end he had explored with parochial devotion what he saw as the national spirit and sectional consciousness. But sections and spirit, unlike the statistics compiled by the United States Bureau of the Census, did not come in political rectangles.[107]

In *The Making of an American Community* "community" jettisons the connotations it had for people like Turner and Royce. "County" and "community" have become working synonyms. A community is a specific geographic region together with its human inhabitants, and its boundaries are determined by legislators and surveyors rather than the historical interaction of physiography and culture. The bureaucratized structure of the census shapes the historian's concepts, methods, and meanings. Knowledge requires standardization. Even though Trempeleau (or any other county) could not claim a distinct sectional consciousness, its study remains of more than local interest so long as it typifies some aspect of a larger American experience. At least in theory the reduction of spirit to system makes it possible to sample, virtually at random, any spatial slice of American experience with reasonable confidence that it replicates the whole. If a certain pattern of functional relations characterizes the American (or the frontier) social system, then one can find that pattern reproduced in the tiniest functional slice, each is a synecdoche of the whole, and microstudies like *The Making of an American Community* offer rigorous glimpses into the overall structure of a particular period of American society.

Despite their love for the language, Curti and his collaborators balked at this positivist prospect. Repeatedly, they declared that while Trempeleau was an "appropriate county" for study, largely because of the abundance and manageability of its documentary records, it was *not* a "typical frontier": "We do not claim, nor do we believe, that our conclusions with regard to Trempeleau hold for frontier areas in general." And their conclusion offered another qualification: "In sum, our study, in both its quantitative and qualitative aspects, lends support to what we believe are the main implications of Turner's thesis about the frontier and democracy, so far as Trempeleau County is concerned." Vulgar empiricism won out, and the authors fled ideology by falling back on the antiquarian formula that history concerns itself with the unique and the particular while science concerns itself with general law.[108]

The debates over historical knowledge had generated new dilemmas, for history seemed unable to replicate the methods of physical science while maintaining the image of human life upheld by liberalism. On the one hand, many scholars believed that science searched out general laws subsuming particular situations. This threatened to subordinate choice, intentionality, and chance to the ordered structures of nature and process. On the other hand, most liberal social scientists wished to affirm the meaningfulness of individual agency. Hence scholars like William Dray could claim that rational reconstruction of the intentions of historical agents was the only method consistent with democratic political philosophy. Curti and his coauthors straddled this fence when seeking to generalize from their study. Was Trempeleau an instance of the operation of more or less codifiable laws of frontier society? Or did the county exemplify the contingent mixing of chance and choice, luck and reason? If the latter, their study would break with what they believed to be scientific method, and method was all that stood between history and propaganda. If the former, if the individuals of Trempeleau were the products of social forces beyond their control, what did this mean for democracy?

Curti, his coauthors, and readers faced the classic problem of parts and wholes. Frontier history had made local archival materials a legitimate field of data. The question was, how would such materials illustrate some larger historical topic of interest to a reasonably broad group of readers? Historians studying particular communities like Trempeleau had to explain the significance of their subjects. Was their community representative? Did it exemplify larger patterns in American history? If so, how would the historian move from part to whole? Whatever the deficiencies of Turner's cosmic story, it had provided a framework for moving from local to universal and back again. The most arcane bit of local trivia could testify to the evolution of spirit, and since the frontier experience shaped America's chapter in that tale, western materials had a special place in universal history. But Curti shared with most of his peers a profound mistrust of big stories. Such narration recalled that speculative European tradition that period commentators often blamed for producing Nazism and Stalinism. And while many historians and presumably many readers were Christians, few of them would openly describe their histories as chapters in the working out of God's narrative will. Those few major scholars of the 1950s who remained committed to Marxist history and whose careers had survived McCarthyism had a grand story to tell, but while some of the new social historians took up this plot, Curti et al. did not.

Instead Curti and his coauthors invested in two distinct but not always explicit stories that pulled Trempeleau out of local oblivion. The first was that tale so nicely summarized by Richard Skotheim in his review of Curti's work: History is the story of a Manichaean struggle between backward-looking reactionary ideas (religion, idealism, narrative history) and forward-looking progressive ideas (science, naturalism, social history). This tacit history is the familiar legitimating narrative told by modern science in its struggle with established religion and tradition, a tale of the long upward march of human progress away from superstition and into certainty. And sitting at the summit of Curti's account is the social historian cum corporate engineer, the "organization man," the white-collar suburbanite with his commitment to teamwork, systems analysis, technical prowess, and obscurantist suspicion of all things mystical, speculative, and abstract. The move from poesy to science, narrative to analysis, faith to knowledge, solipsistic humanism to big social science, culminates in a celebration of corporate society.

The second story is the American frontier narrative that made *The Making of an American Community* national rather than local history. The relation of local and national histories was ambivalent. Trempeleau was only a fragment of America's frontier narrative, and elsewhere the tale might have taken very different forms. To find out if it had, historians would need to study communities all across the country, moving from one county to another, narrating chapter after chapter, and then finally adding them up into a national story. What the proposal entails is fairly staggering. If Trempeleau does not typify American frontier experience, if it is only "a" frontier, and if this sort of history is to have anything more than antiquarian value, then the study must be repeated, county by county, decade by decade, across the entire nation. This envisions intellectual standardization on a colossal scale, with teams of historians, banks of computers, fleets of typists, and tidal waves of research grants pouring out of universities to the archives in the service of histories with identical research problems, compatible test designs, interchangeable data, and commensurable findings. The vision is either utopian or dystopian. Since by 1959 American history had already passed anything approaching a consensus on the importance of Turnerian history, let alone its interpretation, the historiographic agenda of Curti et al. was a prescription for chaos.[109]

The Making of an American Community remains an impressive venture into collaborative research and "local" history. Whether the work is more than that depends on the willingness of readers to ignore its disclaimers and instead project a broader significance for the text. Its meaning for our story lies in its limited role as exemplar of the new social, or structural, or analytic history, a genre of historical literature that echoes *Making*'s materialist (and, in this instance, bourgeois) philosophy of history, the self-conscious identification with the "common people," the combination of empirical rigor with theoretical reticence, and the privileging of analysis over narrative. *Making* also illustrates the dependence of the most devoutly scientific history on the very forces it attempts to hold at bay: philosophy of history, ethical and aesthetic visions, and storytelling traditions. Though Curti et al. blended inductive-statistical hypotheses, theoretical explanation, and imaginative reenactment, Turner's frontier tale gave the book its conflict and plot, and Curti's simplified naturalism shaped both research design and prose style. No amount of number crunching could win over readers hostile to the book's materialism, comic optimism, and naturalization of nineteenth-century American liberalism.

If a "midwestern" school of history grew up around a shared commitment to frontier comedy, still a different group coalesced around tragedy, and the "New Left History" added another antagonistic voice. Stephan Thernstrom, in *Poverty and Progress* (1964), also a pioneering effort in the new social history, contended that American economic and social mobility had been greatly exaggerated. Curti's own data, said Thernstrom, "provide little support for the stark contrast so often drawn between the fluid social order of the frontier and the rigid class-ridden society of the Eastern city." By the time Thernstrom's book appeared, the historical vision of the forties and fifties had even acquired a name, "consensus history," referring to what John Higham saw as its emphasis on stability, continuity, and homogeneity at the expense of dissent. Allan Bogue's important 1960 article "Social Theory and the Pioneer" implied that the functionalist visions of historians like Curti and Elkins and McKitrick paid too little attention to conflict. In 1968 *Towards a New Past: Dissenting Essays in American History,* an anthology of new left history, heralded the breakdown of the "conservative consensus." Its editor, Barton J. Bernstein, tied the new radicalism to social protest and invoked Frederick Jackson Turner: "We should rework our history from the new points of view afforded by the present."[110]

We have grown accustomed to classifying histories by political allegiance: over here, consensus histories like *The Making of an American Community;* over there, new left or new social history (the two are commonly conflated). But in a way Thernstrom and Curti stood closer to each other than to Turner. Their shared vocabularies of postwar social science, naturalism, and materialist philosophies of history set them on the far side of a divide separating modernist historiography from Turner's Victorian idealism. The most radical challenge to traditional frontier history would come not from new left history but from elsewhere. Period commentators noted that *The Making of an American Community* represented a new "cultural" conception of history, and indeed Curti had contributed an essay to *The New Approach to Cultural History* (1940). The anthology had earned an appreciative note from the anthropologist Ruth Benedict, whose phrase "patterns of culture" it had borrowed.[111] But the new cultural understandings of the past could draw attention to the displacement of one culture by another that *The Making of an American Community* ignored.

"Culture" and its histories would not simply cast doubt on happy tellings of frontier history; they would refigure the tale's central conflict. Some thinkers believed that both Turnerians and their critics had devoted a half-century to the wrong plot kernel. Not only was frontier history not a comedy, its central conflict was not between wilderness and civilization or free land and settlement. In the renditions of anthropology the "New World" had contained neither wilderness nor free land but Native American cultural landscapes and the colonization of the Great West was an agonistic struggle between radically different cultural systems. American democracy, in Trempeleau and elsewhere, was born not of material or spiritual discovery but genocide.

BOOK THREE

Time Immemorial

The Indian Trade in Universal History

When thinkers like J. G. Droysen divided the world into analytic categories, they set history on one side and nature on the other. And in Turner's frontier story the interaction of nature and history explained American development. But the tale also emplotted its central conflict as a collision between savagery and civilization and so history could subsume both protagonists. Both Indian and European were *in* history. Civilization was the savage's future, savagery the European's past. The Native American might resist or accept that destiny, but he could not escape it. There was no question of cultural relativism, no hint the ending was ever in doubt. But did the native belong to nature or to history? Depending on the answer, one could read pre-Columbian North America as the historical landscape of savagery or the wild space of nature. Frontier history swung back and forth on this hinge, revealing alternate worlds, pasts, and futures. Turner had described European history as a romance of the elites and a tragedy of the masses. America resolved these diverse subplots into narrative harmony. But the danger remained that this story too might divide itself. And over the course of the twentieth century, it did.

Turner's master's thesis, "The Character and Influence of the Fur Trade in Wisconsin," began his frontier historiography, and he built this paper into a thirty-eight-page dissertation. The result so pleased his mentors that it found its way into the school's premier publication venue, the Johns Hopkins University Studies in History and Politics. "The Character and Influence of the Indian Trade in Wisconsin: A Study of the Trading Post as an Institution" offered mind-numbing detail, thick footnotes, and grand technical ambitions—all the hall-marks of a dissertation. But its refashioning of Francis Parkman placed it near the lonely summit of Indian history in Victorian academia. Turner bequeathed to the profession a narrative account of Native America at once benevolent and benighted, a historical poetics of imperialism measured in its lines. His later essays emplotted this dramatic code of civilization and savagery as a dialectic of master and slave.[1]

Turner brought a fair background to the study. He had grown up in the places he was writing about, and he claimed to have had some contact with the local Winnebagos. As an undergraduate he had explored Wisconsin's archives and written a history of the Grignon tract near his hometown of Portage. He had devoted himself to Francis Parkman's writings, and he knew Henry Rowe Schoolcraft and Lewis Henry Morgan's work in ethnography. These were respectable points of departure for a Victorian study of the fur trade, and Turner embarked with revisionist intent. Parkman had described the trade as an incidental feature of the historical landscape; Turner would elevate it to a new narrative role as a mediating force between two social, political, and moral extremes: the savagery of the Indian forest and the civilization of the European metropolis. This frontier mediation anticipated the democratic synthesis, and trade in furs opened the continent for European settlement. This imperial institution blazed the trail for the increasingly liberal social forms that followed and so played a crucial part in the progressive movement of spirit toward freedom.[2]

The dramatic conflict of savagery and civilization found its most stylish contemporary form in Parkman, and Turner's writing reflected that of his literary hero. The Bostonian's hard-earned familiarity with physical settings, the interest in documents, the romantic prose, and the skillful projection of author and reader back into the scene to reenact the thoughts, feelings, and motions of the protagonists, all these appear in the storytelling of the amateur idealist from Portage. Here is the famous opening passage of Parkman's great history, *The Conspiracy of Pontiac:*

The conquest of Canada was an event of momentous consequence in American history. It changed the political aspect of the continent, prepared the way for the independence of the British colonies, rescued the vast tracts of the interior from the rule of military despotism, and gave them, eventually, to the keeping of an ordered democracy. . . . The history of that epoch, crowded as it is with scenes of tragic interest, with marvels of suffering and vicissitude, of heroism and endurance, has been, as yet, unwritten, buried in the archives of governments or among the obscurer records of private adventure. To rescue it from oblivion is the object of the following work. It aims to portray the American forest and the American Indian at the period when both received their final doom.

Young Turner breathed this air. Europe's opening of the continent, the struggle with the forest people, and the rise of American democracy give his story its sequence of events. He also took up the counterpoint of tragedy and heroism, suffering and endurance. But he did not endorse his precursor's moral vision.[3]

The political and military struggle of Parkman's romance became a social and economic conflict in Turner's comedy. "Indian Trade in Wisconsin" describes the battles and diplomacy of *The Conspiracy of Pontiac* as the surface manifestations of deeper, "buried" structural forces, a larger but "unwritten" history hidden beneath the elite romance which only the social historian could rescue from "oblivion." When in "Significance of History" Turner spoke of the new socioeconomic history, he could easily have referred to his own dissertation. "Indian Trade in Wisconsin" cites Parkman more than any other source even as it transforms his reactionary odes to the *gentilhomme* into populist anthems. Turner likened his conflict to the great encounters of the history of civilization, the collisions of Phoenician and Greek, Roman and barbarian, Christian and heathen. To understand the significance of his analogy, we need to sweep quickly through the conceptual history of savagery and civilization.

The drama of savagery and civilization reached well beyond Parkman's sylvan epics, and the figure of the savage roamed European imagination long before Columbus began searching his Bible for portentous roadmaps to the East. The savage had long stood for all that civilized society was not. Like wilderness and nature, savagery formed one half of a conceptual antithesis breaking the world into "us" and "them," "self" and "other." This equation had an ancient pedigree. The Greeks had divided humanity into "Hellenes," who shared in the civil life of the *polis*, and "barbarians," who did not. The distinction was spatial rather than temporal. Barbarians did not become Greeks, although Greeks bestowed "guest friendships" on those traders and diplomats whose social functions served Greek society. Most "others" fared less well in Hellenic imaginations, and those who fell outside the orderly space of the polis belonged to the beasts, members of nature and not humanity. In Aristotle's *Politics* barbarians appeared as "natural slaves" and the philosopher endorsed Homer's judgment, "It is right that Hellenes should rule over barbarians." The Romans took over this framework as enthusiastically as they appropriated other Greek forms, although at the height of the empire it was rather easier to become a citizen of Rome than it had ever been in Athens.[4]

Christianity offered to dispense with these divisions. Barbarian and Hellene described a fairly static, spatial relationship. One was either born a Hellene or one was not. But anyone could become a Christian, and both Hellenes and barbarians did. Significant boundaries between humans derived not from natural or linguistic distinctions but from differences of belief. In theory if not in practice Christianity was a universal category whose membership was open to anyone who professed the faith. Outside this charmed circle lay heathens and heretics. These categories implied a historical relation between the grand divisions of humanity. Heretics had been Christians in the past, and heathens might become Christians in the future. Both found their place in the larger historico-theological plan. And both shared associations with a series of Hebrew terms that subsequent translators rendered as "wilderness," a word descended from the Old English "wil-deor," a condition of "wildness," or in Latinate form, "savagery." Heretics and heathens belonged to that ferocious space that the King James Bible called wilderness, a state that was at once a territory of climatic extremes, dangerous beasts, and physical suffering and a moral condition bereft of grace, beyond salvation, and beneath civil life.[5]

By the fifteenth century the figure of the savage or the wild man carried all this metaphysical freight. Savagery, wilderness, nature, barbarism, disorder, sin, slavery, and suffering circulated side by side. The wild man stood at once without and within humankind. The savage was both wild nature and unredeemed humanity, a natural slave to be mastered, part of the moral chaos upon which Europeans needed to impose Christian order; and at the same time the savage was an ignorant but potentially fully human being, a child to the European parent who needed only the proper tutelage to be civilized. This dualistic vision crossed the Atlantic with the Spanish, English, and French, and it legitimated competing and sometimes complementary regimes of evangelism and enslavement.

Seventeenth- and eighteenth-century political theory devoted a great deal of speculative space to the origins of civil life and so to the state of savagery or the condition of "natural man." As the phrase suggests, many of these ostensibly secular texts rehabilitated older theological visions by redescribing them in terms of nature. Nature was as orderly as the Christian theogony, human life was part of nature's order, and savagery accounted for one of the temporal links in the great chain of being. Life in a state of nature varied from the brutal bloodfest of Hobbesian nightmare to the idealized stasis of Rousseauian noble savagery. Historical philosophy related civil to savage by placing both within a mechanical series, typically divided into the four ages of man. These stages were determined by modes of subsistence. Savage life depended on economic activities like hunting and gathering which were little removed from natural processes. Civil society lived by commerce. The relative worth of these categories depended on one's view of Europe's emergent capitalism. The suspicion that savagery might have advantages over civilization had always lurked in the radical differentiation of one from the other (in the 1580s Montaigne's famous essay "Des Cannibales" made explicit themes that had been implicit in Tacitus), but not until the Enlightenment did noble savagism become a familiar literary figure. In this period *le bon sauvage* surfaced in the texts of Jesuit missionaries as a reproof of the venality of colonial French traders and in Crevecoeur's *Letters from an American Farmer* as a utopian alternative to the violence of revolutionary British America. Savagery thus took on new political valences but remained an antonym of civilization, firmly if obscurely conjoined with nature, the new key word of Enlightenment vocabularies.[6]

In the nineteenth century the concept that literary historian Roy Harvey Pearce calls "savagism" fell into the contingency of historical change along with everything else, and Morgan's *League of the Ho-de-no-sau-nee, or Iroquois* (1851) and *Ancient Society* (1877) brought savagery into both Victorian history and scientific jargon. If, as geologists and biologists argued, nature evolved, then even "natural man" must develop. As Genesis had claimed for all humans a single origin, social evolutionists described humankind as progressing from savagery through barbarism and into civilization. In this scheme civilization and savagery could be read as differential rather than strictly contradictory signs. They were different moments of a common history. Since the savages of America, Australia, and Africa were analogous to the European savages of prehistory, the best way to understand human development was to use an institution like the family as a point of comparison across societies that stood at different steps on the historical staircase. Comparative method became a favorite tool of social science, and by 1862, the year Turner was born, these new technical uses of savagery and civilization had begun reshaping popular discourse, although they could never completely erase millennia of linguistic experience.[7]

For Turner and other Victorians, nature and wilderness were not necessarily empty of humanity: they were places of wild nature *and* wild people. Turner placed the Wisconsin fur trade in the larger context of colonialism as a practice and colonial trade as an institution. Unlike many of his successors, when he emplotted his savage and civilization antithesis, his frame of reference included the oppositions of Phoenicians with Greeks, Romans with barbarians, and Medieval Christian Europeans with African Muslims. Turner actually introduced his dissertation as a moment in universal history, using comparative method to sketch the interethnic outlines of a frontier situation. The trading post, said Turner, is an *economic* institution built on the exploitation of a "primitive" or "undeveloped society" by a "higher" or "more advanced people." This basic frontier situation is a recurrent historical drama, as evinced by the interaction of Phoenicians and Greeks in the Mediterranean of antiquity, but like any good dissertation topic, the frontier has not yet received the study it deserves, especially in North America. Of course, the European and American experiences are not perfectly analogous: "The Phoenician factory, it is true, fostered the development of the Mediterranean civilization, while in America the trading post exploited the natives. . . . But the study of the destructive effect of the trading post is valuable as well as the study of its elevating influences."[8]

Straightaway we see the essential tension. In Europe the trading post spurred development, while in America it led also to degeneration. For Europeans in America the effect of trade was generally happy, even comic, in the Dantean sense of the word. For Native Americans, however, trade was at best a mixed blessing, perhaps even a tragedy. Turner had already described European history as a double plot, a tragedy for the masses and a romance for the elite. American history threatened to go much the same way, with the relations of civilized and savage reproducing those of bourgeois and proletarian. If the Indians were simply exploited rather than elevated, if the story turned out so differently for its different agonists, why was the tale of the Indian not tragic? The mechanisms that kept Turner's history from breaking into a double plot, a comedy for one society and a tragedy for the other, deserve tracing in some detail.

One strategy subsumed Native America under *nature* rather than under *history*. Turner's story shifted from one dramatic code to another, alternating accounts of America as a natural and a social order. On the one hand, America is a pristine nature of free lands and abundance, the forest wilderness of the New World, both nurturing female and resistant male foe. On the other hand, it is the geography of savagery, the setting of an anachronistic survival of the primitive age of man. As Parkman linked forest and Indian, Turner associated savagery and wilderness, native and landscape (in a 1908 essay, "The Development of American Society," Turner called Native Americans "nature-people"). In the spring of 1888, only weeks before his thesis was due, he wrote his fiancée of his authorial dilemmas.

I am trying to tell how the forest which was to the Englishman a gloomy, repellant, witch haunted realm, lying in its darkness behind his doors, tenanted with lurking foes—not to be entered except with defiant conquering spirit—was to the Frenchman a gay, witching, inviting thing. If it wasn't too flowery I should also like to say that the St. Lawrence flushed an irresistible invitation down its watery course, and whispered to the Frenchman of the Great Lakes from which it came—that the wilderness sang to him in the melody of its waterfalls, thrilled him by the solemn music of its pines, dashed him with the spray of cataracts, awed him by the mystery of its dark glades, and brought to him its untutored children to wonder at his goods and call him master—even as Caliban lay at the feet of Trinculo and the potent bottle on Prospero's enchanted island.

His intuition was right; this was too flowery for a dissertation, and Turner toed the scholarly line, put Parkman behind him, and forswore magical metaphors. What he said in private, to female friends and relatives, diverged substantially from what he said in public to the predominantly male audience of his teachers, peers, and potential employers. But the letter tells us that he intuitively privileged the conflict between Europeans and the natural landscape. The British and the French engage that antagonist differently. To the British nature is masculine foe; to the French, seductive siren.[9]

Despite his apparent sympathy for the French response, Turner finished with an appeal to the dramatic imagination of Elizabethan England, Shakespeare's *The Tempest*. Readings of Shakespeare's comedy as a parable of colonialism probably began as soon as the play hit the stage. But to do justice to Turner's remarks, and at the risk of retracing well-worn trails, we ought to recount its plot and suggest its importance here. The play opens aboard a ship caught in a terrific storm. The vessel goes down and its aristocratic occupants are cast ashore on a remote island. This New World is inhabited by Prospero (a magician cum Elizabethan scientist), the former duke of Milan who had been treacherously overthrown, set adrift on the sea, and given up for dead some years ago. Seeking to restore the old order, Prospero has conjured the tempest that brings his old enemies to him. The island also holds its former owner, Caliban, a savage being Prospero has reduced to slavery. When two of the castaways, Trinculo and Stephano, first encounter Caliban, they wonder if he is man or beast. They resolve the problem by getting him drunk ("the potent bottle") and accepting his submission to their mastery. The comedy ends with the old wrongs righted and its antagonists reconciled to a happy future. Caliban, however, remains outside this comic circle, and the play ends with Prospero's boot still firmly if figuratively planted on Caliban's neck.[10]

Gliding from personification of the St. Lawrence to Shakespearean allusion, Turner moved partway from nature into history, but with Caliban he stopped at the threshold. The dissertation describes a frontier convergence of two historic societies but opens onto the wider gulf between bestiality and humanity. At best, Caliban and the Indians might play children to the higher European parent. But the Indian, like Caliban, belongs to the family of nature, and that bond must first be severed if he is to be adopted into the family of humankind. The ties to wilderness and heathenism must be broken before any further movement can be imagined. In the narrative code of nature and history, this is the best of all possible dramatic outcomes: The Indian might be torn from nature and pulled forcibly into history in a violent act of social evangelism.

A darker reading shadows this one, for to lie at the European's feet and call him master is to enter into a relation whose political energies are not those of the Victorian compassionate family but those of slavery. Caliban and the American Indian, like Aristotle's barbarians, are *natural* slaves, and the position of higher and lower is inscribed in the order of things and not historically conditioned. The two are separated by a time so thick it has become space, and Indians are not going to become Europeans. Moreover, the European does not enslave the Indian. The Indian *is* a slave: Caliban recognizes the natural mastery of the newcomer and submits to his fate. It is right that Europeans rule over Indians, the bond with wilderness is an index of a lower order of being, and this state of affairs is as evident to slave as to master. Between them yawns a gap so great that there can be none of the mutual recognition that characterizes exchanges between equals. The narrative agon of history and nature reproduces the political economy of slavery, and the story resolves with its European protagonists reconciled and its native antagonist subordinated. History and its heroes develop, but nature's children have no share in that brave new world.

Where the expectations of playwright's imagination and audience structured the emplotment of *The Tempest,* Turner's history needed to account for the historical evidence and the displacement of Native American society by European, nature by history. Why did the fur trade succeed so well? One answer is that the Aristotelian dialectic of natural slavery reproduced itself in North America. As expressed by the private Turner, the forest brought its untutored children to lie at the feet of the European master and wonder at his goods. As the public Turner described it, "The early traders were regarded as quasi-supernatural beings by the Indians." And the masters cemented this relationship with the potent bottle, the mythical "firewater," quickly reducing their subjects to "economic dependence." Just as Trinculo and Stephano seal their chattel compact with Caliban by getting the wild man drunk, in North America "firewater" sealed the savage's doom. Economic dependence, political disintegration, commercially motivated warfare, loss of land, and overhunting created a degraded savage, weakened by intermarriage, his once admirable energetic freedom now expressed in the disorder of alcoholism and debt.[11]

Subsuming Native Americans under nature allowed another response to this question of what made possible the success of European trade and settlement: Nature's own economy invited commerce, and geography capitalized capitalism. In Turner's words, "The water system composed of the St. Lawrence and the Great Lakes is the key to the continent" and these riverine passages are "nature's highways." Nature's highways became the trader's supply lines, the arteries linking nature to history and America to Europe. Through them pulsed the goods of civilized life:

Along the lines that nature had drawn, the Indians traded and warred; along their trails and in their birch canoes the trader passed, bringing a new and transforming life. These slender lines of Eastern influence stretched throughout all our vast and intricate water system, even to the Gulf of Mexico, the Pacific, and the Arctic Seas, and these lines were in turn followed by the agricultural and by manufacturing civilization.

Natural process invites historic development, the St. Lawrence whispers a siren song, the European accepts the submission of the forest and its children. Domination is part of nature's economy and the dynamo of American frontier history.[12]

Europe pursued enslavement rather than evangelism in Native America. Turner rebuked his precursor George Bancroft for promoting the "misleading" notion that Europe had first hoped to save souls, that religious enthusiasm had opened the Great West, and that economic opportunism had come only later. "In fact," said the young revisionist, "the Jesuits followed the traders, their missions were on the sites of trading posts, and they themselves often traded." So much for piety. Religion served trade, and evangelism enslavement: "Instead of elevating [the Indian], the trade exploited him." This is not uniquely American; this is the big story of world history and a positive law: In the Great West "a continuously higher life flowed into the old channels, knitting the United States together into a complex organism. It is a process not limited to America. In every country the exploitation of the wild beasts, and of the raw products generally, causes the entry of the disintegrating and transforming influences of a higher civilization." We might substitute "wild men" for "wild beasts," for Turner drew no distinctions between modes of exploitation. Considered in its effects on the lower society, frontier conflict represents disintegration, but seen in light of the cosmic story, it is a single moment in a larger drama.[13]

The integration of two dramatic codes, nature and history, and savagery and civilization, held the story to an upward course. There was no tragedy in the exploitation of natural slaves and little to lament when nature invited development. At the end of the story nature and savagery have been taken up into a higher form, their elements recombining in the evolving tale of humanity. We should stress this point, for the two codes were not autonomous. It was not a matter of nature *or* savagery, but rather both simultaneously, each edging the other. Turner did not always reduce natives to nature. Remember "The Significance of History": History for the savage is the painted scalp. A painted scalp may not be much, but it is still history, more than many philosophers and historians were willing to grant, and more than comes through in "Indian Trade in Wisconsin." On an abstract level, Turner placed his native antagonists inside the developing self-consciousness of humanity.

So we need to ask again, why, when considered as a part of history, did the savage's experience not qualify as tragic? We will see that even if Turner had fully avoided any explicit association of savagery with nature and instead treated it strictly "scientifically" as a mechanical stage of social evolution, he probably would not have imagined savage experience as tragedy. The theoretical frameworks of Victorian social science did not enforce such a reading. Indeed, savagery remained largely a counterconcept for civilization.

Savagery slid into barbarism in many social evolutionist texts. In

Richard Ely's *An Introduction to Political Economy*, which Turner studied and taught, the two words are synonyms. Savage and barbaric social organization are one and the same, characterized by economic absence. Savages/barbarians do not engage in commerce, they do not command the concept of private property, they do not have a cash economy, and they do not exhibit the typical features of nineteenth-century capitalism. They are defined as much by their difference from Victorian Europe and the United States as by internal coherence. Their only common positive property is that they depend on hunting and gathering, activities shared with animals of all sorts and which scarcely qualified as social. Ely's interests lay in the early roots of capitalism and civilization. He saw civilized societies as progressing through a series of stages: pastoralism, agriculture, commerce, and finally industry. Turner, in his 1893 essay "The Significance of the Frontier," adopted this series to describe the frontier advance. In the frontier's most regressive zone, one found white and red hunters living in a state of savagery, not holding any land of their own, not cultivating plants, and often engaged in a barter economy. The next stage consisted of backwoods subsistence farming. Still higher on the scale one found commercial farmers producing surplus for trade. Next came the small town, a center of local commerce integrated into the highest stage and geographic zone, the urban, industrial metropolis. As Turner knew, this was a highly idealized model and not a veridical representation. Categories and divisions were always artificial and the lines could never be drawn with perfect clarity.[14]

Unfortunately, Ely's categories seemed a poor fit for Native America. By his lights the Native Americans were savages lacking the traits of commerce. But as Turner saw it, Indians trading furs for manufactured goods and building trade alliances were clearly engaging in commerce. Ely's stages did not encompass savage traders who did not yet (at least in Victorian eyes) farm or own property. One might imagine Indian commerce as an exotic introduced by Europe. But Turner's sources told him that American Indians had created elaborate trade networks long before Columbus left harbor. The "mound builder" societies of the Mississippi and Ohio river valleys had left behind artifacts from locales as distant as Mexico, articles they could only have acquired through trade. Northeastern tribes had also developed the much discussed *wampum,* an analog to European cash. The Chippewa had adopted Sioux traders, and the "analogy of this custom to the classical 'guest friendship,' " Turner remarked, "needs no comment." The journals of the earliest European explorers attested to an intertribal commerce already in place. The evidence was overwhelming: "It was on the foundation, therefore, of an extensive intertribal trade that the white man built up the forest commerce." Economic taxonomies did not define savagery.[15]

Turner was not the first scholar to chafe at the analytic constraints of savagery. Lewis Henry Morgan's *Ancient Society* (1877) expanded the traditional savage and civilized dichotomy into a continuum of savagery, barbarism, and civilization, each subdivided into lower, middle, and upper stages. Since the production of pottery divided upper savagery and lower barbarism, many Native American tribes, both before and after Columbus, were barbarians and not savages. Morgan likened various American tribal institutions to those of the Greeks, Romans, and Germanic peoples. Turner followed Morgan's comparison of Native Americans and Greeks, but he did not adopt the ethnologist's lexical innovations. Nowhere in his published work did he refer to the Indians as barbarians or press beyond his recognition of the inadequacy of the definitions used by scholars like Ely. Despite his acknowledgment of the problems of the classification, he described Native Americans as savages.[16]

"Indian Trade in Wisconsin" roiled the waters of social evolutionism. Simple economic facts did not define savagery. Savages engaged in commerce and using iron did not rise to civilization. And this suggested a historic distance so great that there was little chance of Native Americans reaching civilized heights. To return to Turner's Mediterranean analogy, the Phoenicians had far surpassed the Greeks when those two societies first collided, but the Greeks had become the new heirs to history and carried the Phoenician heritage forward into a Hellenized European future. In America, European and Indian stood so far apart than there was no similar dramatic reversal. Civilization triumphed, and Europeans came out on top. But they also came out American, and it was difficult to account for this simply by pointing to civilized success. Europe did not reproduce itself in North America. Instead, American democracy replaced both savage society and European despotism.[17]

Social evolution did not offer the subtlety Turner hoped to capture. Neither savage nor civil agonist fit smoothly into the mechanical categories of theory. And Turner did not believe the story related the simple triumph of civilization over savagery. Each had entered into the other and produced a new American form. But the dissertation offered no other outcomes beyond its description of European adaptation to the inviting natural *topoi* of North America. Life developed progressively. Wild rivers invited Indian villages, these encouraged trader's forts, traders opened the country for the farm, and the farm for the city. In later essays dialectical emplotment allowed these developments to commingle and brought savagery and civilization together into democracy rather than simply effacing the one and elevating the other.

Seeing history as the "Know Thyself" of humanity encouraged a more subtle treatment. "The Significance of the Frontier" distilled four polished paragraphs from the dissertation.

Thus the disintegrating forces of civilization entered the wilderness. Every river valley and Indian trail became a fissure in Indian society, and so that society became honeycombed. Long before the pioneer farmer appeared on the scene, primitive Indian life had passed away. . . . The trading posts reached by these trails were on the sites of Indian villages which had been placed in positions suggested by nature. . . . Thus civilization in America has followed the arteries made by geology, pouring an ever richer tide through them, until at last the slender paths of aboriginal intercourse have been broadened and interwoven into the complex mazes of modern commercial lines; the wilderness has been interpenetrated by lines of civilization, growing ever more numerous. It is like the steady growth of a complex nervous system for the originally simple, inert continent. If one would understand why we are today one nation rather than a collection of isolated states, he must study this economic and social consolidation of the country.

Why was the passing of Indian life not tragic? Because all these threads wound into the multicolored fabric of the frontier comedy. Nature invited the Indian settlements; nature and the Indian invited the trader; and the Indian trade, in "spite of the opposition of interests" that clashed over it (Indian and European, French and English, English and American, trader and farmer) "pioneered the way for civilization." Opposing interests have been taken up into a new, more complex synthesis. In the cosmic story the river valleys of nature and the trading paths of savagery have become the constitutive elements of democratic civilization. Civilization and its antagonists moved from relations of opposition and contradiction to differential moments of a greater history, traces of the cosmic past inscribed in the present.[18]

Native America spurred the development of white America's historical consciousness. In Turner's revealing words, "The effect of the Indian frontier as a consolidating agent in our history is important. . . . [The] frontier stretched along the western border like a cord of union." The native antithesis drove the diverse ethnic, class, and religious factions of colonial Euro-America to a more self-conscious recognition of their community. Faced with this opposing self, white Americans took their first groping steps toward a collective identity as master met slave on the American frontier: "Facing each generation of pioneers was the unmastered continent. . . . [D]esolate, grass-clad prairies, barren oceans of rolling plains, arid deserts, and a fierce race of savages, all had to be met and defeated." This dialectic did not encode Euro- and Native American as political equals. Euro-Americans carved out their selfhood against native others, but the true recognition of their identity as a world historic people would have to come from elsewhere. One does not find a satisfactory recognition in the servility of slaves. Turner's American consciousness suspended itself between the objectified other of Native America and the patriarchal other of Europe. Only in Europe could Americans see themselves reflected as historic beings. And by the end of the nineteenth century few could deny that the United States had successfully separated from Europe and created its own social forms. Native America, though, remained an object rather than a person, lacking in historical consciousness.[19]

Imagining someone else's experience as tragedy requires a certain empathy, the ability to project oneself, however adequately, into the place of another. Turner did not lack this quality; he readily intuited the suffering of the voiceless laborers who built the architectural wonders of Europe. But he did not do this for American Indians. Indians do appear, but they own no verbs of their own. In all Turner's published writings there are no passages imaginatively reenacting what it was like to have been a native on the frontier with Europe. Turner kept attention relentlessly focused on the white hero. This focus, of course, helped to hold the plot together. It also reproduced a racism common to the age and one that worked its silent way into the narrative worlds of his intellectual descendants. In his writing this prejudice did not manifest itself in the sort of pseudoscientific racialism that undergirded the eugenics movement, but neither was it irretrievably subtle.

While we cannot locate any passages that re-create Native American consciousness, we can look to other descriptions of "tribal" peoples for clues to the way Turner imagined his story's antagonists. During an 1887 visit to Boston, Turner wrote his younger sister of having accidentally ventured into the city's Jewish district.

I was in Jewry, the street consecrated to "old clothes," pawnbrokers, and similar followers of Abraham. It was a narrow *alley*, we would say in the west—and it was fairly packed with swarthy sons and daughters of the tribe of Israel—such noises, such smells, such sights! . . . The street was . . . filled

with big Jew men—long bearded and carrying a staff as you see in a picture—and with Jew youths and maidens—some of the latter pretty—as
you sometimes see a lily in the green muddy slime. . . . At last after much
elbowing, I came upon Old North [church] rising out of this mass of Oriental noise and squalor like a haven of rest. It no longer stands—

—Among the graves on the hill
Lonely and spectral and somber and still

But it is impressive nonetheless, and I felt paid for my wandering.

This is a remarkable letter, as much for the offhand grace of its prose
as for its typically Victorian anti-Semitism. It describes Turner's passage
from the white sections of Boston through the overcrowded oriental
squalor of the "tribe of Israel." "Jewry" fairly swarms with swarthy
primitives engaged in exotic and unclean practices, it assaults midwestern sensibilities, and offers sexual temptation. The passage ends with
the Christian church rising above this nightmare space, a neat, if
melodramatic, closing. Although Turner drew no intuitive connection
with the Jews, here we see him re-creating a scene from the daily life
of peoples other than white, Anglo-Saxon, and Protestant. The result
is repulsive.[20]

This letter also resonates strangely with Turner's dissertation. We
might, for a start, replace "Jewry" with "savagery," "Abraham" with
"Sycorax," "alley" with "village," and "staff" with "tomahawk." But
there is another, more perverse connection. Many popular writers and
scholars had declared the Native Americans "Orientals" who had wandered from Asia across a presumed land bridge into North America. In
one version of this tale Indians were the remnants, relatives, or former
neighbors of the ten lost tribes of Israel. By 1889 the association of
Native America and Orient had stabilized into something like scholarly consensus, although few still thought the Indians were Hebrews.
Two of Turner's sources made this claim, though, and these links, however tenuous, deserve mention. James Adair's classic eighteenth-century
study, *The History of the American Indians, Particularly Those Nations
Adjoining to the Mississippi, East and West Florida, Georgia, South and
North Carolina, and Virginia,* proposed this pedigree for Native America, as did William H. Warren's 1885 article "History of the Ojibways,
Based upon Traditions and Oral Statements." By the late 1880s Adair's
work roamed that vague frontier between secondary and primary
works, but Warren's piece could claim both contemporaneity and an
author fluent in a Native American language.[21]

William Warren was a mixed-blood descendant of French and "Ojib-way" (Anishinaabe) traders and considered himself a member of the local Indian community. He was also a devout Christian who marveled at the likeness of native oral literature to the versified narratives of the Old and New Testaments. Dabbling in comparative method, he argued that these analogies suggested that if the American Indians were not actually descended from the ten lost tribes, they had at least associated with the Hebrews in their Old World past. Warren saw this as an en-nobling comparison that partially legitimated Ojibway texts and life-ways. Turner doubtless saw it differently. He probably did not place much faith in Hebraic origins for Native America, but he may well have credited Warren's analogies of form. There were some vague common-alities between the customs of the Ojibways and the Jews. And so much the worse for the Indians.[22]

In 1899 American spirit pressed out over the Pacific Ocean and into the Philippines as the nation entered on a new colonial project, and the recurrent drama of "higher" societies exploiting "lower" continued apace. That year the National Herbart Society reprinted "The Signifi-cance of the Frontier" in its yearbook. For this version the historian selected a poetic epigram, "The Foreloper," from the work of a popu-lar contemporary named Rudyard Kipling who introduced millions of readers to sentimental understandings of British imperialism. Turner's poetic sensibility, which like his frontier spirit could encompass both Dante and Shakespeare, selfishness and selflessness, creativity and cru-dity, took up the white man's burden: "For he must blaze a nation's way with hatchet and with brand, / Till on his last won wilderness an empire's bulwarks stand."[23]

William Christie MacLeod and the Tragic Savage

To Turner's credit, he began his career with a formal rec-ognition of just how central the early European and Native American encounters were to American history. Indian history after Turner's dis-sertation scarcely existed. Only in the specialized studies of the fur trade and Spanish borderlands did Native Americans appear with any frequency. For most historians they were an anachronism dispensed with in an introductory paragraph or chapter. More and more, wilderness displaced savagery as the frontier scholar's antagonist of choice and a simple agon replaced Turner's dialectic.

In Frederic Paxson's *History of the American Frontier* the westward march led to the "disruption" and "decay" of the tribes. For Paxson the Indians were important primarily as military opponents who were quickly overrun by the Anglo-Saxons in their "fight with nature and the alien." In 1930 E. Douglas Branch's textbook *Westward: The Romance of the American Frontier* described the history of the American frontier as "a grim merciless conquest" of hostile wilderness. Alongside that basic struggle "the battles with the Indians . . . dwindle in importance. The battle with Nature, the wilderness . . . that is the essential conflict." In Ray Allen Billington's 1949 textbook *Westward Expansion* Anglo-Saxons surmounted various natural barriers in a "series of conquests." The Alleghenies, the Great Plains, the Rocky Mountains, all must be conquered and crossed. Natives turn up in the index in categories like "removal of," "as allies of," and "wars with." The table of contents formalized the conflation of natives and nature, for the author entitled the chapter devoted to Native America "The Indian Barrier."[24]

Indians began creeping out of the frontier narrative. By the 1920s social evolutionism had begun fading from social science, savagery had started slipping out of both popular and scholarly vocabularies, and Indians had all but disappeared from the interpretive horizons of departments of history much as white Americans expected them to vanish from the cultural landscape. "The vanishing American" Zane Grey called Indians in 1925 in his best-selling novel of the same name, and while this disappearance looked tragic enough—who could not lament the passing of a race?—this story and its heroes commanded so little scholarly space there was little chance they might revise American historical imagination.

One period study stands out as a tragic exception. William Christie MacLeod's *The American Indian Frontier* (1928) retold Turner's story in a darker tone. Its preface opened with a lucid statement of the problem: "Every frontier has two sides. Its movement forward or backward is the consequence of two sets of forces. To understand fully why one side advances, we must know something of why the other side retreats." On its own, the claim resembles the introductory passages of Turner's dissertation. But MacLeod meant to focus on Native American experiences, and he believed that this aim enforced a rather different emplotment of the course of events: "North European Indian policies in North America gradually led the aborigines to moral and physical eclipse. . . . The development is one of tragic irony." The statement could hardly have been more pointed.[25]

In MacLeod's telling, Europeans and later white Americans cheat, steal, and slaughter their way across the continent in one long, bloody, and virtually irredeemable imperial misadventure. The trader, so heroically re-created in Turner's dissertation, becomes one of the "ruthless," "cruel," "vicious elements" and "predisposed to villainy." MacLeod repeatedly referred to frontiersmen as "the scum of the earth." And in a series of indictments of the historical profession, he accused his peers of shameless filiopietism: "In the little red schoolhouse it is a sacrilege to intimate that the pioneers suffered from ordinary human frailties. . . . But the masses were no better than the masses of any society." MacLeod occasionally gilded these classist judgments with more dispassionate summations, but these did not transmute the leadshot of his charges. Consider this remarkable passage:

The attitude of the scientific student is not to praise or to blame. . . . Nevertheless we need not overlook the fact that the nastiness of the frontiersmen was an actual problem for the Indian; and it is for the vanished ghosts of innumerable Indians to praise or blame. Perhaps it may be, as Heckewelder insists, that some day they will be called forth in judgment even on the apologetic and intellectually dishonest descendants of the men of the frontier.

Turnerian celebrants of frontier history have inherited the blood guilt of their vicious ancestors. In some millennial future the sins of the fathers will be visited on their academic sons, and perhaps even Frederick Jackson Turner himself will come face to face with a Native American Jesus. There is more than a measure of despair in this picture and little hope that the reckoning will be managed in this year's meeting of the American Historical Association.[26]

MacLeod's *American Indian Frontier* made no appreciable impress on the history profession, but we cannot attribute the fact to poor scholarship. The book was a respectable monograph from a major press, Alfred A. Knopf of New York, a firm that liked to publish scholarly works with potential trade sales. It was competently written, brimming with primary sources, and drawing from an imposing array of secondary literature for just under six hundred carefully footnoted pages. But the two major historical journals, the *American Historical Review* and the *Mississippi Valley Historical Review,* did not accord it so much as a brief notice even though they reviewed a number of much weaker works in Indian history. And the book, though by far the strongest and most systematic assault on Turnerian history prior to the 1940s, elicited none of the defensive reaction from devout Turnerians which followed fast on the publication of minor review essays by Charles Beard and Louis Hacker. Everyone simply ignored MacLeod's book, from AHA President and Turner student Homer C. Hockett on down. The critics of frontier history who might have drawn support from the book probably never knew it existed; they had less interest in Native America than the average Turnerian.

MacLeod's narrative seemed more likely to appeal to the popular taste for primitivism. The notion that modern Indians stood a heartbeat away from death or assimilation underwrote novels, journals, and film. White Americans in the nation's new suburban neighborhoods, comfortably distant from reservations or their great-grandparents' homesteads in Blackhawk country, indulged an expiatory interest in the doom of Native America. If academics found the story antiquarian, romantic, or irrelevant, thousands of less cosmopolitan readers lived these dramas at leisure. And MacLeod's conclusion played a scholarly harmony to Zane Grey's tragedy of the vanishing antagonist.

Some day the last unallotted Indian will be allotted; and within twenty-five years or less thereafter, the last restricted Indian will have become unrestricted, and sell his land to the first white man to offer to buy. . . . The denouement is one in which a proud, numerous, and rich group of heroes are reduced to a remnant of their former numbers, impoverished, degraded, and subjected to the solicitations of social or charity workers. The epilogue will be one in which the last of the degraded former heroes merely walks off a stage on which the properties have been reduced to the utmost shabbiness.

How to read this? If one were an American historian the answer was easy: Do not read it at all. For those who endured McLeod's epic, this final passage reprised its ambivalence. In one reading Indians are the tragic but defeated heroes of a classical agon, completely and agonizingly subjected to their doom. In another and perhaps more likely reading this story has decayed past tragedy. At one point, perhaps in the late eighteenth century when the tribes still commanded a dramatic military presence in large parts of the continent, the story was truly tragic, since the hero's doom was foreshadowed but not foregone. But that story had slipped from tragedy to pathos, with "former" heroes so degraded that they can no longer be counted as agonistic forces in the American narrative.[27]

The ambivalence comes from MacLeod's sense that there was no real alternative to assimilation. As he saw it, the problem was not that Euro-

Americans had expected the natives to accommodate themselves to white culture. The problem was that so many barriers had been placed in the way of assimilation, that so many whites had sought the complete destruction of the Indian, and that so much physical abuse and suffering had resulted. We might wish that he had been more sensitive to cultural pluralism, but given the intellectual dominance of social evolution, it is not surprising that MacLeod believed that natives eventually would have to take up white America's social and cultural conventions. What is remarkable is that he devoted so much print and energy, particularly at the very beginning of his career, to a story that so directly and polemically faced down the dominant figures in American professional history.

If we wish to find other academics telling similar tales in the 1920s and 1930s, we will have to leave history and stroll across the quad to the anthropology building. There, carefully walled off from the historians and their classrooms and readers, we will find a frontier tragedy handed out with each course syllabus. We will also find a sharp swerve off the path of social evolution and into another realm of historical interpretation, a space in which history takes very different shapes and meanings.

Ruth Benedict and the Cultural Turn

A single word broke history in half. A new use for an old term, "culture," fractured American historical imagination.

In a circuitous fashion, frontier history sponsored the break. For centuries Europeans and Euro-Americans had dealt in ways both ingenuous and foolish with the epistemic problems posed by Native America. Where did Native Americans come from? Were they like or unlike Europeans? Did they belong to an identical or different course of history? The nineteenth century resolved these difficulties by locating both groups in a shared sweep of time. Indians came before, Europeans after. Indians were primitive, Europeans civilized. Indians represented the deep past, Euro-Americans the open future. On Turner's frontier of savagery and civilization, two great chunks of history stood face to face without the mediating grace of intervening centuries. From this concordant discord came American democracy, from this division, a pluralized unity. Anthropology placed natives and Europeans into culture, into wildly *different* cultures, and broke the story firmly into halves, dividing national memory straight down the middle. And there seemed to be no way to stop the narrative proliferation. Each half threatened to break into ever smaller stories. Culture rearranged the way that history was imagined. Increasingly, scholars defined their relevant context *spatially* rather than temporally. Native cultures stood beside, rather than behind, Euro-America.

No work illustrated the new style more gracefully than Ruth Benedict's *Patterns of Culture* (1934). This widely read synthesis juxtaposed various tribal communities to show that customs could be so strongly patterned that they amounted to a coherent culture analogous to a single human personality or an object of art. Customs were arranged in systematic wholes rather than in evolutionary stages; social mores were learned habits rather than natural tendencies; and one could judge another culture only from within one's own culture. Just as for Turner and Dewey there was no getting outside history in order to view it as a disinterested observer, for Benedict there was no stepping out of one's own culture in order to condemn another. Few books did as much to popularize the culture concept; few did as much to promote cultural relativism. And in the end few did so much to transfigure historical imagination, for Benedict developed a Nietzschean mythopoesis as an alternative to historical consciousness.[28]

The consequences for the frontier story were profound. While Benedict spent most of her time and energy comparing and contrasting Native American cultures, the implicit comparison of all these groups with white America held the book together. Its frontier conflict described an encounter between competing rather than successive ways of being. As far as Euro-American culture displaced native cultures, and since one could tell the story only from the standpoint offered by one or another of these cultural traditions, the kernel of the narrative became instantly ambiguous. For *whom* was the story a comedy? For *whom* was the outcome democratic? Benedict invited white readers to cross the frontier and read the story from the other side. From this standpoint history took a ruthlessly tragic turn with the European invasion. No scholarly charity could atone for the loss of tribal lifeways. The assimilation of the Indian, however comic it appeared to Turnerians, tragically extirpated an entire style of existence and threatened even white America. And history itself acquired tragic associations. Hope for transcendence, Benedict implied, depended on the suprahistorical worlds of art and science.

In order to understand the appearance of such a book in 1934, we need to sketch a conceptual history of "culture," a term that Raymond

Williams has called "one of the two or three most complicated words in the English language." We can trace it from its beginnings as a verb form associated with historical development to its place in Benedict's text as an abstract noun suggesting a well-wrought aesthetic monad, one of the balanced unities that modernist thought regarded as the consummate end of literature, art, and existence. We might begin with the Latin root, *colere,* a word with a variety of meanings ranging from "cultivate" to "honour with worship." By the fifteenth century "culture" had worked its way into English as a noun of process subsuming the verb "to cultivate." Over the next few centuries it migrated from cultivation of plants to cultivation of humanity: humans, as well as plants, might be cultured. Eventually "culture" referred to the endpoint of development rather than to the process itself, and in the late eighteenth century it surfaced in German as *Cultur,* or *Kultur,* a synonym for the older "civilization." In romantic travel writing and universal histories, "culture" mingled with "spirit," "folk," and "Volk." Herder's *Ideas on the Philosophy of the History of Mankind* (1784–1791) even went so far as to imagine "cultures" in the plural, with European *Kultur* simply one among many. This last innovation, though, did not become common until the twentieth century.[29]

In nineteenth-century English and German, "culture" generally meant the polished, consummate aspect of human development, especially when associated with fine arts and a social elite. Matthew Arnold's influential *Culture and Anarchy* (1862) linked the term with perfection, sweetness, and light. Friedrich Nietzsche, in the first essay of his *Untimely Meditations* (1873), described culture as a "unity of style in all the expressions of the life of a people," and contrasted it with its opposite, "barbarism, which is lack of style or a chaotic jumble of all styles." Culture and *Kultur* acquired elitist connotations, and during World War I German claims to superior *Kultur* inspired hostile British and American responses. In 1918 Turner denounced parochial regions like New England for their "assumption of a superiority of culture, of *Kultur.*" But he also used it more as Herder had done, as a means of differentiating one section from another. In 1922 he declared, "There is a sectionalism of culture . . . a real consciousness of sectional solidarity." "Culture" is a more secular synonym for spirit. It also retains a strong sense of history, as something built, grown, or cultivated. This usage was new for Turner; it had not been in evidence in the late 1880s when he was writing his dissertation, nor did it inform his "Significance of the Frontier."[30]

By 1922 the new use of the term "culture" was common in American anthropology, although its earliest clear statement had been by an Englishman, Edward B. Tylor, in his 1871 book, *Primitive Culture*. Tylor borrowed the word from the German, placed it in his title, and devoted his first paragraph to its definition: "Culture, or civilization . . . is that complex whole which includes knowledge, belief, art, law, morals, custom, and other capabilities and habits acquired by man as a member of society." During the 1890s the word began gracing the titles of monographs in anthropology, and Franz Boas, an Austrian emigré settled into Columbia University as head of its anthropology department, introduced literally hundreds of students to the concept. Two of them, Robert Lowie and Clark Wissler, published early influential books with the term in their titles, *Culture and Ethnology* (1917) and *Man and Culture* (1923). By the middle twenties "culture" was well established in academic discourse, despite its potentially treacherous Arnoldian and Prussian connotations. Scholars debated its proper technical meaning, and even in the most rigorous monographs the word occupied a variety of positions and usages. Lowie, for instance, in a famous phrase, described culture as a "thing of shreds and patches," and Alfred Kroeber suggested that culture represented a "superorganic" integrating force that transformed a community into something greater than the sum of its individual parts. "Culture" generally retained a certain core of associations, and two Tylorian phrases in particular, "complex whole" and "custom," became conventional. By the time Benedict entered anthropology, the word had become an important working part of the language of social science.[31]

We need to know what "culture" replaced as well as where it came from. Turner's usage shows us one of the potential changes. Instead of the spirit of an age or people, one could invoke a culture. The substitution produced new meanings that were both more secular and more technical. Unlike spirit, "culture" had no religious overtones. Culture partook of science and traveled the continent on the title pages of social science monographs. It was a key word of modernism, as new and shiny as jazz and automobiles and as little dependent on philosophical history. If spirit was the stuff of romance and metaphysics, culture betokened realism and technology.

Culture could also displace civilization and savagery. Tylor's famous 1871 definition shows this overwriting of the old by the new: "Culture, *or* civilization . . ." By the 1920s, it had become "culture" *instead* of "civilization," a change with serious implications. For Victorians "civilization" had been an honorific label applied to those developed, urban societies one might wish to claim as historic precursors. Greece and

Rome were civilizations; outside their walls lay savagery, barbarism, and primitivism. Tylor, in 1871, could not easily have entitled his work *Primitive Civilization;* the terms were virtual antonyms. Instead he yoked primitivism and culture in a wonderfully ambiguous trope. "Culture" was a fairly new word with old "civilized" connotations. The new phrase suggested the possibility of civilized primitives without making the connection so explicit as to be jarring. The book's actual title, *Primitive Culture,* thus effected a subtle, relativistic turn. Tylor did not himself imagine all cultures as social equals. The cultures he described were "primitive" rather than "advanced" or modern. Still, while all peoples did not have civilization, all had culture, and so his conceptual leveling opened horizons. By the teens, when Lowie wrote his influential book, he was able to use "culture" and "civilization" as near synonyms.

The replacement of "race" with "culture" showed the transition at its most self-conscious. "Race" was again a fairly new usage that owed its currency to the popularization of biological science. Mainstream social evolution had imagined all humans as descended from a common origin. Morgan's *Ancient Society* conveys the notion quite well: "ancient" Native American societies represented an earlier historic stage in social development, a stage through which European and Euro-American societies once had passed. This basic story line owed a great deal to the biblical account of a common human descent from Adam. Monogenesis underlay Christian universalism; all people could become Christians, for all had sprung from the same source. But in the middle nineteenth century the young discipline of human biology began to market a competing account underwritten by the concept of polygenesis: humans had emerged from a variety of different ancestors; there was no single shared human past; and peoples were biologically distinct races whose social differences could thus be attributed to nature. If some Native Americans were still savage, this was because of genes and not history. Combined with a vulgarized Darwinism, this vision grew popular enough by the end of the century that the United States government supported scientific research into the measurement of racial differences.[32]

One of those researchers was Franz Boas, and he opened his American career by attacking the intellectual tenets of racialism. In the decades that followed, he and his disciples fought what they saw as the allied theoretical positions of social evolutionism and social Darwinism, the one imagining primitive cultures as remnants of a lost age of shared history and the other imagining them as separated from whites by a natural chasm. From the Boasian perspective social differences between races were best ascribed not to physiology but to culture—different peoples participated in different complex wholes of learned and shared customs, and these were the products not of nature or mechanical evolution but of contingent historical circumstance. Culture and Boasian anthropology brought peoples of color back into the theoretical community of a single, shared humanity by means of a series of conceptual displacements. Elevating culture to pride of theoretical place meant transcending spirit, the key word of Christian metaphysics, and nature, the key word of scientific racialism. The turn toward culture also involved a more subtle and much less self-conscious turn, an overwriting of history, the key word of social evolutionism.

Ruth Benedict reacted against particular histories, against history as a process, and against history as a mode of cognition. In the United States the nation's dominant origin tales, Frederick Jackson Turner's frontier history and Lewis Henry Morgan's social evolution, emplotted history as the successive uplifting of the primitive past into a transcendent present. When read against racialism and eugenics, the stories degenerated into mystifying fables of Aryan supremacy, and in reaction Boasians like Benedict inveighed against biology and universal history as explanations of cultural difference. The critique of Turnerian history and social evolution broached deeper dissatisfactions with modernity. In these post-Freudian and post-Nietzschean years critics imagined civilization as the marching black boot of rationality stamping out the last flickering vestiges of meaningful existence. Suspicion of particular histories projected a greater unhappiness with the course of history itself. It is not surprising that critical ethnographers and many of their contemporaries began exploring alternative forms. The etymology of "culture" is the story of a word in motion from verb to noun, from culture as process to culture as product. To see the significance of this shift, we need to return to Benedict's *Patterns of Culture*.

Ramon's Frontier Tale

To know *Patterns of Culture* is to despair of summary. While we cannot do justice to the relations between Benedict's personality and her book, we should note her feminism, her complex sexuality, her successful avocation as lyrical poet, and her renown as a female scholar and author of a major work of scholarship. Boas was one of the rare academic stars who would work with female students. Columbia anthropology became a haven for such talented scholars as Elsie Clews Parsons, Ruth Bunzel, Ruth Murray Underhill, Ella Deloria, Zora Neale Hurston, and Margaret Mead. *Patterns of Culture* took shape in that atmosphere, culminating more than ten years of study, teaching, and fieldwork, and it joined scholarly ambitions with a marketable prose style. Moreover, the work can show us how ethnographers and informants together refigured historical imagination.[33]

The tension between history and the timeless forms of art, myth, and science echoes through *Patterns of Culture*.[34] We can hear it in one of Benedict's key parables, a tale of an encounter years earlier with a Serrano man in Southern California from which she drew the book's epigram.

> In the beginning God gave to every people a cup
> of clay, and from this cup they drank their life.
>   (Proverb of Digger Indians)

The position of this proverb suggests its importance to Benedict. It is similarly important for our exploration of *Patterns of Culture*'s emplotment of history. At virtually every juncture Benedict subordinated history to culture, and in her reading of this verse she emplotted the nation's frontier origin myth as a tragedy while rethinking history itself, a revision negotiated from her own modernist aesthetics and from dialogues with her informants.

The epigram distilled Benedict's frontier allegory to the point of opacity. The fullest recounting of the verse appears at the beginning of chapter 2, "Diversity of Cultures."

A chief of the Digger Indians, as the Californians call them, talked to me a great deal about the ways of his people in the old days. He was a Christian and a leader among his people in the planting of peaches and apricots on irrigated land, but when he talked of the shamans who had transformed themselves into bears before his eyes in the bear dance, his hands trembled and his voice broke with excitement. It was an incomparable thing, the power his people had had in the old days. . . . In those days his people had eaten "the health of the desert," he said, and knew nothing of the insides of tin cans and the things for sale at butcher shops. It was such innovations that had degraded them in these latter days.

One day, without transition, Ramon broke in upon his descriptions of grinding mesquite and preparing acorn soup. "In the beginning," he said, "God gave to every people a cup, a cup of clay, and from this cup they drank their life." I do not know whether the figure occurred in some traditional ritual of his people that I never found, or whether it was his own imagery.

It is hard to imagine that he had heard it from the whites he had known in Banning; they were not given to discussing the ethos of different peoples. At any rate, in the mind of this humble Indian the figure of speech was clear and full of meaning. "They all dipped in the water," he continued, "but their cups were different. Our cup is broken now. It has passed away."

While not using obtrusive terms like tragedy or decay, Benedict's commentary leaves readers little room for interpretive maneuver. This is a tale of loss and decline. From the power and health of the old days to the degradation of these latter days, the Indians have fallen. Technology (tin cans) and capitalism (things for sale) served the European serpents in the New World garden and reduced the natives to Christianity and agriculture. Benedict did not mention Turner, Morgan, or the frontier but the moral is clear enough.[35]

There was a danger that her audience might read the disappearance of the old days as a sad but necessary step in the progress of civilization and so evade the full weight of tragedy. Certainly it was unfortunate that Euro-America had disrupted primitive society, but capitalism was the modern expression of a human instinct of self-aggrandizement and the disappearance of primitivism the reasonable price of progress. Benedict, however, quickly closed off this reading. Capitalism and greed, like other forms of self-aggrandizement, were cultural products, the result of "our particular system of property ownership. . . . Self-support is a motive our civilization has capitalized. If our economic structure changes so that this motive is no longer so potent a drive as it was in the era of the great frontier and expanding industrialism, there are many other motives that would be appropriate to a changed economic organization." There was nothing natural or necessary in the corruption of the Indian by the great frontier.[36]

The conventions of fieldwork reinforced Benedict's tragic vision. Most ethnographers believed Indians on the brink of cultural extinction, and they raced to gather remnants of tradition before primitivism vanished from the globe. "Salvage ethnography" stressed collection, the acquisition of previously unknown rituals, customs, stories, and art objects. Since the natives had been degraded by capitalism and Christianity, ethnographers trolled for the oldest customs and avoided like the plague any habits that synthesized traditional tribal forms with new Euro-American material. Much as historians used source criticism to identify corrupt texts and uncover the purified original, the Ur-text, ethnographers carefully sought out older natives and purged informants' contributions of all traces of cultural borrowing from whites. So Ramon is a highly unusual figure in period ethnography, and it is no accident that a Christianized Indian emblemizes tragedy: "Ramon had had personal experience of the matter of which he spoke. He straddled two cultures whose values and ways of thought were incommensurable. It is a hard fate." The man astride two ways of being, the ultimate outsider, the marginal man—who among Benedict's readers could envy Ramon's fate or dispute the tragic weight of his alienation?[37]

We do not know much about Benedict's encounter with Ramon, but what we do know suggests the power of the ethnographer's will to cultural purity. She based her account on an earlier essay, "Cups of Clay," which is unfortunately lost. We cannot see how Benedict put the passage together, nor can we hear Ramon's entire text or reconstruct that original encounter. She probably met him in 1922 when she visited Southern California to collect material for a monograph on the Serrano ("Digger Indians, as the Californians call them"). This article appeared in 1924 in *American Anthropologist,* but without Ramon. Instead, Benedict named seventy-year-old Rosa Morongo as her chief informant, a woman from the Morongo Valley Serrano, "the only bands whose life can be reconstructed to any extent today." Ramon did not suit a monograph of precontact lifeways; his life was a corrupted text, his Christianity an emblem of inauthenticity. While Boasians disdained the idea of racial purity they reinscribed that border in the search for an authentic other. This was treacherous business. Uncorrupted Indians were rare treasures, and in 1929 the ethnographer William Duncan Strong gleefully reported that Benedict's chief Serrano informant, Rosa Morongo, was not a "Serrano" at all but a Cahuilla who had married a Serrano man. For Strong, Benedict's confusion suggested professional ineptitude. For us, it highlights the dark side of the search for the truly exotic which sent anthropologists scrambling through the backcountry of the western United States.[38]

Benedict's tragedy of cultural mixing typified ethnographic custom in the 1920s and 1930s. Her general conception was fairly conventional, but her metaphors were not, and we need to return to our parable.

In the beginning, God gave to every people a cup, a cup of clay, and from this cup they drank their life. They all dipped in the water, but their cups were different. Our cup is broken now. It has passed away.

So far as we know, this was Ramon's original telling. In addition to her interlinear tragedy, Benedict offered this gloss to her readers.

Our cup is broken. Those things that had given significance to the life of his people, the domestic rituals of eating, the obligations of the economic system, the succession of ceremonials in the villages, possession in the bear dance, their standards of right and wrong—these were gone, and with them the shape and meaning of their lives. The old man was still vigorous and a leader in the relationships with the whites. He did not mean that there was any question of the extinction of his people. But he had in mind the loss of something that had value equal to that of life itself, the whole fabric of his people's standards and beliefs. There were other cups of living left, and they held perhaps the same water, but the loss was irreparable. It was no matter of tinkering with an addition here, lopping off something there. The modelling had been fundamental, it was somehow all of a piece. It had been their own.

Here is the root metaphor of *Patterns of Culture:* Culture is art. A culture is more than the sum of its traits. It is an integrated whole, and its history "is the same process by which a style in art comes into being and persists." More than this, culture is art as object. In these passages all the images are of plastic art rather than music or dance. The first substitution is the cup—culture is a cup of clay, a fragile work that cannot be reshaped, only broken. The next is "fabric," which cannot be rewoven without being unraveled. Cultures and patterns are thus "incommensurable." One cannot fairly compare a cup with a crown. And more to the point, one cannot join the one to the other without first melting them down.[39]

Benedict assured readers that her gloss was not arbitrary. Her interpretation was part of Ramon's original meaning, and she presented their dialogue as a hermeneutic challenge, a process of imaginative self-projection across the frontier border and into the other's world. The very first step in understanding the parable is asking the question, What did Ramon mean? The next is to make associations. What, beyond Ramon's intended meaning, might this text mean? What sort of cultural pattern does this artifact represent? These were big questions, and they demanded some commitments.

Ramon, the Christian Indian, offered at least two traditions against which to situate his text. One could emphasize either his Christian or his Serrano inheritance. His own associations must have included elements from Serrano oral tradition. In the desert, water and its vessels carry more symbolic weight than they might in more humid regions, and Ramon's metaphor doubtless had special force in the Banning pass in August. It also resonated with a Serrano "folktale" that Benedict collected that summer. Its opening scene associates the breaking of a water vessel with violent and unhappy death.

Two sisters travelled east together, and the elder sister carried a pot of water on her back. The younger sister was thirsty and asked for a drink, but the elder sister said no. Three times the younger sister asked for a drink, and the elder sister refused. Then the younger sister could go no farther and she died. The elder sister broke the pot of water over her dead body and went on alone. At last she came to a lake far in the east, and she made her home there.

The narrative goes on much further, though we cannot trust Benedict's transcription very far. It is a prose rendition, likely an abridgment, of what was probably oral verse. Nor can we say with certainty that Ramon knew the tale. It does, however, suggest that the breaking of a water vessel had symbolic importance for the Serrano of that period. The breaking of the cup figures loss of life and serves as a premonition of bad things still to come (it presages the death of another character later in the tale). Read Ramon's parable against this background and the breaking of Serrano society looks both catastrophic and irreversible.[40]

One could situate Ramon's text differently. Ramon was Serrano but he was also Christian and so would probably have known, even if he had not read, many of the biblical passages in which water and vessels figure prominently. For the broken cup we might read the body of Christ broken on the cross. This would dramatically alter the story's complexion, for while the crucifixion of Christ is tragic, it is also the pivotal event taking Christianity beyond tragedy, for the breaking of the body of Jesus underwrites human salvation. The event allows peoples to transcend their differences and join together in the Kingdom of God. It makes *universal* history possible. The breaking of Serrano culture is simply the price of their entrance into the larger community. In this reading the emphasis on the differences between the various cups of culture might suggest Paul's First Epistle to the Corinthians 12:4, "Now there are diversities of gifts, but the same Spirit," and 12:13, "For by one Spirit are we all baptized into one body, whether we be Jews or Gentiles, whether we be bond or free; and have been all made to drink into one Spirit." This would have been a popular text for traveling ministers preaching to Hispano and native audiences in the Banning pass, "bonded" peoples, "speaking in tongues." Ramon's telling, though, at least as presented by Benedict, holds too much nostalgia to imagine that he fully equated the dissolution of the old ways with the Crucifixion.

"Drinking into one spirit" should also highlight the convergence of "Cups of Clay" with the telling of the Last Supper in Mark 14.

22 And as they did eat, Jesus took bread, and blessed, and brake *it*, and gave it to them, and said, Take, eat: this is my body.

23 And he took the cup, and when he had given thanks, he gave *it* to them: and they all drank of it.

24 And he said unto them, This is my blood of the new testament, which is shed for many.

If Ramon were a Catholic, as were many Serrano, he would have participated in Passover and Communion, would have known of transubstantiation. His parable, though, reworks the biblical moral by turning away from the focus on identity (all share in the blood of Christ) toward difference (all the cups were different). Ramon's situation invested the Pauline Gospel with a meaning not fully accessible to white middle-class audiences. The blood of Christ, the water of being, cannot atone for the destruction of the original vessel, and the Serrano entrance into the Christian universe cannot fully recompense that loss.

Benedict probably connected "Cups of Clay" and the Last Supper. Under the pseudonym Anne Singleton she wrote two poems, "This Is My Body" and "Eucharist," reworking the parable. And we may safely imagine that she had Mark 14 in mind when she penned the phrase "things for sale." The Last Supper immediately precedes Christ's betrayal by Judas, who has sold him to the Romans for a handful of silver, much as the Serrano exchanged their cultural purity for modern consumer goods and fell from tribal grace into Christian assimilation. Read against Benedict's frame, Ramon's religiosity signifies Original Sin. However sincere Ramon's faith, Benedict's frame ironized Christian allegory.[41]

The anthropologist's associations differed from those of both Ramon and her general readers. Her most creative borrowings came from outside social science, and the aesthetic metaphors suggest another writer who loved aphorism and parable, Friedrich Nietzsche. We have already heard Nietzsche's description of culture as a "unity of style." Benedict probably knew his *Untimely Meditations*. She first read Nietzsche as an undergraduate at Vassar, mentioned his works often, sent Margaret Mead a copy of *Thus Spoke Zarathustra,* and used *The Birth of Tragedy*'s dialectic of Dionysian and Apollonian attitudes to organize her contrasts of Pueblo and Kwakiutl cultures. "Only as aesthetics do existence and the world justify themselves," said Nietzsche in that early work. The idea fascinated Benedict, who by the 1920s was in quiet rebellion against the Christian dogma and relentless sexism of her world.[42]

The allusions to Nietzsche also hint that Benedict's own reading of "Cups of Clay" went well beyond conventional ethnographic tragedy. One of her biographers, Margaret Caffrey, has suggested a more specific debt for the "Cups of Clay" parable and pointed out its affinity with a passage from the end of Nietzsche's *The Gay Science,* a section later cannibalized for the "Prologue" of *Zarathustra.* The juxtaposition suggests the depth of Benedict's frontier tale. Here again is Ramon's verse.

In the beginning, God gave to every people a cup of clay, and from this cup they drank their life. They all dipped in the water, but their cups were different. Our cup is broken now. It has passed away.

And here is the passage from *Zarathustra.*

Bless the cup that is about to overflow, that the water may flow golden out of it, and carry everywhere the reflection of thy bliss! Lo! This cup is again going to empty itself, and Zarathustra is again going to be a man.
Thus began Zarathustra's down-going.

This cryptic passage appears at the beginning of *Zarathustra,* as the prophetic wanderer stands at the edge of his mountain hermitage and addresses the sun, announcing the end of a ten-year isolation and the beginning of his (and Nietzsche's) return to humanity. Rather than breaking, the cup becomes empty again, as Zarathustra begins to "go down." "Going down" or "under" loads our reading with still more ambiguity, for the German verb, *untergehen,* commonly refers to the setting of the sun but also means to perish or decline. The descent from isolation into sociality suggests both beginning and ending, an overflow of being that is not so much a dissolution as, in another Nietzschean phrase, a self-overcoming.[43]

How does the juxtaposition affect our reading of Benedict?

At the simplest level the passage from *Zarathustra* reinforces the tragic cast of *Patterns of Culture* for it appeared in *The Gay Science* with the frame "Incipit tragoedie," the tragedy begins. But it complicates Ramon's verse. The connotations of sunset, perishing, and loss reinforce Benedict's tragic gloss, but the sense of "becoming man again" suggests return and rejoining. *Zarathustra* builds more nuanced morals than we find on first reading "Cups of Clay."[44] On their own the connections are tenuous, and to make the reading stick we will have to work through Benedict's borrowings from Nietzsche's *Birth of Tragedy.* One of *Patterns of Culture*'s best known features is its contrast of Apollonian with Dionysian cultures. That scheme stood both within and without Nietzschean poetics, and it highlights Benedict's break with the emplotments of history we have seen in Droysen, Turner, and even Dewey. Though not recognized at the time, Benedict's frontier tragedy posed a far greater challenge to Turnerian recountings of national memory than did Dewey's "American Intellectual Frontier," for it challenged the very idea of history.

Friedrich Nietzsche and the American Indians

Benedict's aestheticism emphasized the autonomy of the work of art, and we should at least mention the affinities between her ethnographic style and literary modernism, especially the "New Criticism." The new critics described works of literature as independent of historical contexts. A piece of literature was, in Cleanth Brooks's enduring phrase, "a well-wrought urn." Benedict's own imagistic poems wove cryptic, lyrical verse into balanced meters, and they appeared in magazines under the pen name Anne Singleton, separated from their author and origins. Those modernists who did turn to history, T. S. Eliot, D. H. Lawrence, and Ezra Pound perhaps the most famous, turned, like Nietzsche and Benedict, toward myth. But where Eliot and Pound put *mythos* in the service of reactionary politics, Benedict aimed for democratic ends.[45]

Patterns of Culture devotes one chapter to the problems of individuating one culture from another. Cultural diversity was enormous, Benedict conceded, but ethnographers could do more than catalog chaos. Cultures, like works of art, possessed a unified style, and her aesthetic turn took in the human universe: "A culture, like an individual, is a more or less consistent pattern of thought and action." Individuals are works of art, more or less consistent, more or less whole and unified. Cultures, personalities, and artistic styles all represent a process of development beginning from some contingent starting point in social chaos and migrating toward harmony: "All the miscellaneous behavior directed toward getting a living, mating, warring, and worshipping the gods, is made over into consistent patterns in accordance with unconscious canons of choice." Powerful but unconscious "characteristic purposes" guide the patterning, and so we can understand the resulting forms only by "understanding first the emotional and intellectual mainsprings." Its underlying aim grasped, we can appreciate the method in a culture's stylistic madness, and the history of how it reached its finished stage becomes less important.[46]

The declaration carried Benedict to her principal theoretical target, Oswald Spengler. The book at issue was Spengler's *Untergang des Aben-*

landes (1918), known in English as *The Decline of the West,* a ponderous
venture into metaphysics and world history. Spengler made much of his
debt to Nietzsche, from the *Untergang* in his title with its echoes of
Zarathustra's *untergehen* to his typology of great world cultures. The
work had appeared in 1918, and its grand notion was that all great world
cultures were more or less unified wholes, that they proceeded according to different ends or "destiny ideas," that they reached a final, polished stage of civilization, and that after hitting this high point they
collapsed into darkness and decline. Cultures not only stood apart, they
had life cycles like any other organism. For Germans suffering the losses
of world war, the notion explained a great deal. Spengler's Teutonic
prose found fewer enthusiasts in the United States where metaphysics
was already a term of opprobrium and where his politics looked highly
suspect.[47]

Benedict avoided Spengler's organic metaphors. Having escaped social evolution, she had little interest in another developmental theory.
She described his analysis of "contrasting configurations" in Western
civilization as "far more valuable and original." As she summarized it
in *Patterns of Culture,* Spengler distinguished two great "destiny ideas":
the Apollonian of the classical world, a culture of cosmic harmony with
no place for conflict or egoistic will; and the Faustian of the modern
world, with its deification of rationality, egoism, and conflict. Benedict
praised Spengler's demonstration of the "relativity" and "incommen-
surability" of these opposed forms. But he ran into trouble reducing
the modern world to an underlying "Faustian" idea. While "Apollonian" worked well for describing the simple, homogeneous cultures of
the classical world, Benedict thought modernity far too complex to reduce to a single trait: "It is one of the philosophical justifications for
the study of primitive peoples that the facts of simpler cultures may
make clear social facts that are otherwise baffling and not open to demonstration. . . . The understanding we need of our own cultural processes can most economically be arrived at by a detour." Modern America contained Apollonian, Dionysian, and Faustian elements, along with
enough others to make a full description of culture unlikely. So she
detoured through the simpler cultures of Native America en route to
an understanding of culture itself.[48]

Having surveyed and dismissed alternative approaches, she introduced her own, reworking the Apollonian and Dionysian schema of
Nietzsche's *The Birth of Tragedy* (1872). Benedict described Zuni Indian
society as an Apollonian cosmos of ordered parts with no room for will

and conflict. Her "ceremonious" but "mild" Zuni are an ancient, established, and stable society. "Prayer is never an outpouring of the human heart" but instead an asking for "orderly life, pleasant days, shelter from violence." "Zuni is a strongly socialized culture," "most marriages are peaceful," and "economic affairs are . . . comparatively unimportant." Their placid harmony set the Zuni Pueblos apart from most of Native America as well as from modernity. Benedict drew these existential boundaries in a way that both reproduced and revised *Birth of Tragedy*.

The basic contrast between the Pueblos and the other cultures of North America is the contrast described by Nietzsche in his studies of Greek tragedy. He discusses two diametrically opposed ways of arriving at the values of existence. The Dionysian pursues them through "the annihilation of the ordinary bounds and limits of existence"; he seeks to attain in his most valued moments escape from the boundaries imposed upon him by his five senses, to break through into another order of experience. The desire of the Dionysian, in personal experience or in ritual, is to press through it toward a certain psychological state, to achieve excess. The closest analogy to the emotions he seeks is drunkenness, and he values the illumination of frenzy. With Blake, he believes "the path of excess leads to the palace of wisdom." The Apollonian distrusts all this, and has often little idea of the nature of such experiences. He "knows but one law, measure in the Hellenic sense." He keeps to the middle of the road, stays within the known map, does not meddle with disruptive psychological states. In Nietzsche's fine phrase, even in the exaltation of the dance he "remains what he is, and retains his civic name."

Apollonian cosmos and Dionysian chaos are polar opposites, but they are not homogeneous categories. Benedict distinguished clearly among her Dionysian examples (Plains tribes, the Kwakiutl, the Dobu) while insisting they shared "fundamental Dionysian practices."[49]

A key Dionysian characteristic was the vision-dream, the subject of her dissertation, *The Concept of the Guardian Spirit in North America* (1923). All the Dionysians of Native America seek mystical powers through self-abandonment in ecstatic visions typically induced by ritual fasting, self-torture, or drugs. While the Apollonian Zuni share some of these "objective performances," they do not invest them with Dionysian meanings. What other tribes conceive as a dissolution of self, as a breaking through "into another order of experience," the Zuni imagine as an orderly, calm, and "mechanical taking of omens." For the Kwakiutl, however, dreams and ceremony aim at "ecstasy" and "divine madness," and this "Dionysian slant . . . is as violent in their economic life and their warfare as it is in their initiations and ceremonial dances. They are at the opposite pole from the Apollonian Pueblos." Apollonian and Dionysian, Zuni and Kwakiutl, Benedict's text revolves around conceptual oppositions, and the contrasts made the book both comprehensible and memorable.[50]

Benedict's borrowing actually blurred the debt to Nietzsche, for he had *not* separated Dionysian and Apollonian in quite the way that Benedict did. In *Birth of Tragedy* Dionysian and Apollonian were complementary, rather than contrary, aspects of a *single* culture. Apollonian and Dionysian had been different sides of the same antique coin, and their interplay made Greek tragedy an effective artistic form until corroded by Socratic rationalism. Benedict, in contrast, described them as contraries rather than complements and thus subtly shifted meaning. Her mention of William Blake, sandwiched between quotes from Nietzsche, suggests the turn. "The path of excess leads to the palace of wisdom" is one of Blake's "Proverbs of Hell" from his *Marriage of Heaven and Hell*.

Without Contraries is no progression. Attraction and Repulsion, Reason and Energy, Love and Hate, are necessary to human existence. . . . Thus one portion of being is the Prolific, the other the Devouring. . . .

These two classes of men are always upon earth, and they should be enemies: whoever tries to reconcile them seeks to destroy existence.

Religion is an endeavor to reconcile the two.

Benedict's association of Blake with Nietzsche was not original; by 1934 it had become a tenet of literary modernism. W. B. Yeats had drawn the parallel, as had William Symons. And T. S. Eliot in his 1920 essay "Blake" had chastised his precursor's metaphysical self-indulgence and lack of respect for science. What Blake needed, said the priest of high modernism, was a "framework of traditional and accepted ideas" to give his work some psychic order. Lacking that, the *Marriage of Heaven and Hell* lapses into confusion, and "Confusion of thought, emotion, and vision is what we find in a work as *Also Sprach Zarathustra*."[51]

Blake's Zarathustran confusion terrified Eliot but tempted Benedict. Her careful segregation of Dionysian and Apollonian categories replicates Blake's dyads, and the ethnographer held the two farther apart than did Nietzsche, at least in his early years. We have already seen Benedict's anxiety over cultural integration in the "Cups of Clay," and in her frontier allegory Ramon's situation incarnates Blake's *Marriage of Heaven and Hell*. Recall the Serrano leader's invocation of the old days and his reference to the power of the shaman, the mystic ecstasy of the Bear dance—Apollonian measure has overwritten these Dionysian origins. Ramon and his people have become farmers, they have grown orderly and calm, they have exchanged shamanism for Communion. The blame lies with Christianity, modern religion endeavoring to reconcile two incommensurable ways of being and so destroying the pattern of meaningful existence. Ramon's people have exchanged Dionysian Eden for Christian hell. Benedict placed Dionysian and Apollonian on either side of a cultural frontier, and so distanced herself from *The Birth of Tragedy*.[52]

The most Nietzschean elements of *Patterns of Culture* lie in its emplotment of history rather than in its labels. We can see this debt most clearly if we juxtapose Benedict's work with *Decline of the West*. Spengler, in the middle of his collective biography of great cultures, made this allusion: " 'Only that which has no history is capable of being defined,' says Nietzsche somewhere." An inexact citation to be sure, but a notion that must have struck Benedict and one she could scarcely have avoided in her own reading. Spengler read Nietzsche's comment as marking the bounds between definable nature and indefinable history, the one timeless and knowable, the other a progressive becoming into an unknown future: "Hence, for the one, the necessity of the mathematical, and for the other the necessity of the tragic." But the construction did not fairly capture Nietzsche's meaning, and Benedict engaged the issue with a sensitivity Spengler lacked.[53] Spengler saw cultures as organisms that reach fixed form—unity of style—only in senescence. He used verbs like "harden," "mortify," and "congeal" and described aesthetic unity as a harbinger of death and decay. For Benedict unity marked cultural success. Subordinating history to culture, Benedict went much further than Spengler in developing a mythic or suprahistorical style.

The suprahistorical had reached its theoretical apotheosis in Nietzsche's "The Uses and Disadvantages of History for Life" wherein he surveyed late nineteenth-century Europe and declared it ill. History oppressed Europe, memory besieged it, bits and pieces of the past bore down so heavily from so many directions that Europeans had lost the will to act and create. The cure, Nietzsche believed, was a willful revival of mythic consciousness, the sort of pre-Socratic forgetfulness that allowed genuine artistic self-creation: "A living thing can be healthy, strong and fruitful only when bounded by a horizon. . . . [T]he unhistorical and the historical are necessary in equal measure for the health of an individual, a people, and a culture." Before history "art flees," and we lose the possibility of acting unhistorically, forgetfully, artistically. We have not, as Hegel believed, taken up the highest elements of the Greeks and lifted them and ourselves into a higher realm of existence. In ancient Greece we see a culture that is "essentially unhistorical" and richer for it. To history Nietzsche opposed art. Aestheticizing the world turned it away from history and toward eternity, away from temporal comparison and toward spatial contrast.[54]

Benedict made Nietzsche's suprahistory her own. Whether she read "History for Life," or decoded it from *Zarathustra*, or absorbed it from the modernist aesthetics of her contemporaries in poetry and art, she wove his counterhistoricism into the scholarly imagination far more effectively than had her predecessors. The ethnographic collection of native artifacts, ritual, and myth; the preservation of authentically primitive cultures; the separateness of the Dionysian realm; Benedict turned each of these into an emblem of suprahistory. Nietzsche's *Birth of Tragedy* occasionally anticipated his meditation on history, and in it readers found this pronouncement: "Only a horizon defined by myths completes and unifies a whole cultural movement. . . . [L]et us think of a culture that has no fixed and sacred primordial site but is doomed to exhaust all possibilities and to nourish itself wretchedly on all other cultures—there we have the present age, the result of all that Socratism that is bent on the destruction of myth." For Benedict, poet, ethnographer, amateur philosopher, the passage must have hit hard. She saw the Pueblo Indians as Nietzsche saw the heroic Greeks. The endangered mythic conception of life we find in Zuni is not an earlier mode of existence that we can take up and transcend but an antipode to modern ways of being with their tin cans, capital gains, and threatening Socratic rationalism. In Native America we see cultures that are essentially unhistorical and richer for it.[55]

Ostensibly, Benedict's turn from history was a matter of chance. The first chapter of *Patterns of Culture* assured readers that varieties of culture are "best described as they exist in space" because of the lack of "historical material." Since we do not have reliable records for the histories of Native American cultures, we describe them as we find them. The resulting "bird's-eye view" of cultures is one of convenience, not a "romantic return to the primitive." But this claim was disingenuous. We have already seen, in Benedict's story and metaphor, a subordination of history to culture far too consistent to be a simple matter of circumstance. Moreover, she studiously avoided any reference to historic interaction of European and Indian, any use of typically "historical" data, such as archival sources, or even any mention of the voluminous historical studies by Hiram Chittenden or William MacLeod. History surfaces only in fleeting and tragic moments: the marginalization of Ramon, the disintegration of native cultures, or oblique sentences like "The culture of the Northwest Coast fell into ruin during the latter part of the last century."[56]

Benedict associated history with tragedy, loss, destruction, ruin, suffering, and sin. The strategy had some merit, for it would be difficult to argue that Native America had greatly benefited from the European invasion. But the associations race past this intuition. Benedict's recounting of past native experience withdrew from historical flux into a timeless present tense. She described the nineteenth-century Kwakiutl as if they lived next door, as if one could walk to the corner and witness the oil-burning frenzy of a competitive potlatch. She fixed her subjects in the timeless space of a painting or lyric poem, somewhere outside of the motion of modernity, untouched by the chaos and becoming of the everyday life of the reader. Like most period anthropologists, she emplotted her historic subjects in the ethnographic present. This came partly from a desire to offer generalizations about culture expressed in timeless or predictive formulae true of all societies in all places and times. In this way the turn from history was a turn toward scientism.

For Benedict the turn from history also led toward mythopoesis. The ethnographic present of *Patterns of Culture* represents more than a desire for general laws of culture; Benedict adopted the literary and temporal forms of *mythos* for her rendering of the frontier story. Recall her encounter with Ramon: "A chief of the Digger Indians, as the Californians call them, talked to me a great deal about the ways of his people in the old days." In these crucial passages she relied on markers like "old days" and "new days" and indefinite phrases like "one day." The result is a parable cut loose from historical context and chronology. How else might she have written this? For a start, she might have begun by explaining when and why she was in Banning: In 1922 while gathering data for a research project I met a Serrano man . . . She might have gone on to situate Ramon in both time and space. Her informant was not an example of a lack of historical data imposing spatial contrast on the ethnographer. She knew something of the history of the Serrano and Cahuilla and could have recounted their engagement with Christianity and how life had changed from Ramon's youth to the point of their own dialogue. But instead she used Ramon's own periodization: the old days, latter days, one day.[57]

Benedict assimilated herself to her informant's voice and wrote the anecdote in accord with narrative conventions common to both native oral literature and biblical parable. We have a time so deep it has become space, a place in which cultures scatter across a continent rather than succeed one another in history; we have a recurrent emphasis on the ageless qualities of creation and death; and we find a nearly magical faith in a power, whether existential or supernatural, that exceeds the grasp of science. Like Nietzsche, Benedict sought an escape from the modern developmental understanding of temporality and found it, as she wrote in the late twenties, in "The insubstantial fables, that some day / No stone being shifted, suddenly will bare / The world new-minted, the sky luminous / With stars at noonday, timeless on the air." Zarathustra himself could not have said it better.[58]

We can find some clues to the meanings of Benedict's strategy in an article she contributed to the 1933 *Encyclopedia of the Social Sciences*. Her entry for "Myth" described myths as novelistic folktales about the supernatural. Ethnographers and folklorists typically used similar definitions to contrast mythic distortions of reality with true, rationalistic representations. But Benedict did not end there. After surveying mythic thought in various cultures, including the modern West, she invoked the French radical Georges Sorel. Sorel's notorious *Reflections on Violence* had given myth pride of place in the philosophy of history, arguing that the mythic story of the "general strike," with its generic sequence of events, helped to realize and sanction the revolutionary acts of syndicalism. Sorel's justification of myth was instrumental; he did not contrast mythic with "realistic" representations of social conflict but rather argued that myth embodied the inclinations and dreams of a specific social group, that it *became* true, and that it was best measured in terms of *efficacy*. Benedict did not share Sorel's enthusiasm for violence, but she recapitulated this general view: "Myth is universally the wishful projection of a universe of will and intention. Man in all his mythologies has expressed his discomfort at a mechanistic universe and his pleasure in substituting a world that is humanly motivated and directed. . . . He has recast the universe into human terms." Myths served pragmatic ends in making the world a meaningful place.[59]

In *Patterns of Culture* Benedict danced lightly past Sorel's instrumentalism and deciphered the truth in myth. The West, she said, has given itself over to a mechanized, meaningless world. Commenting on Ramon's "Cups of Clay," she declared that "our social sciences, our psychology, and our theology persistently ignore the truth expressed in

Ramon's figure." The *truth* in Ramon's myth is that it touches a realm of experience unknown to the naturalistic languages of Socratic rationality. His figure is not simply useful, or picturesque, or suggestive but *true* in the way that a work of art or authentic religious faith is true. The myth's timeless events offer a world more livable than that opened up by scientific histories. Like Nietzsche's ancient Greeks, the Serrano inhabit a mythic rather than historical imagination, and the encroaching frontier of modernity threatens to sweep it away.[60]

Benedict held history at arm's length. Like many other period anthropologists, she associated history with specific unhappy notions: Turner's Hegelian sweep of the frontier up and over Native America; the rickety staircase of social evolution; and the jingoistic tropes of progress found in newspapers, journals, and political bombast. America, like Nietzsche's Germany, suffered from an uncritical historical consciousness. In reaction Benedict embarked on a Dionysian flight into the suprahistorical, looking down from this bird's-eye view on a modern democracy ringed round with a stabilizing horizon of myth. Only this last primitive border held America together. What would happen if we collapsed that liminal frontier? The imperial vision of history rolling West, sweeping up all that stood before it, was for Benedict a nightmare. She urged her fellow citizens to conserve a horizon of myth as a passageway into an eternal space of beauty and truth, the dreamtime in which we might momentarily escape history and discover a world "new-minted." If intellectuals had lost faith in magical or hopeful outcomes, as Joseph Wood Krutch believed, they could nourish themselves, however wretchedly, on cultures not yet flattened by rationalism.

Self-transcendence, though, could easily slide into anarchy without some ordering principle to privilege certain types of selves or cultures over others. Seeing history as a developmental process had provided a means of evaluating different forms of culture and selfhood. Take history away, and the forms face off as so many arbitrary alternatives. *Zarathustra* spoke of "One Thousand and One Goals" and imagined universal history fractured into a chaotic array of peoples, plots, and purposes. For Benedict as for Nietzsche, modernity had unraveled history and there remained no shared end against which human actions could be measured. But what if social poesis turned sociopathic? Once aesthetics encompassed existence, how could one justify elevating one aesthetic over another? If mythic truth were real, how to justify privileging Serrano folklore over Christianity?

The End of History:
A World without Culture

Many commentators have read *Patterns of Culture* as a sophomoric exercise in relativism, but that reading is overstated. While Benedict denounced simpleminded Eurocentrism, she did not declare intercultural judgment impossible. True, the comparison of two different artistic wholes is difficult. One cannot fairly measure a Picasso against a Rembrandt. Like works of art, cultures differ because "they are oriented as wholes in different directions. They travel different roads in pursuit of different ends, and the ends and means of one society cannot be judged in terms of those of another because they are essentially incommensurable." But Benedict did not mean cultures could not be compared; comparison is a crucial rhetorical strategy in *Patterns of Culture,* and she did not hesitate to condemn dogmatism, greed, and homophobia. What she seems to have meant was more limited: We own no eternal logical, biological, or moral standards by which to judge human behavior. Lacking a common faith in God and biblical law, we cannot point to Kwakiutl potlatch customs and declare them evil. Absent a shared belief in a fixed human nature, we cannot indict homosexuality as unnatural. And without a universal vision of bourgeois liberty as the ultimate goal of history, we cannot point to Zuni hierarchy and declare it irrational, an anachronism that will or should drop out of human experience as spirit progresses toward freedom.[61]

Benedict took up Nietzsche's notion that only as aesthetic experience do life and the world justify themselves, and she replaced God, Nature, and History with Culture as Art. Cultures could be measured for their artistry, their artistry judged by its patterns, and the patterns assessed by employing another formalist term, "integration." Cultures were more or less successfully integrated, their patterns more or less successfully "interwoven" into a harmonious whole. The Apollonian Zuni and the Dionysian Kwakiutl are not typical cultures. They are more homogeneous than most, they have achieved a "balanced and rhythmic pattern" some groups never reach. Many cultures fail the artistic test with admixtures of conflicting motivations, activities, and behaviors.

This lack of integration seems to be as characteristic of certain cultures as extreme integration is of others. . . . Tribes like those of the interior of British Columbia have incorporated traits from all the surrounding civilizations. . . . Yet in spite of such extreme hospitality to the institutions of others, their culture gives an impression of extreme poverty. Nothing is carried far enough to give body to the culture. Their social organization is little elaborated, their ceremonial is poorer than that in almost any other region in the world, their basketry and beading techniques give only a limited scope for activity in plastic arts. . . . [T]heir tribal patterns of behavior are unco-ordinated and casual.

This is not relativism. The unflattering portrait shows the aesthete at work, and her word choice echoes Nietzsche: a culture is either a stylistic unity or else a barbarous, chaotic jumble. The passage also illustrates some of the consequences of reading culture as finished product, for it revives classist Arnoldian connotations. Unintegrated cultures are un-coordinated and unelaborated. They suffer aesthetic poverty. They lack the body and substance we expect of a classical tragedy or a lyric poem. They are, in short, badly patterned. In the case of the British Columbia tribes, this disharmony is a result of some fundamental inadequacy. Elsewhere, we find poverty of culture as a result of circumstance, for according to Benedict some historic situations encourage disintegration.[62]

Ugliness dominates cultural frontiers. Since cultures are incommensurable, mixing and matching risks aesthetic disaster: "Lack of integration . . . often occurs on the borders of well-defined culture areas. . . . [I]n the cross-section of contemporary primitive cultures, which is all that we can be sure of understanding, many marginal areas are conspicuous for apparent dissonance." Here we remember Ramon, caught in the middle as cups of clay shattered against the tin cans of modernity. Frontier cultures, suggested Benedict, seldom achieve the integration that marks true beauty. Taken at face value, Benedict's understanding entails a radically tragic conception of modernity. By 1934 frontiers had expanded around the globe and the world's cultures had been brought into such intimacy that there was little or no chance that any could exist apart, intact, wholly autonomous and self-contained. If cultural mixing figures death and destruction, then Benedict had pointed her readers toward a story far darker than Spengler's. Unlike his organic civilizations, cups of clay could not regenerate themselves.[63]

Still, *Patterns of Culture* did not reproduce the somber tones of *Decline of the West*. Benedict continuously wove a brighter thread into her prose. Despite the characterization of Ramon as a victim of progress, we sense a happier subtext for "Cups of Clay." The verse itself is an artistic product of cultural blending, a marriage of Ramon's inherited

Serrano patterns of poesy with the imagery and resonance of biblical verse. It mixes incommensurable objects and thus should embody the grim dissonance typical of frontier situations. Yet Benedict would not have chosen an ugly epigram. However tragic her frontier tale, "Cups of Clay" undoubtedly struck her, and many of her readers, as elegant, lyrical, and economical. Ramon's verse offers a glance into creative transcendence, the possibility that one might lift oneself up into the eternal aesthetic concord Benedict so earnestly sought. Despite his status as a marginal man and despite the loss of his culture, Ramon has transcended his alienation. Like *Zarathustra,* he has surmounted history through art. The construction returns us to our earlier reading of *Zarathustra*'s "Prologue," and "Cups of Clay" is both tragedy *and* mythic romance.

Benedict pointed her readers toward a future where they, like Ramon and Zarathustra, might rise above history and revise those culture patterns that limited human freedom. We need to become "culture conscious" and "train ourselves to pass judgment on the dominant traits of our civilization." Here was the story's moral: cultural patterns were inventions and subject to change. Such modern traits as greed, homophobia, and violence were bad old habits rather than unchanging nature. We need to select ways of living that make modernity socially beautiful and reject those that do not, for "not all aspects of life serve equally well the will to power which is so conspicuous in modern life." We see the limits to which Benedict would follow Nietzsche. His will to power was a ubiquituous, monistic energy that might be dangerously repressed but never escaped. For Benedict, will to power was a relational force that might be directed through poetic social engineering.[64]

Benedict escaped vulgar relativism by appeals to both poetic and instrumental truth. All cultures might be translated into a transhistorical standard of beauty within which they could be judged by their congruence with modernist aesthetics: the modern's belief in the unity of artistic style; the faith of the new critics that an aesthetic work transcended the historical circumstances of its production; and the primitivist's devotion to mythic meaning. This could not prove much of a solution, for the "transhistorical" values of modernism came fairly quickly to look like the taste of a limited middle- and upper-class modernist moment. Words like unity, wholeness, and harmony had dominated aesthetic theory since the classical age, but they had a particular class appeal in twentieth-century America, and we may read in them more than a modicum of bourgeois nostalgia. As Benedict worried, celebration of cultural purity could degenerate into the sentimental primitivism that drove intelligentsia into the deserts of the Southwest in search of an authentically premodern consumer experience. At its most venal, it fed demands for keeping the "primitives primitive" and criticizing Native Americans every time they bought a washing machine. The ethnographer's own summertime travels could not be fully separated from those of the other tourists swarming outward from every Fred Harvey house and national monument in the southwestern United States. These too were patterns of culture.[65]

Partly to slip these knots, though with less explanation than the point demanded, Benedict invoked "designated outcomes" as a measure of the efficacy of cultural patterns. The value of a work of art lay in its purposeful aim. Did its pattern minimize the harmful aspects of an unrestrained will to power? Did it open up a future in which culture might become more creative, history less oppressive? Here she escaped the deterministic tendencies of "culture" and "patterns" (the sense that each individual's freedom was overwritten by the customs, structures, and norms into which he or she was born) by displacing free will to the social level. Cultures, as wholes, could become self-conscious and "select" from the "great arc" of possibilities those patterns that might make life freer, more harmonious, more aesthetically pleasing. So why was the Serrano's Dionysian mythic consciousness superior to the Christian rationality of the modern West? Benedict did not answer the question directly, but a line from "Myth" is suggestive: "No other realm of human culture . . . gives to the human imagination the extent of freedom provided by the religious idea that the external world is animate and that man can entreat it and make it propitious." Here stood the pantheistic harmony threatened by Turnerian westering, and here stood a world worth saving, one that could aid modernity in its continual quest for self-transcendence. Dewey might not have approved Benedict's mythic truths or artistic monads, but he could have read his own influence into her political conclusions.[66]

Benedict turned Nietzschean historiography to liberal ends. The irony was profound, for already in 1930s Germany his texts served vicious masters. But in Benedict's America they undercut the cant of progress and demanded that Americans conserve a frontier of myth. *Patterns of Culture* depicted a nation holding in precarious balance its Apollonian, Dionysian, Faustian, and Socratic tendencies and advancing relentlessly on a primitive horizon, intent on assimilating all in its path. If this great frontier marched onward, the result would be a society bereft of borders and balance, without a center, without a fixed identity or selfhood. Drive the story far enough and American democracy would disintegrate into that jumble of styles which is barbarism. Leave history alone and it would conclude in a world without culture.

The Science of Acculturation

Patterns of Culture was both typical and unusual for twentieth-century ethnographies. Its reliance on the ethnographic present and on tragedy and its vision of culture as a comparatively fixed object were all quite conventional. Its invocation of Nietzschean aesthetics (indeed, of any aesthetics whatsoever) was highly unusual. Despite this feature, or perhaps because of it, the book enjoyed an immense popularity with both scholars and general readers, and even after Nietzsche had become a bogeyman for Americans, the work was widely assigned and read. But few ethnographers relied on the book as a model. There was no Benedict school, and her idiosyncratic typologies did not find their way into other major works. When Franz Boas retired as head of Columbia's department of anthropology and urged Benedict as his replacement, the university demurred. Rather than appoint a woman (especially a lesbian; Benedict was by now living with another woman), it brought in an outsider, Ralph Linton, whose sociological approach reshaped the department at Benedict's expense.[67]

The drift toward more scientistic models also conditioned the academic reception of *Patterns of Culture*. As Turnerians read idealism out of Turner, anthropologists read artistry out of Benedict. Her conception of cultures as objets d'art quickly disappeared from the horizons of even her friendly readers. During the late 1940s and 1950s those who continued to find the book valuable used its characterization of culture as "personality writ large" to read it as a precursor of the culture and personality school, an approach that stressed psychological and psychoanalytic vocabularies. For other ethnographers even this reading offered little. As a sympathetic Robert Redfield conceded, the language of *Patterns of Culture* was connotative rather than denotative. What you got out of the book depended on whether you had read Nietzsche, Spengler, or Dilthey. More friendly than some, Redfield saw it as a wonderful artistic contribution, but even he did not hold it up as a model for young scholars.[68]

The model works relied on vocabularies more amenable to scholarly routine. Bronislaw Malinowski's functionalist descriptions were widely invoked. The structural-functionalism of Robert Merton and Talcott Parsons offered similarly adaptable vocabularies. By the early 1960s the linguistic structuralism of Roman Jakobson and Claude Lévi-Strauss had exploded into ethnographic imagination, and systems theory dominated professional discourse. Cultures were systematic arrangements of structures, functions, or patterns, and scholars sought to analyze the interrelations of these multifarious things rather than deduce some single underlying motivation or style. As Renato Rosaldo has characterized the change, "In their zeal to become members of a 'science,' classic writers submitted themselves to the discipline of linguistic asceticism. By their aesthetic standards, 'truth' was a manly, serious business; it was earnest, plain, and unadorned, not witty, oblique, and humanly engaging." From such a perspective Benedict's work looked almost unscholarly. In the 1930s she and Boas had seen the mechanical metaphors of functionalism as evidence of arrested intellectual development. But in the postwar era these figures were a boon rather than a bane, for they were more easily reproduced in expanding university programs than was Benedict's intuitive lyricism or Boas's encyclopedic empiricism.[69]

For the frontier story one concomitant development is especially important, and that is the increasing attention paid to cultural interaction. Ruth Benedict and the other Boasians had worked hard to separate Native American cultures from white contamination. Cultural diffusion from one native group to another excited scholarly interest, but the diffusion of European traits was evidence of cultural decay. At some point the desire to re-create precontact cultures had to collide with ethnographic practice. Informants on the reservation did not much resemble the flint-knapping, skin-scraping primitives of the newest shiny monograph. Still, the Indians in Zuni, Acoma, and Havasupai looked fairly exotic compared with the Smiths and Browns of suburban academia. How should ethnographers describe natives who drove cars, watched John Wayne movies, and ate canned goods? How could one continue to justify a discipline based, as Benedict had put it, on the study of "strange peoples"? Ethnographers faced a surprising cultural diversity. In 1935 anthropologists meeting under the auspices of the Social Science Research Council began discussing Native American and Euro-American interaction. Natives had not disappeared, and some ethnographers now doubted they would. Some tribes had vanished, others seemed to have assimilated, but still others, the Navajo a notable instance, looked to be growing. They were not the people they had been in 1492, but neither were they residents of Middletown. To explain this development, ethnographers took up a new frontier figure, "acculturation."[70]

In 1938 Melville Herskovits traced "acculturation" as far back as 1880 and across several possible meanings: as a description of the cultural give and take between two different groups; as the way in which one particular group adopts a foreign cultural trait; or as the way in which individuals are socialized into the customs of their native culture. Such linguistic flux impeded the production of standardized and commensurable monographs. The SSRC subcommittee on acculturation, Melville J. Herskovits, Robert Redfield, and Ralph Linton, in 1936 defined acculturation as "those phenomena which result when groups of individuals having different cultures come into continuous first hand contact, with subsequent changes in the original culture patterns of either or both groups." Acculturation was a part of culture change, and assimilation was "at times a phase of acculturation." By referring to "groups of individuals" the definition appeased scholars who feared that "culture" had too deterministic a ring to it. By invoking "culture patterns," it assuaged those who worried that an emphasis on individuals reduced cultures to mere arithmetical collections of social atoms. And it enriched the ways of emplotting the interaction of Native American and Euro-American cultures. Assimilation was but one possible outcome of acculturation, a larger concept that was, the subcommittee assured its readers, an interactive and two-way street.[71]

The classic statement came in Ralph Linton's anthology, *Acculturation in Seven American Indian Tribes* (1940). Partly financed by grants from the SSRC and the Works Progress Administration, the book gathered a series of articles into an overview of acculturation. The work as a whole bore Linton's stamp, for he wrote its introduction and three theoretical chapters and also appended an "Editor's Summary" to each of the chapters contributed by his coauthors. The editor imagined the book as a technical report for New Deal social engineering: "As White world dominance declines, the direct and forceful methods which Europeans have hitherto employed in their dealings with other groups become less effective and more dangerous to their users. There is an obvious need for new techniques and for exact knowledge upon which the development of these techniques can be based." As the frontier period of world history drew to a close, Europeans and Euro-Americans needed to learn new, safe, and efficient methods for incorporating the others caught up in the social system. Ethnography was ideally situated to inform policy in a world where cultural frontiers transected nations rather than wilderness.[72]

Each of the chapters in *Acculturation* focused on cultural interaction and historical change. The focus seemed to demand a literary form more conventionally "narrative" than those to which ethnographers were accustomed. Each author narrated a slightly different account. Most measured cultural survival in terms of "adaptation," "adjustment," and "maladjustment." Some cultures successfully adjusted to a world dominated by Euro-Americans; others, the "maladjusted," did not fare so well. As a rule, the contributors placed contemporary cultures into one of three categories. In one the Indians were so nearly assimilated that complete Europeanization seemed a sure bet. Another possibility was that the natives might unrealistically resist white culture and disintegrate entirely. Still another was a sort of equilibrium in which Indians retained certain features of traditional culture while sustaining themselves in a white political and economic system. Few of the authors believed this comic resolution appropriate for their subjects. Most fell back on the conventional tragedy of the vanishing Indian.

Still, the articles mixed analytic confidence with moral ambivalence. Virtually all told tragic stories of maladjusted cultures facing adaptation or extinction; virtually all described aspects of Indian life at odds with this narrative. Marian W. Smith saw the Puyallup of Washington as "acculturated," lamented their tendency to associate with "White trash," and worried that Indians who married whites found "definitely inferior" mates. But Smith rounded off this conventional tragedy with a more romantic conclusion: "None of the Puyallup today consider that the 'old Indians' were superstitious. Belief in the individual supernatural powers never met any real rival. One of the more thoughtful men has worked out a careful parallel between the power concept and the tenets of individual psychology as he understands it and, sometimes, the arguments are not unconvincing." Natives bought cars, married whites, and ate canned goods, but many still saw the world in "native" terms. The picture complicates the tragic account of the Puyallup as "acculturated." And the edgy mix of tragedy and romance weaves through the volume.[73]

Editor Linton blandly smoothed out these wrinkles. His summaries assimilated the discrepant chapters into his own simple story and presented readers with a nearly irresistible temptation to skim the entire volume in a matter of minutes (one suspects that many overworked graduate students and researchers succumbed). In the case of the Puyallup, Linton remarked at their "rapid assimilation," observed that "the bulk of the Puyallup seem to have been killed by kindness," and concluded that "the complete absorption of the remnant into the White population seems only a question of time," an ending note not entirely harmonious with Smith's finale. Linton's mechanical metaphors also filled the theoretical chapters. Cultures were "adaptive mechanisms," acculturation required a meeting of two distinct cultures, and one most often found a "superior" and "inferior" culture side by side. In such cases, assimilation was almost certain, since inferior cultures would normally adapt by voluntarily borrowing from the superior culture, and superior cultures commonly imposed themselves on inferiors. Assimilation, though, was never a simple case of replacement. Linton saw the end product as a "cultural fusion" in which elements of each culture combined. This was the most common outcome of native and white interaction, the melding of both in an overarching Euro-American society with some limited Native American elements. The story could be tragic, especially when natives chose "unrealistic" strategies of resistance and ensured their own doom. It could also find a comic resolution not unlike that projected by Turnerians. Indians might voluntarily assimilate into Euro-American culture, though such instances were rare. Or they might reach that equilibrium that some of the authors claimed to find, a situation in which Native Americans retained some aspects of traditional culture while successfully functioning in white America.[74]

"Equilibrium" seemed to be an instance of acculturation that did not end in assimilation. Natalie F. Joffe's "The Fox of Iowa" offered an example. The Fox Indians had adopted modern technology and held on to their land base while rejecting white religion and values: "When the problem of acculturation of the Fox tribe with the White man is viewed over a long time span, one dominant leitmotif, namely that of vigorous and planned counter-opposition, is apparent." Linton glossed the story in his own words. Although his attention to detail was legendary, he did not possess the literary sensitivity of a Benedict or even a Joffe. For his redescription of cultural equilibrium, he created an ugly organic metaphor: "The Fox present an example of a group which has become encysted within another society and culture." Organic metaphors were no bulwark against vulgarity. Linton's picture of the Fox as a sort of tumorous sac of diseased liquid within the body politic of white America could not have been less happy. Aside from the trope's aesthetic horrors (we could forgive stylistic ineptitude), it made assimilation the only desirable outcome of cultural interaction. If each frontier leads either to the cultural death, the "encystment," or the assimilation of the nonwhite culture, only the morbid or irrational would vote against assimilation.[75]

Ethnographic history had turned its back on sentimental primitivism. The problem was no longer, as Benedict saw it, how to *prevent* the Indians from assimilating but rather how to facilitate their assimilation. What procedures should government administrators follow to help the Native Americans adapt to white middle-class corporate society? Linton struggled with such questions, and as editor of *American Anthropologist* from 1940 to 1953, he published a series of articles on acculturation. During the 1930s the desire of white elites to help Indians resist assimilation had inspired John Collier's Bureau of Indian Affairs and the Indian Reorganization Act of 1934 to provide official recognition of the legitimacy of tribal cultures. Both Collier and the act left ambiguous and sometimes paternalistic legacies, but both had provided state sponsorship for Benedict's ideal, the preservation of a horizon of mythic consciousness for the modern world. Linton's cheerleading for assimilation found a policy counterpart in the "termination" policies of the Eisenhower administration, as the federal government attempted to encourage the privatization of the Indian reservations, a solid first step toward integrating backward primitives into a new social order.

Though many scholars shared Linton's general outlook on Native American and Euro-American interaction, his pathological tropes did not find many buyers. "Encysted" did appear in the 1954 statement of the Social Science Research Council's Summer Seminar on Acculturation, but it was subordinated to the dominant metaphor of postwar anthropology in the United States, the vision of culture as *system*. The SSRC brought its 1936 definition into line with systems theory: "Acculturation may be defined as culture change that is initiated by the conjunction of two or more autonomous cultural systems." "System" had been an intellectual staple since Bronislaw Malinowski's early publications, but now the term colonized the discourse of even those ethnographers unwilling to call themselves functionalists or structuralists. In this regard, historians like Elkins, McKitrick, and Curti were following the lead of their colleagues in the social sciences as mathematical tropes reshaped the humanities. "System" brought hard, reliable, scientific connotations to a discourse previously painted in softer tones. "Pattern," which held a poetic place in Benedict's vocabulary, took on new meanings when juxtaposed against "open" and "closed" systems, "variables," "functions," "codes," and "conjunctive relations."[76]

"System" was as hostile to history as Benedict's artistic tropes had been. Despite the temporal component of "acculturation," imagining cultures as systems did not encourage historicism. The antipathy had a lengthy history behind it, dating back at least to the nineteeth-century distinction between social statics and social dynamics, reinforced by Benedict's divorce of culture and history, and fairly codified by Bronislaw Malinowski's diatribes against Boasian ethnography. In "Culture," his contribution to the 1933 *Encyclopedia of the Social Sciences,* Malinowski categorized the antagonism between functionalist and Boasian approaches to culture as one between scientific analysis and historical description. Boasians wrote antiquarian accounts of the diffusion of culture traits from one group to another, a "historical" approach that escaped social evolution by burying its head in the empiricist sand. Malinowski's critique opposed analysis to history and implied that only those explanations that were not "merely" historical could be fully scientific. Once again, anthropologists defined their practice by setting it against historicism. As the Boasians had associated history with the evolutionary metaphysics of the Victorians, Malinowski associated history with Boasian fact-gathering. By his lights, the method was theoretically naive, and he offered synchronic accounts of functional systems as a more rigorous alternative.[77]

History did not quite disappear, for as Leslie White observed in 1945, anthropology texts and courses typically taught history as the counter-concept of "science." History was the study of the diffusion of elements from one culture to another in "unique events," while science was concerned with "likeness" and "generalization." White found the dichotomy too simple, and he listed three approaches to the study of culture: "(1) the temporal process, being a chronological sequence of unique events, the study of which is history; (2) the formal process, which presents phenomena in their non-temporal, structural, and functional aspects, which gives us studies of cultural structure and function; and (3) the temporal-formal process, which presents phenomena as a sequence of forms, the interpretation of which is evolutionism." White, a neo-evolutionist, saw the third category as the best since it dealt with both time and space while the other approaches dealt with only one or the other. The debate between functionalists and Boasians, he argued, should be superseded by rehabilitating social evolutionism.[78]

White's neo-evolutionist salvo provoked a range of responses, the strongest of which was Alfred Kroeber's 1946 essay "History and Evolution." Kroeber thought that White's reduction of history to chronology painted an "annalistic" portrait of the subject that not even "political historians" (presumably the most plodding) would accept. The evolutionist's simple time/space contrasts did not capture the variety of historiography, since "synchronic" or "ethnographic" works, like Turner's *Frontier in American History,* were a "well recognized and important type," as were histories of the development of sequential social forms. The true division lay deeper. Kroeber separated historical method, which examined phenomena in their "space and time contiguity," from nomothetic sciences, which abstracted events from their contexts in order to see them as instances of general laws. Scientific method had been most successful in dealing with inorganic phenomena. "Pure historical method" was best applied to "human events on the psychocultural level." White had correctly sensed anthropology's opposition of history to science but had mistakenly vulgarized history. History was not just chronology. It dealt in complex ways with human consciousness and the specificity of events. The problem was the "current high prestige of science, which has attained fetishistic proportions in contemporary civilization, with a corresponding depression of history." "The callower our graduate students," Kroeber moaned, "the more concerned they are about getting their anthropology 'scientific.' "[79]

Judging from period language, callow youth was ascendant. Systems existed in space rather than time, and so ethnographers focused on synchronic relations. Since acculturation meant looking at the ways in which different systems joined, the new tropes did not mix smoothly. A system was by definition self-contained. One might speak awkwardly of "open" systems, but what was usually meant was that a system was open to incorporating or, better, assimilating new elements into itself rather than open to transformation. One could not weave computer programs together any more than one could blend cups of clay. The new metaphor gave monographs a harder ring, but it scientized Benedict's antipathy to history and reaffirmed its dualism: a cultural system either remained wholly apart or else assimilated. Since some ethnographers continued to lament assimilation, the language was potentially awkward.

In 1954 the American Anthropological Association officially declared that it no longer considered the "assimilation" of Native America into Euro-American society "inevitable." A sound move, to be sure, but rather modest by some standards. One scholar wrote to *American An-*

thropologist and suggested that the conference had not gone nearly far enough: "It seems to me that the most influential of several assumptions which have underlain policy and which is a major influence now is not that assimilation is inevitable, but rather that assimilation is desirable. . . . It . . . ought to be publicly argued, so that its inconsistency with other basic American assumptions, such as freedom of religion, would become clear and explicit in public policy." Edward H. Spicer's complaint suggested that scholars whose research had policy implications needed to consider what policy should accomplish. The letter did not exactly hide his contempt for assimilationism. A year later the Social Science Research Council brought Spicer and several other ethnographers together in an inter-university summer research seminar, and their final product, *Perspectives in American Indian Culture Change*, appeared in 1961.[80]

Spicer and his coauthors placed their work within the tradition of acculturation studies but projected a radically more pluralistic vision. Linton's narrative had marched from a beginning in which Native American and Euro-American cultures confronted each other to a conclusion in which native society had assimilated or was on the verge of assimilating. Linton was no social evolutionist, but his resolution looked much like that described in William MacLeod's *American Indian Frontier*, and termination lurked in its Aesopian shadows. In Spicer's story the "great majority of Indians" in the United States had not assimilated and did not demonstrate "dominantly . . . assimilative tendencies." In fact, for some natives, prolonged contact with Euro-America actually increased the "distinct sense of identity." The ethnographers differentiated five types of acculturative processes and observed that a group might, at different times and places, demonstrate varying combinations of them. Societies might begin by assimilating but end in "biculturalism." In the case of the Yaqui Indians, Spicer emplotted this outcome as a moral norm, much preferred to the bland landscape of assimilationist stories. More historicist than earlier studies, the anthology's conclusion even cast some tentative doubts on the utility of systems theory for studies of culture change.[81]

With hindsight we can locate Spicer and his coauthors in an emergent interdisciplinary field known as ethnohistory. And a year after the appearance of the *Perspectives* volume, Spicer published his magisterial *Cycles of Conquest: The Impact of Spain, Mexico, and the United States on the Indians of the Southwest, 1533–1960* (1962), a sweeping work of synthesis that has become a canonical text in ethnohistory. It opened up a dramatically new conception of frontier studies and swept past the generic tragedies of an entire century of ethnographic literature, reemplotting frontier history as a tragicomic synthesis of "assimilation and differentiation," a tale in which Native Americans took an active role in the making of a new, pluralistic America.[82]

Ethno-History

With a single word, ethnohistory joined *ethnos* with *historia,* culture with history, bridging disparate academic customs, narrative traditions, and frontier figures. Or at least it promised to do so. At a time when synchronic accounts of culture dominated ethnographic discourse, one might surmise that confronting historical change would kindle highly charged discussions of just how to reconcile systems with history. Such a surmise would be wrong. In its early years neither the new association nor its journal, *Ethnohistory,* devoted the time and attention to "history" that acculturation had provoked. The new discipline catered more to anthropologists than to historians and at the outset displayed a stunningly naive historical understanding. History, as the anthropologists saw it, was a simple matter of method more than content or theory. Historians drubbed archival material for historical facts. String together enough facts, each tied to a particular document, and one had a history. Documents and archival materials thus took on talismanic value, and many ethnohistorians identified history with the culling of legalistic data from piles of aging paper.

Ethnohistory's stress on written documents had a complex resonance, for the evidence researchers sought had to stand up in court, or something like it. In 1946 the United States Congress established the United States Indian Claims Commission to clear up the legal claims made by various tribes who would rather sue than vanish. Claims litigation before the three-judge panel involved armies of lawyers, researchers, and expert witnesses, often spilling out into local and federal courts. Social scientists were in demand as expert witnesses, but a few years earlier, William Fenton, in *American Anthropologist,* had lamented the lack of historical training of ethnographers and the theoretical illiteracy of historians: "Historians without culture are as common as anthropologists without history. Such an historian as Merle Curti is all too rare." The Department of Justice contracted with Erminie

Voegelin to establish an interdisciplinary research center, the Ohio Valley-Great Lakes Ethnohistory Project Archives, the base for *Ethnohistory*. Thus the anthropologist's historical evidence and the expert witness's legal evidence converged. The conception of history and the sort of narratives it produced had to serve duty in the courtroom. Little wonder that ethnohistorians should demonstrate so much respect for parchment.[83]

That respect for written documents concealed a tacit metaphysics that worked its way into the new lexicon. In the first issue of *Ethnohistory: The Bulletin of the Ohio Valley Historic Indian Conference* (April 1954), editor and chairwoman Erminie W. Voegelin, trolling contemporary dictionaries for the term "ethnohistory," found no entries and so offered her own. The definition reflected the practical divide between field and archival research, for Voegelin's ethnohistory was "the study of identities, locations, contacts, movements, numbers, and cultural activities of primitive peoples from the earliest written records concerning them, onward in point of time." The separation of humanity into peoples with and without history had traditionally been predicated on the possession of writing. Literacy had long been considered one of the fundamental indices of civilization, and the distinction between oral and literate cultures had grounded the original separation of departments of history from departments of anthropology. In the fifties this distinction also resonated with the legal phrases "from time immemorial" and "immemorial possession," key concepts culled from judicial precedent which dominated opinions handed down in Indian claims cases. Time immemorial was, literally, prehistoric. History depended on writing; one had history when one had a written record, a seemingly concrete marker tied to differences of disciplinary method rather than any elusive metaphysical abstractions about "history" as a substance. Given this basic idea, ethnologists needed to learn from historians "techniques and methods for locating and controlling . . . primary source material." The data that resulted could presumably be stitched into ethnographic plots without too much difficulty.[84]

Early issues of *Ethnohistory* thus devoted lots of space to educating anthropologists in the location, care, and collating of archival materials. As a result, the early runs looked much like the oldest volumes of the *American Historical Review* and the *Mississippi Valley Historical Review*, featuring actual primary documents, guides to collections, and exercises in Victorian source criticism. Ethnohistory, it seemed, would combine contemporary ethnography with the sort of antiquarian history against which Frederick Jackson Turner had rebelled over a half-century before. Given their situation, it is understandable that for these pioneer ethnohistorians history had to be a solution rather than another theoretical problem.[85]

The main problem was language. As Julian Steward commented in a symposium devoted to Indian claims litigation, "The greatest challenge of the litigation cases lies in the fact that anthropology and law have difficulty in finding a common ground in the use of basic concepts and terms." But words like "property" were not nearly so stable as lawyers might wish; property was a culturally specific concept that not all Native Americans shared with one another, let alone with modern Euro-Americans. Ethnographers needed a "new terminology" better suited to the needs of the courtroom. A. L. Kroeber, in a paper presented at the same conference, argued that the common term "tribe" had not been the typical "land-owning and sovereign political unit" of native North America. Since centuries of popular, scholarly, diplomatic, and legal usage had made "tribe" into a key word of Indian-Anglo relations, any number of technical questions arose. Nonetheless, J. A. Jones believed that a "more rigorous taxonomic system based on land use patterns should evolve out of the research now being undertaken." Nancy Lurie tentatively seconded Jones's optimistic sense that linguistic reform could help rationalize discourse, but she felt that the real problem was the letter of the law: "Had the wording of the Act been less emotionally weighted in terms of fair and honorable dealings and concerned instead with ethnological concepts of cultural integrity and functional expediency it would permit objective presentation of facts on such matters." This presumed that a quorum of scholars would agree on the functional parameters that determined the integrity of a culture. The presumption was too hopeful.[86]

The narrative demands of the law collided with the storytelling traditions of ethnography. As suggested by Lurie's reverential invocation of the adjective "objective," by the journal's obsequious devotion to "historical evidence" and "fact" and by the constant use of "scientist" as a synonym for ethnographer, *Ethnohistory* projected an image of its practitioners as disinterested technicians, a self-image largely at odds with the partisan demands and financial rewards of expert testimony. Another group of professionals better acculturated to the judicial system—lawyers—shared the ethnohistorians' regard for the rhetorical impact of cold, hard facts but did not invest so much credulity in the impartiality of science. Julian Steward professed his offense at the suggestion of one lawyer that "of course witnesses suppressed, twisted, and misinterpreted evidence in order to win their cases." Such imputations discredited anthropology, and so expert witnesses needed to create some forum in which they could clarify the "reasons for disagreement between witnesses," for "if anthropology is to maintain a scientific standing in these cases it must recognize that it would be truly embarrassing were persons holding identical theoretical views to interpret the same body of evidence in opposite ways because they happened to be witnesses for opposing sides in a particular case." Ethnographers needed to get their stories straight or lose their certification as scientists.[87]

Fortunately for ethnohistory the best monographs produced in these years far outstripped the historical understandings found in the journal's first volumes. This would have happened soon enough, as expert witnesses found themselves offering radically different narrative understandings of historical fact in public testimony, as anthropologists read more and more historical monographs, and as the philosophers' debates over the covering law, structuralism, and narrative began drifting across campus. Such developments would have forced ethnohistory's early jejune historiography either to develop or else wall itself off completely from outside irritation. In the 1961 "Symposium on the Concept of Ethnohistory" Nancy Lurie noted that the ethnologist is "beginning to appreciate that the historian has long since ceased to simply chronicle events." But even before the Department of Justice began floating budgetary bread on the scholarly waters, a number of anthropologists had begun reimagining the relationship between history and Native America. Since most thinkers considered immemorial time and life to be literally "pre"-historic, getting the story straight would not be easy.[88]

The Double Plot of Edward H. Spicer

Edward Spicer was one of the scholars trying to historicize Native America without reproducing the dated narratives of social evolution. Professional history did not offer much help. The only place for Native Americans in "mainstream" academic history was in frontier or western history, and this place in the fifties was not an enviable one. Spicer and his colleagues had to find a form mediating the functionalists' rejection of diachronic narratives as antiquarian, the mythicists' figuration of history as a technological juggernaut, and the frontier historian's typical marginalization of natives. Spicer's *Cycles of Conquest: The Impact of Spain, Mexico, and the United States on the Indians of the Southwest, 1533–1960* resulted from this mediation, and the text's ambitions, influence, and realization approach the majestic. But theory was not the primary inspiration of new tropes and tales; Spicer's immediate interest, like that of scholars involved with Indian claims litigation, was more earthbound.[89]

Cycles of Conquest grew out of problems in postcolonial political economy. Spicer conceived the book in 1953 when he joined an official from the United States Department of Agriculture in guiding a group of technicians from India through the southwestern United States (perhaps the nation's closest parallel to third world countries), "pointing out factors for success and failure in government programs among the Indians of the region." "I had been searching for books and articles which would help us to tell the story," but while a wealth of monographs on various tribes and key historic events could be had, "there was almost nothing which attempted to interpret these facts and events in terms of cultural processes or the response of one people to the culture of another." Hence Spicer's task: to synthesize ethnographic detail and historical fact into a narrative explanation of cultural interaction, a story with immediate practical morals suitable for application to the contemporary experience of regions and peoples typically called "preindustrial," "underdeveloped," "third world," or, euphemistically, "developing." The result was a regional frontier history with a global pattern.[90]

Cycles of Conquest integrated historical and ethnographic literary convention. The title of the introduction, "Cultural Frontiers," showed the synthesis. Spicer placed his story inside the narrative traditions of frontier history, but "culture" and "conquest" revised the historian's conventional telling:

The scope of the modern European expansion which began in the fifteenth century far exceeded that of any previous "world" conquest. During the 1500's and 1600's it proceeded to enmesh in its web of domination the natives of the Americas, Africa, southern Asia, and the islands of the South Seas. . . . The lives of several million natives of North America were steadily transformed through systematic efforts to involve them in the European trade lines and political systems and to replace their religions with the various forms of Christianity.

Thus far readers might expect the ethnographer's customary tragedy, but Spicer quickly warned them to prepare for a more twisted tale: "It did not consist of an even and progressive replacement of Indian with European customs and ways of thought," for in a variety of regions and situations, "natives were able to resist successfully." In these cases, instead of death and assimilation, "cultural enclavement" and enduring native identities resulted.[91]

Spicer set himself against the two prevailing scholarly traditions in frontier tales. He did not mean to replicate assimilationist tragedy à la MacLeod or Benedict. Frontiers were often sites of cultural renewal and reinvention, and thus assimilationist emplotments could not do them justice. But frontiers were also places of "conquest," "extermination," and "domination," and while ethnographic tragedy had inspired Euro-Americans to vague stirrings of national guilt, the "old urge for conquest" remained strong, "now expressed in new terms, such as political integration and cultural assimilation." While not fully tragic, the story should not be written in the progressive forms of historians like Ray Allen Billington and ethnographers like Ralph Linton. Neither conventional tragic nor comic emplotments built a livable past:

In the 1950's, a quarter century after the last Indian uprising, the prevailing views among white men of the region in both Mexico and the United States, insofar as they were conscious at all of the Indian population, were that complete submergence was only a matter of time and that Indians were a pitiable people meriting help in their inevitable progress toward assimilation. The long struggle of nearly every Indian group for self-determination had been largely forgotten.

Such forgetfulness Spicer meant to remedy, and the text's six-hundred-plus pages memorialized a new understanding of subaltern heroism.[92]

Native identity endured through various "cycles of conquest." In the Spanish wave of colonization different groups (Spicer focused on ten general linguistic groups) worked through variations on a generic series of events. The Spanish frontiers created "economic exploitation" by civil authorities and "exploitation in a different manner by the missionaries." Where the two fronts succeeded, they generated "familiar phenomena," including

depopulation through war and disease introduced by the Europeans, initial friendliness of many but not all Indians, constructive agricultural introductions of the missionaries, Spanish stimulation of inter-Indian hostilities, Spanish infiltration of Indian communities, Indian reaction and resort to military resistance, Spanish military conquest finally subduing the Indians completely, and outward submission of the Indians. All these phenomena were the stuff of the Spanish frontier.

But all had unforeseen consequences, and while "purposeful planning on the part of the dominant peoples" partly determined native fate, Spicer emphasized peripety, for "much happened that neither Indians nor Whites foresaw or bargained for." Peripety dominated the story.[93]

The outcome was hardly what Hispanos, Anglos, or even ethnographers had expected. "Outward submission" and "political incorporation" did not erase Native American identity, and it did not still resistance. Nor did conquest amount to the enclavement of essentially unchanged pre-conquest peoples within a more modern society. Spicer stressed the synthetic aspects of change, employing time and again verbs and nouns suggesting reciprocity: the "fusion of Pueblo and Anglo culture," the "fusion of two traditions and the production of something new," the "fusion of the Anglo and Navajo cultures," a "distillation of the culture of Spaniards in the process of its transfer to Indians," a "program which knit the elements together" where "the stuff of daily life still had to be largely Indian in origin," and the "diversification of religions." Unforeseen outcomes included the growth of cultural "heterogeneity" and the emergence of tribal identity in groups where political organization had previously been more local. "By the 1950's the sense of tribal identity was strong among the Indians living on reservations." In another ironic twist, "the literature of the Anglo-Americans also played a part. In its various forms, ranging from newspapers to novels and poetry, the distinctions among tribes and their differences in custom from Anglos were made much of and stimulated consciousness of tribal identity." Spicer avoided typical assimilationist reconciliations while retaining a sense of the dramatic breadth of social transformation.[94]

The crux was Spicer's description of differentiation and assimilation. Although he had carefully detailed the unique histories of each group, he concluded with a generalization: "The survival of native groups in the face of successful conquests, followed by vigorous programs for assimilation, has been by no means exceptional in the course of human history. On the contrary it is probably the most common result." Social scientists have been blind to the fact, since until recently "we have been immersed in that phase of triumphant dominance which has made cultural assimilation appear to be the inevitable result of conquest." But the narrative sequence of conquest, incorporation, cultural interchange, and the rise to "self-consciousness" of "newly-invigorated political entities" is actually a "recurring cycle" of the "periodic expansion and withdrawal of nations." He thus placed his work in the tradition of world history exemplified by the grand works of Arnold J. Toynbee, Walter Prescott Webb, A. L. Kroeber, and Leslie White.[95]

Spicer's rendering of world history deserves reconstruction. "At the end of 430 years," he concluded, "despite the intensification of communication among all the peoples of the region through the adoption of common language and a great deal of cultural borrowing and interchange, most of the conquered people had retained their own sense of identity." As Spicer saw it, "two different and opposing processes set in motion by the conquest had attained a balance which favored the persistence of the Indian entities." His amplification is worth quoting in full.

On the one hand conquest stimulated native peoples to a vigorous borrowing of new ideas and ways of doing things at the same time that it stimulated the invaders to active imposition of their ways. This resulted in a steady growth of common culture over the whole region. The Europeanization of the Indian became an accelerating process and from its inception far outshadowed the relatively minor tendency of the newcomers to borrow from the Indian cultures. Almost from the beginning military and political control by the Europeans had assured that the cultural interchange would take this direction.

On the other hand the political domination also stimulated the Indians in a variety of ways to resist submergence in the conquering societies. Moreover in the dominant nations themselves the tendency was ultimately reinforced by recognition of the Indian entities and even encouragement of their continued existence as distinct ethnic groups. The result after four hundred years was the balance of assimilation and differentiation which made extremely unlikely in the foreseeable future the disappearance of such native groups as the Navajos, the Western Apaches, the Tarahumaras, the Yaquis, and the Eastern and Western Pueblos.

Here was neither an assimilationist tragedy nor a comedy. "Differentiation" (not yet a common figure in ethnography) and "assimilation" came together as complementary aspects of the same process rather than opposed alternatives. Their relation was not simply one of contemporaneity. Peripety was more than an ironic ornament, for the directed processes of assimilation tended toward their overcoming by differentiation. The impulse toward cultural sameness produced cultural difference in a "periodic" fashion.[96]

Spicer had joined the histories of sixteenth-century Yaqui warriors and twentieth-century East Indian administrators into a tragicomic *Bildungsroman* of cultural consciousness. The technicians touring the southwestern reservations were products of the same processes of differentiation and assimilation as the Yaquis; European expansion had brought technological and economic change to wide reaches of the globe, transforming both local societies and Europe. But universal homogenization had not been the result. Instead, the process, or better, processes, had created new cultural forms, diversified rather than homogenized the world, and produced a cosmopolitan planet where East Indians, Yaquis, and Anglo-Americans could intermingle in the southwestern United States without losing their unique identities. The double plot, which had for so many decades been broken cleanly along static cultural boundaries, native tragedy and European comedy, found a new form. *Cycles of Conquest*'s global scope, emplotment, and inter-ethnic frontiers today stand out as especially brilliant but atypical of period ethnohistories.

Global horizons were not unknown in 1962, but connecting sixteenth-century Hopi with twentieth-century India was scarcely the stuff of daily monographs. Frontier history had begun in universal history with Turner's dissertation, but he had not developed that larger frame at length. Scholars like James Westphal Thompson and Owen Lattimore took up the frontier figure for histories of Europe and Asia, but not until Herbert Eugene Bolton's "Epic of Greater America" in 1933 did an American historian once again place the frontier firmly within the big story of European imperial expansion. In Bolton's "Epic" the global frontier was primarily a means rather than an end, for it unified his two regions of interest, South and North America, thereby piecing Spain's colonial adventures in the western hemisphere into a grander fabric. The history of the Americas, said Bolton, needed to be researched, read, written, and taught as a single story. As a professional agenda this was not a tale for the times; his fellow historians were carving America into ever smaller bits, and grand synthesis did not look like a fast track to truth, tenure, and an endowed chair.[97]

A few hardy souls told big stories nonetheless. British classicist Arnold P. Toynbee's multivolume *A Study of History* won praise, jeers, and lots of publicity, and Walter Prescott Webb's *The Great Frontier* (1952) earned an admiring note from the English star. American frontier history, said the Texan, was simply an illustrative detail of a "much larger and more important story than one country, however important, could afford." By "frontier" he did not mean frontier in the European sense of a dividing line between nation states but an area "where a civilized people are advancing into a wilderness, an unsettled area, or one sparsely inhabited by primitive people." The rise of ethnographic conceptions of culture left little impress on Webb's frontier, "an advance against nature rather than against men." Cultural relativism did not tangle the story because only one of the protagonists could claim culture:

Once we conceive of western Europe as a unified, densely populated small region with a common culture and civilization . . . and once we see the frontier also as a unit, as a vast and vacant land without culture, we are in a position to view the interaction between the two as a simple but gigantic operation extending over more than four centuries, an operation which may well appear as the drama of modern civilization.

The "cultural center" of Western Europe, the "Metropolis," to use Webb's figure, was the beneficiary of the "windfall" discovery of several vacant continents, and that wealth underwrote the development of capitalism, individualism, and democracy.[98]

Webb's story differed radically from Spicer's, for the Texan's chief interest was with the cultural center rather than the margins.

The major premise is that the sudden acquisition of land and other forms of wealth by the people of Europe precipitated a boom on Western civilization, and that the boom lasted as long as the frontier was open, a period of about four centuries. A corollary of the major premise is that our modern institutions, as distinguished from medieval, were differentiated and matured during a boom, and are therefore adapted to boom conditions.

While the frontier transformed the "static," "half-starved" "ignorance" of medieval Europe, the frontier itself was not the result of free human agency but a "miracle," a "gift," "a vast property which had suddenly been bestowed on the Metropolis." Bestowed by whom? Unlike Toynbee, Webb would not answer, "God." Indeed, he did not answer the question at all. Lacking an unmoved first mover, contingency ruled *The Great Frontier,* and democracy looked more accidental than rational. Worse, if democratic institutions were adaptations to an environment of abundance, how would they fare when abundance disappeared? Though Webb denied that history was a science, he could not resist prediction: "The close of Europe's frontier may mark the end of an epoch in Western civilization, and as a result of that close, many of the institutions designed to function in a society dominated by frontier forces should find themselves in strain and crisis." The book's gloom clashed with period expectations, and Webb speculated that not until 1990 would his story find an appreciative audience.[99]

He was wrong, for in the late sixties *The Great Frontier* helped to inspire social anthropologist Immanuel Wallerstein. Following early fieldwork in Africa amidst the angry excitement of "decolonization," Wallerstein attempted a "natural history" of colonialism. His 1974 book *The Modern World-System I: Capitalist Agriculture and the Origins of the European World-Economy in the Sixteenth Century* echoed Webb's belief that transnational entities should be the subject of history. Wallerstein replaced Webb's frontier and metropolis with periphery and core-states, but he shared the frontier historian's topos of a structural center dominating and incorporating bordering areas, pulling peripheral regions and cultures into an integrated world economic system. *The Modern World-System,* though, found nothing mysterious in the sudden expansion of Europe. From about 1300 to 1450, cyclical economic downturns, changes in climate, epidemic disease, and the extension of Europe's ruling classes beyond the supporting capacity of the laboring classes created a crisis in feudalism and made "territorial expansion" a "key prerequisite" for the solution of that crisis. The result was the transition to a capitalist mode of production linked to geographic expansion and the rise of a world economy. Unsurprisingly, "frontier" remained an important word for Wallerstein, the more so as he synthesized materials from historians of European frontiers, including Lattimore and Archibald Lewis. But the text's new tropes, from system to structure, and its older figures, like appropriation, mode of production, and the epigram from Karl Marx, pointed toward different debts.[100]

Decolonization divided *The Modern World-System* and *The Great Frontier.* Not only did Wallerstein take a dimmer view of European imperialism but the possible range of meanings for the story had changed dramatically. Europe had not reproduced itself in the frontier vacuum. Instead, in Africa, in Egypt, in Southeast Asia, Webb's "scattered" native inhabitants had revolted against incorporation. Wallerstein's concluding paragraph recapitulated, unconsciously to be sure, Spicer's *Cycles of Conquest:* "The mark of the modern world is the imagination of its profiteers and the counter-assertiveness of the oppressed. Exploitation and the refusal to accept exploitation as either inevitable or just constitute the continuing antinomy of the modern era, joined together in a dialectic which has far from reached its climax in the twentieth century." European and Euro-American political economy oppressed and exploited the peoples of the periphery, but the extension of capitalism did not translate directly into cultural assimilation. Natives resisted, rather than simply fading away.[101]

The similarity of *Modern World-System* and *Cycles of Conquest* comes apart if pressed. Wallerstein's prophetic claim that "dialectic" has not yet crested points to a key difference. *The Modern World-System* traces an eschatology, and its faith in a future climax, perhaps even a happy socialist future, keeps the plot from spiraling downward into vulgar ethnographic tragedy. Wallerstein did not lament European expansion for he anticipated a narrative turn that would redistribute the tale's morals. Despite the textual roots in decolonization and emergent third world nationalism, *class* consciousness, rather than ethnic or cultural identity, occupies the center of the book's "Theoretical Reprisal." While we cannot pursue the intricacies of specialized debates, at least one plausible reading of the book sets it far apart from *Cycles of Conquest*. If participation in the world economy is the crucial figure for defining and analyzing local cultures, and if the story narrates the increasing integration of peripheries into a world *system*, then the ethnic diversification described by Edward Spicer is an illusion. What looks like cultural reinvention is actually assimilation, if only the gradual effacing of ethnic borders by rising class consciousness. In this sense, and despite the appeal to the "counter-assertiveness" of the oppressed, the world-system story is an assimilationist narrative in which the tragic incorporation of natives into the world economy allows their comic integration into a revolutionary global working class.[102]

The assimilationist drift of *The Modern World-System* carried it away from the interests of those seeking to show the importance of non-European actors. Wallerstein's introductory comment that "in general, in a deep conflict, the eyes of the downtrodden are more acute about the reality of the present" acquires a certain irony as one vainly scans the book for the views of the downtrodden. Given the narrative logic of the world system, native voices are "peripheral"; insofar as European processes of production and exchange govern frontier incorporation, the driving force of the story remains at the center. If one is looking for causal forces and if the cause of incorporation lies in the making of the world system, then the "frontier" itself demands less attention. Wallerstein's radical faith held his telling to a hopeful course, but if we strip the plot of eschatology and read it against the tradition of assimilationist tragedy, it can underwrite a brutal narrative of declension.

In 1983 historian Richard White's impressive *The Roots of Dependency* demonstrated just how bleak a Wallersteinian frontier history *could* look. In White's view the world system's incorporation of natives resulted not in ethnic reinvention but abject "dependency." In language reminiscent of Linton's acculturation studies, White argued that "the collapse of [North American Indian] subsistence systems and their integration into world markets brought increasing reliance on the capitalist core, lack of economic choice, and profound political and social changes within their societies." He denounced "crude materialism," but the recurrence of words like "chaos," "entrapment," "fatal," "underdevelopment," "disruption," and of course "dependency" pressed his actors firmly into well-worn dramatic formulae. Indians "succumb," are "crippled," and their subsistence systems "fail." The chapter titles outlined the stark plot: the Choctaws "Collapse," "The Pawnee Decline," and "The Navajos Become Dependent." If for Wallerstein authentic resistance surfaces as class rather than ethnic consciousness, in White's book the periphery's resistance becomes, in a word, peripheral.[103] But this necessitarian tragedy, so well attuned to the sensibilities of earlier decades and so evident in the older ethnographies that filled White's footnotes, no longer typified ethnographic imagination.

The Trouble with Tragedy

The narrative politics of anthropology had changed, and the tragedy of the vanishing Indian, which had been the main critical alternative to the celebratory history of civilization, now looked like that tale's demonic twin. Whether happy or sad, assimilationist narratives projected a past of victimization and a future of assimilation for native protagonists, and many readers did not see either as desirable or realistic. In a 1986 essay, "Ethnography as Narrative," anthropologist Edward M. Bruner traced the shift: "In the 1930s and 1940s the dominant story constructed about Native American culture change saw the present as disorganization, the past as glorious, and the future as assimilation. Now, however, we have a new narrative: the present is viewed as a resistance movement, the past as exploitation, and the future as ethnic resurgence." Tragicomic or even romantic tellings of the heroic reinvention of Native American identity in the face of Euro-American oppression had overwritten ethnographic tragedies. As Bruner saw it, the change had been fast, dramatic, and complete. There was "little historical continuity" between the two traditions. Like one of Kuhn's paradigmatic shifts, the new simply sprang up and displaced the old.[104]

Had the old ethnographic tragedy been wrong? Did the change in plot represent an advance in scientific knowledge? Bruner did not believe it did, and he ruminated at some length about what that meant. He made clear his debts to Hayden White, but if he meant to follow the historiographer he needed to argue that neither assimiliationist tragedy nor resistance romance corresponded to the past, that each arbitrarily imposed narrative order on chaos. Instead, Bruner struggled to describe, in an almost Deweyan way, how informants and ethnographers negotiated shared stories from larger structures of narrative experience. Both acculturation and resistance had characterized interethnic exchanges from the earliest colonial periods and continued to do so, but different periods placed more emphasis on one process or the other. The "world conditions" of "history" explained the transition.

New narratives do not arise from anthropological fieldwork research, as we sometimes tell our graduate students, but from history, from world conditions. The Indian acculturation story was part of the American dream, the expansion of the frontier, the conquest of the wilderness, and the Americanization of immigrants. After World War II the world changed, with the overthrow of colonialism, the emergence of new states, the civil rights movement, and a new conception of equality. Narrative structures changed accordingly.

Hayden White might justifiably express some skepticism of "history" explaining changes in "histories." Bruner's explanatory history of world conditions is itself just another story, and a fairly conventional one at that in which the tail of traditional history (wars and political events) wags the dog of daily life and narrative style.[105]

Bruner's careful segregation of "stories" from "history" or "world conditions" frustrated his desire to understand narratives as shared communal events rather than private textual artifacts. The appeal to radical discontinuity between storytelling traditions also undermined the project (if stories are radically discontinuous, how can they be shared?). And the claim that the new romance of resistance appeared *ex nihilo* in the postwar period and rose quickly to dominance does not fairly capture the complex genealogies of emplotment. Worse, it reproduces at the literary level the bad old vocabularies of assimilation. The notion of paradigm or episteme mirrors the concept of culture as closed system or organic whole, the idea that drove assimilationist tragedies. Assimilation has disappeared at the level of tribal community, but it resurfaces as "paradigm shifting" in ethnographic imagination. Ethnographers assimilate themselves to new narrative cultures or else vanish. Natives do not assimilate, but narrators do. The construction simply relocates the archaic tropes and tales. But Bruner's emphasis on interethnic dialogue, the construction of interpretive communities, and his conclusion that "all of us then, anthropologists and informants, must accept responsibility for understanding society as told and retold" opened more promising paths. To do justice to Bruner's essay, we now need to contrast storytelling traditions in anthropology and history.

In anthropology the appearance of more hopeful emplotments of subaltern experience followed trails much messier and continuous than the clean breaks of an epistemic or paradigmatic shift. Spicer's double plot was striking, original, and influential, but the possibility of celebratory assessments of native history had run like a coded thread through earlier works. Remember Benedict's *Patterns of Culture,* with its ambiguous epigram and Christianized informant, Ramon, simultaneously figuring both the tragedy of assimilation and the romance of self-fashioning. And as Bruner says, more sympathetic accounts of historical change in Native American cultures had begun showing up in journals and monographs in the early fifties, especially in the writings of anthropologists like A. Irving Hallowell, Anthony F. C. Wallace, and Nancy Lurie. Retelling the big frontier tale as a tragicomedy or even a subaltern romance of resistance was not an overnight revolution. We might single out two factors as important in the changes. First, some Native Americans had long envisioned their own stories as subaltern romance rather than assimilationist tragedy, and shifts in ethnographic fashion reflected this insistence. Second, by painting its subjects as passive victims, ethnographic tragedy appeared to strip Native Americans of agency, a tendency at odds with the politics and experience of many ethnographers. We cannot safely abstract the changes from the local situations of both tribal communities and ethnographers, whether in the field or in the courtroom.[106]

Ethnographers turned away from assimilationist tragedy at least partly because some Native American informants, critics, and scholars questioned the story's adequacy and efficacy. And those questions grew pointed in the sixties. A Sioux political scientist, Vine Deloria Jr., in a celebrated essay in the October 1969 issue of *Playboy,* "Anthropologists and Other Friends," caustically satirized the conventions of ethnographic fieldwork and weighed in with especially heavy criticism of the tragic topos of the "vanishing" Indian. The lonely few who did not read Deloria's diatribe could see members of the American Indian Movement on the nightly news demonstrating in less genteel ways the continuing Native American resistance to assimilation. Deloria and AIM represented spectacularly visible rejections of assimilationist tragedy, but they were not the first to assure academia that Native American cultures had not gone the way of the dodo.[107]

While the history of informants still awaits scholarly narration, scattered evidence suggests that subaltern romance was conventional among Native American interpretive communities long before it surfaced in monographs. But ethnographers committed to a darker course could search out informants whose narrative tastes were closer to their own. Tribes were hardly unified in their understandings of the course of history. At a special symposium at the 1970 meeting of the American Anthropological Association, Margaret Mead recalled that she and her colleagues had sought out "Indian intellectuals who had the same interests we did," namely, older, conservative individuals "who knew most and cared most about their past." Abbott Sekaquaptewa, official interpreter for the Hopi Tribal Council, observed that when "anthropologists have become involved in local matters" they usually took sides with "what are commonly referred to as the traditionalist people." Competing narratives legitimated different ways of living, and ethnographers could seldom avoid native debates between "progressives" and "traditionalists." Bruner's point about informants and ethnographers finding each other on the basis of a shared predilection for one story or another depicts ethnographic storytelling as more than a simple exchange between academic and informant. Entire communities of interpretation crystallized and dissolved in these events. While never an egalitarian sharing, ethnography seldom constituted a one-sided imposition of literary form on malleable native material, and so stylistic change rarely approximated an instantaneous gestalt switch. The various forms of tragedy, though hegemonic in anthropology from the twenties to the fifties, never enjoyed the stability of a paradigm.[108]

Interest in *agency* also eroded necessitarian tragedy. The problem was that the simplest frontier tales described Native Americans as passive victims of history and so left little room for native agency. Such stories bore other burdens as well, for a narrative of disintegrating tribal culture commonly projected a future in which the culture had disappeared. Though ethnographers often understood the story as a critique of assimilationism, it could help to place natives in the dependent, degraded state they were presumed to inhabit, for assimilated or acculturated peoples could scarcely claim the special legal status accorded "authentic" Indians. Deloria followed Mead on the panel at the 1970 AAA and indicted the political work done by assimilationist tales. He first quoted from a study of the court battles in the Pacific Northwest in which a judge had ruled that there existed no authentic Puyallup tribe to claim treaty rights: "Part of the basis was the statement of an anthropologist that Puyallup culture is dead. The only thing that survives are memories. They are now Americans by cultural assimilation. What was two cultures has become blended into one.' " Deloria did not care whether the anthropologist saw culture death as comedy or tragedy. In the context of the trial, it was the outcome and not the emplotment that underwrote the verdict. He was indignant: "I would submit that this is a terrible use of the word 'culture.' It is an even more appalling analysis of property rights. We will no longer have our property rights trampled because of the inexact use of language by scholars." Assimilation, acculturation, culture death: "We can no longer be smothered by this use of language."[109]

If "culture death" was fading in ethnography, it still had legs in history. The adoption of peripetic tales of resistance and cultural reinvention in anthropology did not immediately transform the historian's terms of understanding. For anthropologists in the sixties wishing to create a usable past for Native Americans, assimilationist tragedy looked like something to be revised, for its characterization of Indians as victims not only obscured the important role of native agency in culture change but also implied that Indians were largely irrelevant to the new world of urban technology and capital gains. For historians wishing to create a usable past for Native Americans, textual politics were rather different. American history as a discipline had no tradition of ethnographic tragedy, for in it frontier history had traditionally been told as a happy tale of the rise of American democracy. The frontier tragedies that did exist, Dewey's, for example, had generally ignored Indians and suggested simply that the making of American democracy had been harder on its white male heroes than Turnerians realized. In departments of history the crudest assimilationist tragedies still looked like radical revision.

Tragedy could trigger defensive reactions in historians. In 1966 Ray Allen Billington, one of the country's leading frontier historians, helped write a report on "national bias" in history textbooks. "Unconscious bias is rooted in the commonplaces of our lives," said Billington. "It is taught us at our mother's knee, deepened by the folktales of youth, and perpetuated in our daily conversation with friends or strangers." While pure objectivity was an impossible goal, one could cleanse historical discourse of effeminate, childish figures. Billington offered this example of the dangers of bias.

Loaded language can be used to convert innocent sounding descriptions into instruments of propaganda. Witness this statement from a recent Russian publication dealing with the treatment of red Indians in the United States: "The entire history of embattled America is one of unheard-of violence and treachery, of mass destruction of native peoples and their enslavement. The Indians resisted in despair but were defeated." There is little actually inaccurate with that appraisal, and no modern American historian would defend the harsh policy that drove them from their homelands. But the use of such terms as "mass destruction" and "enslavement" creates the impression that a ruthless slaughter of Indians occupied the entire population of the United States for at least two centuries. There is nothing in the language to suggest that this unhappy policy was formulated by a relatively few officials and enforced by a small number of frontiersmen.

Communism, propaganda, and folktales taught at mother's knee: The irony is that the sentence from the "Russian" text could have been lifted from any number of ethnographic monographs reaching back to the twenties and thirties. William MacLeod could have written it in 1928. Indeed, we can imagine Edward Spicer agreeing with most of it, save only the bit about Indians being defeated in despair. While Billington bridled at "mass destruction" and "enslavement," as he noted, the terms are not incorrect. They carried no more ideological baggage than the chapter title "The Indian Barrier" in his own frontier history. His implication that the violent occupation of Native American homelands was a quirk, contrived by a handful of venal politicians and rednecks, should also strike us as suspect. Unfortunately, while Billington was more forthright in his apologia for American imperialism than were many of his colleagues, the general position was not uncommon.[110]

It is little wonder that some historians writing ethnohistories in this discursive climate and aiming primarily at an audience of historians could narrate a tragic course as relentless and polemical as MacLeod's 1928 *American Indian Frontier* or the assimilationist postmortem of the Puyallup delivered by Deloria's unnamed expert witness. In 1973 Francis Jennings delivered a presidential address before the American Society for Ethnohistory entitled "The Legacy of Conquest." Jennings railed at the historian's use of the civilization and savagery equation. This dichotomy was a "moral sanction," a "cliché" not "susceptible to objective measurement." It mischaracterized the European conquest of Native America as the triumph of civilized society over savage wilderness. Historians from Turner to Billington had subscribed to the myth, scientized it, and "glorified the devastation" wrought by the conquerors. "Reason must struggle to break the bonds of ideology," said Jennings in one especially hyperbolic burst, and "employ semantic instruments designed for measurement rather than attack." The "conceptual tools" of anthropology could rationalize historical language: "The alternative to the historian of frontier semantics and mythology is the ethnohistorian. In the lexicon of the ethnohistorian savagery and civilization become the morally neutral and relatively descriptive categories of 'societies' and 'cultures.' " Jennings divided specialties by narrative loyalty: frontier historians tell happy stories about the progress of white people; ethnohistorians tell tragic stories about the suffering of Native Americans. Objectify language, and the story would change.[111]

An earlier essay had suggested which conceptual tools should replace the historian's ideological rhetoric. In a 1965 article, "Virgin Land and Savage People," Jennings traced the development of a Puritan "virgin land" myth that subordinated Native Americans to the providential sweep of history and legitimated their displacement by the English. "Students of historical relevance," wrote Jennings, "may perceive here a precedent for such later American national ventures as Theodore Roosevelt's intervention in Panama and the current prolonged invasion of southeast Asia." From his reading of the history of Puritan New England as an allegory of the Vietnam war, Jennings drew some historiographic morals: "The frontier theory in its pure form has no existence except in terms of civilization and savagery." He described Alden T. Vaughan, author of *New England Frontier,* as the "most thoroughgoing modern apologist for Puritan Indian policy" and called intellectual historian Bernard W. Sheehan a proponent of "mythological conceptions" of history. We must "replace myth with history," said Jennings. "What is needed is a theory in terms of what anthropologists call acculturation—a single process involving plural cultures and societies." He referred his readers to Ralph Linton's theoretical chapters in the *Acculturation* anthology.[112]

In 1975 "Legacy of Conquest" turned up as the opening chapter in Jennings's influential monograph, *The Invasion of America: Indians, Colonialism, and the Cant of Conquest.* We may easily gloss its sanguinary frontier history: "[Europeans] invaded and displaced a resident population." Over the course of 326 pages the invading hordes cheat, steal, maim, torture, kill, infect, oppress, and rationalize, marching inexorably from the introduction to the ironic and extremely bitter end. Some Indians are displaced, many die, others survive in "subjection and debauchery," but all have descended tragically from their secure position in precontact North America. The story ends with European domination but not in triumph. Jennings ironically undercut the apparent military success of the invaders, describing the conquest as "a fiasco for its victors. Instead of easy plunder, the Puritans netted massive debts and smoking ruins, to say nothing of heavy casualties." Not even the most resolutely ethnocentric Turnerian could read success into this narrative: "The Puritans and their historians have never acknowledged that the victories of the Puritan conquest were only defeats for themselves."[113]

Some historians might have dismissed *Invasion of America* as over-wrought political demagoguery, but one of the works cited by Jennings, a 1972 dissertation by Neal Salisbury, was on its way to book form, and in 1982 *Manitou and Providence* told much the same story in more mea-sured tones. "From a global perspective," Salisbury concluded on a Wal-lersteinian note, "the expropriation of Indian lands in New England and elsewhere was a variation of the process that drew feudal and peas-ant lands in Europe into a commercial orbit." As a "consequence of colonization," the Native Americans suffered a "descent to the position of a sub-proletariat." Ironically, degradation ensured their survival: "Al-though the structural foundations of Indian society had been all but obliterated, the Indians' very marginality and isolation permitted the survival of strong tribal identities in several enclaves." Salisbury gin-gerly skirted the edges of the topos of the vanishing Indian. Natives had indeed survived, but this was simply evidence of how thoroughly they had been marginalized by colonization. What could remain of any culture once its "structural foundations" had been obliterated? While not going so far as Jennings in the direction of victim's history, *Mani-tou and Providence* carefully guided readers toward a fairly grim inter-pretation of Native American survival in New England.[114]

The difficulty of rendering the tragic horrors of the colonization of Native America vexed more than one competent work. Wilcomb Wash-burn's *The Indian in America* (1975) cautioned that while the "Indian's loss . . . might suggest a simple and unrelieved tragedy," the history of Native America has a "brighter side." "The Indian has fructified and regenerated the character of the larger society of which he constitutes a part, and in the process has established a degree of autonomy and pride." The series editors, Henry Steele Commager and Richard Brandon Morris, noted the "tragic story" and offered this gloss: "De-spite this long record of past injustices, mistakes, and mutual misun-derstandings Dr. Washburn ends on a hopeful note. . . . [H]e foresees a period of healthy coexistence between Indian and white, one which will make amends in some part for earlier efforts at total destruction or total assimilation of the Indian presence." We might possibly read this as a double plot, but it is more easily read as melodrama: Once upon a time, Native America was a place of beauty and stability; white invaders slaughtered their way across the continent; now, having escaped those dark days, we have joined hands and are marching into a happy future. Aside from the way this interpretation served as a sop for white liberal guilt, the gloss, if not Washburn's text, vulgarized ethnographic tragedy. At its most stark, tragedy claimed a certain purity like that which Aristotle had ascribed to it, a cathartic mix of awe and fear of the darkness stalking the world. But Commager and Morris's summation calls to mind the cliché of the literary comedian: Americans like a tragedy with a happy ending.[115]

We cannot reduce the intricacies of plot to stark contrasts of bad assimilationist tragedies (or comedies) told by historians and good subaltern narratives of resistance told by ethnographers and informants. By the early sixties historians like William Appleman Williams had firmly linked Turnerian history with the ideology of imperialism. Others, Wilbur Jacobs and Robert V. Hine, for instance, had ventured into shadowy regions of the West even as Billington warned of communist propaganda. A few others, like Robert Berkhofer, had begun revising ethnographic tragedy. And despite Bruner's optimistic assessment of his discipline, some ethnographers continued to believe in necessitarian tragedy and assimilation. Worse, simply dropping texts into labeled boxes devolves quickly into formula. Stories draw morals, but particular plots do not always lead to predictable futures, and stories are seldom chosen simply by deciding which outcome one hopes to see in the courtroom. Stories impose themselves on tellers, as much as the other way around. Perhaps Commager and Morris were right: The history of Native American communities prior to the mid-twentieth century had been tragic, but now it was happy; the division in mode replicated a temporal division of experience with either Boasian ethnography or the civil rights movement (take your pick) serving as the watershed.[116]

In *Cycles of Conquest* the two threads of history, homogenization and differentiation, tragedy and comedy, interwove through centuries, if not millennia, in a single variegated figure. The strength, or weakness, of the telling was that it integrated its agonists into a common narrative universe. It did not distribute its plot along strict cleavages of specialty, epoch, region, or race, with a happy story for Europeans and a sad one for all the others. Homogenization and differentiation structured, although in locally varying ways, the imperial course of modern world history. A grandiose telling, perhaps, verging on the sort of universal history that modernism claimed to have deconstructed. Yet more geographically circumscribed "local" stories of assimilation and acculturation, for all their empirical modesty, projected equally demanding visions. Linton's *Acculturation* anthology, like Curti's *Making of an American Community* and many other works of the period, had projected a universal history composed of commensurable social atoms described singly and then recombined by addition. The vision was neither more nor less ideological or figurative than Spicer's narrative of culture change.

One need not be a Curti or a Linton, however, to suspect Spicer's great sweeps of fabulation. What affinities join tragedy and comedy? What integrates the double plot into a tragicomic or dialectical form? What prevents it fracturing down the center, as it did for Benedict and her contemporaries?

In 1988 James Clifford's *The Predicament of Culture* subtly criticized accounts such as Spicer's. "There is no master narrative that can reconcile the tragic and comic plots of global cultural history," declared Clifford. Indeed, "modern ethnographic histories are perhaps condemned to oscillate between two metanarratives: one of homogenization, the other of emergence; one of loss, the other of invention. In most specific conjunctures, both narratives are relevant, each undermining the other's claim to tell 'the whole story,' each denying to the other a privileged Hegelian vision." Wallerstein's incorporation of the peripheral cultures is indeed tragic. But it is accompanied by the reinvention by local cultures of new ways of being, even the creation of new cultures. Neither pure progress, nor pure entropy, nor even a fusion of the two, history flashes like a strobe light from loss to invention of cultural difference. Homogenization and differentiation, tragedy and comedy, are distinct events, and we cannot reduce one to the other, nor can we join them in a unified tragicomedy, as Spicer seems to have done.[117]

Predicament of Culture's pastiche of styles, pictures, and fonts placed the book in an expanding conversation within and about cultural anthropology. Experimental ethnographies, like Vincent Crapanzano's work on the Navajo, *The Fifth World of Enoch Mahoney* (1969), or even Carlos Castaneda's freewheeling renditions of "Yaqui" culture, had been a focus of debate for some years. By the early eighties anthropology journals brimmed with ethnographic soul-searching, lamentations of the colonial implications of fieldwork, and plaints of the impossibility of "objective" social science. Clifford's writing did not descend into the often self-indulgent modes of many experimental works, but it did exemplify the intense interest in subjectivity. Identity, of both students and the studied, had become a thing of wonder and concern. Clifford argued that cultures remade themselves through imaginative reconstruction and creative differentiation from a variety of evolving others along interethnic frontiers. But form was not a simple matter of choosing whatever shape one wished. Stories and cultures were mediated by forces not quite within the grasp of either ethnographers or their subjects. We will return to this revision of the double plot, for it opens onto much broader vistas, but we first need to reconsider the position of frontier, culture, and their associated words in ethnohistory.[118]

Margins, Borders, Boundaries

Despite the later academic apartheid of frontier history and ethnohistory, Edward Spicer's *Cycles of Conquest* made the two complementary if not identical. On his "Cultural Frontiers," two or more cultures meet. Frontier recurs throughout the book as the geographic and imaginative space where Native American, European, Euro-American, and Mexicano come together. That mingling involves the taking of colonized cultures into the colonizers and the invention of new ways of being Indian, Mexicano, Anglo, or some other novel identity. Frontiers, Spicer declared, are and were places of both destruction and creation, forgetting and remembering, though the degree and forms of that equation differ through situation. Spicer's employment of "frontier," a term Francis Jennings and Neal Salisbury later eschewed, owed something to its use by ethnographers and ethnohistorians in the fifties as well as an older source, the histories of Herbert Eugene Bolton, one of Turner's students. Bolton was best known for his voluminous studies of Spanish colonialism in the Americas, a field in which racial and cultural mixing, *mestizaje,* constituted a legitimate research interest. And in works like "The Mission as a Frontier Institution" (1917), *The Spanish Borderlands* (1921), and "Epic of Greater America" (1933), Spicer could find frontiers somewhat less constrictive than those featured in most history textbooks.[119]

"Frontier," despite its service as a line between wilderness and civilization, had, even in the depths of its Latin origin, troped a place where different communities came up against one another. From the militarized walls of Rome's imperial possessions to the frontiers of the

United States and the Indian nations, "frontier" had figured a meeting, typically hostile, of differentiated human groups. Turner's earliest usage, in his dissertation, had engaged these interethnic connotations and placed the word in its global context, the world-historical encounters of Greek and Phoenician, Saxon and Roman, Christian and Muslim, European and Indian. His frontier also marked the high point of the westward sweep of human consciousness raising itself up into the historical light, and so his focus on Euro-America and national identity drew highly partisan morals. MacLeod's 1928 *American Indian Frontier* had indignantly addressed the point: Since frontier implies two sides, historical understanding must engage equally the memory of both agonists.[120]

While frontier historians from Paxson to Billington had largely ignored the strictures of MacLeod and the scholarship of ethnographers, thereby partly emptying "frontier" of its historical meanings, the word remained, as late as the fifties, an attractive trope for anthropologists retelling the story of the European occupation of Native America. In a 1952 article for *American Quarterly,* "Handsome Lake and the Revival in the Great West," Anthony F. C. Wallace employed both Turnerian metaphors (West and frontier) in his study of a Native American revitalization movement. Where MacLeod had seen the interethnic connotations of "frontier" pointing toward darkening tales of assimilation and suffering, Wallace pioneered an early telling of the reinvention of new ways of being Indian, tracking the Seneca's syncretic adoption of Christian religiosity into a new frontier synthesis that allowed Seneca identity to create a space for itself in the heart of Benedict's modernist America. In 1957 A. Irving Hallowell's "The Backwash of the Frontier" appeared in Clifton B. Kroeber and Walker D. Wyman's anthology *The Frontier in Perspective.* Hallowell explored the obverse side of the syncretic coin, looking at the ways in which native thought and cultures imprinted Euro-American community. The reading of frontier and West as syncretic, if often exploitative, processes was available to Spicer before he ever began work on *Cycles of Conquest.*[121]

Ethnohistorian Jack D. Forbes elucidated the ethnographic usage of "frontier" in a series of articles and books begining in 1959. A Native American scholar of mixed Powhatan, Delaware, and Saponi heritage, he embodied the modern cultural mixture unthinkable with figures like assimilation. Where for a Turner or MacLeod "frontier" held echoes of social evolution, Forbes took up the post-Boasian meanings of culture. He indicted the "one-sidedness" of meaning in writers like Paxson and

Billington and then returned to the word's roots: "In its narrowest and most non-ambiguous usage . . . frontier refers to a boundary or border region—a place where two groups confront each other." Forbes suggested that we define frontier as an "*inter-group contact situation,* that is, as any instance of more than momentary contact between two ethnic, cultural, or national groups." "Frontier" connoted any interethnic situation, any place where two different cultures met. Forbes's essay implied a radical revision of frontier history and national memory. Ethnohistory was not a relative of frontier history or a subset of it. Ethnohistory *was* frontier history. And frontier histories, while they might focus on the experiences of whites in remaking locales recently emptied of indigenous inhabitants, always presupposed a meeting of different cultural regimes if only in the replacement of one cultural landscape by another.[122]

Forbes's idea of frontier as a space where two opposed cultures came together aligned with broader trends in contemporary thought. If the juxtaposition of two distinct cultures created a frontier, the question was, what made a culture distinct? At what point would culture change mean that the original culture had ceased to exist? Boasians had treated cultures as given social units characterized by a variety of behavioral and intellectual traits. So-called "trait-lists" chronicled a culture's contents. One culture made baskets while its neighbors did not; one group moved seasonally while another occupied permanent villages. Presumably, once a group had given up or exchanged its defining traits, it would have disappeared—assimilated. Hence the anxiety over American Indians adopting the fixtures of modern life, from canned goods to cars. More systematically minded ethnographers might fix on a particular trait as critical. For a strict Marxist the distribution and relations of means of production were the determining traits, and all the others were epiphenomenal. Hence the anxiety over the incorporation of Native Americans into the capitalist economy. For Benedict it was not the traits that defined a culture but the end toward which they moved. Groups sharing identical traits might move toward different goals and so create very different meanings for their lives. In all of these concepts the very notion of frontier or border was problematic. At borders, cultures mixed and matched traits with their neighbors; aims and goals blurred; natives might participate in a cash economy and yet retain more "traditional" forms of gift exchange. Hence the ethnographer's disdain for "frontier" informants straddling two cultures, the "marginal man." And yet even as the Puyallup bought radios and Papagos borrowed Lakota headdresses for their own ceremonials, and even as literacy swept across their pre-Columbian verbal innocence, many tribes persisted in calling themselves tribes and acting on that belief.[123]

Culture was still shifting meaning. In 1969 Norwegian anthropologist Fredrik Barth's *Ethnic Groups and Boundaries* fairly leapt into the canon of social science literature on ethnicity and culture. His introduction declared that ethnic boundaries persist despite the flow of traits, cash, and even people back and forth across them. The thesis that social interaction necessarily leads to the disappearance, dilution, or assimilation of at least one of the cultures is wrong. Interaction creates ethnic identity, for ethnicity "depends on the maintenance of a boundary." Boundary markers may change, and cultural content may change, and ethnicity may yet survive. It is the "ethnic *boundary* that defines the group, not the cultural stuff that it encloses." The book's subtitle, "The Social Organization of Culture Difference," distributed its themes across three closely related but not quite identical concepts: ethnicity, society, and culture. The diversification suggested ever more nuanced ways of engaging the interactive production of culture difference. The affinities with Forbes's frontier stand out. The interethnic spaces where Lakota and Crow, Zuni and Spanish, Serrano and Anglo come together are not forever darkling plains of cultural death. They are the places and processes whereby groups set themselves apart from others and create a distinct sense of self. From Turner's thin red line to Spicer's dual process, frontier was not just a place where two cultures met: it figured the historic process of cultural differentiation, with all the potential violence and creativity that implied.[124]

These changing frontier figures pointed obliquely toward the discursive forms we now call "multiculturalism." In 1972 Edward Spicer coedited an anthology, *Plural Society in the Southwest,* that linked his earlier work with the meanings of ethnicity and culture limned by Barth. The telling of different histories, the creation of collective memories for particular ethnic groups, these were frontier processes, ways of drawing boundaries that differentiated an "us" from a "them." The complex affinities of border, boundary, frontier, margin, and edge, especially when set against words like culture, society, and ethnicity, provided a semantic depth that both Spicer and his coauthors turned to good advantage. Another of Spicer's contemporaries, anthropologist Paul Bohannon, joined frontier history to "post-colonialism." "Today," said Bohannon in the introduction to *Beyond the Frontier: Social Process and Cultural Change* (1967), "frontiers have reversed themselves. Westerners are becoming doubly aware of boundaries and frontiers. They themselves are the people who are in the way, who are beyond the frontiers of non-Western peoples experimenting with new and effective technologies. Things look different from this side—and the world looks different to everyone from its look in 1945." The book's table of contents described the new world as a "post-colonial" place of "margins, action, counter-acculturation and new nations," and its map set post-colonialism inside the United States. Its chapters presented selected writings of Billington, MacLeod, and A. Irving Hallowell but concluded with a dramatic excerpt from Frantz Fanon's Third World manifesto, *The Wretched of the Earth*.[125]

Borders, boundaries, ethnicity, and culture difference placed frontier figures inside works like Clifford's *Predicament of Culture*. Eventually, frontier and *frontera* became key words for multicultural textuality. The new genre of "critical anthropology" or "ethnographic criticism," featuring literary and critical analyses of ethnographic situations, concepts, and texts, has become a locus of debate over the meanings of postcolonial frontier tales. But to appreciate the full breadth of such works, we need a better sense of the development of literary criticism in American academia, and so we will need to postpone our discussion while we drop back several decades and explore that ground. The trails will lead us through the history of American Studies and the search for an American mind, character, or culture.

The End of Ethnohistory

We might read ethnohistory as having preserved the older, historical meanings of frontier as a civil border between distinct societies until "mainstream" historians were ready to rediscover them. By the 1980s Native American history was a growth field. And theoretical statements by leading western historians took up the anthropological understandings of frontier developed by authors like Spicer and Forbes. "Culture" dominates most important recent definitions, from Howard Lamar and Leonard Thompson's "Comparative Frontier History" (1981) and Paul Kutsche's "Borders and Frontiers" (1983) to William Cronon, George Miles, and Jay Gitlin's "Becoming West: Toward a New Meaning for Western History" (1992). Cronon, Miles, and Gitlin took "frontier" through a list of defining verbs, from species shifting, state forming, and market making to the Barthian processes of "boundary setting" and "self shaping." The 1986 *Dictionary of Anthropology* associated the word with the study of "inter-ethnic relations" while also packing "colonization" and "domination" into its brief abstract. And Annette Kolodny's "Letting Go Our Grand Obsessions: Notes toward a New Literary History of the American Frontiers" (1992) specifically invoked the Romance languages: "In my reformulation the term 'frontier' comes to mean what we in the Southwest call *la frontera*, or the borderlands, that liminal landscape of changing meanings on which distinct human cultures first encounter one another's 'otherness' and appropriate, accommodate, or domesticate it through language." In a way, ethnohistory had helped to realize the original promise of scholarly frontier narrative by returning the colonial encounters with Native America to the very heart of national memory.[126]

Unfortunately, that happy reading is a partial one. The American Society for Ethnohistory had not created the first confluence of academic ethnography and history. Turner's dissertation had been in most senses of the word an ethnohistory. It had employed the theoretical vocabularies of contemporary anthropology. It had footnoted the current scholarly ethnographies on its native subjects. Indeed, its account of the reduction of Native Americans to dependency through the fur trade as well as its evocations of earlier global frontiers resurface in the ethnohistories of the postwar era. In 1893 Turner had declared that the history of America up to that time had been the "history of the colonization of the Great West." Spicer or Wallerstein might well have agreed with that proposition while finding in it new meanings. But Spicer and Wallerstein did not stand in the "main" stream of American history. By the seventies the "frontier thesis" had become a museum piece on the dusty edge of the profession, and its alternate tellings, from Benedict's ethnographic tragedy to Deloria's romance of resistance and Spicer's double plot, suffered much the same fate.

Turner's frontier history had set its white male subaltern heros adrift in a marginal West, roaming up to and sometimes over the edge of civilized life. If one took its savagery and civilization dichotomy seriously, Native Americans were fully one-half of frontier experience and a necessary element in defining a frontier situation. And even if one privileged the nature and history equation, as most writers did, the natives remained an essential element of American wildness. Nonetheless, Indians appeared in most history courses and texts, if at all, as fringe characters, a dramatic obstruction, or as Billington's textbook described them, a "barrier." The conflation of natives with nature predominated; Merle Curti's *Making of an American Community* did not treat Indians except as peripheral characters, marginal when community life first began and absent by the time it reached political maturity. Even where the details of Turnerian history were criticized, this basic framework remained. Eventually, it passed into the *doxa* of the discipline. Lecturers had traditionally begun courses on colonial United States history with the arrival of whites on the Atlantic seaboard, the story's triumphant conclusion already prefigured in this choice of beginnings, but they now had a theoretical justification for that telling, even if it remained largely implicit.

During the 1950s and 1960s anthropologists and historians began rediscovering the historicity of Native America, but by that time racial divisions of the past had been canonized in print and academic ritual, the historical imagination blinkered, and the pedagogic ruts carved so deep that the discipline was hung-up, high-centered on ignorance, ethnocentrism, inertia, and unreflective habit. Specialization made it possible for young scholars to justify dissertations in the history of Native America, but it also made the situation worse. By the time ethnohistory had become a recognized specialty, it was too late for it to be anything else. Ethnohistory did not transfigure "mainstream" American history but became another note, paragraph, page, or lecture shoehorned into an already overloaded semester. One added an "ethno" lecture or article or chapter or book in a typically well-meant but poorly conceived effort to achieve diversity through arithmetic, revision by addition. The relentless *westward* march of Anglo-Saxons remained the grand narrative framework, any hint that things might have worked out differently lost in the opening scene, the focus firmly fixed on the European agonist, now redescribed as antihero in keeping with the ironic spirit of the age, the plight of ethnic others lamented in a suitably indignant tone.

Ethnohistory: The very word raises questions. Why call the history of Native America "ethno-history" at all? Why not just history? Or anthropology?

Originally Indians had fallen under the tender care of anthropologists because, as people without history, they needed a special "ethno" method. The method was fieldwork conducted by participant-observers interviewing informants and recording data, and it employed the oral texts, observed behavior, and material culture of Native Americans to create a printed past. By the end of the twenties ethnographers could also point to the culture concept as a boundary marker differentiating their discipline from sociology and history. As anthropologists turned away from history, ethnohistory created a space where ethnographers and historians could exchange methods and monographs. By the 1980s many anthropologists not associated with ethnohistory had turned to historical interpretation. Many historians not associated with ethnohistory interviewed informants and used oral texts as historical evidence. Today the "library dissertation" and historical narrative are becoming popular fixtures in anthropology. Oral interviews and the culture concept are commonplaces in history. The transitions have gradually emptied "ethnohistory" of its methodological content. The word no longer points unambiguously to a method distinct from what other ethnographers and historians do.

What remains in the word is a specialty without departmental status. What remains are traces of a decade when academia could historicize Native America only as a special category. What remains is the remembered excitement of a new institution fostering shared projects in scholarship and community activism. What remains is the metaphysics, the division of the world into peoples with and without history shining through a cold war neologism.

BOOK FOUR

Histories of Language

The Fourth Frontier of Henry Nash Smith

The turn away from historicism in philosophy, history, and anthropology has a counterpart in departments of English that by 1950 had institutionalized the "New Criticism" and its close readings of canonical works. But most of the scholars relevant to our story were not "New Critics." Bernard DeVoto, Perry Miller, Henry Nash Smith, Roy Harvey Pearce, and Leo Marx all produced historical studies of literature while their colleagues were busily insulating texts from history. Together with their students and audiences, they cleared a new interdisciplinary field, "American Studies," that mixed literary criticism and cultural history. Sermons, pulps, and pamphlets mingled with Nathaniel Hawthorne and Henry James as scholars traced the historical terms of American identity. Once again the frontier tale supplied narrative order, though the story now looked less happy than it had in more innocent academic seasons. The new field reproduced the analytic quest for scientific vocabularies by trying to separate figurative from literal language in ways that set false consciousness against historical actuality. "Culture" replaced the older fascination with an unmediated nature, and its associated figures, such as ideology and discourse, displaced myth and symbol. The displacements were not painless. Though it did not turn away from history, American studies did turn historical imagination.

The turn curves through a complex figural landscape of "myth," "history," "nature," and "culture." From these tropes early American studies abstracted an "American Mind," and Turner's frontier dialectic became a topic of inquiry for historicist literary criticism. Now his stories were read *as stories* and his favorite tropes mined for mythic content. Scholars living in the technological society found little value in celebrations of the yeoman farmer. The frontiersman seemed irrelevant in an atomic age. Others found the "agrarian myth" reactionary and placed frontier history in traditions of nature worship stretching back to Virgil. The Deweyan frontier tragedy found a new currency, and many historians even read Turner primarily as mythologist and spokesman for the Victorian interests of the rural white Anglo-Saxon Protestant middle class. Ultimately, it became almost trite to say that Turnerian history had engendered a false historical consciousness.

The relation of myth and history dominated scholarly attention to the point of acquiring its own label, "myth and symbol studies," a genre popularized by Henry Nash Smith's *Virgin Land: The American West as Myth and Symbol* (1950). Smith placed the frontier dialectic at the center of national consciousness but criticized Turnerian history by implicitly contrasting it with a "true" or nonmythic history much as the new historians contrasted narrative with analysis. In 1986 Sacvan Bercovitch and Myra Jehlen put together an anthology on American literary history, *Ideology and Classic American Literature*. Smith contributed the essay "Symbol and Idea in *Virgin Land*," which drew intriguing links between his old work and some of the newest theoretical manifestos. This passing of the torch gained a sudden poignancy when Smith, in his eighties, died in a car crash as the book rolled off the press. For four decades his book had been a touchstone of American literary and cultural history, and it seemed destined for years of life as an ongoing event in American historical imagination.[1]

Virgin Land has been so influential that it is easy to imagine the book as self-grounding. Smith did not view it thus grandly, however, and we should disentangle several traditions interwoven in his study and its narrative heirs. One is an older lineage in American literary historiography, for a number of scholars, generally in departments of English, explored frontier tales in the decades before the Second World War. A second is the growing chorus of anti-Turnerian voices in history. And a third is a loose association of texts and authors that in the late forties and fifties coalesced into "myth criticism."

Smith's book appeared so original partly because its publication coincided with the institutionalization of American studies. American studies did not really emerge as a discipline until after the war partly because it took almost that long for *American* literature (let alone frontier or western literature) to gain footing in departments of English. At the time of Vernon Louis Parrington's *Main Currents in American Thought* (1927–1930), no major scholarly journal devoted itself to American literature, and few universities offered postgraduate work or even courses in American texts. Melville had not yet been fully discovered by the critics; D. H. Lawrence's famous essays on American letters were only a few years old; and Mark Twain was still considered a semi-tragic figure so brutalized by frontier Missouri that he had lost whatever talent he might have owned at birth. There were some serious writers, a few of them critics, who took the western United States and frontier materials for their topics—Edward Eggleston, Hamlin Garland, Moses Coit Tyler, Frank Norris, and Willa Cather among them. But these were voices in the wilderness, and English pedigrees ruled the academy.[2]

Into this vacuum rushed Parrington's work. By 1938 *Main Currents in American Thought* had narrowly edged Turner's *Significance of the Frontier in American History* as the leader in *Books That Changed Our Minds,* and although initial enthusiasm faded, *Main Currents* bequeathed two lasting legacies to American studies. First, it effectively formalized the canon of myth and symbol studies. Parrington publicized authors who might otherwise have remained hidden in antiquarian darkness. Some names were familiar to historians but still exotic for critics. D. H. Lawrence, for instance, had devoted an essay to Crevecoeur, and Jefferson, Franklin, and Cooper were well worn by the time Parrington found them, but few had seriously considered their texts as literary works. Others—the scatological journalism of Col. William Byrd's *The History of the Dividing Line* (1728), the stylistic excess of Robert Montgomery Bird's *Nick of the Woods, or the Jibbenainosay* (1837), and the plebeian humor of *A Narrative of the Life of David Crockett, of the State of Tennessee* (1834)—were fresh for most readers, and they became standard sources in American studies. At this distance, it is difficult to imagine the liberating effect Parrington's eclecticism must have had, and though from a postmodern perspective his roll call of authors looks quite limited, with only two women and no people of color in a list centuries long, in the twenties it represented a radical democratization of scholarly interest.[3]

Parrington's other legacy is a tradition of cultural criticism he inherited and passed down. *Main Currents* consistently criticized the American mind, pointing up excess, sentimentality, crudeness, narrowness, and destructive egotism. And it pilloried triumphal frontier tales even as it elevated the masculine backwoods philosophy of agrarianism over the effeminate urban doctrines of capitalism. In grand outline the story was more than vaguely Turnerian, and later readers like Lionel Trilling and Richard Hofstadter saw this narrative debt as evidence of the book's failure to transcend the nostalgic climate of the twenties.[4] Yet its detailed readings unraveled the glossy, sentimental frontier tales found in movies, pulps, and undergraduate textbooks. In its skeptical moments *Main Currents* carved passages like this one: "The history of the western frontier is a long, drab story of hardship and privation and thwarted hopes, of men and women broken by endless toil, the windows of their dreams shuttered by poverty, and the doors to an abundant life closed and barred by narrow opportunity." Such constructions anticipated myth and symbol studies and facilitated reading the "farce" in ever darkening tones.[5]

The oppositions of mythic and real, romance and realism, and the metaphors of uncovering, demythologizing, and unmasking also passed down into critical language. The book's crude dualisms contributed to its declining reputation. Parrington mobilized an army of contraries ("good" realism and "bad" romance was one of his favorites) which later critics found heavy-handed. Still, American studies would find such formulae easier to identify than escape.

In the thirties the book inspired both admiration and reaction. Parrington dished out derogatory adjectives with zeal. His secularization of the colonial mind also elicited objections. One young graduate student, Perry Miller, found Parrington's treatment of Thomas Hooker so improbable that he devised a counter essay, "Thomas Hooker and the Democracy of Connecticut," that carefully, but gently, set Hooker on a less secular course. Years later Miller included the piece in an anthology and there, at the height of his career, introduced it less circumspectly: "Parrington simply did not know what he was talking about." In 1931 the article was Miller's first scholarly publication, and subsequent works like *Orthodoxy in Massachusetts* (1933) and his imperial *The New England Mind* (1939) established him as one of the leading intellectual historians in the United States, a major force behind Harvard's American Civilization program.[6]

Miller's ventures into Puritan theology seemed to lie far afield of frontier history, and yet the scholar consistently returned to that grand story. In the early thirties the frontier and Harvard were still materially connected. Turner remained, in retirement, part of the institution, and after his death Frederick Merk assumed his chair. And Miller's mentor, Percy Holmes Boynton, had written in 1931 on *The Rediscovery of the Frontier*. The mature Perry Miller, in his 1956 anthology *Errand into the Wilderness*, declared that he had devoted twenty-five years to elucidating the "massive narrative of the movement of European culture into the vacant wilderness of America." He did not see himself as a Turnerian, nor did he envision his writings as a contribution to the testing of the frontier thesis. But he did locate himself in a way that hints at his narrative debts. Miller described an epiphany, years earlier, that had set him on his scholarly path. Like Edward Gibbon, conceiving the *Decline and Fall of the Roman Empire* while listening to Christian friars chanting inside a Roman temple, "It was given to me, equally disconsolate on the edge of a jungle of central Africa, to have thrust upon me the mission of expounding what I took to be the innermost propulsion of the United States, while supervising, in that barbaric tropic, the unloading of drums of case oil flowing out of the inexhaustible wilderness of America." These frontier figures—the colonial mission, the extractive industry, the "barbaric" jungle, the "vacant" wilderness of Africa devoid of civil (that is, "white") society—serve not merely to ornament an anthology but to orient Miller himself.[7]

Still another Harvard academic found frontier interests more existential than academic. Bernard DeVoto, a native of Ogden, Utah, and a novelist, editor, and lecturer in English, devoted much of his career to explaining the West to easterners in danger of getting it wrong. In his 1931 book *Mark Twain's America,* DeVoto set out after critics like Waldo Frank, Lewis Mumford, Mark Van Doren, and Albert Paine for telling vulgar frontier tragedies. Scornful of rural America, they projected its imagined faults back on frontier society and figures like Mark Twain, lamenting the vulgar inheritance this past had handed down. DeVoto would have none of it, though he himself had eagerly fled Utah and lived much of his adult life in and around Cambridge. In *Mark Twain's America* he built an articulate defense of folk art and frontier literature into what one reader called a "social history of Mark Twain." Twain inhabited the border between folk culture and high art, and DeVoto's book was one of the first critical texts to construct the Twain that most of us have grown up with, one of America's great authors.[8]

DeVoto described Twain's literary realism as a frontier product. The pragmatism of a Huck Finn was "created by wilderness life, derived from the chief skill of the Indians, and almost imposed as a condition of success by the westward exploration." "Essential to frontier life" and "native to the frontier mind," it occupied the "very center of American experience." Avoiding Melvillian metaphysics, Twain made art from the stuff of experience, and though even Victorian experience was terrifically pluralistic (DeVoto was the first to kick when others used phrases like "the frontier mind"), it had a definitive center.

In whatever mood of poetry or psychological curiosity one examines the passage upland from the Atlantic, with whatever instrument of precision one tries to test its nature, one at once perceives that the symbolism of the Westward journey is tremendous. It has given the commonplace word "frontier" a meaning for the Americans that it has had for no other people. Inseparable from that meaning and immediate in the symbolism, is the beauty of the land across which the journey passed. Whatever else the word means, it has also meant water flowing in clear rivers, a countryside under clean sun or snow, woods, prairies and mountains of simple loveliness. . . . Layer after layer of experience or frustration may come between but at the very base of the American mind an undespoiled country lies open to the sun.

DeVoto's writing refracted Turner's narrative ethnocentrism, nature worship, and Emersonian shimmer into some of the best prose American studies has created. The drama of civilization and nature, DeVoto insisted, *is* American experience. The subordination of natives to nature charted the formal horizons of expectation for Henry Nash Smith's *Virgin Land* and many lesser works that later surveyed the undespoiled country of the American past.[9]

Virgin Land was a possibility before it was a concept, a concept before it was a dissertation, a dissertation before it was a book manuscript, and a much-rumored presence before it was a finished commercial product. First submitted to Alfred Knopf, it wound up with Harvard University Press, and its reception largely justified the word-of-mouth publicity attending its printing. Historians read *Virgin Land* with much more enthusiasm than they had accorded Parrington's *Main Currents*. Parrington's book, though praised by Henry Commager, was not even reviewed in any of the major historical journals, and while Commager's *The American Mind* (1950) continued Parrington's project, historians did not devote themselves to *Main Currents* the way they did *Virgin Land*. Prizes and acclaim showered down, the American Historical Association's Bancroft and Columbia University's Dunning prizes among them.[10]

One of the reasons *Virgin Land* so impressed historians was that it opened and closed with the controversy over the frontier thesis, still near the center of professional interests in 1950.

One of the most persistent generalizations concerning American life and character is the notion that our society has been shaped by the pull of a vacant continent drawing population westward . . . The present study traces the impact of the West, the vacant continent beyond the frontier, on the consciousness of Americans and follows the principal consequences of this impact in literature and social thought down to Turner's formulation of it. Whatever the merits of the Turner thesis, the doctrine that the United States is a continental nation rather than a member with Europe of an Atlantic community has had a formative influence on the American mind and deserves historical treatment in its own right.

Though ultimately quite critical of Turner ("whatever the merits" quickly became a catalog of *de*merits), the book appealed to partisans on both sides of the frontier feud. While its critique harmonized with a growing chorus of voices, its empirical content and artful discussions of frontier figures gave devout Turnerians a readable reconstruction of the western *Volksgeist*. Still, *Virgin Land* ventured morals more tragic than those told by most western historians.[11]

Henry Nash Smith's background gave the book a depth that must have helped its credibility with historians accustomed to happier stories. *Virgin Land* was no beginner's book. The Texan had been reading and writing frontier history for some years. Smith's 1935 essay "What Is the Frontier?" distinguished four frontiers in the early nineteenth century. The first was Turner's "social and political frontier." The second was the technological border between European and "primitive" societies. The third was the line between regions known in scientific description and those yet uncataloged. And the fourth was a frontier of "scientific intension," marking the boundary between a thinking subject and the edge of experience "wherever knowledge ceases and we enter the realm of conjecture and uncertainty." Smith clarified contemporary usage rather than inventing these meanings, but the essay points up how early and carefully he had begun thinking about the topic. The four frontiers directed his writing for years to come, and the fourth, with its sublime encounter with the great unknown, fascinated Smith, though he was the harshest of critics when he suspected others of treading its metaphysical margin.[12]

Returning to Harvard to study with Frederick Merk and Howard Mumford Jones allowed Smith to expand these ruminations into a dissertation cut to continental dimensions. Logistics and common sense eventually stopped the project at the Rockies, and in 1940 Smith filed his thesis, "American Intellectual and Imaginative Attitudes toward the Great Plains and the Rocky Mountains, 1803–1850," earning the first Ph.D. in Harvard's program in American Civilization. From there he went on to positions at Texas, Minnesota, and the Huntington Library in California. As a fellow he immersed himself in the Huntington Library's western Americana and published "Rain Follows the Plow," a brief exploration of the scientific frontier between the arid West and an early nineteenth-century Euro-American agriculture better suited to humid climes. Teaching English and reading western history (he reviewed DeVoto's majestic *1846: The Year of Decision* for the *New England Quarterly*) focused his writing. In 1948 he taught "The West in Nineteenth-Century American Thought" at the American Studies Salzburg Seminar in Austria. And in 1949 he shipped off his manuscript, a work that, if we take "What Is the Frontier?" as its germinal point, had been fifteen years in the making.[13]

Three internal books structure *Virgin Land*'s account of frontier mythology and narrate a historical prologue to Frederick Jackson Turner. The first, "A Brief Passage to India," surveys two centuries of conflict between competing visions of American empire. In the Anglocentric vision America looked across the Atlantic to Europe. In the Jeffersonian vision America faced west across the mythical overland passage to India. Lewis and Clark converted mythic anticipation into physical reality, and by the early nineteenth century Manifest Destiny had won out. From this ancient tale America made its origin myth. Imperial rhetoric and the sense that the nation would inherit the torch of universal history structured the lives and language of politicians like Thomas Hart Benton before Frederick Jackson Turner was even born.

Book 2, "The Sons of Leatherstocking," focused on the frontier figure who personified the westward movement. Leatherstocking, James Fenimore Cooper's archetypal frontiersman and the model for countless subsequent coonskin-capped and Colt-waving heroes and heroines, was a synecdoche of Manifest Destiny and bore the full symbolic weight of the larger narrative. As Smith described him (and, more awkwardly, her), the frontiersman did not spring fully grown from the earliest frontier writing but developed with the nation's political consciousness, from a peripheral character in Cooper's early upper-class romances to a hero in his own right, the rugged individual of dime novels massproduced for a dream-starved middle class. By the end of book 2 Turner's democratization of frontier narrative, the historian's shift of heroic focus from the Washingtons toward the Boones, looked less like a revelation of true subaltern heroism and more like the last moment of a mature literary convention, the movement of mythical into historical thought.

Book 3, "The Garden of the World," traced spatial figurations of the West. From Puritan notions of a city in the wilderness to the republican language of the Homestead Act, images of the West as threatening wilderness and Edenic utopia had struggled for dominance. Unfortunately, Smith argued, those rural ideals had diverged sharply from the realities of industrialism and urbanization. In the end, and even into the modern twentieth century, the hero of the myth of the garden, the archetypal yeoman farmer, independent, virtuous, middle-class, and free, stood beside the more primitive Leatherstockings, Calamity Janes, and Virginians as synecdoche of national consciousness. These were America's historic heroes before Turner put pen to paper.

Virgin Land's format reproduced in outline the frontier narrative while projecting new morals. "A Brief Passage to India" encapsulates the story's movement from east to west, upward, progressive, and hopeful. "The Sons of Leatherstocking" figures the protagonist, the frontiersman who stands in for both civilization and primitivism. "The Garden of the World" tropes the wilderness antagonist against which the hero works out both national identity and destiny. And *Virgin Land*'s conclusion, "The Myth of the Garden and Turner's Frontier Hypothesis," achieves the critical demolition of Turnerian history that Smith had disavowed in his opening pages. Frontier history had been frontier myth long before it grew footnotes. Turner had committed himself and the country to a story unsuited for modernity. In scholarship the frontier thesis diverted attention from modern problems. In politics it fostered a false consciousness, dividing farmers from factory workers and preventing both from seeing their common class interests. Worst of all, it kept Americans from thinking of themselves as "members of a world community." By the end of *Virgin Land* frontier narrative, not long ago the historical profession's favorite story, had condensed into clouds of myth and symbol obscuring the historical landscape.[14]

Smith placed Turnerian history at the end of a long tradition of frontier folktales. In 1890 that folk tradition conferred on Turner a social authority any scholar would envy. But instead of using its imaginative language, Turner allowed it to use him. As Smith put it,

Rebirth and regeneration are categories of myth rather than of economic analysis, but ordinarily Turner kept his metaphors under control and used them to illustrate and vivify his logical propositions rather than as a structural principle or as a means of cognition: that is, he used them rhetorically not poetically. . . . But sometimes, especially when the conception of nature as the source of occult power is most vividly present, Turner's metaphors threaten to become themselves a means of cognition and to supplant discursive reasoning.

Under the critical chisel the Turnerian text split into halves: metaphor, myth, poesy, and falsehood on one side and logic, reason, cognition, and truth on the other. We have seen this operation before, and if we did not make the association immediately, Smith's footnotes can help us out: "I am deeply indebted to Professor [George] Pierson for many ideas," such as the "suggestion that Turner's 'poetic interpretations' revived 'the grandest ideas that had gone to make up American legend.' "[15]

Virgin Land historicized Turner's mythopoesis and brought frontier tragedy to fruition. Pierson had warned that the house of Turner stood on quicksand. Turner had forsaken masculine reason for effeminate poesy, his metaphors had opened a "Pandora's box" of scholarly horrors, and he had succumbed to "social theory." Like Pierson, Smith spoke in gendered language of the "veil of literary convention, class prejudice, [and] social theory" and lamented the "apparatus of theory that had so often beclouded the vision of observers." European metaphysics likewise beclouded Turner's vision, and Smith described the Victorian idealist as a vulgar social evolutionist, committed to a primitivist conception of democracy unfit for an industrial age. Believing that democracy sprang from wilderness, Turner could not account for democracy once wilderness was gone. In senescent despair Turner finally turned, said Smith, to "unconvincing" rhetorical appeals to education as a replacement for a lost frontier.[16]

Smith's feminization of myth, metaphor, and theory fell on many friendly ears. New critics like I. A. Richards had eagerly employed the figures of "hard science," of technique, test, experiment, and analysis. Robert Spiller, a leading literary historian, spoke of historical criticism as a process of hypothesis construction and testing. Perry Miller later declared that a metaphor is a "vastly different thing" from a "thesis." In 1957 Max Lerner's epic *America as Civilization* invoked Smith's dissection of Turnerian "legend." In 1965 Edwin Fussell's *Frontier: American Literature and the American West* noted Turner's "astonishing confusion" and sniffed at his "sentimental-antiquarian-West-mongering." And in 1968 Hofstadter's *Progressive Historians* adopted *Virgin Land*'s treatment of Turner. By the end of the sixties the story was solid: Seduced by the feminine wiles of poesy, Turner surrendered the intellectual freedom of masculine science for the slavery of storytelling.[17]

Smith's contrast of frontier myth and modern reality stood on monographs critical of Turnerian tradition. Chester Eisinger's description of the yeoman farmer as a tool of political propaganda; Paul Wallace Gates's analysis of corporate exploitation of land law; a youthful Richard Hofstadter's assaults on "frontier myth"; Smith cited all these works in support of a nonmythic history. The strategy seemed designed to appeal to professional historians who might otherwise have suspected the book's assault on a founding father, its ambiguous professional allegiances, and its vaguely leftist politics. The vocabulary of myth and symbol harmonized with period concerns about the "official histories" and distortions of the past by authoritarian regimes in Russia and Asia, and its insulation of contemporary historiography from the effeminate idealism of earlier generations allowed historians to secure a scientific place in an increasingly technical academy.[18]

Virgin Land's vocabulary was as influential as it was ambiguous. Its original preface opened with this famous statement:

> The terms "myth" and "symbol" occur so often in the following pages that the reader deserves some warning about them. I use the words to designate larger or smaller units of the same kind of thing, namely an intellectual construction that fuses concept and emotion into an image. The myths and symbols with which I deal have the further characteristic of being collective representations rather than the work of a single mind. I do not mean to raise the question whether such products of the imagination accurately reflect empirical fact. They exist on a different plane. But as I have tried to show, they sometimes exert a decided influence on practical affairs.

Turner's "fusions" mixed too much emotion with too much theory. Smith's qualification, that he did not mean to question "whether such products of the imagination accurately reflect empirical fact," was quite disingenuous. The book stands on ironic juxtapositions of false mythical consciousness with historical reality, and lacking these contrasts, the study's moral, that frontier myth generated a slavish devotion to bad political habits, would not work.[19]

By the end of the fifties *Virgin Land*'s lexicon of "myth" and "symbol" loosely affiliated the book with a school of "myth criticism" that was giving new critics a run for their money. But *Virgin Land* appeared before such studies as Northrop Frye's *Anatomy of Criticism* (1957) and owed few debts to Joseph Campbell's *The Hero with a Thousand Faces* (1949). Like Ruth Benedict and unlike Smith, Campbell and Frye were interested in myth *as myth*, not just as bad history. Campbell's *Hero with a Thousand Faces* traced the changing forms of "the one, shape-shifting yet marvelously constant story," a timeless vision of the heroic quest that he believed surfaced in all narratives. Smith was less interested in universal archetypes; he wanted to unmask specifically *American* forms. He would not have approved *Hero*'s conclusion that the happy endings of comedy represent "transcendence of the universal tragedy of man," and he stood entirely opposed to its moral, that "consciousness" could not control collective symbolism, that such things worked themselves out on "another level" in "what is bound to be a long and very frightening process." Smith kept a similar distance from Northrop Frye, whose *Anatomy of Criticism* detailed an elaborate typology of narrative form. All literature articulated some version of the heroic quest, emplotted as romance, tragedy, comedy, or satire, each of which could be subdivided into infinity. Frye noted the imprint of these *mythoi* on historical monographs, but he believed that the historian's "scientific treatment" of evidence separated history from legend: "The presence of science in any subject changes its character from the casual to the causal."[20]

Smith's method scarcely resembled the myth criticism of Campbell and Frye. Both of these contemporaries wished to uncover "timeless" universal forms rather than historical accounts of emplotment. Both placed a single Ur-narrative in a collective human unconscious. Both tried to demonstrate the presence of myth in modernity, the way that consciousness continued to reproduce deeper and not fully rational archetypal patterns. Both used methods that complemented the new critical axiom that a text was a self-contained object with a unifying structural principle. And both rehabilitated myth. Frye invoked Ruth Benedict and Campbell quoted Nietzsche in service of claims for the efficacy, even the *necessity*, of myth. Nothing like this appeared in *Virgin Land*, and from one obvious convergence, Smith's agreement with Campbell and Frye that mythic thought is subconscious and irrational, the myth critics and the American studies scholar drew wildly divergent morals. Unlike Hayden White, Smith had no interest in adapting myth for modernity.[21]

The one debt Smith shared with the myth critics was to Sir James Frazer's *The Golden Bough*, one of the classic works in Victorian "armchair" anthropology. Frazer's text assembled and analyzed under the general rubric of myth everything from Hesiod's *Works and Days* to Polynesian cosmologies. Frazer treated myths as primitive stories about phenomena that were more realistically explained by science. Myths were simply picturesque and significant but incorrect tales told by ancient or primitive peoples. But Frazer's stylized prose and appreciation of the literary qualities of his materials made *The Golden Bough* required reading for modernists like Ezra Pound and T. S. Eliot who had stronger sympathies for mythic truth. By 1959 it had become required reading for their students as well, and Lionel Trilling's famous essay "Teaching Modern Literature" singled out the text as a prerequisite for critical analysis of the modern canon. This Frazerian sense of myth, rather than the technical variations of other myth critics, drove Henry Nash Smith's readings.[22]

Virgin Land opposed a vaguely defined "myth" to an indefinite "history" and an even more ambiguous "art." While some readers linked the book with works closer to the mainstream of myth criticism, it owed more to "common sense" academic usage of myths as false stories. It fell nearer to the meanings projected by Richard Hofstadter's "frontier myth" than to the analytic figures found in contemporary ethnographies. To the extent that *Virgin Land* invoked cultural anthropology, it returned to *The Golden Bough* and many of the unfortunate Victorian notions that Smith attributed to Frederick Jackson Turner. Some of this ambiguity disturbed otherwise adulatory reviewers. Merrill Peterson worried about the "extremely difficult question of the cultural value of myth." Marvin Wachman asked, reasonably enough, when does historical interpretation become myth? "When revisionist interpretation is no longer accepted, is it also to be considered myth?" And Fulmer Mood noted the "reader wearies a little" of Smith's amorphous labels: "It is to be hoped that his use of these terms will not prove catching, for in less skilled hands such terms could lead to pernicious results." The words were more than catching; they became virtual fetishes for American studies scholars attracted to their fusion of older humanist figures with the scientific resonance of modern ethnography. But the hybrid was more than a bit enigmatic, especially in a work that one reviewer, Richard Hofstadter, declared a major methodological innovation.[23]

In 1952 Barry Marks, one of Smith's students, turned the rule of reason back on *Virgin Land* and denounced its many "logical contradictions." To begin with, after declaring that he had no intention of exploring whether myths corresponded to actuality, Smith made such comparisons the heart of his book. Worse, the comparisons were muddy. By Marks's analytical lights, the relation of myth and reality could be discussed in at least two ways: as propositions of fact (the myth says that "x is the case") and as propositions of value (the myth says "x should be the case"). *Virgin Land* confounded these categories, and while the book's tone emphasized factual accuracy, its examples more often involved difficult questions of value. And since the examples frequently contradicted one another, confusion resulted. For instance, Smith argued that the Southern Plantation myth failed to captivate westerners because it was unrealistic; large-scale cotton farming was impossible in the arid lands. But the myth that did win, the myth of the garden, was equally unrealistic. And while Smith described the myth of the garden as a "timeless" set of stories celebrating subsistence farming, an ideal at odds with the real capitalist practice of American agriculture, many of his examples described farmers using mechanized tools in commercial settings. If myths were "timeless," then how could they change?[24]

Despite Smith's disclaimers, myth carried a tremendous analytical weight, and so *Virgin Land*'s theoretical reticence was problematic. His insistence on retaining myth as a special form while refusing to define it encouraged readers to superimpose the Platonic essence of their choice. The construction grated against his harder linguistic analysis, which privileged a tough-minded empiricism. If myth was so elusive, how could one be sure that it even existed?

In 1950 *Virgin Land*'s final chapter, "The Frontier Thesis and the Myth of the Garden," appeared in a new journal, *American Quarterly*, which Smith was helping to edit. The journal became a power nexus for American studies, and Smith contributed regularly to its early issues. A specialized publication is one of the first steps in the making of a discipline, and the creation of the American Studies Association followed soon after *American Quarterly*'s 1949 debut. *Virgin Land*'s timely appearance and enthusiastic reception guaranteed that its study of myth and symbol would be bound up with questions of method and matter. R. W. B. Lewis, in a 1951 essay on Faulkner's *The Bear*, rewrote Christian metaphysics into the *Virgin Land:* "The frontier, as Turner and Constance Rourke were the first to make clear, was the major source of this uniquely American idea: the idea, I mean, of a new, unspoiled area in which a genuine and radical moral freedom could once again be exercised—as once, long ago, it had been, in the garden of Eden." Shortly afterward this essay appeared in book form, as Lewis redescribed the frontiersman in *The American Adam* (1953) (praised in reviews by Smith for its rich exploration of American mythology and by Sherman Paul who appreciated its "mature and liberating" tragic sense of life). Meanwhile, one of Smith's students wrote a dissertation on the key political incarnation of Turner's Adamic frontiersman. John Ward's *Andrew Jackson, Symbol for an Age* (1955) explored the "structural underpinnings of the ideology of early nineteenth-century America, for which Andrew Jackson is *one* symbol." Ideology and structure, myth and symbol, wound in and out. In the end, one of these thematic pairs would subvert the other, and *Virgin Land*'s marriage of naturalistic linguistic analysis and idealistic myth criticism would not survive the coming of "culture."[25]

In 1957 Smith published his first theoretical essay on myth and symbol, "Can American Studies Develop a Method?" He placed the field in the no-man's-land separating literary criticism from social science. American studies stood at this intersection of art and culture ("by 'American Studies' I shall mean 'the study of American culture, past and present, as a whole' "), but Smith doubted the utility of any further discussion. Scholars needed to do American studies rather than talk about it. And there was much to do, for conventional scholarship had left a great gap. Any great work of art was made of "cultural, not merely private and individual, images." But neither criticism nor social science dealt with this level of experience. New criticism removed texts from their historic contexts, refusing to address the political and social forces involved in their writing and reading. Social science flattened all literature, treating great books like potboilers. Sociological criticism, especially content analysis where researchers quantified the usage of particular words, produced a "mutilated image of man and society." By marginalizing "imaginative" and "poetic" language, the "only instruments we have for embodying and communicating the full content of consciousness," the social sciences built a mechanized world in which "freedom is entirely absent and in which consciousness itself is rudimentary." Where the new criticism produced art without society, the social sciences created "society without art."[26]

Smith proposed that American studies mediate these extremes with the aid of a new key word: "The concept 'culture' seems, in the abstract at least, to embrace the concepts 'society' and 'art.' Why may we not say quite simply that the problem of method in American Studies can be solved by presupposing a value implicit in culture which includes and reconciles the apparently disparate values assumed in the disciplines of, say, literature and sociology?" "Culture," though, was as much a question as an answer. In this essay Smith wandered from ethnographic to Arnoldian meanings for the word. And "culture" had not figured greatly in *Virgin Land*. Despite his belief that science threatened to banish poesy from human life, Smith repeatedly identified poesy with myth, ideology, falsehood, irrationality, and social evils. His critique of Turner depended on a crude dichotomy of fact and figure. And even "Can American Studies Develop a Method?" concluded that the value of individual masterpieces lay in their embodiment of some aspect of culture which could be rigorously verified: "At the very least one might hope for suggestions capable of being formulated as hypotheses and then tested against more extensive evidence." But content analysts meant to do just that, and by concluding with their self-justification, Smith diluted his polemic against technocracy.[27]

"Culture" could not save Smith's humanism. The Arnoldian sense of the word justified the new critics' refusal of history, and the sociological sense of the word emptied culture of consciousness as thoroughly as any statistical reduction. And Smith's enthusiasm for culture hid deeper ironies. He had chastised scholars and the masses for their agrarian nostalgia. They eulogized the wilderness as they civilized it out of existence. Now Smith clung desperately to the memory of an Edenic humanism untrammeled by the academic equivalents of assembly line and smokestack. He rejected the linguistic turn's mechanization of thought and culture much as Leatherstocking had lamented the clearing of the American forest. And like Leatherstocking, Smith ushered in the new order he feared.

Culture opened the temple to the technocratic barbarians. In 1963 Richard Sykes stepped into the opening created by "Can American Studies Develop a Method?" with an article in *American Quarterly:* "American Studies and the Concept of Culture: A Theory and Method." "There comes a point," said Sykes, "when the justification of a new field must exceed a reaction against the narrow perspectives of New Criticism or a purely quantitative social science." If, as Smith said, American studies was the study of American culture, then it was a specialized branch of cultural anthropology: "The materials studied may be literary, but the approach will be that of the student of culture, not the critic. It is time to recognize this fact openly and to start working out its implications." As he saw it, the study of culture demanded the content analysis of social science. Myth and symbol "confuse the issue," said Sykes, "not only because they are words with long and devious histories from which it is difficult to disassociate them, but because they have a certain connotation of the divine and the mysterious." Only a language emptied of divinity, mystery, and "devious history" could be fully rational. Sykes's method looked familiar. The researcher must posit a hypothesis; devise a means of sampling data to test it; prove it "true or false"; and then present the "findings" to other scholars.[28]

By 1963 the philosophers' debate over what constituted a hypothesis and what counted for verification or falsification had reached a frenzy. And it was about to get worse, with Kuhn's *Structure of Scientific Revolutions* in print and structuralism drifting into view. "Culture" broke over American studies like napalm over Da Nang, and within five years Seymour Katz could claim that "the word 'culture' has appeared in almost every attempt at explaining or justifying the aims and methods of American Studies." Katz noted that this did not reflect a utopian consensus. "Culture" had a long and devious history, and critics seldom used the word precisely. He promptly introduced his own definition (borrowed from Leslie White). By 1972, when Robert Berkhofer's "Clio and the Culture Concept" showed up in the *Social Science Quarterly,* "culture" was the new keyword of American studies, and it frequently promoted the methods, if not the avowed values and aims of hard social science. Systems theory had taken the linguistic turn to American studies, and humanism was feeling the pressure.[29]

Culture versus Art: Leo Marx

Virgin Land ended where Turner had ended, with Turner himself. Despite its talk of the idiocy of rural stories for an urban age, the book did not carry that critique through the twentieth century in a way that brought out the gritty texture of modern life. The problem of technology in American culture remained unresolved, almost unexamined, but Henry Nash Smith's vilification of mass culture rang familiar bells. In the fifties one could not open a popular or academic journal without reading some jeremiad against the mechanization of life. Vance Packard's *The Hidden Persuaders* (1957) warned readers that their neighbors were gullible consumer lemmings manipulated by venal advertising executives. Dwight Macdonald warned of the encroachment of "masscult," a middle-brow confection that wrapped artistic dreck inside a genteel crust. Jacques Ellul denounced the new "technological society," C. Wright Mills called it the "fourth epoch," William H. Whyte declared the conformist "organization man" its typical personality, and Arnold Toynbee coined its enduring name: "The Post-Modern Age." Joseph Wood Krutch's pessimistic predictions about the modern temper seemed to be fulfilled, and intellect and art appeared on the verge of an industrialization as complete and painful as that which had overtaken Emerson's New England.[30]

American studies took up these issues with grim enthusiasm. Smith's books on Mark Twain, *Mark Twain: The Development of a Writer* (1962) and *Mark Twain's Fable of Progress* (1964), featured extended readings

of *A Connecticut Yankee in King Arthur's Court,* a work about technology's devastation of an idealized preindustrial society. Twain, like
Turner, could not reconcile progressive ideology with actual experience.
Smith offered no panaceas, and even warned, in tones sadly ironic given
his suspicion of agrarian nostalgia, of the growing ominous presence
of the machine. Perry Miller took a different path and argued in "The
Responsibility of Mind in a Civilization of Machines" that Americans
had always prayed for an industrial world, and now that it was here they
should quit whining about dignity and the price of progress. There was
no point in beating a dead humanist horse and feeling sorry for oneself
simply because one's colleagues in the physical sciences were raking in
grant money hand over fist. America had always prided itself on rewarding people who made things, and if engineers made modern plumbing,
electric light, and airplanes, then they would get the money and the
glory. Miller placed the essay in *The American Scholar,* journal of the
Phi Beta Kappa honors society for excellence in both the humanities
and science, where it was read by a skeptical James Hiner. Hiner fired
back in *American Quarterly.* In assuaging humanist fears Miller had
concentrated on "machines," which, as concrete bits of technology,
were not to be feared. But he subtly elided a truer anxiety, the inarticu-
late but correct sense that the machine was part and parcel of a larger
system of social relations that mechanized human life as locomotives
reduced coal. Hiner warned readers to distinguish a "machine" from
its "system."[31]

One of Miller's students, Leo Marx, had explored these themes in
his 1950 dissertation on Hawthorne, Emerson, and machine technology. From that work Marx refined a series of articles, including a 1956
piece in *The New England Quarterly,* "The Machine in the Garden."
The article debuted a new trope for postindustrial frontier tales, "the
machine," and sketched a Jungian understanding of symbols ("cultural
images") that extended the dualisms of *Virgin Land:* "History peri-
odically renews man's sense of the perils attendant upon the conquest
of nature. This obvious fact lends force to the view, tacit postulate of
much recent criticism, that what we value in art derives from (and resides in) a realm beyond time, or, for that matter, society." Along with
other essays, like "Literature and Covert Culture," coauthored with
Bernard Bowron and sociologist Arnold Rose, "The Machine in the
Garden" helped make Marx a star. His first book, *The Machine in the
Garden,* appeared in 1964 and was probably the single most influential
work in American studies after *Virgin Land.* It inherited Smith's lexi-

con and picked up its thesis where he had left off. How did Euro-Americans incorporate the machine, synecdoche of the new industrial order, into traditional frontier tales? The central American origin myth, declared Marx, took the form of *pastoral,* a genre characterized by a thematic resolution of contradictory forces in an idealized middle state. American culture had emplotted the frontier synthesis as a domesticated rural haven mediating urban civilization and howling wilderness.[32]

Marx imported the pastoral from William Empson's *Some Versions of Pastoral* (1935). Empson called pastoral a "puzzling form which looks proletarian but isn't." Pastoral employs a double plot, which gives each agonist his or her own plot mode but resolves in a way that leads the audience to identify with the protagonist, or even identifies the antagonist with protagonist, or else provides a happy reconciliation of the two. Its conclusion projects a unification of divided social groups under a single symbolic hero. "Clearly," said Empson, "it is important for a nation with a strong class-system to have an art-form that not merely evades but breaks through it, that makes the classes feel part of a larger unity or simply at home with each other." And the double plot allows multiple readings. While most readers identify with the happiest possible resolution, others may highlight the dark side of the story, and Empson's study made room for the role of an active reader in defining a text.[33]

Machine in the Garden used pastoral duplicity to resolve two of the problems raised but not retired by *Virgin Land:* How could one explain the presence of frontier myth in great works of literature? And how did Americans reconcile their romanticization of wilderness, personified by Leatherstocking, with their adulation of civil society, exemplified by the yeoman farmer? As Marx saw it, pastoral was not an irremediably evil myth, as *Virgin Land* had suggested (Marx did not even use the term "myth"). Pastorals could be "sentimental" or "creative." Sentimental pastoral tended toward escapist nostalgia for an imaginary golden age while offering a basically happy ending. The myth of the garden, with its yeoman hero, complemented the more primitive Leatherstocking stories because the yeoman partook of Leatherstocking's independence, pragmatism, and close relation to nature. Leatherstocking could be reconciled with civility because that middle state incorporated the virtues of wilderness without the vices. Marx associated sentimental pastoral with infantilism, ideology, and mass culture. *Creative* pastoral, however, turned the frontier agon into high art. Authors from Hawthorne forward had used it to illuminate the contradictory depths of experience, teasing out its darker morals and turning it back on itself. The duplicity of nature, which figured both as wilderness and garden; of civilization, symbolized both as civil society and threat to personal freedom; and their narrative combination, which might be paradoxical or dialectical, comic or tragic, provided virtually inexhaustible interpretive possibilities.

Leo Marx recast Turner's frontier dialectic. Industrialism and its dark trope, the machine, had generated a counterforce to Arcadian conclusions, and pastoral brought locomotives, factories, and steamboats into frontier tales with varying degrees of success, optimism, and irony. Marx invoked Lionel Trilling's critique of Parrington to summarize the broader meaning of his story: "What Trilling is proposing . . . may be called a dialectical theory of culure. The 'very essence' of a culture, he says, resides in its central conflicts, or contradictions, and its great artists are likely to be those who contain a large part of the dialectic within themselves." For Marx American culture was uniquely dialectical from its origin: "The contrast between the machine and the pastoral ideal dramatizes the great issue of our culture."[34]

Marx traced the history of pastoralism. With a nod to Paul Johnstone, he began with Virgil's *Eclogues* but moved quickly to *The Tempest*, whose comic resolution anticipated "the moral geography of the American imagination." Marx placed *The Tempest* against Elizabethan discovery of the New World in order to illuminate technology's mediation of wilderness and civilization. Prospero's engineering (his magic, derived from scholarly study of arcane texts) has converted a demonic wilderness into an idyllic landscape of beauty and comfort. Caliban, embodiment of the wild, still wanders the island as both evil foil for Prospero's aristocratic justice and partly sympathetic tragic figure. The story ends with Prospero restored to his throne in Milan and the young lovers married, but while this does not endorse primitivism or even the pastoral as anything more than a temporary solution, the dramatic passage from civilization to wilderness transforms the narrative universe: "The model for political reform is neither Milan nor the island as they existed in the beginning; it is a symbolic middle landscape created by mediation between art and nature." The journey prefigures the great themes of American literature as well as Turner's frontier narrative.[35]

In the tales most often treated by *Machine in the Garden*, technology assumed shapes more modern than Prospero's books. The industrial revolution, with its technical innovation (especially the steam engine) and its new ordering of human relations (especially the factory system), entered American literature through the emblem of the machine: the locomotive in Hawthorne, the steamboat in Twain, the dynamo in Adams. In the eighteenth and early nineteenth centuries American intellectuals believed they could assimilate the machine to the garden. For one thing, the machine offered democratic hope. Labor-saving devices promised to free workers for the cultivation of artful virtue. Enlightenment faith in reason allowed a Jefferson to separate machine from system and imagine technological innovation as a thing apart from the alienation, exploitation, and pollution of the factory system. And American belief in the redemptive power of nature allowed a symbolic rehabilitation of machines in rural settings. Machines facilitated the democratic domestication of desolate wilderness, and, framed in a softening green, locomotives and factories became part of the rural republic. By the end of the century, however, voices had begun to undercut the conflation of moral and technical progress. In Thoreau, Twain, and Adams pastoralism declined (or evolved) from comic hope to tragic knowledge of the ironic divorce of literary dream and political experience.

Where Jefferson's pastoral generated a "conservative quietism," the newer fables rewrote the tale as farce. As Nietzsche, Adams, and Krutch had foretold, paradox replaced synthesis, diremption replaced reconciliation, and alienation replaced communion as modernity's metaphors of choice.

This recurrent metaphor of contradiction makes vivid, as no other figure does, the bearing of public events upon private lives. It discloses that our inherited symbols of order and beauty have been divested of meaning. It compels us to recognize that the aspirations once represented by the symbol of an ideal landscape have not, and probably cannot, be embodied in our traditional institutions. It means that an inspiriting vision of a humane community has been reduced to a token of individual survival.

Marx refused to blame the dissolution of pastoralism on "artistic failure." The failure was social: "The machine's sudden entrance into the garden presents a problem that ultimately belongs not to art but to politics." We should point up the situational irony in Marx's ending a historicist study of the ideological work of canonical texts with one of the axiomatic figures of new criticism, the separation of art and politics. Additional ironies dwell in his "divestment of meaning" from traditional symbols, the erosion of traditional institutions, and the dispirit-

ing of humane community. Marx's own story sounds much like sentimental pastoralism's anxieties of decline from a golden age and speaks
to more than Victorian frontier tales.[36]

Machine in the Garden allegorized the decline of humanism. While
Marx identified the "machine" and "technology" with the industrial
revolution, the book belongs, with *Virgin Land,* to debates over the
role of mind, art, and humanism in a computerized consumer world.
The machine stood in for the harder sides of the linguistic turn, the
flattening of historical consciousness, abstract thought, and artistic
creation by the industrial tropes of social science. By the sixties the
machine had clearly extended its imperial grasp to the ivory tower. In
1964, the year Marx's book rolled off the Oxford University presses,
the Free Speech Movement at Berkeley exploded onto national head-
lines and television screens. Atop a parked car, modern primitive Mario
Savio indicted the university for its complicity in the military-industrial
complex and exhorted his fellow students to hurl their bodies against
"the machine." Some did. By 1968 the wildness had spread, and Lionel
Trilling complained of "modernism in the streets." Some academics
joined in. Others saw civil disorder as the sad result of raising an entire
generation in a bureaucratized mass culture. Humanists cultivated their
own special fears, and some of these harmonized with Savio's pastoral
manifesto. From the library, the auditorium, and the faculty lounge,
besieged humanists peered out over the campus green and worried
about evil machinery humming behind the well-financed doors of the
physics departments.[37]

If the physics department seemed safely distant, techno-barbarians
lurked in corridors closer to home. Linguistic analysis had overtaken
departments of philosophy, content analysis dominated pyschology and
sociology, and historians spent more and more time reading regression
coefficients. Even dyed-in-the-wool humanists took up the new languages. Henry Nash Smith had condemned the tendency of social science to strip the world of human meaning and significance. He had
not, however, recognized *Virgin Land*'s attempt to rationalize history
as part and parcel of the technologizing of thought. Marx, in an address
in 1967 before an interdisciplinary conference on history and public
opinion, reprised Smith's defense of methodological pluralism but distanced himself from the elder scholar's vocabularies of verification.
The title said it all: "American Studies—A Defense of an Unscientific
Method."[38]

Marx had wandered far from *Virgin Land*. He now believed American studies had to consider three levels of experience. The first was history or society, the brute facts of existence. In the case of his own work, these were the economic indices of industrialism, rates of production, changes in technology, and so on. The second level was culture, as in "the general culture." This was the system of values and meanings humans attached to their lives. Content analysis had its greatest utility in reconstructing these patterns of popular ideology. But a third level, art, or "high culture," demanded traditional humanist tools. Art was the most abstract of the three categories, and though it ultimately depended on a canon established by scholarly consensus across time, it remained crucial to understanding the other categories. Creative art, more than the other levels, opened up the contradictions at the heart of experience, generating that "enlargement of meaning" found in Hawthorne, Melville, and Twain.

Art recuperated humanist custom, reserved a place for abstract thought in the social sciences, and reconciled the machine of content analysis and the garden of humanist critique. Much as his subject authors had married locomotives to meadows, thereby resolving the tragic doubleness of American life, Marx cleared an Arcadian space between the dismal wilds of modern primitivism and the decadent rationality of hard science. And like Empson's pastoral, this curious form looked proletarian but wasn't. Scientific machine and humanist garden came together in a new academic middle state that saved a place for the democratizing force of technology while identifying it with a more aristocratic order of great texts and their critical keepers. Content analysis sampled the daily lives of common folk, but only high art and the critical class that defined and tended it could tell what it all meant. Marx thus rejoined the frontier and postfrontier worlds left asunder at the conclusion of *Virgin Land*. Pastoral was not just an old frontier tale that slid into the ideological underground with the coming of assembly lines, radio, and bathtub gin; more than false consciousness, pastoralism remained, for both good and evil, the narrative shape of modern life.

Marx returned to history to reconcile art and culture. Appropriately, the great unread, and thus unrepresentative, Herman Melville served as example. A content analysis study of nineteenth-century American culture would probably not sample any work of Melville's. But if one wished to understand nineteenth-century America, one should read *Moby Dick*, even though contemporaries ignored it, because Melville's writing still shaped experience in ways that once popular but now obscure documents did not. In the long run, that is to say, into the twentieth century, *Moby Dick* had profoundly affected American life. "And yet, to say that the novel had a greater influence *upon* the culture is a misleading way of putting it, for it obscures the literal sense in which the enduring work of art *becomes* the culture which produced it. With the passage of time, that is, books of the stature of *Moby Dick* comprise a larger and larger portion of the consciousness of nineteenth-century America that remains effectively alive in the present." History held culture and art in dialogue. Each age passed down its highest elements and these became the new culture, regardless of whether they had been statistical averages at the moment of their creation. As Marx saw it, the endurance of works like *Moby Dick* depended on the "choices" of living individuals, and these, he concluded, formed the "ultimate basis for the method we would call humanistic."[39]

Where Smith used culture to revise history, Marx called on history to save culture. He identified history with consciousness and emplotted it as an "irreversible" progression of "unique events." The construction approached Collingwood's idealism but clashed with the naturalism of a Carl Hempel or a Morton White. It ran head on into Robert Berkhofer's behaviorist text on historical analysis, and Berkhofer, in a 1972 article, identified the idealism of American studies with the "conservative" thinkers of the fifties—Talcott Parsons, Daniel Bell, Daniel Boorstin, Richard Hofstadter, and Louis Hartz, all of whom were denounced by new left historians for having told glossy "consensus" histories of America in which all citizens agreed on aims, ends, and evils.[40]

The problem is not just that Leo Marx (and Smith) avoided the materialist tales that usually underwrote oppositional politics. The difficulties lie in the way they developed their ostensibly proletarian heroes. The masses of *Virgin Land* and *Machine in the Garden* always appear on the side of myth, ideology, and error. Where a Frederick Jackson Turner, a Merle Curti, or a Stephan Thernstrom imagined the new technologies of social science as democratizing forces, Smith and Marx saw the system to which those developments belonged as an engine of enslavement. The real bearers of history, consciousness, and freedom were those critical intellectuals with the talent and training to demythologize the cultural products of industrial capitalism. Despite the recurrence of ideology as a frontier figure, there was little *Capital* or *The German Ideology* in either of these great books in American studies. Marx and Smith re-created the Jeffersonian attitudes that both wished to critique. The idyllic community of artful virtue to which both appealed, the hilltop of green with citizens engaged in contemplation of truth, looked more like an Arcadian company of educated republicans than a mass of pulp-swilling urban proletarians, eyes glazed by consumer narcosis.

What was reaction in one institutional context could be radical in another, and some saw *Machine in the Garden* as a tool of cultural revolution. The politics of mass culture became more, rather than less, tangled as the decade ended. The new scientistic languages facilitated democratic revisions of history, but they also facilitated the delivery of napalm to the fields of Southeast Asia. There were affinities, if not systematic relations, between the statistical analyses of the new left historians, government grants for interdisciplinary social science research, marketing surveys of consumer behavior, and the anonymous body counts and computerized draft rolls of the American military. In such an atmosphere one could read *Machine in the Garden* in a number of ways, and as Kenneth Lynn later observed, the green-covered book found a left-of-center place on many middle-class bookshelves alongside Joseph Reich's *The Greening of America,* Barry Commoner's *The Closing Circle,* and Rachel Carson's *Silent Spring.* Some read *Machine in the Garden* as an allegory of environmentalism, and for these readers the text opened up a new green world and suggested that Henry Nash Smith had been wrong: frontier tales could still inspire revolution.[41]

Explanations of the crisis of humanism and the desacralization of the world came from all corners. Marx and Smith began their stories with the industrial revolution. Jacques Ellul's *Technological Society* (1957) concluded that Baconian method was the source of mechanized modernity. "Technique" characterized thought before it appeared in material culture. Philosopher Martin Heidegger followed Nietzsche's lead in finding the "thingification of Being" implicit in Socratic rationality. The Socratics had conceptualized thought, and once that step had been taken scientific method, assembly lines, and Sputnik were, if not foregone conclusions, hidden potentialities of a way of living that saw the world as an object. These different beginnings projected different morals. If mass culture, bureaucracy, content analysis, and atom bombs resulted from the industrial revolution, one could recuperate humanism. If the story began with Francis Bacon, one could reclaim Christianity. And if one blamed Socratic rationality, then virtually all Western philosophy went out the window. If one went this far, and many did, then pre-Socratic or non-Western tradition looked better and better. One might even, as Benedict had hinted, reclaim myth as an alternative to the rationality of social science and the Euro- and androcentrism of traditional humanism. One could also read myth into historical discourse, as Hayden White argued in *Metahistory*. Before we move on to these developments, we need to hold on to history a bit longer and take another look at *Virgin Land,* historicism, and frontier tales.[42]

Myth, Method, and Manliness

Being an American historian means that one studies American history. The label implies three basic questions.

1. What is history?
2. What is American?
3. What is American history?

To the first query—What is history?—Frederick Jackson Turner responded with Droysen's aphorism, "History is the 'Know Thyself' of humanity," the dialectic of past and present as each remakes the other. To the second—What is American?—he answered that the American was the democratic product of European history's interaction with the wilds of North America. In response to the third question—What is American history?—he synthesized his first two replies: The history of America is the development of human consciousness in the colonization of the Great West. However sophisticated or naive his answers, his forthright delivery suggests the depth of his sense of the historian's responsibilities. Henry Nash Smith believed that theory flirted with metaphysics, and so he bypassed question 1 and went directly to questions 2 and 3. Still, to that unasked question, What is history? *Virgin Land* addressed an oblique response: History is the collective sum of material facts revealed by rational empirical research purified of emotion and ideology. Like George Pierson and Merle Curti, Smith imagined the historian as organization man, a corporate engineer solving discrete problems in a respectably professional setting far from the effeminate metaphors of the masses.

Responding to charges of naive dualism, Smith wrote a new *mea culpa* preface for the 1970 edition of *Virgin Land* and admitted that he had, despite the best intentions, conceived of myths as simple "distortions of empirical fact." He believed the book permitted a richer reading, but his reformulation was paradoxical: "History cannot happen—that is, men cannot engage in purposive group behavior—without images which simultaneously express collective desires and impose coherence on the infinitely numerous and infinitely varied data of experience." Much turns on "purposive group behavior." The phrase marries the Christian and humanist connotations of "purposive" to the naturalistic and behaviorist senses of "group behavior." If we read "purposive group behavior" as that which is intended by a collection of rational agents, then Smith read history in a very traditional sense à la William Dray. The construction does not substantively transform *Virgin Land*'s original contest of myth and reality. As Smith said, "If the impulse toward clarity of form is not controlled by some process of verification, symbols and myths can become dangerous by inciting behavior grossly inappropriate to the given historical situation." He did not spell out what sort of verification would be best, a crucial question since methodology had obviously not prevented his own early confusion and since he had asserted the superiority of an ad hoc humanism. Still, one did not need a compass to chart the vectors of words like "verification" and "behavior." He would not follow Leo Marx in historicizing art and science.[43]

In the event, Smith's distaste for theory, combined with his appeals to reason, amounted to a sophomoric defensive maneuver. Pressed by his critics to justify the description of myth as timeless, deterministic, and evil, Smith invoked the need for rationality and verification; pressed to define the rules that set rationality and verification apart from myth, he refused on the grounds that this would lead down the slippery slope to metaphysics. It was late in the day for such tactics, and at about the same time that Smith was writing his new preface, philosopher Morton White was reprimanding Richard Hofstadter for waving "the rules of rational discourse" while refusing to specify them.

In later years Smith complained that critics had engaged only his preface and that the monograph itself did not suffer from the careless facility of its author's gloss; however vague the theory, the practice remained sound. His suggestion that we reread *Virgin Land* with a new vocabulary is intriguing, but it will not do simply to go back through *Virgin Land* and replace "myths" with "ideologies" or masculine pronouns with feminine pronouns. Relabeling the work's original semantic oppositions will not escape the reverberations set off by its linkage of women and nonwhites with myth, metaphor, and irrationality. Smith's gendering of myth (*virgin* land, the *veil* of literary convention) and his easy conflation of savagery, barbarism, and wilderness place women and natives into the timeless sphere of emotion, affect, and determinism, something to be fought, compartmentalized, and dominated by the masculine reason of history. And given his desire to locate necessity on the darker, feminine side of the equation and to place free will and truth on the other, we should not follow Smith in his proposed readerly revision.

Henry Nash Smith simply adopted the self-understandings, story lines, and gender codes of historians like Pierson and Hofstadter. History was a given sum of reasoned temporal facts. The problem was art. If myth was timeless and history temporal, what was art? Smith, his interest in popular materials notwithstanding, left little doubt that he believed in the intrinsic superiority of great books to pulp. The key was the *relationship* of culture and art. Art was the vernacular transcending the determinism of myth and raising itself to consciousness. Art was a mediating frontier where neither pure rationality nor absolute fantasy held sway. In art the creative individual set his stamp on traditional materials, confronting the unknown with the known while avoiding the horrors of a hyperrational world. Hence Smith's enduring fascination with Mark Twain, the popular American author who carried out the Emersonian project of transfiguring American materials into a universal form.

It takes little work to "textualize" or "contextualize" Henry Nash Smith, but there is some justice in his suggestion that *Virgin Land* might survive the changing of critical calendars. While we cannot rehabilitate its method or even its aims (a simple critique of Turner does not hold for us the fascination it did for the white male academy of 1950), *Virgin Land* continues to teach. Smith held forth scholarly obligation and social responsibility. He disciplined himself for ten years of immersion in what he felt to be "sub-literary" prose. And so we should pay special attention to those rare moments when *Virgin Land* indulges in a canonical text, such as its dialogue with Herman Melville. Why does *Moby Dick* appear in a study of popular culture? *Moby Dick* had virtually no contemporary readers. Even by Smith's theoretical lights, the novel offered no special access to the popular mind. But it did give a brief glimpse into freedom. *Moby Dick* and other "literary" works transcended the workaday metaphysics of popular culture. In these rare moments, thought doubled back on itself and not only pointed up the divide between reality and myth but also *commented* on that chasm.

Melville's West served Smith's own hidden metaphysics. The West was not simply place or process. It was not merely a geographical region or a technical, biological, or cultural border. In a crucial but unusual passage Smith loaded art and let it fly. For Melville the "Wild West, like nature in general, came to seem entirely ambiguous. It was not more certainly good than bad, yet in either case it was terrible and magnificent." What was this existential other against which the American mind created its own identity? Smith relied on Melville to articulate the faith he dared not voice: "Though in many of its aspects this visible world seems formed in love, the invisible spheres were formed in fright." Years after his early essays Smith put to work his fourth frontier, the "violently figurative" border of imaginative intension. Against this terrible, magnificent blankness on the far side of experience and consciousness, humanity raised up its identity.[44]

Our sporadic comments on gender converge at the intersection of art and history in *Virgin Land*. What ought history to be? Smith imagined three potential answers: history as reason, history as art, and history as myth. The first, history as reason, held all the traditional advantages of rational discourse, but in its modernist forms, the mechanistic analyses of the behaviorists, it looked pretty scary. History as art was almost a contradiction in terms, for great art was timeless. And history as myth was what Turner had written, so many fairy tales creating a false consciousness. In some way history had to remain both artful and rational. Recall Smith's claim that some common value held sociology (reason) and literature (art) together. Art and reason were joined by their shared opposition to history as myth. Art and reason invert myth's falsity, unconsciousness, and *effeminacy*. Reason had long been characterized as masculine, active, and virile. Art too, for Smith, held itself apart from myth by its masculine qualities. His treatment of Melville reproduced romantic ideals of artistic creation: the artist as lone individual genius, manfully imposing pattern on chaos, courageously penetrating the dangerous spaces where feminine beauty is transfigured into a masculine *sublime*.[45]

History must remain manly, and a purified masculine intellect must balance reason and art to resist the feminization of culture, thought, and life. Smith believed that American studies was the place where that could happen, so long as its practitioners did not succumb to the wiles of theory. He repeatedly cast "doing" American studies, in contrast to "theorizing" American studies, in agonistic metaphors of work, struggle, and masculine triumph. "Doing" *Virgin Land* was, in his pugilistic phrase, "mixing it up." We will leave to his biographers the joys of psychoanalytic readings, but it is easy to imagine that a professor of litera-

ture molded by 1930s Texas might have felt some social pressure to mas-
culinize his own practice. But we should situate Smith within the academic study of American literature, which, Elizabeth Renker has
shown, was taught at women's colleges long before it was admitted into
"serious" departments of English at leading universities. Little wonder
that an Americanist legitimating his field of study might whip out so
many masculine metaphors. Smith's gender codes also typified the tendency of high modernism to imagine mass culture as feminine in order
to distinguish genuine art from commercial mystification. As Andreas
Huyssen has argued, "Mass Culture as Woman" served as modernism's
other. And we should point up the tradition of gendering specific texts
as part of a process of objectification. For Smith as for Pierson and generations of other thinkers, serious analysis was a masculine endeavor;
narrative was not. At all of these levels American studies would bond
reason with a masculinized art.[46]

Virgin Land's conflicted linguistic loyalties allowed one reviewer
to call the work "fundamentally rationalistic" while permitting a humanist like Roy Harvey Pearce to declare it "a rational book dealing
sympathetically with the irrational." Smith's poesy provoked the suspicions of other readers that he had not understood the real import of
the new languages of verification, system, and rationality. By 1970 the
battlefield between older humanistic approaches to literature and new
naturalistic approaches had heated to incandescence. Behaviorists and
linguistic analysts in the social sciences assimilated "art" and "literature" to other tropes, such as culture, behavior, and language. Smith
and Marx defended the border between high and low culture: reduce
Moby Dick to *Deadwood Dick* and you surrender one of the final sources
of human dignity in a secular world. For believers in hard social science,
even manly appeals to poesy re-created a bad old metaphysics.[47]

In 1972 intellectual historian Bruce Kuklick sharpened such criticisms to a killing point with his essay "Myth and Symbol in American
Studies." "American Studies humanists make a strict dichotomy between consciousness and the world," said Kuklick. This crude "Carte-
sian dualism" (how could one escape "mind" and reach an unmediated
physical reality?) invested consciousness, myth, and art with the force
of Platonic ideas or worse. Kuklick invoked philosopher Gilbert Ryle,
one of the pioneers in the analytic turn. Ryle had denounced spirit,
collective consciousness, and like constructions as a "ghost in the machine," a last residue of a defunct faith in the soul. Exorcise this final
spirit and only actions and propositions remained. In fact, these were

the only data that scholars could properly know; all others (poetic truth, mythic archetypes, God) were, as logical positivists had put it, "meaningless," since they could be justified only with supra-empirical appeals, and "if myth-symbol generalizations have any substance, they must be subjected to falsification by the conclusion of 'lower-level' historical research." While *Virgin Land*'s figures offered easy targets, Leo Marx's constructions demanded a different tack, and Kuklick denounced them for defining great texts in terms of their importance for present-day critics rather than searching for the original intentions of their authors. The claim that great books were great because they had been so defined through time by critical consensus legitimized a humanist "mandarin caste."[48]

Few of Kuklick's contemporaries would so readily invoke Gilbert Ryle as a theorist of choice, but Kuklick's attack on humanism had sympathizers on all political and epistemic sides. *New Literary History,* the journal in which Marx's "Defense of an Unscientific Method" appeared in 1969, had by the seventies become one of the principal sources of antihumanist theory for literary critics who had not found time in the sixties to read Claude Lévi-Strauss, Roland Barthes, or Michel Foucault. Structuralism, along with its "poststructuralist" critics, would dissolve both Smith's myths, Marx's humanistic metaphors, and even Kuklick's authorial intentions into the postindustrial tropes of "system" and "sign." In its more aggressive forms, the works of Michel Foucault the most powerful, the new critical theorizing would claim that humanism, which had seen itself liberating humanity from ignorance and hierarchy, had produced ruthlessly totalitarian systems of intellectual and physical repression.

Structuralism found a place in the so-called "Crisis in American Studies," and while Smith and Marx assailed the movement head on, others attempted to assimilate the new methods. Works like John Cawelti's *The Six-Gun Mystique* (1971) and Will Wright's *Six-Guns and Society* (1975) imported Lévi-Straussian vocabularies. And Cecil F. Tate's *The Search for a Method in American Studies* (1973) turned the codes and arrows of structuralist method back on the field and concluded that "the results and discoveries of American Studies are completely compatible with the method of analysis popularly called structuralism." Henry Nash Smith was justifiably skeptical: "It's startling how much discussion of theory can be generated without any practical enterprise." Smith's reticence here had some grounds, for Tate largely failed to disaggregate the methods of his subjects; the stacks of punched computer cards lying behind Lévi-Strauss's monographs lay worlds away from Smith's archival notes. While American studies had produced creative accounts of dualisms in American life, and some structuralists spent volumes working out binary equations, not all dyads were created equal. While Smith's opposition of nature and civilization, or Leo Marx's dialectic of culture, or Richard Chase's contradictions of American romance *could* be assimilated to structuralist equations, their common appeals to consciousness, free will, and individual agency would not survive the operation.[49]

While structuralism and its epigoni struggled with older vocabularies, political critique produced a host of important studies. Annette Kolodny's *The Lay of the Land* (1974) satirized *Virgin Land*'s gendered title, and she pursued a feminist analysis of the ways in which centuries of masculine discourse had gendered the landscape, producing images of a feminine nature awaiting conquest and exploitation and legitimating patriarchal structures in the society that dreamed the myths of the garden and the desert. Another period work, Richard Slotkin's *Regeneration through Violence* (1973), struck more sparks, whether because of its timely linkage of Turnerian history with the military debacle in Vietnam or because of a heavily male academe's disinterest in feminist critique. Both works, though, reproduced traditional American studies methods, Kolodny narrating a heavily footnoted story based on archival and primary accounts and Slotkin a Jungian study of archetypal myths in American discourse. And both stepped to the left of their narrative parents. Still, "left" may be too simple a term; by 1973 the politics of opposition was not a simple matter of location on an ideological line. A new politics of difference—gender, ethnicity, and sexual orientation—complicated class politics. Democratization took on new colors, some of them bright and hopeful, others depressingly shadowed.[50]

Culture opened new doors, and in the seventies Henry Nash Smith ventured through them. He was ready to admit that *Virgin Land, American Adam, Machine in the Garden,* and even *Lay of the Land* owed more to Turnerian frontier tales than their authors intended or realized. None disagreed that the frontier was the preeminent creative force in the making of an American consciousness. All echoed the opposition of wilderness and civilization, nature and history, as the dominant conflict, contradiction, or dialectic of American culture. While all effectively inverted Turner's morals and found darker, more ambiguous themes, subplots, and endings for the story, all had adopted his basic conflict and made white middle-class males (in Kolodny's case, white middle-class females) the tale's protagonists. As a result, American democracy looked much more shadowy and tragic than it had in Turner's conclusions, but an essentially Euro-American conception of the frontier made up the narrative kernel of American history.

Smith chose a "third world" forum for his most confessional public essay. In "*Virgin Land* Revisited," originally delivered at the 1972 Modern Language Association conference but contributed to the *Indian Journal of American Studies,* Smith conceded that "even though the last chapter of *Virgin Land* questions the historical accuracy of the Turner thesis, I had at that time still not fully extricated myself from his unconscious assumptions." Whitman's "Passage to India," Turner's *Frontier,* and Smith's *Virgin Land* all pointed down the textual path to Vietnam. Smith, who had recently presided over an explosive season of the MLA, an institution now regarded by student protesters as a bastion of the military-industrial machine, credited those who had contributed to his political education: "I owe the dawning recognition of my own naiveté to the revisionist historians and even to the young agitators who have discovered in recent years that by identifying themselves with Native Americans as another oppressed minority they acquire an additional set of slogans with which to abuse the Establishment." While disavowing his earlier idealism, Smith was not yet ready to endorse a new theoretical language. He did, however, recognize the currency of an entirely new set of frontier figures and embraced the double plot: "If the conquest of the continent was a glorious triumph for progress and civilization, it was also a prolonged act of genocide."[51]

Culture had truly come to American studies.

Queer Frontiers

Henry Nash Smith's recognition that the American mind was a mind against itself was laudable if belated. With the clarity of hindsight, we can find diversity in even that blandest of decades, the fifties. While period monographs generally characterized the American frontier hero as white, middle-class, male, and heterosexual, a handful of works followed different paths. When in 1973 Smith alluded to revisionist historians who had helped him reimagine the frontier narrative, one of those he had in mind was Roy Harvey Pearce. Even in 1953 Pearce's *Savages of America,* later reprinted as *Savagism and Civiliza-*

tion, ought to have been a scholarly triumph. Its Lovejoyan "history of ideas" method, humanist convictions, careful research, and lucid prose ought to have won for the work a position near the summit of American studies. They did not. Years later Pearce recalled that the manuscript had been rejected twice before Johns Hopkins University Press decided to chance it, and even that press demanded he partially subsidize the printing.[52]

Pearce had studied with philosopher Arthur O. Lovejoy, best known as the author of *The Great Chain of Being* and chief spokesman for the method he called "the historiography of ideas." Lovejoy's seminal 1938 article called for investigation of "unit-ideas." Critics often denounced these as neo-Platonic forms, but his programmatic definition was more concrete, and expansive, than critics allowed. Unit-ideas were, in his many words, "types of categories, thoughts concerning particular aspects of common experience, implicit or explicit presuppositions, sacred formulas and catchwords, specific philosophical theorems, or the larger hypotheses, generalizations, or methodological assumptions of various sciences—which have long life-histories of their own." His work tended toward bookishly abstract discussions, but his student's dissertation, *Savages of America,* exemplified Lovejoy's ideal history. Pearce called "savagism" an "Idea . . . a predication, explicit or implicit, which offers a solution of a major human problem"; he described the "Indian" as the "Symbol" derived from the Idea; and he called each of the symbol's particular textual manifestations an "Image." Unlike the timeless myths of *Virgin Land,* these were historic figures read within larger temporal and cultural horizons of meaning.[53]

Savagism was the counterconcept of civilization. By defining savagery, early Euro-Americans had, through negation, defined themselves: "The Indian as savage defined precisely what the civilized man was not." The process of marking out some opposing force against which to create a sense of selfhood was part of "our fundamental psychological character as humans." Euro-Americans resolved the tension between savagism and civilization by historicizing them. Universal history avoided "cultural relativism" by imagining savage and civil life as sequences in a cosmic drama rather than radically opposed alternatives. The tale followed a more than vaguely Hegelian plot. Europeans had brought notions of wildness and states of nature with them to native North America. Savage society and its figures were from the first encounters highly ambiguous: Indians could be noble or ignoble, appealing or threatening. From these antitheses came savagism, a complex combination of Christian theology and Scottish philosophies of the stages of humanity made into a moralistic narrative into which Native America could be fitted. The resolution placed both noble and ignoble savages safely in the "past" of universal history and legitimated Anglo-American ideology.[54]

Pearce's summation integrated history and culture in a manner unusual for the early fifties.

The American solution was worked out as an element in an idea of progress. Cultures are good, it was held, as they allow for full realization of man's essential and absolute moral nature; and man realizes this nature as he progresses historically from a lesser to a greater good, from the simple to the complex, from savagism to civilization. Westward American progress would, in fact, be understood to be reproducing this historical progression; and the savage would be understood as one who had not and somehow could not progress into the civilized. . . . For the Indian was the remnant of a savage past away from which civilized men had struggled to grow. To study him was to study the past. To civilize him was to triumph over the past. To kill him was to kill the past. History would thus be the key to the moral worth of cultures; the history of American civilization would thus be conceived of as three-dimensional, progressing from past to present, from east to west, from lower to higher.

The practical problems of cultural conflict stimulated the rise of historical consciousness. Universal history held cultural relativism at bay and allowed Turnerians to admire the tribal past while believing that modern Euro-American life was better still. But the passage holds more than a culture critic's garden-variety denunciation of naive faith in progress.[55]

Pearce's reading of Victorian frontier tales allegorized the historical treatment of Native America by his own contemporaries, for the tropes he described in an impressive selection of primary texts still shaped scholarly stories. From a series of early national narrative poems, Pearce neatly abstracted the emplotment that allowed Euro-Americans to mingle pity and censure, regret and joy, when explaining the vanishing antagonist: "The Indian is described for what he is, a noble savage. The coming of the white man is described for what it is, the introduction of agrarian civilization. And the Indian is shown dying or moving west, often with a vision of the great civilized life which is to come after him, occasionally with the hope that he himself can become civilized." From Turner's dissertation to Billington's textbook, from the assimilationist narratives of MacLeod to those of Linton, all the *topoi* are here, all the conventions that allowed twentieth-century readers to enjoy a frontier tragedy one minute and a comedy the next with no sense of conflict. And the telling enabled a *Virgin Land* or *Machine in the Garden* to conflate savages with wilderness, imagining the Indian as "man out of society and out of history," and turn its attention to modernity.[56]

Savages of America did not itself escape these traditions. Pearce hoped his story would speak to postwar America, and he closed with Melville's Queequeg: "We cannibals must help these Christians." But his sophisticated tolerance grew partly out of a sense that he and his readers could afford it, since "the Indian is no great personal issue to us." So far as Pearce saw the problem in 1953, the study was a postmortem. So far as the Library of Congress was concerned, he was right, and they cataloged the book this way: "1. Indians of North America—Cultural assimilation." So we should not be surprised to learn that many, if not most readers read the book inside the assimilationist tragedy it sought to elucidate.[57]

Reading *Savages of America* as an assimilationist tragedy meant walling it off from the mainstream of American studies. It is interesting that one of the only appreciative reviews came from Henry Nash Smith, who later lamented that *Virgin Land* had not taken advantage of the materials opened up by *Savages of America*. Of course, Pearce's work had not been unknown to Smith in the late forties. *Virgin Land* had cited Pearce's 1947 article "The Leatherstocking Tales Re-examined," and Smith ought to have read another Pearce essay, "The Significances of the Captivity Narrative," published that same year in *American Literature,* the premier journal in the field. But neither these nor *Savages of America* nor Pearce's 1957 *Ethnohistory* essay, "The Metaphysics of Indian-Hating: Leatherstocking Unmasked," became canonical texts for American studies. Pearce's work could not be added to the wilderness and nature narratives at the center of the conversation. Read the story of the westward movement as the imperial subordination of savagism to civilization and even the high art of Emerson, Hawthorne, and Thoreau—all those primitivist voices of radical protest with which white male literary historians identified in their revolt against the mass society—turned bloody, their "enlargements of meaning" revealed as oblique legitimations of imperialism, their leafy landscapes magically emptied of tribal life, Caliban quietly exiting stage left as the new hero, the urban proletarian cum critical intellectual, entered stage right.[58]

The significance of *Savages of America* was the more easily missed as it fell into a stylistic netherworld bounded by the mechanistic tropes of social science, the multilingual abstractions of Arthur Lovejoy, and the splendiferous figures of myth criticism. Culture, as Pearce used it in the fifties, closely resembled the trope of ethnographic discourse, save that the intellectual historian allied it with the more humanistic and organic constructions of a Benedict or a Lovejoy. (The work that came closest to the topical focus of *Savages of America* was anthropologist A. Irving Hallowell's "The Backwash of the Frontier.") Avoiding "myth" made it difficult for readers to place the text in the mainstream of American studies or myth criticism, the two chief alternatives to new criticism. And Pearce's brand of idealism found few enthusiasts. In a 1958 article, "Historicism Once More," he charted a synthesis of literature and history that, compared with the discussions in *American Quarterly*, offered a sophisticated historicism and explored a refigured *humanitas* that might have escaped the debate's naive polarities of humanism and science. But the piece was widely ignored. Pearce's *Savages of America* had opened up its story twenty years earlier, and when American studies finally faced the topic, the book's idealistic vocabularies looked positively antediluvian to a new group of young scholars socialized into an electronic age.[59]

Roy Harvey Pearce was not the only literary historian to lament the narrative politics of savagism. In 1958 another author complained of the "glorification of the Plains savage at the expense of the semicivilized sedentary Indian of Mexico." According to Américo Paredes, "After the 1870s, when the Indian danger was past, it was possible to idealize the Plains savage. But the 'Mexican problem' remained." In popular and scholarly Anglo-American discourse, "A distinction was drawn between the noble Plains Indian and the degenerate ancestor of the Mexican." The ethnographer's love of cultural purity, the idealization of the vanishing antagonist, and the ascendancy of assimilationist morals ensured the academic marginalization of the Mexicans, peoples derived from the mixing of European and native. *"With His Pistol in His Hand": A Border Ballad and Its Hero* (1958) tried to pull that margin into the center of scholarly attention. Like Pearce's *Savages of America*, Paredes's text was an innovative study that might have reoriented American studies but did not, at least not immediately.[60]

In 1930s Texas, while Walter Prescott Webb completed his *Texas Rangers* and *Great Plains* and a young Henry Nash Smith taught at Southern Methodist University and checked the proofs of "What Is the Frontier?" Américo Paredes was becoming an accomplished musician in the caste society of south Texas, gaining fluency in the musical tradition known as the *corrido*, a fast-paced heroic ballad popular in the Rio Grande region. After serving in the military in the war, Paredes took a bachelor's degree at the University of Texas, Austin. Baccalaureate in hand, he armed himself with a tape recorder (funded by a research assistantship courtesy of Mody Boatright, one of Turner's early critics) and worked through the field studies for his dissertation, quickly published by University of Texas Press. The book did what Pearce's study had only suggested: it gave voice to a traditional antagonist of academic frontier tales, describing the rise of historical consciousness along a cultural border, a popular memory based in both indigenous and European oral tradition and encouraged by interethnic conflict. A compact paragraph framed the subject: "*El Corrido de Gregorio Cortez*, then, is a Border Mexican ballad, 'Mexican' being understood in a cultural sense, without reference to citizenship or to 'blood.' But we must stress 'Border' too. It is as a border that the lower Rio Grande has made its mark: in legend, in song, and in those documented old men's tales called histories."[61]

"*With His Pistol in His Hand*" reclaimed frontier *topoi*. The border, *la frontera*, and its social landscape bore all the pseudo-Turnerian and Boltonian marks of its frontier past one might expect to find in a period work: "Isolated by natural barriers, the country was still unexplored long after the initial wave of Spanish conquest had spent itself," and its "colonization" followed the familiar pattern, "settled much like the lands occupied by westward-pushing American pioneers." Paredes's use of "settlement," "colonization," and "occupation" distanced his telling from naive celebrations of noble savagery and distinguished the Mexican frontier from the better-known Anglo and Spanish frontiers: "The Indians seem to have given little trouble. They were neither exterminated in the English way, nor enslaved according to the usual Spanish way. . . . [T]he Indians, who began as vaqueros and sheepherders for the colonists, were absorbed into the blood and culture of the Spanish settlers." The result was a "basically Spanish culture" with the usual democratic existence that "fostered a natural equality among men," where the typical "borderer" was a "self-sufficient landholder," where the "peon" "could and did rise in the social scale," and where devotion to individual rights did not erode social loyalty.[62]

Into this pastoral idyll broke the Anglo invasion, culminating in the war between the United States and Mexico and memorialized in the Treaty of Guadalupe Hidalgo. The treaty added the "final element" to this prelude to the rise of the *corrido:* "a border." "The river, which had been a focal point, became a dividing line. Men were expected to consider their relatives and closest neighbors, the people just across the river, as foreigners in a foreign land. A restless and acquisitive people, exercising the rights of conquest, disturbed the old ways." By page 15 Paredes had resolved the original dialectic of native and European into a fundamentally "Spanish" folk culture, now threatened by the march of the Anglo-American empire. As in the ethnographic tragedy, the Turnerian protagonist became antagonist. The "new ways" of Anglo-America provided the counterforce, the Texas Ranger its principal personification. Democracy and the "old ways" stood at risk, and the *corrido* formalized an oppositional historical consciousness for its defense.[63]

It must have demanded some restraint for Paredes not to thoroughly demonize the Texas Rangers. Webb's and J. Frank Dobie's studies of the Rangers plumbed the depths of hagiography, but with the author of *The Great Plains* himself installed across the campus, discretion was the better part of scholarly valor. Paredes adopted an ingenious approach, one that has since become a convention of subaltern scholarly narrative. He called Anglo historiography "legendary" while denying it the redeeming status of an authentic folk art. The Anglo-Texan "disappoints us in a folkloristic sense," said Paredes. Typical elements of Anglo-Texan literary culture include depictions of Mexicans as cruel, cowardly, and degenerate. But this legend does not appear in "cowboy ballads" or the "folk tales of the people of Texas," Paredes declared (though he adduced no evidence in support of this suspect claim). One found the legend in print, reproduced by historians. He had no difficulty culling benighted racist passages from Webb's books; in *The Great Plains* Webb had claimed that the blood of the Mexican Indian, "when compared with that of the Plains Indian, was as ditch water." *The Texas Rangers* offered even more egregious constructions, and behind the "superhuman Ranger" Paredes espied "Beowulf, Roland, and the Cid." But Webb's history was not genuine folk memory elevated to historical scholarship.

The difference, and it is a fundamental one, between folklore and the Texas legend is that the latter is not usually found in the oral traditions of those groups of Texas people that one might consider folk. It appears in two widely dissimilar places: in the written works of the literary and the educated and orally among a class of rootless adventurers who have used the legend for very practical purposes. One must classify the Texas legend as pseudo-folklore. Disguised as fact, it still plays a major role in Texas history.[64]

The distinction was crucial. Like Ruth Benedict and unlike Henry Nash Smith, Paredes wished to redeem folk memory. But this raised the specter of relativism. If Anglo histories were as mythic as the Mexican border ballads, why justify choosing one tale over the other? For Benedict the grounds had been both artistic (native myths accessed transcendent truth) and pragmatic (mythic thought had instrumental value for a rationalized age). For Paredes less rode on transcendent values and more on narrative politics. The pseudofolklore of the Anglos belonged to elites and served to legitimate political repression and manipulate popular opinion. Authentic folklore, in contrast, issued spontaneously and "naturally" from within the organic "traditions" of a people. It belonged to people "one might consider folk," and Webb and his "rootless adventurer" contingent did not count. When Turner positioned himself against the narratives of Great Men, he had set up the midwestern frontiersman as a democratic hero. When Webb decried the midwesterner's colonial mistreatment of the Southwest, he portrayed the southwesterner, the Plainsman, as the authentically subaltern voice of the people. Now cheering for the underdog took its toll on the Anglo male hero.

The *corrido* had deep roots. Paredes traced it back to the *romances fronterizos* of medieval Spain, the balladry of the Cid, stimulated by the interethnic conflict between Christianity and Islam and nourished by the "democratic spirit in the folk communities of medieval Europe." It also owed something to the Scottish border ballads and their themes of "resistance against outside encroachment." Curiously, but in keeping with his insistence on the Hispanicism of Border Mexican culture, Paredes did not mention Native American oral tradition, although he would have been familiar with the burgeoning work in this area, if only as a reader of the *Journal of American Folklore*. He did, though, acknowledge the significance of Great Mexican balladry. As these traditions interwove, formal conventions solidified, and "the *corrido* of border conflict assumes its most characteristic form when its subject deals with the conflict between Border Mexican and Anglo-Texan, with the Mexican—outnumbered and pistol in hand—defending his 'right' against the *rinches* [Rangers]."[65]

"The Ballad of Gregorio Cortez" reproduced this plotline and commemorated an historic event known in Paredes's childhood. In 1901 a *vaquero*-turned-farmer named Gregorio Cortez shot and killed an Anglo sheriff in a gunfight, a needless confrontation not uncommon in encounters between Anglo-Texas political authorities and Mexicanos.

A bad translator, a troublesome history, and a misunderstanding left a man dead. Cortez fled and eluded capture through a series of suitably heroic adventures. Finally taken, he was acquitted of the murder of the sheriff but convicted of the murder of one of the pursuing Rangers. After nine years in a Texas prison, he received a pardon from the governor. Cortez was for some time the center of attention in south Texas, and his cause was celebrated by Mexicanos harboring generations of resentment of Anglo dominance.

Paredes redeemed folk romance as a subaltern narrative form. Folk tradition was, he said at the outset, local, democratic, organic, and peaceful. Threatened by outside forces, it created a heroic story that focused political resistance and reasserted the power of an older pastoral order against the pressure of Anglo modernity. As Northrop Frye had pointed out a year earlier, romance held its "genuinely proletarian element," which Paredes meant to exploit. Rather than transcribing directly his interviews and conversations with the "folk," Paredes pushed the limits of what in the fifties was still considered legitimate scholarly license and glossed the exegesis of the ballad as it might have been told by an idealized informant. The result drew a stylized (and Anglicized) border Mexican vernacular into a scholarly text. In lesser hands the maneuver might have proved disastrous; Paredes's literary skill carried it off, and a selection offers a sense of it: "No man has killed more sheriffs than did Gregorio Cortez, and he always fought alone. For that is the way real men fight, always on their own. There are young men around here today, who think they are brave. Dangerous men they call themselves, and it takes five or six of them to jump a fellow and slash him in the arm. Or they hide in the brush and fill him full of buckshot as he goes by. They are not men. But that was not the way with Gregorio Cortez, for he was a real man." For twenty pages such prose imparts to the monograph the authority of authenticity. Like his ideal *corrido,* it seems to flow "naturally" out of local tradition.[66]

"With His Pistol in His Hand" also disentangled the ballad's descriptions of events from the documentary record, comparing "legend" with "fact," while encouraging writer and reader to identify with the ballad's hero. Paredes found that although fact, fancy, and mythology blended in the *corridos,* "one of the most striking things about Gregorio Cortez is the way that the actual facts of his life conformed to pre-existing legend. . . . It was as if the Border people had dreamed Gregorio Cortez before producing him, and had sung his life and his deeds before he was born." The mythic truth in the "Ballad of

Gregorio Cortez" lay not in some transcendent realm but in the narrative texture of daily life, in cultural experience organized according to
the forms of frontier romance.[67]

Many commentators have described *"With His Pistol in His Hand"*
as a counterhegemonic discourse resisting the assimilationist politics of
Anglo society, but the book is both more and less than that. For a start,
there are subtle tensions between Frye's claims for the proletarian resonance of romance and Paredes's insistence on the need for a folk art to
authenticate its subaltern standpoint. The "folk" and the proletariat are
not identical. Gregorio Cortez represents Paredes's idealized frontiersman, the self-sufficient man of property defending his rights against
usurpers. He is not a classically "revolutionary" figure but a bourgeois
landholder refigured in a new scholarly context. There did exist Border
Mexican *corridos* that described more traditional proletarians, usually
outlaws, but the "proletarian ballad's concept of the hero as an outlaw
who robs the rich to give to the poor does not gain acceptance. . . . The
hero . . . is not the highwayman or the smuggler, but the peaceful man
who defends his right." The central figures of the "Ballad of Gregorio
Cortez" are less a subversion of the tenets of private property (as many
Rangers and Anglo capitalists believed) and more a conservative affirmation of the value of a stable, propertied order against the revolution
threatened by Anglo modernity.[68]

"With His Pistol in His Hand" likewise took up many scholarly traditions in frontier narrative. Its pseudo-Turnerian celebration of the
Mexican "settlement" of the native lands of south Texas celebrates
Mexican rather than Anglo imperialism. Where the Anglos exterminated and the Spanish enslaved the Indians, Mexican culture peacefully
absorbed them. Paredes's description of the ensuing society as "basically" Hispanic, his enthusiasm for Spanish tradition, and his mysterious omission of native oral tradition (even though he does mention the
importance of Coyote, the trickster, to the *corrido*) push the story
toward this moral. Significantly, the frontier synthesis on which the
book ends is not native and European but Mexican and Anglo, "an
international phenomenon straddling the border between Mexico and
the United States and partaking of the influences from both cultures."
And Paredes projected a further reconciliation as Mexican and Anglo
find a common enemy in world war: "Thus the old folk communities
straddling the international line at the Rio Grande were absorbed into
their respective countries. The era of border conflict had passed, but its
heroes survived in the *corridos* and the legends, to linger in the memo-

ries of a new generation until the last old man dies." The story sweeps from culture to nation, from the local to global, from the isolated folk communities of the premodern world to the integrated postindustrial society.[69]

Of all the figures we have read, Paredes falls perhaps the closest to Turner, for the poet of Anglo-American imperialism and its Hispano critic share certain narrative conventions, historical tastes, and even political morals. The likeness rests partly on genetic connections, notably the willingness of Paredes to locate his study in a tradition of frontier historiography which he extended, à la the Boltonians, into medieval Europe. But affinities run deeper. In his pastoral, as in Turner's, we see the frontiersman defending his property rights against the illegitimate incursions of the state. The projected moral order is an idealized rural, patriarchal, and petit bourgeois American paradise standing out in stark relief against the political reaction of Europe. To legitimate this folksy affair, each imagined popular memory or myth as somehow continuous with historical consciousness. For Turner history migrated from the "painted scalp" to the printed page but remained history throughout its journey. With local pride, he described his scholarly endeavors as a western *Volksgeist* raising itself up into national consciousness. For Paredes myth and history represented complementary aspects of a single realm of human imagination. The lack of a true folk origin delegitimated Webb's hagiographies, while historical source criticism authenticated the *corrido*. Moreover, the generic forms of folk memory actually structure experience. Turner would have loved the construction.

Each saw his story as a subaltern discourse gathering hidden heroes into the scholarly light. Arrayed against the Great White Men of New England and the AHA, Turner's potentially reactionary pastoral could serve fairly radical ends. Set against the Great White Frontiersmen of the University of Texas, Paredes's potentially reactionary pastoral could do the same. The politics of each, as Dewey might have said, resided not in some narrative essence but shifted with each reading. And *"With His Pistol in His Hand"* still circles uneasily about its patriarchal morals.

If narrative politics changes with telling, reading, and textual situation, then much rides on who does the telling and situating. Recall Paredes's description of history as "tales told by old men." Its ironic inversion of "old wives' tales" aside, the construction is quite serious. Not only did Paredes see the *corrido* as a traditionally masculine form (written and performed by men) but for him it modeled historical imagination generally. A patrilineal historical consciousness may be expected to privilege experience encoded as "male," and the "Ballad of Gregorio Cortez" does just that. Its agonistic emplotment and celebration of model masculine behavior ("a real man always fights alone") project a universe of manly conflict reminiscent of the romances of heroic ages: the ancient Greeks, the Icelandic Norse, and more directly the balladry of the Cid. This is a world and a history in which women remain as silent as Turner's pioneer mothers. We should not uncritically conflate the patriarchy of Turner's Midwest with the patriarchy of Paredes's south Texas, but the kinship suggests the potential for even subaltern discourse to project a hero by marginalizing others. Radical in one position but reactionary in the next, *"With His Pistol in His Hand"* helps illuminate the politics of memory.

While scholars often imagine interest in cultural conflict as a product of the sixties, Pearce and Paredes had opened that door before the decade opened. Other themes associated with postmodernism and sixties-era rebellion also surfaced well in advance of the better publicized academic upheavals. In 1948 a young critic named Leslie Fiedler placed gender, sexuality, and miscegenation at the center of American historical imagination. In "Come Back to the Raft Ag'in, Huck Honey!" Fiedler declared that the Negro and the homosexual had become interwoven "stock literary themes" because they expiated the nation's historic guilt. Where classic European literature centered on "heterosexual passion," great American novels turned on the "mutual love of *a white man and a colored*." Think of Huck and Jim in *Huckleberry Finn;* Ishmael and Queequeg in *Moby Dick;* Natty Bumppo and Chingachgook in *The Deerslayer;* these are the key relationships of those books, all are forcefully homoerotic, and all of the texts are common assignments for the edification of young children. Fiedler dramatically rendered the subtext for white male readers:

Our dark-skinned beloved will take us, we assure ourselves, when we have been cut off, or have cut ourselves off from all others, without rancor or the insult of forgiveness; he will fold us in his arms saying "Honey" or "Aikane!", he will comfort us, as if our offense against him were long ago remitted, were never truly *real*. . . . It is a dream so sentimental, so outrageous, so desperate that it redeems our concept of boyhood from nostalgia to tragedy.

These were not words to win the heart of a Perry Miller. Outrageous they were indeed, with the nation still segregated, assimilation a word of the hour, and homosexuality identified by McCarthyites as a characteristic communist tendency.[70]

Fiedler instantly earned a reputation for flamboyance, though none of the canonical texts in American studies followed his lead in exploring the politics of sexuality; indeed, it is difficult to identify a major work of American studies prior to the seventies which dealt seriously with gender. Fiedler had this field to himself, and if his synaptic leaps and stylistic flourishes were trendy to the point of suspicion, much of his work today looks prescient. In 1968 *The Return of the Vanishing American* again showed the critic in eruption. While most reviewers dwelled on its outrageous advocacy of psychedelic drugs for healing the nation's shattered memory, we should focus our attention on different themes. The dedication, "With thanks to the Blackfoot tribe who adopted me," and the epigram, a passage from Claude Lévi-Strauss eulogizing the Indians "destined for extinction," explained the book's self-description as a "venture in literary anthropology." "It is the presence of the Indian," declared Fiedler, "which defines the mythological West. . . . The heart of the Western is not the confrontation with the alien landscape . . . but the encounter with the Indian." That encounter generally followed one of two distinct plots ending in either the "metamorphosis" of the white or the "annihilation" of the Indian. "In either case, the tensions of the encounter are resolved by eliminating one of the mythological partners." The white could transform himself through ritual or symbol (including drugs) or else resort to "genocide" and "eliminate the Indian" ("our homegrown Final Solution").[71]

After considering Caliban and Shakespeare's *The Tempest* ("a paradigm of the tragi-comedy of the plantation"), Fiedler was ready to revise some of his own work. In *Love and Death in the American Novel* (1960) he had painted the "Battle of the Sexes" as America's impoverished substitute for the class struggle. But this, he had come to understand, was merely the "comic version of the class struggle; race conflict constitutes the pathetic, or even tragic version." *Return of the Vanishing American* returned homosexuality to the center of the story and the "real West": "a place to which White male Americans flee from their own women into the arms of Indian males, but which those White women, in their inexorable advance from coast to coast, destroy." The book also, albeit briefly, treated the works of several homosexual authors, Truman Capote, James Purdy, and Hart Crane. Fiedler singled out *In Cold Blood* as an especially pure rendering of the basic plot, a white man and an Indian (Perry's mother, he explained, was Cherokee), "bound in homosexual alliance against the respectable White world around them." Readers thus far might have expected Fiedler himself to trot out the old assimilationist morals for yet another swing at the reeling white bourgeois conscience, but he had a different end in view, one that was generally missed by reviewers in their concern for what Fiedler might have been taking.[72]

Fiedler captured a note from D. H. Lawrence and made of it an anthem for a queer multicultural world. We should see the quote in full, partly for its own period wonder as one of Lawrence's many gems and partly to understand the ends to which his successor turned it: "The moment the last nuclei of Red life break up in America, then the white man will have to reckon with the full force of the demon of the continent . . . within the present generation the surviving Red Indians are due to merge in the great white swamp. Then the Daimon of America will work overtly, and we shall see real changes." As Fiedler put it, "His *then* is our *now.*" But he quickly damped the assimilationist spin Lawrence had given the passage. "To be sure, the Indian has not disappeared at all 'into the great White [sic] swamp,' but has begun to reinvent himself—in part out of what remains of his own tribal lore, in part out of the mythology and science created by the White men to explain him to themselves." Fiedler, his finger to the winds of fashion, had already detected the shift in ethnographic storytelling, and his choice of verb, "to reinvent," pointed up a key word for a later decade. But he was racing to radical morals. "The 'New Race' which Lawrence foresaw . . . demands a New Myth." "The heart of the matter," what Lawrence sensed dimly but could not quite articulate, was that "from the nonconsummated marriage of males the New Race would come." Fiedler exhorted Americans to follow the frontier trail leading to white metamorphosis rather than Indian genocide. He offered three rites of symbolic passage pointing toward a redemptive ending. Two of them, the use of hallucinogens and dialogue with insanity, provoked reviewers, but the third solution was the truest: "What we demand," he concluded, is "the old, old fable of the White outcast and the noble Red Man joined together against home and mother, against the female world of civilization." Fiedler had queered the frontier and made it the nation's future.[73]

The queer frontier did not draw the attention that allusions to psychedelia and psychosis excited. Cynical readers might even blame the homoeroticism of the work on its author's other enthusiasms and imagine it as a predictable by-product of drug abuse or perhaps the last resort of a critic desperate to shock a jaded audience. But Fiedler did not claim that his brave new world was an invention of contemporary counter-culture. He appealed to national memory: "It is easy to forget how those first hippies of the Western World, Raleigh, Marlowe, and company, cultivated a life-style based on homosexuality, a contempt for Established religion, and 'drinking' tobacco." Whatever merits Fiedler's account might claim as social history, and they were not many, as an exploration of recurrent patterns of story and history it had legitimate claims on scholarly imagination. At the very least, one could never again read Frederick Jackson Turner quite the same (the wilderness brought to the Frenchman her "untutored children to wonder at his goods and call him master").

Fiedler's work helped to open up several new topics in American studies. His concern for gender was still unusual in 1968, and only in the late eighties did the construction of masculinity fully rise to monographic view. *Return of the Vanishing American* demonstrated that one could study gender without being exactly feminist. *Love and Death in the American Novel* had lamented the subjugation of women in American literature. But by 1968 Fiedler had taken the argument in directions as misogynistic as homophilic. The vision of two gay males allied across racial and ethnic borders against the female world of civilization did not seem to hold any place for women. And where his early works simply depicted this situation as the dominant image of the white male subconscious, he ultimately held it out as a program for the future. In 1974 Annette Kolodny's *The Lay of the Land* showed that European and Euro-American males had long described the North American landscape in gendered terms that invited the domination, conquest, and mastery of the white male over feminine nature. The language had naturalized patriarchy and environmental despoliation. Scholars from Turner to Fiedler had unselfconsciously reproduced that language until misogyny had literally been inscribed into the nation's geography. By the end of the seventies Fiedler's contributions to the development of gender studies were clouded. *Return of the Vanishing American* imagined a world in which male homosexuals emancipated themselves at the expense of female subjectivity. Some feminists might read the book as one more reactionary example of the patriarchy lashing out at women just as they began to make some headway.

The Return of the Vanishing American pointed less equivocally toward another growth industry in American studies, namely, monographs exploring white America and Europe's "othering" of Native

America. Pearce had led the way, and the reprinting of *Savagism and Civilization* in 1965 likely gave some impetus to Fiedler's own work. By the seventies major studies were appearing at regular intervals, with Richard Slotkin's *Regeneration through Violence* in 1973, Fredi Chiappelli's anthology *First Images of America* in 1976, and Robert F. Berkhofer's *The White Man's Indian* in 1978. This was just the tip of the scholarly iceberg. By the early eighties reading great works in American literature for conceptions of race and ethnicity had become a central critical pastime. Stephen P. Greenblatt, a pioneer in what became "New Historicism," had published an early article in *First Images of America*. "Learning to Curse: Aspects of Linguistic Colonialism in the Sixteenth Century" took *The Tempest* as a launchpad for a ranging exploration of Caliban as symbol of the colonized natives, the overwriting of orality by literacy, and the meanings of cultural relativism for traditional humanism. Greenblatt quoted both Roy Harvey Pearce and Hayden White en route to his concluding salvo: "Reality for each society is constructed to a significant degree out of the *specific* qualities of its language and symbols. Discard the particular words and you have discarded the particular men." The three themes of the passage, the social construction of reality, the systems of culture and language, and the particularity of historical situation, were key themes in new varieties of literary history.[74]

Fiedler's work in many ways anticipated much of what is now called "New Historicism." His generic label, "literary anthropology," pointed toward an increasingly popular convergence of ethnographic and literary criticism we have already seen working its way, via culture, into journals like *American Quarterly*. For Fiedler the label referred to method as much as to content. He often related the lives of authors to their texts, a practice that the new critics derided as the intentional fallacy. But he had joined the new critics in renouncing the genetic fallacy, the practice of seeing a work as genetically rooted only in those older works with which it could be definitively linked by source criticism. Fiedler instead read texts against any other text that might possibly offer a useful surface to push off of, any opening, parallel, or affinity that suggested a homology of structure. He was looking for mythic patterns, but new historicists justified similar concerns with "confluence," rather than "influence," by taking up ethnographic conceptions of culture as a system of shared meanings. Fiedler's interests also pointed toward shifting topics and morals: a radical revaluation of myth; enthusiasm for alternative modes of selfhood; and a focus on interracial sexuality.

"Post-humanism," Fiedler called it in a 1965 essay, a break with the canonical histories and conceptions of human nature in favor of radical pluralism.[75]

Such works raised the question of whether any study of "two" groups, including such metacommentaries as our own exploration of Euro- and Native America, can do justice to the pluralism of modern experience. We have scarcely traversed the outskirts of the literature on interethnic borders in America. If Turner's rustic white male was one frontier synthesis, then the *métis* and Mexicano were others, and it needs no prophet to imagine that even these syntheses might be divided by region, class, gender, and sexuality. The questions of myth and symbol studies—queries like, what does it mean to be American?—had been subverted by even more basic questions, such as, what does it mean to be human? Smith and Marx had been steeped in traditions that defined humanity by the models figured in the canonical texts of Western civilization, models of agency and subjectivity cast in white, male, and even upper-class terms. By the end of the sixties behaviorism and structuralism had pressed "humanity" to the wall. In 1967 Michel Foucault's *Les Mots et les choses,* later translated as *The Order of Things,* described "Man" as a social fiction constructed by changing linguistic codes, a figure scribbled in the tidal sands of history. Fiedler's post-humanism, like Toynbee's postmodernism, so completely refigured American studies that the very topic might come to seem problematic. Once again, a detour and a brief glimpse into an alternative landscape can suggest the breadth of the changes the new languages portended for both history and America.[76]

Dialectica Fronterizos: Gloria Anzaldúa

Thus far we have concentrated on canonical works that represented the strengths of American studies. These texts also reveal its limits. In period discourse "America" referred strictly to the United States and its territories, and its scholars studied works in English circling around a recognizable canon: Hawthorne, Melville, Twain. Alternative visions did exist, however, and we need to open a window onto other ways of imagining literary histories of "American" frontiers. *"With His Pistol in His Hand"* appeared in 1959 and was fairly contemporaneous with other works important in the emergence of "Chicano" historicisms. José Vasconcelos's *Making of the Cosmic Race* had shown conceptual events in motion as early as the twenties. But its translation into English, in 1957, together with the publication of Edmundo O'Gorman's *The Invention of America* (1957); the translation of Miguel Léon-Portilla's *La Filosofía Nahuatl* as *Aztec Thought and Culture* (1963); and especially Octavio Paz's *The Labyrinth of Solitude* (1950, revised and translated into English in 1959) created a larger horizon of scholarly significance for Paredes's "old men's tales." To situate the new criticism, we need to sketch the outlines of Hispanic frontier history prior to the sixties.[77]

Herbert Eugene Bolton, one of Turner's graduate students, virtually created the Spanish borderlands as a field of professional history. His 1917 essay "The Mission as a Frontier Institution" formalized the story as it came to shape academic thought. Throughout the Western hemisphere Spain had opened new frontiers, frontiers that Bolton's many works described as cultural regions. Indians were the resource that civil and military authorities mined for "profit," and they were the spiritual rationale for the Church's own authority in the New World. Though Bolton concerned himself almost exclusively with Spanish agents, the equivalents to Turner's Anglo frontiersmen, the story resisted the naturalization suffered by frontier tales elsewhere in North America. Eliminate the natives from the Spanish borderlands, and you had no story; for borderlands scholars natives could not be swept as easily into the wilderness as they were for "mainstream" historians. And while Bolton seldom ventured beyond the age of Spanish hegemony, his narrative revised Turner's. In the borderlands cultural and racial mixture produced a new ethnicity, society, and nation. The Mexicano (as in Gregorio Cortez) would eventually replace the Spanish padres and conquistadores as a leading frontier figure.[78]

As we have seen in the Boasian ethnographies of the twenties and thirties, products of cultural mixture held ambiguous positions. Sociologist Robert Parks's "marginal man" stood at the center of George Sánchez's history of Hispanic New Mexico, *Forgotten People* (1940). In keeping with period convention, Sánchez adapted the ethnographer's assimilationist tragedy for the telling of his subjects, describing the Anglo sweep across Mexicano culture as a judgment on modernity. Harmonies of pathos and hope timbred his conclusions, as he lamented the loss of organic community but looked forward to a day in which even the villages of the Rio Grande Valley could enjoy the benefits of social democracy. Sánchez's groundbreaking study, later denounced for its reactionary "assimilationist rhetoric," did not much sway the storytelling of other frontier historians, but the writings of Carey McWilliams drew more attention. Though not a professional scholar, McWilliams's visibility as national journalist and political activist, as well as the readability of books like *North from Mexico,* placed Anglo oppression of Mexicans and Hispanic Americans firmly within California history, if not quite inside *America's Frontier Heritage.* By the end of the fifties ethnographers like Robert Redfield and Oscar Lewis and folklorists like Paredes had rewritten Mexicano culture as a viable identity rather than a degraded crossbreed. In their texts a new frontier *topos,* the "village," figured organic community and certified the cultural authenticity of a formerly "intercultural" society.[79]

If we are looking for an analog to Henry Nash Smith's *Virgin Land,* then *Labyrinth of Solitude,* by poet and essayist Octavio Paz, stands out. First published in 1950, then slightly revised and translated into English in 1959, this cultural history opened with an epigram from Antonio Machado: "The *other* refuses to disappear; it subsists, it persists; it is the hard bone on which reason breaks its teeth." Paz meant to give voice to the other of Europe's historical imagination, and his book created a national mind for a Mexico on "the margins of universal history." Gender was crucial. As Mexico was other to Europe, so the Mexican fashioned "his" own selfhood against another figure: "Woman is another being who lies apart and is therefore an enigmatic figure. . . . She attracts and repels like men of an alien race or nationality." Paz peered into the etymological depths of a popular exclamation, "Viva México, hijos de la chingada!" *Chingar,* perhaps from an Aztec origin (*chingaste,* seeds, residue, or sediment), took up a universe of tones in its Hispanicization, but "the ultimate meaning always contains the idea of aggression, whether it is the simple act of molesting, pricking, or censuring, or the violent act of wounding or killing." The verb is gendered: "The *chingón* is the *macho,* the male; he rips open the *chingada,* the female, who is pure passivity, defenseless against an exterior world." Paz broadened this into a philosophy of history by reading it against the Mexican past. *La Chingada,* the mythical mother, had origins not only in Eve, the Virgin Mary, and Tonantzín, the Aztec goddess of fertility, but also in *La Malinche, La Malintzín,* or *Doña Marina,* the Indian woman who served Cortés as both translator and mistress.[80]

The frontier encounter of European and Indian had been gendered from the beginning with masculine conqueror violating the passive female to produce the mestizo. Memory judged the event, and "the Mexican people have not forgiven La Malinche for her betrayal." Paz found an existential significance in Mexico's allegorical descent from La Malinche. Woman was the other, the negation of man, and as *La Chingada*, "She loses her name . . . she *is* Nothingness." Mexicans, said Paz, the "sons of Nothingness," had created an identity for themselves through a desperate negation of history.

When we shout "Viva México, hijos de la chingada!" we express our desire to live closed off from the outside world and, above all, from the past. In this shout we condemn our origins and deny our hybridism. The strange permanence of Cortés and La Malinche in the Mexican's imagination and sensibilities reveals that they are something more than historical figures: they are symbols of a secret conflict that we have still not resolved. When he repudiates La Malinche—the Mexican Eve as she was represented by José Clemente Orozco in his mural in the National Preparatory School—the Mexican breaks his ties with the past, renounces his origins, and lives in isolation and solitude.

Mexican liberalism had institutionalized the denial of history by founding a state on an abstract conception of "man" rather than on the historical figures of criollos, Indians, and mestizos. "The Reform movement," said Paz, was the "great rupture with the Mother." That break was "necessary and inevitable," since every truly autonomous life must break with its family and its past, but Mexico must now transcend its solitude by reclaiming history: "For the first time in our history, we are contemporaries of all mankind."[81]

Paz's frontier synthesis of native and European, like that of Paredes, pointed up the amazing complexity of cultural mixture at a time when such themes were not easily treated within American academia. Cultural borders, for most anthropologists, remained regions of death and destruction. Mexicano culture, however, could not pretend to an uninterrupted holism. It was a product of *mestizaje,* biological and cultural mixing. Even the simplest of all possible tellings, an even blend of two cultures, ethnicities, nationalities, or races, forced some critical choices on any narrator. One could stress either the European or native heritage. Authors like George Sánchez and Américo Paredes had emphasized continuity with Europe. The choice was reinforced by strong academic traditions: the dominant focus of borderlands history on the Spaniard and the hegemony of peninsular literature in departments of Romance languages. And we have seen its psychology and gender politics limned in *Labyrinth of Solitude.* But the possibility of stressing native identity, *indigenismo,* had a tradition all its own, embodied in the great works of art, literature, and philosophy of the revolutionary era, articulated by writers like Vasconcelos and artists like Orozco, Diego Rivera, and Frida Kahlo.

During the sixties American activists revised *indigenismo* into *Chicanismo*. Some of the clearest expressions of the new genealogy could be found in novels like Rudolfo Anaya's *Bless Me, Ultima* (1972) and in political manifestos like *El Plan Espíritual de Aztlán*, from the First Chicano National Conference in 1969.

In the spirit of a new people that is conscious not only of its proud historical heritage but also of the brutal "gringo" invasion of our territories, we, the Chicano inhabitants and civilizers of the northern land of Aztlán from whence came our forefathers, reclaiming the land of their birth and consecrating the determination of our people of the sun, declare that the call of our blood is our power, our responsibility, and our inevitable destiny.

This was frontier romance in revolt: spirit, consciousness, heritage, blood, power, destiny, all rooted in the soil, the homeland described in Aztec tradition as Aztlán, the place of origin. While the scholarly works in Chicano history that appeared from the late sixties typically eschewed romance in favor of the more straightforward phrasing of community studies or political narratives of resistance, the mystic tribalism of *Chicanismo* always hovered in the distance as a potential horizon. Founders of the major scholarly journal in Chicano studies adopted the name of the homeland: *Aztlán*. And most monographs implicitly identified Chicano culture as indigenous victim of Anglo invasion. The title of an early important synthesis, Rodolfo Acuña's *Occupied America* (1974), made the point clear enough for the slowest frontier historians.[82] In 1984 John R. Chávez, in *The Lost Land: Chicano Images of the Southwest*, did for Aztlán what Henry Nash Smith had done for the West and Octavio Paz for Mexico. Chávez resolved the old dialectic of Spanish and Indian into the Chicano, a new culture hero rooted in the homeland Aztlán which stretched from northern Mexico into the greater southwest of the United States.[83]

Chicano history and literature typically identified protagonists with native mother rather than European father but effectively masculinized that descent. The native mother, La Malintzín, La Malinche, Doña Marina, became the dominant half of the cultural genealogy, but the resolution, the Chicano, commonly appeared as the hero of a patrilineal historical consciousness. The gendering rested partly on grammar. Where English had long used "man" as a universal figure subsuming both male and female, the masculine -*o* ending of Spanish meant that "Chicano," "Hispano," and "mestizo" were gender coded in much the same way. For Chicanas, as for other women hidden under masculine labels, the figures handed down painful traditions of patriarchy along with a politicized ethnic consciousness. More than grammar was involved. In an important 1981 essay, "Chicana's Feminist Literature: A Re-Vision through Malintzín / or, Malintzín: Putting Flesh Back on the Object," graduate student Norma Alarcón carefully unraveled the "male myth" of La Malintzín. As Chicanas embrace feminism, said Alarcón, "they are charged with betrayal *à la* Malinche." But they could not simply exchange "one male ideology for another," and the replacement of Anglo by Chicano patriarchy was "no choice at all." Alarcón rendered Malintzín as a slave stranded between patriarchies. She cited Paredes and Paz but focused on the writings of Chicanas, reminding readers, in a footnote, that while women "in their assigned roles as transmitters of culture have often adhered to these views, they have not created them."[84]

Alarcón's "Putting Flesh Back on the Object" recalled the epigram from Machado that framed Octavio Paz's discussion of identity politics. As Mexico was the other for Europe, woman, symbolized by La Malintzín, was the other for the Mexican male, "the hard bone on which reason breaks its teeth." Putting flesh back on the object meant imagining Chicanas as subjects of history. Alarcón's essay appeared in a 1981 anthology, *This Bridge Called My Back: Writings by Radical Women of Color*, which over the course of several years became a major work within academic feminist discourse, and Alarcón's subtitle encapsulated its aims. Stung by accusations of homophobia and racism, "mainstream" feminist journals and organizations were trying to listen to women of color who insisted, eloquently and repeatedly, that, in the words of Audre Lorde, "assimilation within a solely western-european herstory is not acceptable." Much as the largely white, male, and affluent academic authors of the "American mind" had fashioned their subject after their own image, the fabulation of sisterhood had obscured crucial differences of race, class, and sexuality. "Assimilation" had become a word of opprobrium, and making women of color into historical subjects did not simply mean, as many historians appeared to believe, depicting them as so many anonymous social atoms locked in decaying orbit around the capitalist sun.[85]

In the writings of Gloria Anzaldúa, one of the editors of *This Bridge*, historical subjectivity and frontier history took highly unconventional forms. In *Borderlands/La Frontera: The New Mestiza* (1987) she mixed genres as thoroughly as history had mixed cultures. Part autobiography, part historical essay, part literary criticism, part poetry, and liberally salted with Spanish, Spanglish, and occasional fragments of Nahua, the book formalized the "code-switching" that Anzaldúa saw as a feature of her daily life. The result was eclectic enough to make questions of genre complicated, to say the least. Many, if not most, academics would balk at describing it as a scholarly work. Its author, though she had some graduate training, did not hold a Ph.D. The book was not published by an academic press. While portions of it were footnoted (a key paratextual test of the scholarly genre) others were fictionalized or written in verse. And while many historians and literary critics were Christians, or Buddhists, or Muslims, few raised their religiosity to the surface of their monographs, as Anzaldúa did. But we should proceed carefully, for such books asked questions like, what *counts* as scholarly history? Who defines it? And whose interests are served by defining history one way rather than another? With such issues before us, we might read the book against a century or more of frontier and literary history, from Paredes to Benedict to Turner.[86]

Borders, boundaries, and frontiers had by the middle eighties become key words of new varieties of discourse, from academic strains of postmodernism and feminism to mass media debates over multiculturalism and education.[87] Anzaldúa's book grew out of the United States and Mexico border region, but the title troped more than land: "Borderlands are physically present wherever two or more cultures edge each other, where people of different races occupy the same territory, where under, lower, middle and upper classes touch, where the space between two individuals shrinks with intimacy." Psychological, spiritual, and sexual as well as regional and ethnic, "border" took up many of the old connotations from borderlands history, notably region, interethnicity, and colonialism. It picked up the heavy symbolic weight *la frontera* carried for Mexican nationals and Chicanos/as. And it swept through the range of meanings cataloged by writers like Smith and Forbes in their essays on the frontier. One of the text's most vivid images placed writer and reader inside this semantic wild, moving up and out from the most literal meanings to the most distant.

The U.S.-Mexican border *es una herida abierta* where the Third World grates against the first and bleeds. And before a scab forms it hemorrhages again, the lifeblood of two worlds merging to form a third country—a border culture. Borders are set up to define the places that are safe and unsafe, to distinguish *us* from *them*. A border is a dividing line, a narrow strip along a steep edge. A borderland is a vague and undetermined place created by the emotional residue of an unnatural boundary. It is in a constant state of transition. The prohibited and forbidden are its inhabitants. *Los atravesados* live here: the squint-eyed, the perverse, the queer, the troublesome, the mongrel, the mulato, the half-breed, the half-dead; in short, those who cross over, pass over, or go through the confines of the "normal."

This was a long way from Turner, and yet enough history glimmers through for us to recognize it as more than a trendy, "politically correct" inversion of academic frontier figures. Long before the appearance of professional frontier history, the border had been understood as the nethermost dangerous margin of country inhabited by social outcasts. For social scientists, well into the century, borders had made marginal men. And Anzaldúa did not simply choose, as a polemic against academic taste, the language of injury and pathology; that tradition had been passed down in good academic words like "encysted." Turner's frontiers had inscribed themselves in blood and barbed wire along the international divide, around the perimeters of the Indian reservations, and in the psychic chasms crossing selves and others. Still, Anzaldúa's tone pointed toward a reclamation. If the border grates, bleeds, hemorrhages, edges, distinguishes, and divides, if it is what "Reagan calls a frontline, a war zone," it is also a place of intimacy where two different identities touch, merge, and form a third.[88]

The making of that third identity, the mestiza, demanded a substantial rewriting of Chicano history. The first hundred pages of the work, "*Atravesando Fronteras*/Crossing Borders," came the closest to recognizably academic text, with seven multilingual chapters of mixed autobiography, historical narrative, lengthy quotation, original poetry, and syncretic spirituality all punctuated with footnotes. The notes ranged widely: ethnohistorians and anthropologists like Jack Forbes, Eric Wolf, and June Nash; historians like John R. Chávez, and Arnoldo De León; and philosopher cum psychologists Nietzsche and Jung. The chapters, anecdotes, and poems, though scarcely straightforward chronologies, narrate a repeating pattern of invasion, injury, recovery, and resistance, much akin to the emplotment grown popular in ethnography and ethnohistory. Prophecy flashed through the memory of endurance: "We know what it is to live under the hammerblow of the dominant *norteamericano* culture. But more than we count the blows, we count the days the weeks the years the centuries the eons until the white laws and commerce and customs will rot in the deserts they've created, lie bleached." The "other" had been inverted. Not Woman nor Mexico but the "dominant white culture" served as the "hard bone" of the other against which the mestiza created her own identity.[89]

For Anzaldúa the separation from Anglo domination prefigured a more difficult differentiation from Chicano patriarchy. Freeing mestiza consciousness from mestizo homophobia and sexism meant revising cultural genealogy. In her telling, the Spaniards had conquered a patriarchal, class-stratified, militaristic, and imperial Aztec state; neither Cortés nor Montezuma looked like a desirable parent. Instead, citing the work of anthropologist June Nash, Anzaldúa imagined an alternative matrilineal history originating in the gender-balanced world of the Toltec, precursors to the Aztec. Their "egalitarian traditions" had been distorted by Aztec patriarchy's development into a "predatory state." Male oppression had ended that empire: "The Aztec nation fell not because *Malinali* (*La Chingada*) slept with Cortés, but because the ruling elite had subverted the solidarity between men and women and between noble and commoner." Anzaldúa's new history did not look much like Paredes's tales told by old men. It originated in a matriarchal culture, was quietly handed down in oral texts from mother to daughter, and was reconstructed by feminist scholars. The mestiza had endured through the changing seasons of patriarchy: "My Chicana identity is grounded in the Indian woman's history of resistance." Identity did not mean the well-wrought holism of functionalist anthropology or the integrated personality of Freudian psychology: "The new mestiza copes by developing a tolerance for contradictions, a tolerance for ambiguity. . . . She learns to juggle cultures. She has a plural personality."[90]

Anzaldúa's description of the mestiza as a plural identity carried the book out on strong tides of period fashion, theory, and politics. An influential essay by French theorists Gilles Deleuze and Félix Guattari, *Anti-Oedipus* (1973), described schizophrenia, plural identity, as the mode of existence characteristic of late capitalism. In a mass consumer society, fragmented by the proliferation of experience, information, and the market's demand for novelty, the old bourgeois ego described by Freud had splintered into a modernist collage. Anzaldúa's new consciousness exemplified the age. Mestiza experience doubtless varied from other plural identities by virtue of its specific contents and situations, but even the selfhood of the "dominant white culture" had changed dramatically from the secure bourgeois individualism of nineteenth-century Europe. Contradiction and ambiguity ruled everyone's world.[91]

The growing sense of contradiction and fragmentation evident in works like *Borderlands/La Frontera* had led Hayden White to demand historiographic revolution. In the nineteenth century, when Europe and Euro-America still had urban centers rather than endless sprawl, when individuals still fashioned integrated personalities suited to performing in a world of industrial capitalism, and when painters still made paintings that looked like photographs, the conventions of traditional narrative (White called it "historical realism") had some mimetic value. A Dickens novel, while fictional, fairly captured the understanding of experience shared by middle-class Londoners. A Parkman history adequately depicted the sense of time and event white Americans found in their own lives. But after a century of world war, genocide, revolution, atomic anxiety, environmental crisis, video technology, and modernist, even postmodern art, historical realism was archaic, and not just in the innocent sense of being unstylish. Invented in an earlier age, "realist history" no longer served its original purpose: it could not adequately represent the authentic chaos of modernity. "Historical realism" was no longer "realistic." Historians, White concluded, needed to emancipate themselves from the Victorian forms by which they were (unconsciously) enslaved and consciously experiment with the modes of representation common in modernist art: juxtaposition, collage, genre-mixing, multiple voice and viewpoints.[92]

Standing against this theoretical backdrop, we might make a case for describing *Borderlands/La Frontera* as what White would call a "modernist" history and what other critics might call postmodern. The book's assemblage of voices, styles, genres, and languages seems a fair example of literary collage. And the ego emerging from the debris of the postindustrial border looks much different from Turner's masculine heroes or Benedict's ideal Apollonian selves. Yet Anzaldúa's insistence on "consciousness" and her attempts to breathe history back into the marks on the printed page bore little resemblance to the aesthetics of theorists like Deleuze and White. "My 'stories' are acts encapsulated in time, 'enacted' every time they are spoken aloud or read silently," said Anzaldúa. "When invoked in rite, the object/event is 'present'; that is, 'enacted,' it is both a physical thing and the power that infuses it." These metaphysics, however "exotic" they might be made by the indigenous goddess, *Coatlicue,* could not be assimilated to the structuralist suspicion of presence and concepts of language as self-referential systems of signification. Anzaldúa did not see code switching as an artifice adopted for a calculated effect. It grew directly out of experience, it was faithful to the world. And the world, for all its contradictions, ambiguities, and fragmentation, was not a flattened jumble of self-contained shards.[93]

Pluralistic experience demanded pluralistic forms, but pluralism was not chaos, and Anzaldúa's narrative description of the new mestiza consciousness emplotted an ascending dialectic:

> That juncture where the mestiza stands is where phenomena tend to collide. It is where the possibility of uniting all that is separate occurs. This assembly is not one where severed or separated pieces merely come together. Nor is it a balancing of opposing powers. In attempting to work out a synthesis, the self has added a third element which is greater than the sum of its severed parts. That third element is a new consciousness—a mestiza consciousness.

We have seen history as dialectic before, and while Anzaldúa scarcely reproduced the historical imagination of a Frederick Jackson Turner or an Américo Paredes, in some ways the book lies closer to those traditions than to the works dominating the canon of modernist and postmodern literature. The code switching of *Borderlands/La Frontera* does not share much with that in, say, John Barth's *Lost in the Funhouse* (1969). Their senses of history and language stand too far apart. For Anzaldúa this was history, not an ironic parody. And like Benedict's mythic narratives, history had a pragmatic value as well: The future will "belong to the mestiza," because "it depends on the straddling of two or more cultures." Decolonization was shifting the margins to the center, and in the coming world Droysen's torch of history and consciousness would pass on to still another people.[94]

A Note on Form

With Anzaldúa's *Borderlands/La Frontera* we have come far enough to build our discussion of Frederick Jackson Turner's legitimation of folk memory into some generalizations about the narrative construction of disciplinary, specialty, and cultural identities, at least within the academic context of our topic.

We can discern a pattern in the development of scholarly narrative traditions. The making of new frontier tales has traditionally begun by marking out a new hero. Typically, a new field or tale begins by identifying itself with an outsider, a subaltern hero (Turner's middle-class westerner; Webb's arid westerner; MacLeod's natives; Paredes's Gregorio Cortez; Anzaldúa's lesbian mestiza). The story initially looks tragic; the hero roams the margins, subordinated by the dominant culture (in Turner's case, the Great Men of Europe and the Atlantic seaboard; for Webb, all the Yankees; for MacLeod and Chávez, white America; for Anzaldúa, the dominant white culture but also the patriarchal and heterosexist Mexicano culture). The immediate response is to break the account into multiple plots. The stories of the elites are happy ones, but this glossy surface ironically obscures the real story, the tragic isolation of the hero (the European masses, the westerner, the southwesterner, the Native American, the lesbian mestiza). The next turn is romantic; the subaltern has been tragically oppressed but heroically surmounts these barriers and emerges triumphant, autonomous, and independent. Subaltern history has great actors and deeds of its own. The next turn carries the story in more "realistic" directions. Antagonists are never fully vanquished; the story is not a linear ascension but a peripetic struggle between real social forces. Conflict integrates both agonists into a larger social order of their own making, a world that may be less than perfect, but one built by the actors and their relationships and thus amenable to reconstruction. Finally, the story may turn ironic. All of these figures are imaginative instruments of the narrative will to power, and they cannot be reconciled without epistemic and political violence.[95]

As a *Bildungsroman* of scholarly imagination, this pattern is more than slightly idealized (we should not imagine it as a universal evolution of narrative form), but it is strong enough to remark and suggestive enough to help us understand our interpretive conflicts. Privileging the subaltern frontiersman allowed Turner to invert the romance of Great Men, elevate the western male to heroic status, and subvert the parochialism of eastern elites. Imagining Native American societies as autonomous, rule-ordered systems provided ethnographers a distinct subject and a template on which to inscribe critiques of modernity. These themes framed the postwar and postcolonial proliferation of oppositional narratives, the emergence of an academic culture of subaltern storytelling against an increasingly technical, bureaucratized, and fragmented intellectual landscape. When a George Sánchez or an Américo Paredes or even a Gloria Anzaldúa cast their prose into intellectual life, they took up these patterns, and while the trends might be altered or resisted, their trajectories could not be completely redirected. Indeed, the very possibility of a new history depended on its conforming sufficiently to these traditions that it could be recognized as a narrative, read within some imaginable variant of these habits, and adapted.

The development of Chicana/o and other ethnic, feminist, and gay and lesbian historicisms took place in this chaotic academic context. Where Turner's subaltern hero, the white middle-class male frontiersman, enjoyed many years of narrative supremacy before confronting directly the claims of competing subalterns, the new protagonists entered an interpretive arena in which the possibility of rejoining their experiences with those of their multiple others appeared both epistemically impossible and politically undesirable. Critics worry that any attempt to integrate these various histories risks the subjugation of "local" experiences. The conflict between the metaphors of history and culture, hidden for so many years by their segregation in different departments and plots, here occupies center stage. Different cultures, some feel, cannot share a history in common. Today the key words of American studies, "history" and "culture," clash as often as they complement one another, and their complex relations inspire volumes of theoretical debate.[96] We have touched briefly on the debates in postmodernism running in and out of the texts we have been reading. We need now to address the topic directly, for in the last two decades postmodernism has fairly transformed what counts as American studies.

Postwestern

Henry Nash Smith's 1986 theoretical testament, "Symbol and Idea in *Virgin Land*," situated that book within debates raging over postmodernism and narrative. His work had not been so naive as many of its critics assumed. "I present the collective representations I discuss as having quite various relations to the reality of American history as this is defined by scholars," said Smith, "and I do not accord to that reality a 'scientific accuracy.' The book does indeed assume that both myth and ideology in American culture belong wholly or partly to what Fredric Jameson has recently labeled the 'political unconscious.'" Representations, ideology, culture, and the unconscious; these are key words of the new historicisms, connected through "myth" to older nineteenth-century vocabularies. The invocation of Jameson's *The Political Unconscious: Narrative as a Socially Symbolic Act* (1981) al-

lied *Virgin Land* with neo-Marxist critical discourse and returns us to
our opening discussions of history, philosophy, and narrative. Though
Smith stressed the historical continuity of American and cultural studies, the discussion will quickly lead us back to the double plot and
that division of historical imagination we have already seen in anthropology.[97]

We do not know how far Smith wished to follow Jameson in the
latter's insistence on Marxian "History" as the final horizon of interpretation, but Smith's "collective representations" suggest an affinity
with Jameson's interpretive apparatus. *The Political Unconscious* argued that all texts inhabit a series of levels of interpretation. At the
immediate literal level, a text is a discrete literary artifact produced at a
particular date by a specific author. It is an individual text. But a text
also inhabits a horizon of collective representations, the stories a group
(whether a class, culture, or nation) tells itself about itself and its place
in the world. Since the way we understand a text is conditioned by the
ways that readers and critics before us have understood it, we need to
reconstruct an entire series of horizons a text has occupied. The same
text can be (and has been) rewritten by different groups placing it inside
different traditions. Given the variety of historical experience, there
seems to be no limit to the number of traditions against which a text
could be read; this sort of reconstruction could go on forever. But textual meaning does not multiply endlessly into the great beyond, according to Jameson, because of the third interpretive level, the ultimate
horizon of "History," with its Germanic capital indicating the Hegelian
and Marxist traditions Jameson had in mind.

> Only Marxism can give us an adequate account of the essential *mystery* of
> the cultural past. . . . These matters can recover their original urgency for
> us only if they are retold within the unity of a single great collective story;
> only if, in however disguised and symbolic a form, they are seen as sharing
> a single fundamental theme—for Marxism, the collective struggle to wrest
> a realm of Freedom from a realm of Necessity.

Only when interwoven into a single variegated story can the voices
of the past be brought to bear on our present world and its future.
Every text, no matter how modest or ahistorical, projects a philosophy
of history in order to be recognized, read, and understood (or misun-
derstood). Not all texts deliberately emplot history as the struggle between necessity and freedom; consumer capitalism has produced so
many competing histories that they seem to preclude any synthesis.

For Jameson, this apparent diversity masked a deeper unity. These different histories offer only partial glimpses, fragments of history which may be truthful representations of some particular regional, ethnic, or gendered experience of the world. But they ultimately must be subsumed into that one overarching narrative.[98]

In the early eighties Jameson's recuperation of Marxist philosophy of history amounted to a sharp polemic. American studies aside, few regions of literary scholarship seemed open to historicism. Many literary scholars saw great texts as great just because they transcended their historic contexts. Others employed theoretical vocabularies in which history barely figured. And Jameson's appeal to the unavoidable *need* for philosophy of history would have struck even many philosophers as absurd. Both vulgar Baconians and logical positivists had denounced philosophy of history (in all but its narrowly empirical and analytic forms) as unscientific; indulge in speculative philosophy of history, as Marx did, and you were on the downhill slide to Stalinism or worse.

By 1981 Jameson's "History" also struck sparks off French philosopher Jean-François Lyotard's *La Condition postmoderne: Rapport sur le savoir* (1979), which appeared in English in 1984 as *The Postmodern Condition.* "Postmodern" already held a host of meanings. Toynbee's *Study of History* had introduced the word in the fifties. Since then it had circulated as the name of an historical epoch that followed the modern or modernist period; as an aesthetic fashion in the arts and architecture characterized by centerless forms, juxtaposition of different styles, and random historical quotation; and as an interpretive attitude implying a radical (yet non-Marxist) politics. Lyotard ranged from one sense to another and his classic definition struck directly at Jameson's big story. Science has always been in conflict with stories, said Lyotard, but in order to legitimate itself, it had created narratives of its own, a "discourse called philosophy."

I will use the term *modern* to designate any science that legitimates itself with reference to a metadiscourse of this kind making an explicit appeal to some grand narrative, such as the dialectics of Spirit, the hermeneutics of meaning, the emancipation of the rational or working subject, or the creation of wealth. . . . Simplifying to the extreme, I define *postmodern* as incredulity toward master narratives.

Those "master" or "meta" narratives obviously included Jameson's "History" as the dialectical struggle of freedom and necessity (the emancipation of the working subject). But they also included Hegel's and Turner's histories as the development of consciousness (dialectics of Spirit) and Curti's history as the progress of science (creation of wealth). Modernity had produced diverse experiences, knowledges, and languages, but it no longer commanded the power of belief to join them into a single meaningful whole. The Deweyan faith in open communication did "violence to the heterogeneity of language games." Different cultures could be contained or persuaded only within what Lyotard saw as a totalitarian system of education and information. "Consensus" meant that dissent faced one of two choices: assimilation or exclusion.[99]

Lyotard spun a story of the postmodern as an historical epoch. Western science had carved out an identity for itself by differentiating its own mode of discourse from narrative. "The scientist," said Lyotard, "questions the validity of narrative statements and concludes that they are never subject to argumentation or proof." Viewed like this, narratives belonged to a different mentality: "savage, primitive, underdeveloped, backward, alienated, composed of opinions, customs, authority, prejudice, ignorance, ideology. Narratives are fables, myths, legends, fit only for women and children." This distinction, from Francis Bacon to Henry Nash Smith, underwrote "the entire history of cultural imperialism from the dawn of Western civilization." The marginalization of story and oratory legitimated and facilitated the conquest of non-Western peoples. But even science could not sustain its claims to authority without narrating an account of its own place in the world. Those stories, modeled on Judeo-Christian theologies of history and honed to a fine secular edge, became the master narratives of Hegelian Spirit, Marxist emancipation, and technical progress. But they contained internal contradictions and produced alternate accounts and critiques. Pressed by the twentieth century's massive proliferation of technologies of knowledge, the sheer mass of information and media, and the atomism of consumer societies, they fractured beyond repair. Today, in postmodernity, "the grand narrative has lost its credibility," and "most people have lost the nostalgia for the lost narrative."[100]

Lyotard also cast the postmodern as a style and a politics. The postmodern is characterized by a widening array of incommensurable language games, each with its own players, rules, and ends. Among these are local narratives (*petit récits*), which Lyotard set against meta- or master narratives. The crucial difference is that the "local stories" we find in, say, Native American communities, always contain as their referent or subject the tribe itself. The names most tribal cultures give them-

selves translate as "the people" or "the humans." All others fall outside
that charmed circle. By Lyotard's account, such texts as Pueblo creation
tales tell only of the origins of the Pueblo; the stories never emplot a
narrative that would wind the Pueblo *and* their neighbors into a single
tale. Judeo-Christian theology, Hegelian or Marxist universal history, and evolutionary biology all do. The difference was crucial. In *The
Differend* (1983) Lyotard invoked a French ethnography of a South
American group, the Cashinahua. Of their stories he claimed "the bond
woven around 'Cashinahua' names by these narratives procures an identity that is solely 'Cashinahua.' " To take them up into another narrative, whether Turner's colonization of the great West, Spicer's global
frontiers of loss and creation, or Jameson's struggle between necessity
and freedom, is to erase their original identity: "The little stories received and bestowed names. The great story of history has its end in
the extinction of names (particularisms). At the end of the great story,
there will simply be humanity." All the great frontier tales and their
philosophical underpinnings extinguished cultural difference in the
service of some imagined cosmopolitan future. Hence the postmodern
as politics: To denounce metanarratives and applaud the proliferation
of local narratives is to resist Western capitalism and its totalitarian tech-
noculture.[101]

The interpretations of Jameson and Lyotard faced off. For Jameson
the postmodern proliferation of histories disguised the true tale of the
struggle between necessity and freedom. For Lyotard capitalism's obliteration of local narratives and cultures will and must be opposed by the
radical differentiation of histories. Some reader was bound to split the
difference, and in 1986 Stephen Greenblatt's "Towards a Poetics of Culture" argued that the general question Jameson and Lyotard meant to
address simply did not have a single satisfactory answer. Capitalism is
"not a unitary demonic principle" producing either false difference or
bad homogeneity but a "complex historical movement in a world without paradisial origins or chiliastic expectations." The world was becoming both more homogeneous and more diverse. Indeed, in late capitalism "the drive toward differentiation and the drive toward monological
organization operate simultaneously, or at least oscillate so rapidly as to
create the impression of simultaneity." The construction should remind
us of Edward Spicer's *Cycles of Conquest* (1961) and its thesis that European imperialism had produced a globe in which cultural differentiation and homogenization interwove in a periodic tragicomedy. With
Greenblatt's influential brand of new historicism, we have returned to

the oscillating double plot we first saw in ethnographic criticism, specifically in Clifford's *Predicament of Culture* (1988). We have come far enough now to reach back for that loose thread and begin pulling together the last strands of our story.[102]

The Predicament of Culture

I should briefly rehearse the situation as we left it at the end of our discourse on ethnohistory. Ethnography had broken Turnerian and social evolutionist frontier tales along ethnic lines and made of them a double plot, comic for the Europeans, but tragic for the natives. By the fifties and sixties ethnographers had begun transforming assimilationist tragedy into peripetic tales of cultural continuity and native resistance. Spicer's *Cycles of Conquest* (1962) emplotted a frontier tragicomedy of differentiation and homogenization. And James Clifford's *Predicament of Culture* (1988) critiqued that sort of synthesis: the history of European colonialism and native cultures, in America and elsewhere, demands dual narratives in which the tragic loss of cultural difference and the comic creation of new ways of being native "oscillate." Neither telling can be reduced to the other or reworked as a tragicomic "metanarrative" à la Spicer. Each remains relevant at most points in history, declared Clifford, each denying to the other a "privileged Hegelian vision."

Clifford was right to say that his and Greenblatt's verb of choice, "oscillate," strikes a very un-Hegelian tone. It suggests a rapid mechanical movement back and forth between essentially distinct forms rather than the more fluid moments of dialectic. The figure calls to mind Hegel's "bad infinity": The static repetition, aimlessly into eternity, of mutually hostile alternatives, black against white, the two never creating any of the multifarious patterns that even so stark a contrast as black and white could achieve. Since *Predicament of Culture* described cultures as refashioning themselves in Technicolored shadings with each new context, we should wonder at its mechanical description of narrative form. Like Edward Bruner, Clifford displaced the problems of autonomy and assimilation to the level of literature. None of his described tribal communities was anywhere near so starkly individuated and eternally self-identical as his opposed modes of emplotment. The crux is the insistence, drawn partly from Hayden White's *Metahistory* (and thus Northrop Frye's Platonic *mythoi*), that a story either *is* tragedy or comedy. A specific brief digression can amplify Clifford's concerns and illuminate the "oscillation" of history. Along with its affinities with Lyotard's denunciation of narrative and Greenblatt's oscillating stories, *Predicament of Culture* opens into even wider circles of interpretation.[103]

Predicament of Culture mediates two influential theoretical visions, structuralism and "poststructuralism" as exemplified by French intellectuals Claude Lévi-Strauss and Jacques Derrida. Lévi-Strauss thus far has figured only briefly in our tale, but his thought has cast a bright shadow across virtually all ethnographic productions undertaken in recent America, and his ruminations over the global frontier narrative still surface in unlikely texts far from their original source. Nostalgia for the vanishing primitive drove his confessional essay, *Tristes Tropiques* (1955). In a masterwork of travel writing, autobiography, and ethnographic criticism, the author limned the significance of deteriorating memory, worried about the duplicity of the past, and contrasted the world of his youth with the homogenized globe of colonial capitalism. Little remained now but "contaminated memories." As a novice ethnographer, fresh from an abandoned career in philosophy, he had ventured into the Brazilian backcountry in search of a proverbial lost tribe, the Nambikwara. What possible meaning could their American lives have for the young scholar? Lévi-Strauss hinted the meeting was of world historical significance.[104]

The frontier encounter of French ethnographer and Native American informant reprised older dramas. An enthusiastic reader of American anthropology (a taste unusual among French intellectuals), Lévi-Strauss declared that the great authors like Lowie, Kroeber, and Boas (Europeans by birth) represented a "synthesis reflecting, on the level of knowledge, that other synthesis that Columbus had made possible four centuries earlier: the synthesis of a strong scientific method with the unique experimental field offered by the New World." In the case of his own subjects, the Nambikwara, the synthesis of ethnographer and informant might replay even more ancient relationships. Reconstructing the "highly charged atmosphere" of period research on American prehistory, Lévi-Strauss posited a connection between the Neolithic revolution in Europe, the event in which we find the origins of history, and the cultures of the New World. Post-Columbian Native America had no historical dimension, but this did not necessarily mean that its inhabitants had always suffered the "deep silence" of peoples without history. Research might uncover hidden traces of contact between primitive tribes like the Nambikwara and the great literate civilizations of the Aztec and the Maya, linkages evincing a pre-Columbian world of historical dimensions, affiliated, either by homology or actual transoceanic contact, with the historical cultures of Europe.[105]

Lévi-Strauss's own expedition from urban Brazil through the "Pioneer Zone" and into the wild "Lost World" of the Nambikwara traversed all the colonial *topoi* of frontier history. Once encamped in the backcountry, he ruminated on the meanings of the imperial exchange. What differentiated European self from American other? One night he distributed sheets of paper and pencils as gifts and was intrigued to watch the chief, in emulation of the ethnographer's own note taking, lord it over his kinsmen by pretending to read from a text of "preliterate" scribbling. From the event Lévi-Strauss drew a moral. Writing, he said, is an "artificial memory." Of the many criteria used to distinguish "barbarism and civilization," it is "tempting" to retain the division of literacy: "peoples with and without writing." But the division is not so clear; some Neolithic groups built civil life without developing literacy. The only phenomenon reliably associated with writing is the "creation of cities and empires." From this the structuralist derived his hypothesis: "The primary function of written communication is to facilitate slavery."[106]

Writing is not only the precondition of the artificial memory we call history, it is also the instrument of human enslavement. The imposition of literate reason on mythic orality lies at the heart of the destruction of cultural difference. For the ethnographer the conflict between native and European echoed the thematic of nature and culture which he saw as a deep structure of language and cognition. The overwriting of natural orality by literate culture made up the great tragedy of modernity. The telling had strong affinities with the classic Boasian ethnographies, Benedict's *Patterns of Culture,* and even the assimilationist tragedies of the forties and fifties, though Lévi-Strauss hoped to provide a more rigorous sense of the differences between modern and primitive. A few years later, in *The Savage Mind* (1962), he described the cognitive and discursive frontiers separating native and modern cultures. Mythic and scientific thought were not evolutionary stages but parallel and equally valuable ways of thinking. Myths, rooted in orality and memory, subordinated change to a timeless order and relied on analogy, classification, and metaphor; science, including historical knowledge, sought explanation of change through temporal continuity and metonymy. The book concluded with a critique of Jean-Paul

Sartre's existential Marxism by denying that history had a central subject such as "humanity" or "existence." History consisted solely in method: "Even history which claims to be universal is still only a juxtaposition of a few local histories." The structuralist had prepared the ground for its subsequent occupation by postmodernism.[107]

In a work released in 1967 at the peak of structuralism's reign, philosopher Jacques Derrida criticized both Lévi-Strauss and the structuralist tradition he exemplified. *Of Grammatology* placed the anthropologist's noble savagism within a history of "writing." In affirming his subjects' "lack" of writing, even while suggesting that this absence ensured them a certain Edenic grace, Lévi-Strauss re-created a metaphysical tradition of ascribing radical but intelligible alterity to another. But tragedy, the ascription of violated innocence to the observed natives, was not, as Lévi-Strauss believed, firmly centered on a single equation, in this case, the erasure of orality by writing. Its meaning depended on its implicit opposition to some other theme, some other telling, some other plot, some other figure. As with Forbes's frontier and Barth's boundaries, the interrelation of forms provided their content. Derrida meant to dismantle the ancient conception of speech and writing as fundamentally opposed ways of being. But he also commented briefly on Lévi-Strauss's frontier tale: "What is going to be called *enslavement* can equally legitimately be called *liberation*. And it is at the moment that this oscillation is *stopped* on the signification of enslavement that the discourse is frozen into a determined ideology that we would judge disturbing if such were our first preoccupation here." Freezing discourse, culture, or being on a presumed "center" of meaning (writing, orality, primitive, modern, myth, science) was, as it had been for Dewey, "classically ahistorical" and potentially totalitarian. In effect, Lévi-Strauss reified the Hegelian division between peoples with and without history. Derrida followed the path into regions Dewey never wished to tread, but the resonance with Clifford's and Greenblatt's oscillating stories deserves comment.[108]

Predicament of Culture appears to narrate a Derridean history, but appearances are deceptive. Clifford feared discourse might stop on one metanarrative or the other, and so to Lévi-Strauss's tragedy of loss he attached the comedy of cultural invention. The endless alternation of the two stories seemed to avoid dogmatic closure. But Clifford's "oscillation" differed significantly from Derrida's. For the philosopher both liberation and enslavement flickered through Lévi-Strauss's story, despite the ethnographer's best efforts to stick to one telling and one telling alone. Clifford, in assigning specific plots to enslavement and liberation, simply went Lévi-Strauss one better. Tragedy and comedy are not the true alternatives. The alternative is a *different* combination of plot and figure. The narrative of tragic loss and comic invention of cultural difference is shadowed by the old assimilationist comedy in which cultural loss is emplotted as comedy and invention as tragedy: Europeans brought history, science, and civil reason to North America. Some Native Americans joined happily into this comically integrated society. Others, unfortunately, resisted, and today they tragically press factionalizing and ultimately undemocratic claims for tribalism, quotas, and separatism. This is the true alternating other whose absence defines *The Predicament of Culture.*[109]

The story of comic assimilation and tragic fragmentation remains popular in polemics against multiculturalism, and while Clifford's politics pointed him toward a happier reading of multiculturalism, it calls forth its own reactionary counternarrative, each denying to the other a "privileged Hegelian vision." Indeed, the conflict surfaces in *Predicament of Culture.* In Clifford's narration of the Mashpee Indians' suit for tribal status, we can see the frontier antinomies of orality and literacy, myth and history, ethnography and historiography, shaping the political geography of recent America.

The longest essay in *Predicament of Culture,* "Identity in Mashpee," recounts the civil suit by the Mashpee Wampanoag Tribal Council, Inc., for the legal right to an Indian identity and title to "tribal" lands. At issue was "whether the group calling itself the Mashpee was in fact an Indian tribe, and the same tribe that in the mid-nineteenth century had lost its lands through a series of contested legislative acts." The trial was much like those touched on in our discussion of ethnohistory. Once again, a court adjudicated competing frontier tales. An array of historians and anthropologists testified. The old anxieties about language, the rewards of expert testimony, and interpretive conflict surfaced again, as did the disparity between narratives of assimilation and narratives of resistance. Clifford cast the suit and its defense as two ways of imagining the Mashpee and America's past: "The Mashpee were a borderline case. . . . Looked at one way, they were Indian; seen another way, they were not. Powerful *ways of looking* thus became inescapably problematic. The trial was less a search for the facts of Mashpee Indian culture and history than it was an experiment in translation, part of a long historical conflict and negotiation of 'Indian' and 'American' identities." The construction implied a *Rashomon*-style relativism, with the same events retold through the eyes of different spectators, emplotted, like one of Hayden White's neutral historical series, as tragedy or comedy depending on aesthetic and political tastes. And Clifford's denial of metanarrative pointed in this direction. Yet the result thwarts expectation, for the essay leads to some fairly straightforward conclusions and morals.[110]

The contrast of plaintiff and defendant, comedy and tragedy, invention and assimilation, at first exemplifies Clifford's oscillating stories. "The case against the plaintiffs [the Mashpee] was based on a reading of Cape Cod history. . . . The story emerged of a small mixed community fighting for equality and citizenship while abandoning, by choice or coercion, most of its aboriginal heritage. But a different, also coherent story was constructed by the plaintiffs, drawing on the same documentary record. In this account the residents of Mashpee had managed to keep alive a core of Indian identity over three centuries against enormous odds." In the courtroom Edward Bruner's older story of acculturation came up against the newer ethnographic romance or comedy of resistance. Some of the other conflicts we have discovered in our journey also turn up as ways of framing this equation. According to Clifford, "the trial can be seen as a struggle between history and anthropology." History, characterized by expert witness for the defense Francis Hutchins (actually trained as a political scientist), relied on written documents to produce a "seamless monologue." Anthropology, led by expert witness for the plaintiffs James Axtell (actually a historian), relied on oral interviews and produced a babble of "contending voices." History won out, and the jury returned a verdict that effectively refused the Mashpee claim to tribal status.[111]

Despite the alternation of tragedy and comedy in the expert testimony, only one mode dominates Clifford's narration of the trial and that is the Lévi-Straussian tragedy of history. "The law," observed Clifford, "reflects a logic of literacy, of the historical archive rather than changing collective memory. . . . The Mashpee trial was a contest between oral and literate forms of knowledge." On this note the writing lesson with the Nambikwara sneaks into the plotline: "Indian life in Mashpee—something that was largely a set of 'oral' relations, formed and reformed, remembered in new circumstances—had to be cast in permanent, 'textual' form." Textualizing (historicizing) oral experience brutalizes its subtle shapes. The metanarratives of history efface local orality, collective memory, and plural voices. Writing facilitates enslavement and erases local names. Few readers will be left wondering where

Clifford's sympathies lie, for "Identity in Mashpee" projects a clear moral: We ought to reform our ways of seeing, reading, and remembering so as to create a world of freer, more expressive collective and individual identities. Orality, local narrative, collective memory, and ethnography—all associated with peoples of color—come out of the story looking very good. History, excluded from these figures and associated with the whitened one-thing-after-another facticity of simple chronology, looks very bad indeed.[112]

"Identity in Mashpee" emplots history's narrative enslavement of "others." And as Derrida warned in his reading of *Tristes Tropiques*, the story of enslavement depends on its alternative tale of liberation. Clifford clearly hoped that the tragedy of the historicization of Mashpee identity and their consequent courtroom "setback" would be followed by an oscillation back into a story of heroic cultural invention. Perhaps the Mashpee, denied offical recognition as a tribe, could still find "new ways of being Indian." But the defendants who denied the "Indianness" of the Mashpee had not depicted the disappearance of tribal culture as a tragedy. In the summation, counsel for the defense described the Mashpee's acculturation as a " 'slow but steady progress' toward 'full participation' in American society." Conflicting, alternating, "oscillating" in the courtroom with Clifford's tragedy of homogenization and comedy of differentiation, was an assimilationist comedy and a warning that the recognition of Mashpee identity would balkanize America. *Predicament of Culture* keeps this counterhistory hidden in the shadows. Of *Tristes Tropiques* Clifford noted that it captured a great truth, but "it is too neat, and it assumes a questionable Eurocentric position at the 'end' of a unified human history, gathering up, memorializing the world's local historicities." The critique applies, with less force perhaps, to "Identity in Mashpee."[113]

The formal distinction between "meta" and "local" narrative comes apart in "Identity in Mashpee." Trying to avoid the sentimental noble savagism dogging Lévi-Strauss's account, Clifford worked hard to escape metanarrative.

The Mashpee were trapped by the stories that could be told about them. . . . Tribal life had to be emplotted, told as a coherent narrative. In fact, only a few basic stories are told, over, and over, about Native Americans and other "tribal" peoples. These societies are always dying or surviving, assimilating or resisting. . . . But the familiar paths of tribal death, survival, assimilation, or resistance do not catch the specific ambivalences of life in places like Mashpee over four centuries of defeat, renewal, political negotiation, and cultural innovation. Moreover most societies that suddenly "enter the modern world" have already been in touch with it for centuries. . . . Indians in Mashpee lived and acted *between* cultures in a series of ad hoc engagements.

Only oscillating tales can capture the vagaries of a subject between cultures. The courtroom's demands for narratives of continuous identity clash with the discontinuities of real life. For Clifford the problems with the stories told about Mashpee are problems of form: the law demands metanarratives of homogeneity when local narratives would be more realistic. But the merits of Clifford's own tale, while it may tell a better story than the simpler narratives at war in the courtroom, do not lie in its postmodern escape from master narrative. Indeed, "Identity in Mashpee," with its multiple subjects and modern primitives, allegorizes the *impossibility* of avoiding "metanarrative."[114]

As *Predicament of Culture* illustrates, the desire to identify with "local historicities" or "local narratives" against the tyranny of narrative mastery contains more than a grain of modernist nostalgia. *The Postmodern Condition*'s tale of the destruction of names by history sounds suspiciously like Linton's "encystment" of the last pitiful remnants of Native American culture within the body politic of a whitened West. "Identity in Mashpee" convincingly demonstrates the dangerous naiveté of Lyotard's construction: "Most societies that suddenly 'enter the modern world' have been in touch with it for centuries." The Mashpee lost *because* they were expected to produce what Lyotard would see as an authentically "local" narrative of a subject whose single name has not been contaminated through imaginative incorporation of other identities. But neither the Mashpee nor most "tribal" peoples can or should construct stories of cultural purity untainted by the press of other subjectivities, whether American, European, African, or Asian. Disturbed that the Mashpee, and us with them, are "trapped" by bad stories, Clifford, a good historian, tries to tell a better one. From such acts come revision, but we need not appeal to some magic essence to demonize the stories we critique.[115]

Narrative mastery comes not from "meta" form but from social position. Some groups have been more effective at institutionalizing their tales and imposing them on others. The imposition can be crude or subtle, openly contested, as in the Mashpee trial, or implicitly negotiated, as with ethnographic fieldwork. But there is no literary legerdemain behind the event, no hidden circuitry of masterful cognitive power to be unmasked and deactivated. There is no simple easy choice between "meta" and "local" narratives, no special way of telling that will safeguard a particular tale against slipping silently into a hegemonic or oppressive position. Virtually overnight, the chanting of subaltern discourse may modulate into the crack of the historical whip.

We do need stories of greater subtlety than the either-or, all-or-nothing tales of pure assimilation, absolute resistance, and unbroken continuity. But Derrida, Greenblatt, and Clifford's metaphor, "oscillation," reinforces such stories. It implies an ahistorical repetition of two distinct entities into an unchanging future, surely not the world Clifford wishes to open up. Like his cultures, narratives—tragedy and comedy, "meta" and "local"—are not aesthetic monads. They define each other through interaction, shifting meaning and morals with each new juxtaposition, taken up into each other en route to changing aims, reinvented with each new situation in processes not fairly captured by A-C images of electrical engineering. Their differences, like those of Clifford's subject cultures, will be anchored at our peril. "If the word 'history' did not carry with it the theme of a final repression of *différance*," said Derrida in 1968, "we could say that differences alone could be 'historical' through and through and from the start." The philosopher wished to describe the play of language, the movement of meaning from one sign to another, as basically historical. The differentiation of tragedy and comedy, mastery and slavery, is not out of history or a mechanical representation of a more subtle historical world, but history itself. He could not say "history" without a disclaimer because he feared that the word still evoked Hegel: History as the "repression of *différance*" refers obliquely to the peoples with and without history. It was, after all, Hegel's history that the well-meaning Lévi-Strauss denied to his natives.[116]

In *Tristes Tropiques* Claude Lévi-Strauss recalled having been socialized into an educational system that immersed aspiring philosophers in a suffocating, pseudo-Hegelian language of ascending dialectic. Little wonder that he found liberation in the sharp edges of positivism and structuralism. And so he associated the ahistorical vocabularies of structural linguistics with the political interests of his colonized subjects. He returned again and again to Hegel's people with and without history. Lévi-Strauss offered at least three ways to circumvent or subvert the equation and its celebration of European empire. First, one might posit a pre-Columbian historicity for Native America; perhaps, he mused in *Tristes Tropiques*, one could find traces of historical consciousness in the wilds of South America contemporary with Europe's Neolithic revolution. A second possibility located the roots of historical consciousness in the mythic thought of natives. But this sounded too much like the old stories of cultural evolution. The third option inverted Hegel and encoded history as evil. Lévi-Strauss's texts emplotted history-as-events as the march of imperial oppression facilitated by literacy and science. They depicted history-as-method as one option among others. As he noted in *The Savage Mind*, "History may lead to anything, provided you get out of it." Getting out of history became a critical obsession for intellectuals after structuralism, and many unfortunately followed Lévi-Strauss in *not* positing, and perhaps inadvertently closing off, a fourth option: History might be dramatically transfigured by new voices.[117]

Clifford's narration of the trial over Mashpee as a collision between ethnography (local, oral, fluid, and subaltern) and history (universal, written, static, and hegemonic) reenacted the escalating conflicts between the key words "culture" and "history." But the divisions no longer look so clear; the expert testifying for "history" and the defendants, Francis Hutchins, was a political scientist. The expert testifying for "anthropology" and the plaintiffs, James Axtell, was a historian. And the author encoding history as one-thing-after-another and ethnography as an inventive engagement with multiple subjects and voices was a historian trained at Princeton. Clifford might have described the trial as a clash between different conceptions of history rather than between anthropology and history, but he did not. And his story conserved a deepening border between the people with and without history.[118]

The Problem of History

The frontiers between Native America and Europe have been figured in ways verging on the theological as scholars discounted the internal diversity of both colonist and colonized by stressing the extremity of their difference from each other. In the scholarly imagination of the European occupation of Native America, an old European folk convention—Lyotard's antinomy of myth and reason—was elevated to an ontological division of humanity, figured as a moral principle of the development of consciousness, redescribed as an empirical difference dividing the disciplines of history and anthropology, and eventually hidden deep in the forgetful bliss of "common sense." Scholars from Benedict to Clifford have wondered if "history" is a desirable form of imagination. As Michael Roth has observed, "In the 1950s and 1960s, Nietzschean suspicions about the burdens of historical consciousness were linked to new social scientific accusations about the superficiality and fuzziness of historical thinking." In American studies and elsewhere, scholars speculate that perhaps the shapes of time, memory, and event cannot be assimilated to anything we might recognize as historical. Or perhaps such an assimilation would so brutalize native experience that historicizing frontier encounters is actually a force for evil. Lyotard's contrast of local and metanarratives hints at morals this grand. And the equation echoes Hegel's people with and without history. Contemporaneous with works like *Postmodern Condition* and *Predicament of Culture* came demands that scholars renounce history altogether.[119]

In *The American Indian and the Problem of History* (1987) ethnohistorian Calvin Martin followed paths opened by Benedict's rehabilitation of mythic truth, Lévi-Strauss's encoding of literacy as instrument of enslavement, Hayden White's depiction of historical narrative as an artistic falsification of a pluralistic world, and the postmodern suspicion of narrative mastery. "The traditional historian colonizes the Indian's mind, like a virus commandeering the cell's genetic machinery," declared Martin. "The typical procedure is to make Amerindians into what might be termed a 'people of history.' " Invoking the great modernist critics of history from Yeats to Lévi-Strauss, Martin counseled that "we historians need to get out of history if we are to write authentic histories of American Indians." Where would this leave natives? "In eternity, I believe." Martin's "Epilogue" troped the frontier as a boundary line cleanly separating "people of myth and people of history."[120]

Myth is the most ambiguous of frontier figures. Those theorists from Frederick Jackson Turner to Américo Paredes who understood history as a narrational form had imagined myth and history as more or less continous since both were emplotted. But some intellectuals preferred more antagonistic formulations. When imagined as an alternative to authentic historical consciousness, myth could be either good or bad. Understood pejoratively, from George Pierson to Henry Nash Smith, myth was a compound of fairy tale and affect standing between social science and rational knowledge of the world. Understood sympathetically, from Ruth Benedict to Calvin Martin, myth was a discursive or cognitive form that engaged the deep meaning of existence in ways naturalism could not. All three views ran through *The American Indian and the Problem of History*. While some contributors, like Richard Drinnon, criticized history's displacement of myth or urged the recuperation of mythology for scholarship, others, like Neal Salisbury and Henry Dobyns, returned to pejorative descriptions of myth as an ideological language preventing white social scientists from writing more rational histories of Native America. And Robert Berkhofer, Mary Young, and Michael Dorris questioned the efficacy of elaborating a "pan-Indian" mind as an alternative to the idealized "mind" or national character that had dominated American studies texts in the fifties and sixties. Only bindery glue could hold together visions so opposed.[121]

The interpretive conflicts within *The American Indian and the Problem of History* amplified broader disagreements. Few scholars agreed on a definition of myth, but some common features recurred throughout the literature. One opposed mythic temporality to historical chronology. The most explicit accounts, like Mircea Eliade's *Cosmos and History*, prominent in Calvin Martin's footnotes, described mythic thought as cyclical or timeless, in contrast to the linear histories of Judeo-Christian and modern thought. Another stressed the highly affective or figurative nature of mythic language. Myth was somehow connected to metaphor. Another highlighted religiosity as a defining feature. Myth dealt with transcendental and spiritual content. Still another, as with Claude Lévi-Strauss, pointed to orality—oral cultures and texts functioned in mythic rather than scientific ways. In the broad sweep of academic discourse myth was both an intellectual error to be renounced *and* the form natural to Native American storytellers.[122]

All these equations imply revisions of the narrative conflicts of frontier history and the boundaries differentiating savage and civil, primitive and modern, prehistory and history. Set virtually any of them out in the open and they begin to fade. If we are looking for cyclical accounts of history, we might invoke any number of western scholars from Spengler to Benedict to Toynbee who invoked or evoked circularity. If we are looking for figural language, then virtually any monograph might serve. After White's *Metahistory* we have learned to decode "mythic" literary elements in the most secular, bejargoned structural histories. As for religiosity, while few historians explicitly appealed to Providence, Toynbee a notable exception, equally few texts of the nineteenth and early twentieth centuries were untouched by it (*Sursum corda*—Lift up your hearts!). The only hard-and-fast distinction that could consistently differentiate "mythic" from "historical" texts was the division between orality and literacy, the venerable boundary marker dividing "prehistory" and history. Since by the late twentieth century most Native Americans (and all Native American scholars) were literate, it was not entirely clear how this last wall could be maintained. If it were to be reaffirmed for their ancestors (once upon a time, natives had mythic imaginations, now many of them suffer from historical consciousness), then the division between myth and history had become one more index of how far Native Americans had assimilated, one more chasm standing between them and their lost tribal origins.

Cultural identity hung in the balance. Did American Indians relinquish mythic imagination, and with it cultural authenticity, when they took up pen, pencil, and computer? Did the telling of "linear" stories by Native Americans mean they were no longer native? What of the many Indian scholars, from Ella Deloria to Russell Thornton, who had written in scholarly idiom on the European occupation of Native America? Calvin Martin's division of Native America into bad historical Indians, like the Aztecs and Maya who had chirographic systems, and good mythic natives, hints at answers. Historical Indians indulged in imperialism and class oppression. Mythic natives communed with nature. The classification has obvious dangers. And the perils cannot be contained by simply limiting mythic texts to those purporting to represent American Indian religiosity, for then the questions become even messier. What *counts* as an authentically "native" spirituality? Martin, in a new variant of salvage ethnography, sought to revitalize an imagined pre-Columbian pan-Indian cosmology, but many Native Americans are (and have been) Baptists or Buddhists or Scientologists. How would the historian respond to the Native American voice demanding entrance to historiographic debate in the service of evangelical creationism? One suspects it would be treated as many federal judges treated other "assimilated" plaintiffs.[123]

Martin's manifesto reinscribed the old Hegelian *topos* of the peoples without history, but now it was *good* to be without history. The posture had served noble savagism from Montaigne to Lévi-Strauss and the "hippiefication" of Native America. At worst, it reinforced the bad old essentialist notions of Indian identity which it sought to dissolve by deploying antihistorical and racialized conceptions of culture that were, as one reviewer put it, "outmoded" and "chillingly monolithic." At best, it created a space for popular native voices to reenter historiographic debate behind a velvet rope. In courtrooms, classrooms, and administrative offices the conflict between oral "myth" and "historical" evidence had worked itself out in very unhappy ways. "To be an Indian in modern America is in a very real sense to be unreal and ahistorical," said Vine Deloria Jr. in 1969. Mythicists bear the burden of persuading him and the Mashpee that unreal and ahistorical are good things to be. Benedict's double plot here returns with a vengeance. To make history look less inhabitable, critics identify it with master narratives, imperialism, industrialization, and political oppression. History is a tragedy of enslavement. It is ringed round with a horizon of myth, of brighter nonlinear local stories of liberation. We need either to end history or step lightly out of it into a brave new world. We need to stop the world's plot and get off.[124]

If we avoid confronting history directly and devise new labels, categories, and boxes for a "new" approach to the past, we effectively renounce any claim to revise history. If we wall off a separate space for "non-Western" or "tribal" or "oral" voices, then history-as-given may continue merrily on its way, untouched, unconcerned, unreclaimed. The notion that history encodes strictly the experience and epistemes of the West and that myth or countermemory articulates the voice of others is drifting toward dubious ends. We have outdistanced straightforward problems about Western academia's representations of the "others." We are all others now. Every culture is multicultural. This does not mean that we have assimilated into a level postmodern plain of ethnic community. It means that, imagined from a postcolonial perspective, "Euro-America" has become the other against which ethnic consciousness marks itself out. Patriarchy has become the alter image against which feminism works out its complex identities. "Dominant culture" has become the counterreferent for new communities of interpretation. Ethnographers, historians, and literary critics come in all shapes, sizes, colors, genders, sexualities, and tribal affiliations, and our new narratives should transfigure history. The old modernist cultural apartheid, where each community was presumed to live in a room apart, sheltered from the others by its isolation in a closed system or story of self-referential signs, is coming undone, and the undoing reaches well beyond video vernacular and into classroom, conference, and courtroom. Appeals to a stable horizon of myth, still ringing round the West and giving both self and other stable identities on which we may affix different values, have taken on an air of desperation.

We might even read the mythicist's suspicion of history as a subconscious defensive maneuver. Right as he sees the Nambikwara becoming part of "history," the ethnographer declares history something to be escaped. In the midst of decolonization, just as Droysen's torch of historical consciousness passes from the "West" to the "rest," European and Euro-American intellectuals declare history ended. Frances E. Mascia-Lees and Patricia Sharpe have noted that the sort of skepticism they see in Clifford's *Predicament of Culture* surfaces just as competing voices—women, natives, others—begin pressing their truth claims in the academic arena. Essayist Richard Rodriguez, in *Days of Obligation,* links the new suspicion of history to changing emplotment. Once upon a time optimistic Euro-Americans imagined their history ascending comically into a brightening tomorrow. Mexicans, in contrast, inhabited a place of deeply tragic contours where the past weighed down the future. Today, says Rodriguez, we have reversed roles, traded plots. Anglos suffer the angst they formerly associated with decadence and age, and they imagine history has turned tragic. It is Mexico, with its centuries of colonial suffering, that now looks to a brighter tomorrow and a past commemorated as a comic ascension from enslavement to liberation. A bit glib, perhaps, this vision, but provocative. We will not conjure happy stories through sheer force of will, and the chanting of subaltern mantras will not dissolve the border patrol, but *Days of Obligation*'s inversion of the double plot should give pause to our reflections on the use and abuse of history.[125]

The problems with the antinomies of myth and history, tragedy and comedy, reprise the grander patterns we have been tracing. Academia's slow, painful cultivation of cultural pluralism has gone hand in hand with compartmentalization. Listening to "other" voices in historiographic debate *ought* to have transformed history itself. New forms ought to have shaken the foundations of Turner's Great Library of the Universe. Too often new voices were assigned new offices, extra wings added in a mechanical process of incorporation through addition, a process that could isolate as well as expand. Adding ethnographic textuality to history did not transfigure history so thoroughly as we might wish. Instead, "ethno-history" and its occupants acquired a room of their own tacked onto the original structure, the marginality of the enterprise encoded in the "ethno-" prefix, holding in its very name the mark of that crucial difference that keeps it from remaking history. It is easy to understand the frustration of Martin and others, but hanging a sign above one's door, "This Room Is Better Than the Rest," will not bring down the walls.

Hard and fast categories like "local" and "metanarrative," myth and history, orality and literacy, no longer offer the sure grip on the world they afforded our scholarly ancestors. The ethnography of communication has eloquently insisted on the complexity of the matter, as early practitioners urged on anthropologists the need, both epistemic and moral, to take seriously the voices of informants. Linguist Dennis Tedlock, in a series of provocative articles begun in the middle seventies, denounced the Lévi-Straussian antinomy of mythic and scientific thought: "When Claude Lévi-Strauss states that myth is an instrument for the 'obliteration of time,' this is not an insight into the nature of narrative but an artifact of his choice of a method of analysis based on phonology." The savage "timelessness" celebrated by Lévi-Strauss was a function of his ahistorical method rather than a fair rendition of native thought and culture. Though not sympathetic to Derrida, Tedlock shared his suspicion of Lévi-Straussian method, and by the end of the eighties many others did as well. The year Martin delivered his manifesto on myth, an anthology of work by linguists in Native American oral texts, Joel Sherzer and Anthony C. Woodbury's *Native American Discourse* (1987), angrily declared that "there is no simple dichotomy between oral and written discourse."[126]

The comparison marks the limits of our own exploration, for careful discussions will build on thorough readings of oral texts typically located outside any survey of "scholarly" storytelling tradition. While we might read Martin's posthistorical vision as a product of white liberal academia's growing awareness of the burdens of history, we ought to heed his admonition that different philosophies of history face off every time we listen for other voices. In the end, the ways we differentiate "traditional" texts (whether oral, poetic, or religious) from "modern" printed texts can be disentangled only by the sort of careful source criticism and interpretation that originally grounded historical scholarship. Interpretation has changed since historical and biblical hermeneutics drifted apart, and what counts as a text, narrative, or "history" has changed too. As native voices shape more directly the forms of national memory reproduced in education, mass media, and commemorative acts of the state, ways of remembering will change as well. A study such as this can offer only a prolegomenon, but we can hint at the possibilities.[127]

Like the familiar distinctions between oral and printed texts, texts and contexts, and myths and histories, the stories we have drawn upon will continue to metamorphose. Where historians enter into dialogue with the figures of times deceased, the narrative conventions we accept as meaningful enter into the terms of negotiation. R. G. Collingwood made the point back in the forties: a tragedy or a comedy will have strange meanings for an interpretive community lacking a tradition of comedy or tragedy. And while the abstract *mythoi* of romance, tragedy, comedy, and satire may find equivalents in various tribal languages, they will be transformed yet again by Native American historicities. Linguistic anthropologist Keith Basso, for instance, tells us that the Cibecue Apache distinguish at least seven generic forms in their own discourse: "The people of Cibecue classify 'speech' (*yat'i'*) into three major forms: 'ordinary talk' (*yat'i'*), 'prayer' (*'okaahi*), and four major and two minor genres. The major genres include 'myths' (*godiyihgo nagoldi';* literally, 'to tell of holiness'), 'historical tales' or (*'agodzaahi* or *agodzaahi nagoldi';* literally, 'that which has happened' or 'to tell of that which has happened'), 'sagas' (*nlt'eego nagoldi';* literally, 'to tell of pleasantness'), and stories that arise in the context of 'gossip' (*ch'idii*)." Neither an ontological nor a generic divide between myth and history, savage and scientific, local and meta, will fairly differentiate the stories of the most "traditional" Apache from the narratives of their "whitest" neighbors, nor do justice to their own classifications of form.[128]

History does not stand on one side of a sundered humanity but rather shapes darkly the spaces that join and divide changing worlds. History *is* the difference, the frontier, the event, the dialogue from which we abstract ourselves and our stories, and the deep silence of its opposed figure, the other outside of language and time, marks the very limit of imagination and the ragged edge of what can be thought, told, and lived. As Langston Hughes told us back in the twenties, "History is a mint of pain and sorrow." Little wonder that so many people, of so many persuasions, might search for an exit, an end to the story, some magic way of living and reading that could deny the onrushing force of temporal experience and conjure a new existence free of debt and doubt.

Yet despite Lyotard's suspicion of dialogue, even the pseudocolonial encounters we have traced did not enforce a simple assimilation of difference to sameness. As Ruth Benedict's engagement with Ramon shows, while ethnography often reduced informants to faceless bits of objectified data in the service of scholarly empires, native voices could shape academic texts in ways that were as powerful as they were obscure. In some murky but important sense, the "history" projected by *Patterns of Culture* is not just Benedict's but also Ramon's. And for just this reason we ought to resist characterizing it as "mythic" in opposition to "historical," for dialogue between different histories is what we should seek. Without history, however contested or contingent, we have no meaningful engagement, only so many incommensurable cultures speaking past one another into the arithmetic chaos of uncritical pluralism. History holds Benedict and Ramon together, and if the mistrust of historicisms reflects a healthy unhappiness with assimilation, it also projects a fear of miscegenation, the modernist's horror of the mutual contamination of pure primitive and autonomous modern. If to be modern is to divide and conquer, then past modern is where we should place ourselves, cultivating new varieties of historical imagination.

"History is what hurts," says Jameson in one of his more prophetic moments, and while we may wonder at the facility with which he hopes to make us whole, there is much to consider in his claim that we have repressed rather than escaped the great horizons of narrative. The most modest descriptions of culture and history cannot avoid larger stories of history and culture. This is not to say that all histories presuppose an axiom of History from which they deduce plots, heroes, and morals, but rather, as Paul Ricoeur says, that each projects a metaphor, "History is . . . ," thereby engaging a narrative much broader than the discrete local experiences in which it originates. As Jameson argues, the "master" narratives of history have become our new political unconscious, displaced to the blank spaces between the lines where, like a crazy uncle locked away in the attic, they roam back and forth, breaking out at inopportune moments, subverting the intentions of author and auditor. While Jameson has specific European tales in mind, neither narrative mastery nor sweeping horizons is essentially European. Not even those among us from Cibecue can escape telling big stories, nor should "we." The idea of narrating a single experience, naming only one name, fuels the ultimate Eurocentric nostalgia for psychic autonomy. What we know of pre-Columbian America is handed down through textualized frontier memories indelibly impressed with multiple cultures and subjects. In the Pueblo creation tale, says Laguna storyteller Leslie Silko, "there is even a section of the story which is a prophecy—which describes the origin of the European race, the African, and also remembers the Asian origins."[129]

Silko described Pueblo metanarrative in an oral presentation that Leslie Fiedler and Houston Baker printed in a 1979 anthology on "opening up the canon" of English literature. She was not aiming directly at Lyotard's meta and local antinomy, but the shot found the mark. Her comments also underlined how little had changed in the study of American literature since it was first developed by writers like Parrington, DeVoto, Mathiesson, and Smith. While critics wielded the analytic categories of race, class, and gender like meat cleavers, their subjects remained predominantly white, middle class, and regionally parochial. As ethnohistory had not transfigured "mainstream" history, ethnolinguistics had not remade the literary canon. Leo Marx's vision of the best elements of culture being handed down through the ages looked less benign than it had a decade earlier, as Native American oral texts continued to slip through the hands of the custodians of history. So we should listen with special care to Silko who, as a Native American woman, embodied the racialized and gendered qualities conventionally associated with narrative. Her words can stand as a caution to all of us who venture on the treacherous waters of historical criticism.

I suppose the task I have today is a formidable one because basically I come here to ask you, at least for a while, to set aside a number of basic approaches that you have been using and probably will continue to use in approaching the study of English or the study of language; first of all, I come to ask you to see language from the Pueblo perspective, which is a perspective that is very much concerned with including the whole of creation and the whole of history and time. . . . [L]anguage *is* story.[130]

Language Is Story

The quest for scientific certainty led scholars through a series of linguistic turns that encoded narrative and knowledge as antonyms and opened the door for assaults on historical imagination. At key points the suspicion of historical discourse converged with doubts about the social justice of Europe's imperial sweep across the globe. In fits and starts, scholars synthesized those scientistic and political critiques of historical narrative. For some thinkers attempting to bring "people without history" into the academic picture, "culture" seemed a good way to begin. People without history became people with culture. But that shift whitened history, since the adoption of "culture" was facilitated by its association with ahistorical ways of thinking, speaking, and being. Few noted that the new languages reinscribed the old frontier metaphysics of the western edge of History. In America, History collided with its others, and democracy commemorates the moment.

These various attempts to empty language of ideology changed academia's narrative habits without ending narration. Storytelling became suspect, but it did not disappear. Unfortunately, even as the new linguistic shifts created new heroes, they reproduced older, unhappy traditions. George Pierson's "Pandora's box" of metaphor, Henry Nash Smith's "veil" of symbolic language, Ray Allen Billington's "folktales" learned "at mother's knee," Hayden White's historians "indentured" to "fiction-making," Claude Lévi-Strauss's timeless "myths" of the savage mind—story and metaphor had been consistently gendered, racialized, and devalued. The encoding reaches back at least to Plato, but it grew frantic in the twentieth century, and several decades of revisionist scholarship have set it in stark relief. Racial and gender codes helped scholars to separate narration from "rational" modes of discourse. They let historians like Merle Curti and Richard Hofstadter define the frontiers of scholarly practice without fully realizing the contradictions within academia's idealized attempts to rationalize linguistic behavior. They lent weight to critics like Calvin Martin who hoped to get out of history. And they have structured even those histories devoted to revising our ethnocentric renderings of the past.

By the time Leslie Silko delivered her presentation, the scholarly revaluation of narrative had already begun. Arthur Danto had imagined narrative as a form of explanation, W. V. O. Quine had described scientific hypotheses as "plausible stories," and a host of other scholars had begun to delineate the significance of narrative in the physical as well as the human sciences. With occasional nods to John Dewey, some intellectuals now describe disciplined knowledge as an evolving collection of stories we tell ourselves about our contributions to our communities. That new pragmatic approach hardly amounts to a stable consensus on the ways and means of storytelling, but it urges us to imagine narrative as a point of convergence for folk, popular, and scholarly histories rather than a diacritic of their separation. Still, we will not abruptly unburden ourselves of linguistic tradition. "Language" and "culture" have so long served as antonyms of "history" that they will not be easily reconciled. Today, many people talk about the return of history to the social sciences, but the social sciences routinely plaster historical figures over antihistorical foundations. Scholars still build critiques of history that depend on the coded dissociation of narration and cognition. The unhappy connotations of story and poesy run too deep to efface with the stroke of a computer key.

"Language is the archive of history," said Ralph Waldo Emerson, and like so many of his other aphorisms, this one gives back more meaning than its brevity seems to promise. For a Silko or an Emerson, naming and narrating are not trivial glosses applied after the event to the real stuff of an extralinguistic world. To name an identity, to narrate a happening, is to engage a world of pasts both remembered and forgotten and to open new futures both anticipated and unexpected. To say we live in worlds of words and to say that language *is* story is to say that we live out our lives according to the narratives we can make of them. We should not speak lightly of stories. We should not forget that figuration is not always fiction and that naming and narration entail obligation as well as reward. We will continue to revisit the frontiers of historical imagination.

Notes

Introduction

1. Hayden White, *Metahistory: The Historical Imagination in Nineteenth-Century Europe* (Baltimore: Johns Hopkins University Press, 1973); White, *The Tropics of Discourse: Essays in Cultural Criticism* (Baltimore: John Hopkins University Press, 1978); White, *The Content of the Form: Narrative Discourse and Historical Representation* (Baltimore: Johns Hopkins University Press, 1987); Joyce Appleby, Lynn Hunt, and Margaret Jacob, *Telling the Truth about History* (New York: W. W. Norton, 1994), 262.

2. Peter Novick, *That Noble Dream: The "Objectivity Question" and the American Historical Profession* (Cambridge: Cambridge University Press, 1988).

3. François Furet, *In the Workshop of History*, trans. Jonathan Mandelbaum (Chicago: University of Chicago Press, 1982), 54–67; Fernand Braudel, *On History* (London: Weidenfeld, 1980), esp. 11–12.

4. See especially Patricia Limerick, *The Legacy of Conquest: The Unbroken Past of the American West* (New York: Norton, 1987), 25; Limerick, "What on Earth Is the New Western History?" in Limerick et al., eds., *Trails: Toward a New Western History* (Lawrence: University Press of Kansas, 1991), 85; Limerick, "The Adventures of the Frontier in the Twentieth Century," in James R. Grossman, ed., *The Frontier in American Culture* (Chicago and Berkeley: The Newberry Library and the University of California Press, 1994), 66–102; Limerick, "Turnerians All: The Dream of a Helpful History in an Intelligible World," *American Historical Review* 100 (June 1995): 697–716; Donald Worster, "New West, True West: Interpreting the Region's History," *Western Historical Quarterly* 18 (April 1987): 141–156; Worster, "Beyond the Agrarian Myth," in *Trails*, 3–25. See also Kerwin Lee Klein, "Reclaiming the 'F' Word, or Being and Becoming Postwestern," *Pacific Historical Review* 65 (May 1996): 179–216.

5. Evelyn Fox Keller, *Reflections on Gender and Science* (New Haven: Yale University Press, 1984), 77 and passim; Worster, "Beyond the Agrarian Myth."

6. James Axtell, "History as Imagination," in *Beyond 1492: Encounters in Colonial North America* (Oxford: Oxford University Press, 1992), 19; William Cronon, "A Place for Stories: Nature, History, and Narrative," *Journal of American History* 78 (March 1992): 1347–1376. Cronon argued that we may use David Carr's *Time, Narrative, and History* (Bloomington: Indiana University Press, 1986) to show that narratives are veridical. Carr argued that narratives are inscribed in human actions with natural beginnings, middles, and ends. But Cronon's essay argued that while historians can agree on collections of factual statements, they may begin and end their stories on different sentences. The construction falsifies Carr's claims about "natural beginnings" and destroys Cronon's attempt to escape skepticism.

7. Richard Rorty, "Solidarity or Objectivity?" in Michael Krausz, ed., *Relativism: Interpretation and Confrontation* (Notre Dame: Notre Dame University Press, 1989), 35–50.

8. Loren Baritz, "The Idea of the West," *American Historical Review* 66 (April 1961): 618–640; Edward Said, *Orientalism* (1978; reprint, New York: Vintage, 1979).

9. Georg Wilhelm Friedrich Hegel, *Lectures on the Philosophy of World History: Introduction: Reason in History,* trans. H. B. Nisbet (Cambridge: Cambridge University Press, 1975).

Book One: The Language of History

1. Compare, for instance, Herman Ausubel, *Historians and Their Craft: A Study of the Presidential Addresses of the American Historical Association, 1884–1945* (New York: Columbia University Press, 1950), especially 46–47, 211–213, 326–329; H. Hale Bellot, *American History and American Historians: A Review of Recent Contributions to the Interpretation of the History of the United States* (Norman: University of Oklahoma Press, 1952), 1–40; Michael Kraus, *The Writing of American History* (Norman: University of Oklahoma Press, 1953), 271–314; Harvey Wish, *The American Historian: A Socio-Intellectual History of the Writing of the American Past* (New York: Oxford University Press, 1960), 181–209; Jürgen Herbst, *The German Historical School in American Scholarship: A Study in the Transfer of Culture* (1965; reprint, Port Washington, N.Y.: Kennikat, 1972), esp. 99–128; John Higham, *History: Professional Scholarship in America* (1965; reprint, Baltimore: Johns Hopkins University Press, 1983), esp. 171–181, 201–204; and Peter Novick, *That Noble Dream: The "Objectivity Question" and the American Historical Profession* (New York: Cambridge University Press, 1988), esp. 91–94, 103–104, 184–185.

2. The single best account of Turner and his legacy is Ray Allen Billington's monumental study *Frederick Jackson Turner: Historian, Scholar, Teacher* (New York: Oxford University Press, 1973). For supplementary overviews see Wilbur R. Jacobs, *On Turner's Trail: One Hundred Years of Writing Western History* (Lawrence: University Press of Kansas, 1994); Richard Hofstadter, *The Progressive Historians: Turner, Parrington, Beard* (1968; reprint, New York: Vin-

tage, 1970); and Gerald D. Nash, *Creating the West: Historical Interpretations, 1890–1990* (Albuquerque: University of New Mexico Press, 1991). More specialized treatments are too numerous to list. For an annotated bibliography of writings on Turner, see Vernon E. Mattson and William E. Marion, *Frederick Jackson Turner: A Reference Guide* (Boston: G. K. Hall, 1982). The most thorough study of Turnerian origins is Ray Allen Billington's *The Genesis of the Frontier Thesis: A Study in Historical Creativity* (San Marino, Calif.: Huntington Library, 1971). Among the many works in this genre, several are especially important for my purposes: Lee Benson, *Turner and Beard: American Historical Writing Reconsidered* (Glencoe, Ill.: The Free Press, 1960), 1–94; Ronald H. Carpenter, *The Eloquence of Frederick Jackson Turner* (San Marino, Calif.: Huntington Library, 1983), 3–112; W. Stull Holt, "Hegel, the Turner Hypothesis, and the Safety-Valve Theory," *Agricultural History* 22 (July 1948): 175–176; William Coleman, "Science and Symbol in the Turner Frontier Hypothesis," *American Historical Review* 72 (October 1966): 22–49; and Merrill Lewis, "Language, Literature, Rhetoric, and the Shaping of the Historical Imagination of Frederick Jackson Turner," *Pacific Historical Review* 45 (August 1976): 399–424.

3. Frederick Jackson Turner, "The Significance of the Frontier in American History," State Historical Society of Wisconsin, *Proceedings*, 1893, reprinted in *The Early Writings of Frederick Jackson Turner*, ed. Fulmer Mood (Madison: University of Wisconsin Press, 1938), 183–232; quotation from pp. 185–186. Subsequent references are to this edition.

4. Ibid., 187–188.

5. For comparisons of the different versions of this essay, see Fulmer Mood's invaluable appendix to *Early Writings*, 273–294. The *Cyclopedia* entry is reprinted in Fulmer Mood, ed., "Little Known Fragments of Turner's Writings," *The Wisconsin Magazine of History* 23 (March 1940): 328–341; quote from p. 339.

6. *The Frontier in American History* (1920; reprint, New York: Holt, Rinehart, and Winston, 1962); Ray Allen Billington, *America's Frontier Heritage* (New York: Holt, Rinehart, and Winston, 1966), 16; Turner, "The Development of American Society," *Alumni Quarterly* 2 (July 1908): 120–121, cited in Billington, *Frontier Heritage*, 18. See also Wilbur R. Jacobs, "Turner's Methodology: Multiple Working Hypotheses or Ruling Theory?" *Journal of American History* 54 (March 1968): 853–863.

7. "The Significance of the Frontier in American History," in Mood, *Early Writings*, 219–220. The first version of the essay included sections with subheadings. Later revisions deleted these section breaks and titles.

8. Ibid., 227–228.

9. W. H. Walsh, *Philosophy of History: An Introduction* (1951; reprint, New York: Harper and Row, 1960), 59–64. See Walsh's revision of the concept in his "Colligatory Concepts in History," in W. H. Burston and D. Thompson, eds., *Studies in the Nature and Teaching of History* (London: Routledge, 1967), 65–84. Walsh borrowed the term from logician William H. Whewell. See his "Of the Colligation of Facts" (1840), reprinted in Yehuda Elkhana, ed., *Selected Writings on the History of Science* (Chicago: University of Chicago Press, 1984), 206–217. For accounts of Walsh's work, see L. B. Cebic, "Colligation and the

Writing of History," *Monist* 53 (1969): 40–57; C. Beham McCullagh, "Colligation and Classification in History," *History and Theory* 27 (1978): 267–284; and William H. Dray, "Colligation under Appropriate Conceptions," in L. Pompa and Dray, eds., *Substance and Form in History* (Edinburgh: University of Edinburgh Press, 1981), 156–170. Historian Edward N. Saveth, without reference to Walsh, says that "frontier is a composite concept." See his "The Conceptualization of American History," in his *American History and the Social Sciences* (New York: The Free Press, 1964), 3–24; quote on p. 18.

10. Jack D. Forbes, "Frontiers in American History," *Journal of the West* 1 (July 1962): 63–71, and "Frontiers in American History and the Role of the American Historian," *Ethnohistory* 15 (Spring 1968): 203–235; Patricia Limerick, *Legacy of Conquest: The Unbroken Past of the American West* (New York: W. W. Norton, 1987), 25; Limerick, "What on Earth Is the New Western History?" in Limerick et al., eds., *Trails: Toward a New Western History* (Lawrence: University Press of Kansas, 1991), esp. 85; Limerick, "The Adventures of the Frontier in the Twentieth Century," in James R. Grossman, ed., *The Frontier in American Culture* (Chicago and Berkeley: The Newberry Library and the University of California Press, 1994), 66–102. See also Donald Worster, "New West, True West: Interpreting the Region's History," *Western Historical Quarterly* 18 (April 1987): 141–156; Worster, "Beyond the Agrarian Myth," in *Trails*, 3–25; Richard White, "Trashing the Trails," in ibid., 26–39; and Kerwin Lee Klein, "Reclaiming the 'F' Word, or Being and Becoming Postwestern," *Pacific Historical Review* 65 (May 1996): 179–216.

11. John T. Juricek, "American Usage of the Word 'Frontier' from Colonial Times to Frederick Jackson Turner," *Proceedings of the American Philosophical Society* 110 (February 1966): 20. See also Fulmer Mood, "The Concept of the Frontier, 1871–1898: Comments on a List of Source Documents," *Agricultural History* 19 (January 1945): 24–30; Jack D. Forbes, "Frontiers in American History"; Walter Rundell Jr., "Concepts of the 'Frontier' and the 'West,' " *Arizona and the West* 1 (Spring 1959): 13–41; J. R. V. Prescott, *The Geography of Frontiers and Boundaries* (London: Hutchinson University Library, 1965), 9–55; and Lucien Febvre, "Frontière," *Revue de Synthèse Historique* 45 (June 1928): 31–44. Turner's frontier was bound up with another term, "West," which was even more loaded with historical freight. See Loren Baritz, "The Idea of the West," *American Historical Review* 66 (April 1961): 618–640.

12. Juricek, "American Usage," 33.

13. See Nash, *Creating the West*, 3–48.

14. Frederic Paxson, "A Generation of the Frontier Hypothesis, 1893–1932," *Pacific Historical Review* (1933): 45, 51; Paxson, *History of the American Frontier, 1763–1895* (1910; rev. ed., Boston: Houghton-Mifflin, 1924). On Paxson's influence see Richard W. Etulain, "After Turner: The Western Historiography of Frederic Paxson," in his *Writing Western History: Essays on Major Western Historians* (Albuquerque: University of New Mexico Press, 1991), 137–165.

15. Charles A. Beard, "The Frontier in American History," *New Republic* 25 (February 16, 1921): 349–350, and "Culture and Agriculture," *Saturday Review of Literature* 5 (October 20, 1928): 272–273; John Dewey, "The American Intellectual Frontier," *New Republic* 30 (May 10, 1922): 303–305; John C.

Almack, "The Shibboleth of the Frontier," *Historical Outlook* 16 (May 1925): 197–202; Arthur M. Schlesinger Sr., "The Influence of Immigration on American History," *American Journal of Sociology* 27 (July 1921): 71–85; Benjamin F. Wright, "American Democracy and the Frontier," *Yale Review* 22 (December 1930): 349–365; Louis M. Hacker, "Sections—or Classes," *Nation* 137 (July 26, 1933): 108–110. None of the critiques appeared in major scholarly journals, save perhaps Wright's piece in *Yale Review,* a journal that published both scholarly and popular articles. For good overviews see Gene M. Gressley, "The Turner Thesis—a Problem in Historiography," *Agricultural History* 32 (October 1958): 227–249, and Nash, *Creating the West,* 3–48.

16. George W. Pierson, "The Frontier and Frontiersmen of Turner's Essays," *Pennsylvania Magazine of Biography and History* 64 (October 1940): 465, 470, 471; and "The Frontier and American Institutions: A Criticism of the Turner Theory," *New England Quarterly* 15 (June 1942): 229, 250, and 252.

17. Pierson published the questionnaire and results in two articles: "American Historians and the Frontier Hypothesis in 1941 (I)" and "American Historians and the Frontier Hypothesis in 1941 (II)," in *Wisconsin Magazine of History* 26 (September and December 1942): 36–60 and 170–185. For convenience citations will be by page number; the cites are from pp. 180, 189, 173.

18. Ibid., 43.

19. Ibid., 172, 45, 43, 46, 48, 180. Pierson attributes the quote denying the existence of a Turner hypothesis to "one of Turner's pupils who knew him best." Historians J. D. Hicks, Homer C. Hockett, Edward Everett Dale, John L. Harr, and W. A. Mackintosh, all are quoted to the effect that the "hypothesis," if there was one, was not a self-contained testable proposition and should not be treated as such.

20. Charles Victor Langlois and Charles Seignobos, *Introduction to the Study of History* (1898; Eng.-lang. ed., London, 1898); Ernst Bernheim, *Lehrbuch der historischen Methode* (Leipzig, 1893); Herbert Baxter Adams, *Methods of Historical Study* (Baltimore: Johns Hopkins University Press, 1884); Edward A. Freeman, *The Methods of Historical Study* (London: Macmillan, 1886); E. Benjamin Andrews, *Brief Institutes of General History* (Boston: Silver, Burdett, 1897); Fred Morrow Fling, *The Writing of History: An Introduction to Historical Method* (New Haven: Yale University Press, 1920); and C. G. Crump, *History and Historical Research* (London: Routledge, 1928). A less naive account appeared in Allen Johnson, *The Historian and Historical Evidence* (New York: Charles Scribner's Sons, 1926), 157–176. The most sophisticated treatments appeared in works in philosophy of history, but these received little attention apart from a handful of historians and philosophers. See Frederick J. Teggart's works: *Prolegomena to History: The Relation of History to Literature, Philosophy, and Science* (Berkeley: University of California Press, 1916), *The Processes of History* (New Haven: Yale University Press, 1918), and *Theory of History* (New Haven: Yale University Press, 1925); Morris R. Cohen, *Reason and Nature: An Essay on the Meaning of Scientific Method* (New York: Harcourt and Brace, 1923), 347–385; Morris R. Cohen and Ernest Nagel, *An Introduction to Logic and Scientific Method* (New York: Harcourt, Brace, 1934), esp. 323–357; and Maurice Mandelbaum, *The Problem of Historical Knowledge: An Answer to Relativism* (1938; reprint, New York: Harper and Row, 1967). On the impact of

these works see Ausubel, *Historians and Their Craft*, 189–255, and Novick, *That Noble Dream*, 164–165, 262–264.

21. Homer C. Hockett, *Introduction to Research in American History* (New York: Macmillan, 1931), and the revised edition, *The Critical Method in Historical Research and Writing* (New York: Macmillan, 1955). On the popularity of this text, see Walter Rundell Jr., *In Pursuit of American History: Research and Training in the United States* (Norman: University of Oklahoma Press), 4. Hockett quoted in Pierson, "American Historians and the Frontier Hypothesis," 46, 55.

22. Social Science Research Council, Bulletin 54, *Theory and Practice in Historical Study: A Report of the Committee on Historiography* (New York: Social Science Research Council, 1946), viii, 42–44, 44–45. On this report see Allan Bogue, "The Attempt to Write a More Scientific History" (1967), in Robert A. Skotheim, ed., *The Historian and the Climate of Opinion* (New York: Garland, 1985), 167–187, and Novick, *That Noble Dream*, 387–400.

23. Gilbert J. Garraghan, S.J., and Jean Delanglez, S.J., *A Guide to Historical Method* (New York: Fordham University Press, 1946), 153. This work appears in none of the major contemporary bibliographies of methods texts.

24. Paxson, "A Generation of the Frontier Hypothesis," 36; Pierson, "American Historians and the Frontier Hypothesis," 172.

25. Karl Popper's *Logik der Forschung* (1935) appeared in English as *The Logic of Scientific Discovery* (New York: Harper and Row, 1959). My account follows that in Popper's *The Poverty of Historicism* (1944; reprint, New York: Harper and Row, 1964), where he more explicitly discusses history. Morris Cohen's *Reason and Nature* anticipated Popper's work but had nothing like its impact.

26. Carl G. Hempel, "The Function of General Laws in History," *Journal of Philosophy* 39 (January 1942): 35–48. Key contributions to this conversation are anthologized in Patrick Gardiner, ed., *Theories of History* (New York: The Free Press, 1959), and William H. Dray, ed., *Philosophical Analysis and History* (New York: Harper and Row, 1966). The single best overview is found in Paul Ricoeur, *Time and Narrative*, vol. 1, trans. Kathleen McLaughlin and David Pellauer (orig. ed., 1983; Eng.-lang. ed., Chicago: University of Chicago Press, 1984), 96–149. See also Christopher Lloyd, *Explanation in Social History* (Oxford: Basil Blackwell, 1986), 42–70; F. R. Ankersmit, ed., *History and Theory*, Beiheft 25: *Knowing and Telling: The Anglo-Saxon Debate* (Baltimore: Johns Hopkins University Press, 1986); Richard W. Miller, *Fact and Method: Explanation, Confirmation, and Reality in the Natural and the Social Sciences* (Princeton: Princeton University Press, 1987), 15–59; and Wesley C. Salmon, *Four Decades of Scientific Explanation* (Minneapolis: University of Minnesota Press, 1989). It is instructive to compare Hempel's article with three others that ran almost simultaneously yet did not generate a comparable amount of attention: Frederick J. Teggart, "Causation in Historical Events," Morris R. Cohen, "Causation and Its Application to History," and Maurice Mandelbaum, "Causal Analysis in History," all in *Journal of the History of Ideas* 3 (1942): 3–50.

27. Hempel, "The Function of General Laws in History," 35, 37, 40. The label "covering law model" was applied by William H. Dray, *Laws and Explanation in History* (London: Oxford University Press, 1957).

28. SSRC, *The Social Sciences in Historical Study* (New York: Social Science Research Council, 1954); SSRC, *Generalization in the Writing of History,* ed. Louis Gottschalk (New York: Social Science Research Council, 1962). See also Novick, *That Noble Dream,* 387–400, and Higham, *History,* 129–139. Louis Gottschalk's popular methods text, *Understanding History: A Primer of Historical Method* (New York: Alfred A. Knopf, 1963), oscillates between verificationist and falsificationist accounts of historical explanation; see especially pp. 223–227 and 259–269. In 1962 the New York Institute of Philosophy brought together philosophers and historians. Historian Lee Benson endorsed the covering law model, but most other historian participants remained skeptical. See the essays collected in Sidney Hook, ed., *Philosophy and History: A Symposium* (New York: New York University Press, 1963).

29. Mink, *Historical Understanding,* 62; SSRC (ed. Gottschalk), *Generalization,* 6; Carl G. Hempel, "Explanation in Science and History" (1962), reprinted in Dray, ed., *Philosophical Analysis and History,* 95–126.

30. Ibid., 110. In this reading Hempel veered dangerously close to his severest critics, followers of idealist philosopher R. G. Collingwood. Collingwood's *The Idea of History* (Oxford: Oxford University Press, 1946) argued that the historian ought to imagine himself in the place of the person or persons involved in the event at issue and thus reconstruct their thoughts and actions. Hempel's reconstruction of Turner's argument accords well with Collingwood's account of historical reenactment.

31. Lee Benson, one of the few persuaded by Hempel's account of historical laws, in "Causation and the American Civil War" (1961), in *Toward the Scientific Study of History* (Philadelphia: J. B. Lippincott, 1972), 81–97, declared the Turner thesis falsified, but his brief analysis advanced a highly idiosyncratic understanding of the hypothesis, namely, that Turner had declared that the end of the frontier would lead to economic collapse. Historical geographer James Malin, *Essays on Historiography* (Ann Arbor: Edwards Brothers, 1946), 26, held to the unity-of-method thesis as tightly as did Benson but nonetheless arrived at a sharply different reading of Turner: "Turner asserted that 'American democracy is fundamentally the outcome of the experiences of the American people in dealing with the West.' This is the kind of question about which one person can say 'It's true' and another 'It's false,' neither being able to produce proof." Robert V. Hine's *The American West: An Interpretive History* (Boston: Little, Brown, 1973), 321, concluded that "acceptance of Turner's thesis was based on the remarkable accuracy of his predictions," especially those which claimed that American capitalism would expand into overseas markets since the internal frontier had closed. More recently, William Cronon, "Turner's First Stand," stresses Turner's naturalism but laments that his science was not what it might have been. Of Turner's many hypotheses, says Cronon, "few could be falsified."

32. Beard, "Culture and Agriculture"; Pierson, "The Frontier and the Frontiersmen"; Turner, "The Significance of the Frontier," 186.

33. Morton White, *Foundations of Historical Knowledge* (New York: Harper and Row, 1965), 65. See J. H. Hexter's scathing review in the *New York Review of Books,* March 9, 1967, pp. 24–28, and White's response in ibid., March 23,

1967. Also useful are Rudolph H. Weingartner, review of White in *History and Theory* 7 (1968): 240–256; Louis O. Mink, "Philosophical Analysis and Historical Understanding" (1968), reprinted in *Historical Understanding*, 118–146; William H. Dray, "On the Idea of Importance in History" (1970), reprinted in Dray, *On History and Philosophers of History* (Leiden and New York: E. J. Brill, 1989), 74–92; and Raymond Martin, *The Past Within Us: An Empirical Approach to Philosophy of History* (Princeton: Princeton University Press, 1989), 19–25. White's earlier works in the philosophy of history include "Historical Explanation" (1943), reprinted in Patrick Gardiner, ed., *Theories of History* (New York: The Free Press, 1959), 357–373; "The Attack on the Historical Method," *The Journal of Philosophy* 42 (1945): 314–331; "New Horizons in Philosophy" (1960), rev. in *Pragmatism and the American Mind: Essays and Reviews in Philosophy and Intellectual History* (Oxford: Oxford University Press, 1973), 171–185; and "The Logic of Historical Narration," in *Philosophy and History*, 3–31.

34. White, *Foundations of Historical Knowledge*, 107, 115.

35. Ibid., 119, 126.

36. Weingartner, review of White, 251. See also Weingartner, "The Quarrel about Historical Explanation," *Journal of Philosophy* 58 (1961): 29–45. Other commentators had voiced similar concerns in regard to White's "The Logic of Historical Narration." See Lee Benson, "On 'The Logic of Historical Narration,'" *Philosophy and History*, 32–41, and Maurice Mandelbaum, "Objectivism in History," in ibid., 43–58.

37. Morris R. Cohen, *The Meaning of Human History* (LaSalle, Ill.: Open Court, 1947), 106. See also David L. Hull, "Central Subjects and Historical Narratives," *History and Theory* 14 (1975): 231–275.

38. White, *Foundations of Historical Knowledge*, 77; White, "Horizons of the New Philosophy." See also Martin, *The Past within Us*, 19–25. For an attempt to address this problem, see Dray, "On the Idea of Importance in History." Weingartner made much the same point in his earlier article, "The Quarrel about Historical Explanation," 44–45.

39. Richard Hofstadter, *The Progressive Historians: Turner, Beard, Parrington* (1968; reprint, New York: Vintage, 1970), 164. All subsequent references are to this edition. See also his "Turner and the Frontier Myth," *American Scholar* 18 (Autumn 1949): 433–443.

40. Hofstadter did sketch a demythologized frontier thesis: "Much of the Turner thesis boils down, in this sense, to the understanding, sound enough, but hardly so distinctive as the frontier rhetoric suggests, that the United States was a rural society before it became an urban one and that many of its traits were shaped by the requirements of a fast-developing capitalistic agriculture expanding into a rich terrain" (*Progressive Historians*, 124). See also Hofstadter, "History and Sociology in the United States," in Seymour Martin Lipset and Hofstadter, eds., *Sociology and History: Methods* (New York: Basic Books, 1968), 3–20, and "Introduction," in Hofstadter and Lipset, eds., *Turner and the Sociology of the Frontier* (New York: Basic Books, 1968), 3–6.

41. Morton White, review of Hofstadter's *The Progressive Historians*, in *American Historical Review* 75 (December 1969): 601–603, rev. ed. in White, *Pragmatism and the American Mind*, 204, 207.

42. By the early 1970s even this semblance of order was eroding. The work of G. H. von Wright splintered this debate by rehabilitating teleological causation. See his *Explanation and Understanding* (Ithaca: Cornell University Press, 1971); Juha Manninen and Raimo Tuomela, eds., *Essays on Explanation and Understanding* (Dordrecht, Holland: D. Reidel, 1976); and Rex Martin, *Historical Explanations: Re-enactment and Practical Inference* (Ithaca: Cornell University Press, 1977).

43. See especially Dray, *Laws and Explanation in History*. An earlier study, Patrick Gardiner, *The Nature of Historical Explanation* (London: Oxford University Press, 1952), anticipated Dray's work. Hempel's own position had evolved considerably by this point. See his *Aspects of Scientific Explanation and Other Essays in the Philosophy of Science* (New York: The Free Press, 1965), esp. 331–489. Again, Ricoeur's *Time and Narrative,* vol. 1, offers the best overview.

44. See, for instance, Fernand Braudel, *On History* (London: Weidenfeld and Nicolson, 1980), 11–12. The narrative/social history opposition has been assumed more often than analyzed. For discussions by social historians, see Lawrence Stone, "The Revival of Narrative: Reflections on a New Old History," *Past and Present* 85 (November 1979): 3–24; Philip Abrams, "History, Sociology, Historical Sociology," *Past and Present* 87 (May 1980): 3–16; and June Philipp, "Traditional Historical Narrative and Action-Oriented (or Ethnographic) History," *Historical Studies* 20 (April 1983): 339–352. For more critical discussions see William H. Dray, "Narrative versus Analysis in History," *Philosophy of the Social Sciences* 15 (1985): 125–145, and Alan Megill, "Recounting the Past: 'Description,' Explanation, and Narrative in Historiography," *American Historical Review* 94 (June 1989): 627–653.

45. For overviews see Novick, *That Noble Dream,* 440–445; Lloyd, *Explanation in Social History,* 1–24; Alice Kessler-Harris, "Social History," in Eric Foner, ed., *The New American History* (Philadelphia: Temple University Press, 1990), 163–184; Laurence Veysey, "The 'New' Social History in the Context of American Historical Writing," *Reviews in American History* 7 (1979): 1–12; and Olivier Zunz, "The Synthesis of Social Change: Reflections on American Social History," in Zunz, ed., *Reliving the Past: The Worlds of Social History* (Chapel Hill: University of North Carolina Press, 1985), 53–114. For views of two influential practitioners, see Braudel, *On History,* and Charles Tilly, *As Sociology Meets History* (New York: Academic Press, 1981).

46. Murray G. Murphey, *Our Knowledge of the Historical Past* (Indianapolis: Bobbs-Merrill, 1973), 81. As a result, Murphey's model differs logically from Hempel's. Reducing generalizations to probabilities means that the covering law model is no longer deductive. We now have an inductive-statistical syllogism, for conclusions may only be *inferred* and not *deduced* from probability statements. Hempel also introduced a statistical version of the covering law model. See his "Deductive Nomological vs. Statistical Explanation," in Herbert Feigl and Grover Maxwell, eds., *Minnesota Studies in the Philosophy of Science* (Minneapolis: University of Minnesota Press, 1962), 3:98–169. See also Miller, *Fact and Method,* 118–126, and Salmon, *Four Decades of Scientific Explanation,* 50–60. Beyond this, the ways and means of establishing probability relationships are quite complex. Murphey worried that evidentiary problems might prove insurmountable. Peter McClelland, *Causal Explanation and Model*

Building in History, Economics, and the New Economic History (Ithaca: Cornell University Press, 1975), reached a similar conclusion, although, for economic historians at least, such uncertain procedures remain the only game in town. And where in Hempel's statistical model the strength of an explanation is measured by the strength of the correlation, still another modification makes probabilistic explanations dependent on the accuracy of the correlation, regardless of how strong it might be. See Wesley Salmon et al., *Statistical Explanation and Statistical Relevance* (Pittsburgh: University of Pittsburgh Press, 1971). For a more recent treatment of empirical justification of causal claims, see C. Behan McCullagh, *Justifying Causal Descriptions* (Cambridge: Cambridge University Press, 1984), and Raymond Martin, *The Past within Us.* Murphey has recently amended his earlier stance by describing probabilistic models as "covering generalizations" and admitting that they need not be "causal laws," but he leaves his understanding otherwise intact. See his "Explanation, Causes, and Covering Laws," in *History and Theory,* Beiheft 25, pp. 43–57, and his *Philosophical Foundations of Historical Knowledge* (Albany: SUNY Press, 1994), 97–134.

47. Murphey, *Our Knowledge of the Historical Past,* 70, 85.

48. Ibid., 121. For Hempel and the strict unity-of-method theorists, such functional descriptions were not truly explanatory. See his *Aspects of Scientific Explanation,* 297–330; Miller, *Fact and Method,* 118–126, and Salmon, *Four Decades of Scientific Explanation,* 111–116. See also Murphey's more recent work, *Philosophical Foundations of Historical Knowledge,* 97–134.

49. I am grouping a number of theorists into a camp that is sometimes defined more narrowly. All, however, share the root metaphor of system, a belief in the preeminence of structural relations over individuals, and (in varying degrees) a commitment to a social science agenda of hypothesis construction and testing. Whether all structuralist explanations may be categorized as what Hempel calls "functional analysis" is not clear. The original texts are Jean Piaget, *Structuralism* (London: Routledge, 1971); Noam Chomsky, *Language and Mind* (1962; rev. ed., New York: Harcourt, Brace, and Jovanovich, 1972); and Robert K. Merton, *Social Theory and Social Structure: Toward the Codification of Theory and Research* (Glencoe, Ill.: The Free Press, 1949); Claude Lévi-Strauss, *Structural Anthropology,* trans. Claire Jacobson and Brooke G. Schoepf, (orig. ed., 1958; Eng.-lang. ed., New York: Doubleday, 1967), 31.

50. Elazar Weinryb, "The Justification of a Causal Thesis: An Analysis of the Controversies over the Theses of Pirenne, Turner, and Weber," *History and Theory* 14 (1975): 32–56. Stanley Elkins and Eric McKitrick, "A New Meaning for Turner's Frontier, Part 1: Democracy in the Old Northwest" and "Part 2: The Southwest Frontier and New England," *Political Science Quarterly* 69 (September and December 1954): 321–353 and 565–602. For convenience subsequent references will be to page numbers. Weinryb also mentioned Merle Curti et al., *The Making of an American Community: A Case Study of Democracy in a Frontier County* (Stanford: Stanford University Press, 1959). Hofstadter too invoked both these works as support for Turner's general argument.

51. Elkins and McKitrick, "A New Meaning for Turner's Frontier," 325, 602. See Merton, *Social Theory and Social Structure,* 3–111. Elkins and McKitrick refer frequently to Merton, Patricia S. West, and Marie Jahoda's massive commu-

nity study, *Patterns of Social Life: Explorations in the Sociology and Social Psychology of Housing* (Bureau of Applied Social Research, Columbia University, n.d.).

52. Elkins and McKitrick, "A New Meaning for Turner's Frontier," 334, 339, 348, 349.

53. Weinryb, "Justification of a Causal Thesis," 46. This sort of justification is usually called "theoretical." See Wilfrid Sellars's classic article, "Theoretical Explanation," in Joseph C. Pitt, ed., *Theories of Explanation* (New York: Oxford University Press, 1988), 156–166.

54. Allan G. Bogue, in "Social Theory and the Pioneer," *Agricultural History* 34 (January 1960): 21–34, made a similar point in his critique of Elkins and McKitrick, arguing that Merton's functionalism paid too little attention to conflict.

55. See the worries expressed in W. N. Davis Jr., "Will the West Survive as a Field of American History? A Survey Report," *Mississippi Valley Historical Review* 50 (March 1964): 672–685. One index of this shift is the change in the title and focus of one of the by-products of Turnerian history, a journal called *Mississippi Valley Historical Review*, which had effectively devoted its first fifty volumes to topics associated with western and frontier history. In 1967 it became *The Journal of American History*. See William D. Aeschbacher's historical summary "The Mississippi Valley Historical Association, 1907–1965," *Journal of American History* 54 (September 1967): 339–353. Within six years, frontier and western historians had their own journal, *Western Historical Quarterly*, compelling evidence that western history had moved out of the mainstream and become a subspecialty.

56. Thomas Kuhn, *The Structure of Scientific Revolutions* (1962; 2d ed., Chicago: University of Chicago Press, 1970). All subsequent references will be to this edition. Patricia Nelson Limerick, "The Trail to Santa Fe: The Unleashing of the Western Public Intellectual," in *Trails: Toward a New Western History*, 64.

57. Kuhn, *Structure of Scientific Revolutions*, 147. For introductions to this literature, see Imre Lakatos and Alan Musgrave, eds., *Criticism and the Growth of Knowledge* (Cambridge: Cambridge University Press, 1970), and Gary Gutting, ed., *Paradigms and Revolutions: Appraisals and Applications of Thomas Kuhn's Philosophy of Science* (Notre Dame: University of Notre Dame Press, 1980).

58. Many historians believed systematization was possible and desirable. See David Hackett Fischer, *Historian's Fallacies: Toward a Logic of Historical Thought* (New York: Harper, 1970), and Robert F. Berkhofer Jr., *A Behavioral Approach to Historical Analysis* (New York: The Free Press, 1969).

59. See Murray Murphey, *Our Knowledge of the Historical Past*, 26 and 86; Gene Wise, *American Historical Explanations* (1973; 2d rev. ed., Minneapolis: University of Minnesota Press, 1980).

60. Margaret Masterson, "The Nature of a Paradigm," in *Criticism and the Growth of Knowledge*, 59–90. See Kuhn's postscript to the second edition of his *Structure of Scientific Revolutions*, 174–210.

61. David Hollinger, "T. S. Kuhn's Theory of Science and Its Implications for History" (1970), in *Paradigms and Revolutions*, 195–222.

62. Gene Wise's 1973 study *Historical Explanation in American History*

met with a rough critical reception, partly because of these sorts of difficulties. Wise sometimes substitutes his own neologism, "explanation-forms," for Kuhn's paradigms, but the alternative taxonomy did not excite those intellectual historians who found the project unpersuasive. Little of what is valuable in *American Historical Explanations* derives from specifically Kuhnian insights. Wise, in fact, abjures any systematic reconstruction of a Progressive paradigm (in terms of formal propositions, heuristics shared, students trained, or exemplars studied) by explaining that so many historiographers have described the group that any additional definition is unnecessary.

63. And it is not at all clear that even this sort of procedure is entirely useful. For claims that the social sciences cannot be usefully described in terms of disciplinary matrices, see Douglas Lee Eckberg and Lester Hill Jr., "The Paradigm Concept and Sociology: A Critical Review," in *Paradigms and Revolutions,* 117–136, and Paul A. Roth, *Meaning and Method in the Social Sciences: A Case for Methodological Pluralism* (Ithaca: Cornell University Press, 1987). Among the many works that engage philosophy of social science, I have found the following especially helpful: Jürgen Habermas, *On the Logic of the Social Sciences,* trans. Shierry W. Nicholsen and Jerry A. Stark (orig. ed., 1967; Eng.-lang. ed., Cambridge: MIT Press, 1988); Mary Hesse, *Revolutions and Reconstructions in the Philosophy of Science* (Brighton: Harvester Press, 1980); Barry Barnes, *T. S. Kuhn and Social Science* (London: Macmillan, 1982); Richard Rorty, "Method, Social Science, and Social Hope" in *Consequences of Pragmatism* (Minneapolis: University of Minnesota Press, 1982), 191–210, and *Objectivity, Relativism, and Truth: Philosophical Papers,* vol. 1 (Cambridge: Cambridge University Press, 1991); and Hilary Putnam, *Reason, Truth and History* (Cambridge: Cambridge University Press, 1981).

64. Louis O. Mink, "The Autonomy of Historical Understanding" (1965), reprinted in Brian Fay et al., eds., *Historical Understanding* (Ithaca: Cornell University Press, 1987), 73–75. See also Mink, "History and Fiction as Modes of Comprehension" (1970) and "Narrative Form as a Cognitive Instrument" (1978), in *Historical Understanding,* 42–60, 182–203. Michael Oakshott had anticipated Mink's argument. See his *Experience and Its Modes* (Cambridge: Cambridge University Press, 1933), 126–145. Mink's discussions of history are treated in Richard T. Vann, "Louis Mink's Linguistic Turn," *History and Theory* 26 (1987): 1–14. This observation about historical hypotheses parallels that in Rolf Gruner, "Historical Facts and the Testing of Hypotheses," *American Philosophical Quarterly* 5 (April 1968): 124–129.

65. Arthur C. Danto, "Mere Chronicle and History Proper," *Journal of Philosophy* 50 (1953): 173–182; Danto, "On Historical Questioning," *Journal of Philosophy* 51 (1954): 89–99; and Danto, "On Explanations in History," *Philosophy of Science* 23 (1956): 15–30.

66. "Narrative Sentences" (1962) appeared in his book *Analytical Philosophy of History* (New York: Columbia University Press, 1965). This book, plus two additional chapters, was reprinted as *Narration and Knowledge* (New York: Columbia University Press, 1985). All page references will be to the 1985 edition; the citations are from pp. 132, 152, and 167. Danto's argument about narrative sentences addressed an already old debate over whether there were such things as statements specifically about the past. See Clarence Irving Lewis, *Mind and*

the World Order (New York: Charles Scribner's Sons, 1929), esp. 150–152; A. J. Ayer, "Statements about the Past," (1950), reprinted in *Philosophical Essays* (London: Macmillan, 1954), 167–190; and Jack W. Meiland, *Scepticism and Historical Knowledge* (New York: Random House, 1965). See also Kerwin Lee Klein, "Anti-History," *CLIO* 25 (Winter 1996): 125–143.

67. Some have claimed Danto defers to the covering law model. Mink, "Philosophical Analysis and Historical Understanding," 118–146, makes this argument, as does J. H. Hexter's review in *New York Review of Books*, March 9, 1967, pp. 24–28. My reading is supported by Danto himself, in his response to Hexter in *NYRB*, March 23, 1967, and in the new preface to *Narration and Knowledge*. See also Alan Donagan's review essay in *History and Theory* 6 (1967): 430–435, and Habermas, *On the Logic of the Social Sciences*, 33–35, 155–160. Danto was attacked for his narrative relativism by Maurice Mandelbaum. See Maurice Mandelbaum, "A Note on History as Narrative," *History and Theory* 6 (1967): 413–419; Richard G. Ely, Rolf Gruner, and William H. Dray, "Mandelbaum on Historical Narrative: A Discussion," *History and Theory* 8 (1969): 275–294; and C. Beham McCullagh, "Narrative and Explanation in History," *Mind* 78 (1969): 256–261.

68. Danto, *Narration and Knowledge*, 233; Turner, *Early Writings*, 220.

69. *Narration and Knowledge*, 255. Indeed, we might as easily reform general laws into narratives. As Danto pointed out, Hempel's most famous example, that of a radiator bursting in an automobile, was written in narrative form.

70. Mink, *Historical Understanding*, 77, 133. I do not claim that all historical hypotheses will take the form of narrative sentences, although this seems to be the case with most of Turner's equations.

71. Narrative and stories are not to be conflated with the literary forms known as "realist fiction," such as are found in Dickens novels. For a discussion of the ways in which we might profitably broaden conceptions of narrative, see Ricoeur, *Time and Narrative;* Terry Pinkard, "Historical Explanation and the Grammar of Theories," *Philosophy of the Social Sciences* 8 (1978): 227–240; George A. Reisch, "Chaos, History, and Narrative," *History and Theory* 30 (1991): 1–20; and Donald N. McCloskey, "History, Differential Equations, and the Problem of Narration," *History and Theory* 30 (1991): 21–36. It may be, as some critics have argued, that Danto had in mind an archaic style of historical narrative, but this does not mean that his general argument cannot be applied to social history. For the critiques see Murphey, *Our Knowledge of the Historical Past*, 113–132, and Phillip, "Traditional Historical Narrative."

72. Danto, *Narration and Knowledge*, xii, xiii; Mink, "History and Fiction as Modes of Comprehension." See also Danto's recent reformulation, in "Narrative and Style," *Journal of Aesthetics and Art Criticism* 49 (Summer 1991): 201–210.

73. In Mink's words, " 'Events' (or more precisely, descriptions of events) are not the raw material out of which narratives are constructed; rather, an event is an abstraction from a narrative." See *Historical Understanding*, 192. Compare with Donald Davidson, *Actions and Events* (Oxford: Clarendon Press, 1980), and Bruce Vermazen and Merrill B. Hintikka, eds., *Essays on Davidson: Actions and Events* (Oxford: Clarendon Press, 1985).

74. Mink, *Historical Understanding*, 199. The larger question was, Could

narratives be verified? See Leon J. Goldstein, *Historical Knowing* (Austin: University of Texas Press, 1976), and the responses to Goldstein's constructionist position in "The Constitution of the Historical Past," *History and Theory*, Beiheft 16 (Baltimore: Johns Hopkins University Press, 1976). Also important here are Maurice Mandelbaum, *The Anatomy of Historical Knowledge* (Baltimore: Johns Hopkins University Press, 1977); Pinkard, "Historical Explanation and the Grammar of Theories"; Leon Pompa, "Truth and Fact in History," in Pompa and W. H. Dray, eds., *Substance and Form in History* (Edinburgh: University of Edinburgh Press, 1981), 171–186; William H. Dray, *On History and Philosophers of History* (Leiden: E. J. Brill, 1989); and Paul A. Roth, "Narrative Explanations: The Case of History," *History and Theory* 27 (1988): 1–13.

75. *Metahistory: The Historical Imagination in Nineteenth-Century Europe* (Baltimore: Johns Hopkins University Press, 1973). An earlier article, "The Burden of History" (1966), reprinted in his *Tropics of Discourse: Essays in Cultural Criticism* (Baltimore: Johns Hopkins University Press, 1978), 272–250, had suggested the directions in which White was moving. See also his *The Content of the Form: Narrative Discourse and Historical Representation* (Baltimore: Johns Hopkins University Press, 1987).

76. Northrop Frye, *Anatomy of Criticism: Four Essays* (Princeton: Princeton University Press, 1957), and *Fables of Identity: Studies in Poetic Mythology* (New York: Harbinger, 1963); Kenneth Burke, *Permanence and Change: An Anatomy of Purpose* (1935; rev. ed., Berkeley: University of California Press, 1965); *Attitudes toward History* (1937; rev. ed., Berkeley: University of California Press, 1961); *The Philosophy of Literary Form: Studies in Symbolic Action* (1941; 3d ed., Berkeley: University of California Press, 1973); *A Grammar of Motives* (1945; reprint, Berkeley: University of California Press, 1962). See also Frank Lentricchia, "Reading History with Burke," in Hayden White and Margaret Brose, eds., *Representing Kenneth Burke: Selected Essays from the English Institute* (Baltimore: Johns Hopkins University Press, 1982), 119–149.

77. See Burke, *A Grammar of Motives*, 503–517. This scheme preceded Burke by many centuries, however, and White here also draws directly on eighteenth-century philosopher Giambattista Vico. See *The New Science of Giambattista Vico*, trans. Thomas G. Bergin and Max H. Fisch (Ithaca: Cornell University Press, 1968).

78. The argument is most clearly spelled out in the introduction to White's *Tropics of Discourse*, 1–25. For discussions of White's tropology, see John S. Nelson, review in *History and Theory* 14 (1975): 74–91; "*Metahistory*: Six Critiques," *History and Theory*, suppl. 19 (Baltimore: Johns Hopkins University Press, 1980); Wallace Martin, "Floating an Issue of Tropes," *Diacritics* 12 (Spring 1982): 75–83; Hans Kellner, "The Issue in the Bullrushes: A Reply to Wallace Martin," *Diacritics* 12 (Spring 1982): 84–88; Fredric Jameson, "Foreword," in Algirdas Julien Greimas, *On Meaning: Selected Writings in Semantic Theory*, trans. Paul J. Perron and Frank H. Collins (orig. ed., 1976–1983; Eng.-lang. ed., Minneapolis: University of Minnesota Press, 1987), vi–xiii; and Wulf Kansteiner, "Hayden White's Critique of the Writing of History," *History and Theory* 32 (1993): 273–295. White further complicated his scheme by correlating plot modes and tropes with Pepper's forms of argument and Mannheim's ideo-

logical systems. I have focused on the tropes and *mythoi* as those elements that proved most influential. Significantly, White's own work after *Metahistory* does not use the labels of Pepper or Mannheim.

79. See the essays in "Metahistory: Six Critiques"; Paul Ricoeur, *Time and Narrative*, 1:161–168; Perry Anderson, "On Emplotment: Two Kinds of Ruin," in Saul Friedlander, ed., *Probing the Limits of Representation: Nazism and the "Final Solution"* (Cambridge: Harvard University Press, 1992), 54–65; Carl Ginzburg, "Just One Witness," in ibid., 82–96; Dominick La Capra, "A Poetics of Historiography: Hayden White's *Tropics of Discourse*" (1978), reprinted in *Rethinking Intellectual History: Texts, Contexts, Language* (Ithaca: Cornell University Press, 1983), 72–83; Sande Cohen, *Historical Culture: On the Recoding of an Academic Discipline* (Berkeley: University of California Press, 1986), 80–85; Didier Coste, *Narrative as Communication* (Minneapolis: University of Minnesota Press, 1991), 15–32; Russell Jacoby, "A New Intellectual History?" *American Historical Review* 97 (April 1992): 405–424; Fredric Jameson, "Figural Relativism, or the Poetics of Historiography," *Diacritics* 6 (Spring 1976): 2–9; David Carroll, "On Tropology: The Forms of History," *Diacritics* 6 (Fall 1976): 58–64; and Kansteiner, "Hayden White's Critique."

80. See Vincent Leitch, *American Literary Criticism from the Thirties to the Eighties* (New York: Columbia University Press, 1988), especially 249–251, where he associates Hayden White with structuralism rather than formalism or myth criticism. Compare with Kansteiner, "Hayden White's Critique."

81. White, *Metahistory*, 21, 428; White, *Tropics of Discourse*, 85; Jacoby, "A New Intellectual History?"; Kansteiner, "Hayden White's Critique"; W. V. O. Quine and J. S. Ullian, *The Web of Belief* (New York: Random House, 1970), 43; Max Black, *On Models and Metaphors* (Ithaca: Cornell University Press, 1962); Mary B. Hesse, *Models and Analogies in Science* (Notre Dame: University of Notre Dame Press, 1966); Reisch, "Chaos, History, and Narrative"; McKloskey, "History, Differential Equations, and the Problem of Narration"; McCloskey, *If You're So Smart: The Narrative of Economic Expertise* (Chicago: University of Chicago Press, 1990); Joseph Margolis, *Texts without Referents: Reconciling Science and Narrative* (Oxford: Basil Blackwell, 1989); N. Katherine Hayles, *Chaos Bound: Orderly Disorder in Contemporary Literature and Science* (Ithaca: Cornell University Press, 1990).

82. Mink, *Historical Understanding*, 199.

83. On narrative and the natural sciences, see n. 81 above, and Haskell Fain, *Between Philosophy and History: The Resurrection of Speculative Philosophy within the Analytic Tradition* (Princeton: Princeton University Press, 1970), 277–308; Hayden White, "The Fictions of Factual Representation" (1976), reprinted in *Tropics of Discourse*, 121–134; Alasdair MacIntyre, "Epistemological Crises, Dramatic Narrative, and the Philosophy of Science," in *Paradigms and Revolutions*, 54–74; and Hull, "Central Subjects and Historical Narratives."

Book Two: From Spirit to System

1. Naturalistic readings of Turner began early and have proliferated. See Carl Becker, "Frederick Jackson Turner," in Howard W. Odum, ed., *American*

Masters of Social Science (New York: Holt, 1927), 273–318; Merle Curti, "The Section and the Frontier in American History: The Methodological Concepts of Frederick Jackson Turner," in Stuart A. Rice, ed., *Methods in Social Science* (Chicago: University of Chicago Press, 1931), 353–367; John Higham, *History: Professional Scholarship in America* (1965; rev. ed., Baltimore; Johns Hopkins University Press, 1983), 174–179; William A. Coleman, "Science and Symbol in the Turner Hypothesis," *American Historical Review* 72 (October 1966): 22–49; Wilbur R. Jacobs, "Turner's Methodology: Multiple Working Hypotheses or Ruling Theory?" *Journal of American History* 54 (March 1968): 853–863; Richard Hofstadter, *The Progressive Historians: Turner, Parrington, Beard* (1968; reprint, New York: Vintage, 1970); Ray Allen Billington, *The Genesis of the Frontier Thesis: A Study in Historical Creativity* (San Marino, Calif.: Huntington Library, 1971); Billington, *Frederick Jackson Turner: Historian, Scholar, Teacher* (New York: Oxford University Press, 1973); Peter Novick, *That Noble Dream: The "Objectivity Question" and the American Historical Profession* (Cambridge: Cambridge University Press, 1988), 91–104; William Cronon, "Revisiting the Vanishing Frontier: The Legacy of Frederick Jackson Turner," *Western Historical Quarterly* 18 (April 1987): 157–176; Cronon, "Turner's First Stand: The Significance of Significance in American History," in Richard W. Etulain, ed., *Writing Western History: Essays on Major Western Historians* (Albuquerque: University of New Mexico Press, 1991), 73–101; and Wilbur R. Jacobs, *On Turner's Trail: One Hundred Years of Writing Western History* (Lawrence: University Press of Kansas, 1994). Ernst Breisach, *American Progressive History: An Experiment in Modernization* (Chicago: University of Chicago Press, 1993), 21–28, is one of the few that engages Turner's early, more idealistic work.

2. Dorothy Ross, "American Historical Consciousness in the Nineteenth Century," *American Historical Review* 89 (December 1984): 909–928; Ross, *The Origins of American Social Science* (Cambridge: Cambridge University Press, 1991), 266–274. This book describes Turner as part of the historicist reaction against the first wave of Americanists trained in Germany. For a millennialist reading of Turner, see David W. Noble, *Historians against History: The Frontier Thesis and the National Covenant in American Historical Writing* (Minneapolis: University of Minnesota Press, 1965). Republican readings, which followed quickly on the heels of J. G. A. Pocock's work on republicanism and civic virtue, may be found in David W. Noble, *The End of American History: Democracy, Capitalism, and the Metaphor of Two Worlds in Anglo-American Historical Writing, 1880–1980* (Minneapolis: University of Minnesota Press, 1985), and Donald R. Pickens, "The Turner Thesis and Republicanism: A Historiographical Commentary," *Pacific Historical Review* 61 (August 1992): 319–340.

3. "The Significance of History," *Wisconsin Journal of Education* 21 (October/November 1891): 230–234, 253–256, reprinted in *The Early Writings of Frederick Jackson Turner,* ed. Fulmer Mood (Madison: University of Wisconsin Press, 1938), 43–68; all references will be to the Mood edition of the essay (hereinafter "Significance of History"). Although this piece did not become well known among Americanists, European historiographers have treated it as one of the most important elements of Turnerian history. In 1956 Fritz Stern

reprinted it in his influential teaching anthology *The Varieties of History* (1955; reprint, Cleveland: World Publishing, 1963), 197–208, the only essay in the volume written by a nineteenth-century Americanist and one of only five written by Americans at all. See also the discussion of Turner in Ernst Breisach, *Historiography: Ancient, Medieval, and Modern* (Chicago: University of Chicago Press, 1983), 316.

4. "Significance of History," 43, 48. This should be compared with a similar passage in one of Turner's sources, the 1882 edition of J. G. Droysen's *Grundriss der Historik* (1858–1882), reprinted in Peter Leyh, ed., *Historik: Historisch-kritische Ausgabe von Peter Leyh* (Stuttgart-Bad Cannstatt: Frommann-Holboog, 1977), 415–417. Turner later acquired the translation of this work, *Outline of the Principles of History*, trans. E. Benjamin Andrews (Boston: Ginn, 1897). References will be to Leyh's German edition, with references to the *Outline* in parentheses.

5. "Significance of History," 43, 49, 50. Turner is actually quoting Lord Acton, "German Schools of History," *English Historical Review* 1 (January 1886): 7–42, reprinted in *Selected Writings of Lord Acton*, vol. 2: *Essays in the Study and Writing of History*, ed. J. Rufus Fears (Indianapolis: Liberty Classics, 1985), 327. Turner does not quote Herder. Much of his summation seems to be based on Acton's but with one telling difference: Turner described Niebuhr and Ranke as *continuing* rather than breaking with the romantic idealists. On Adams and scientific history see R. J. Cunningham, "The German Historical World of Herbert Baxter Adams, 1874–1876," *Journal of American History* 68 (1981): 261–275; John Higham, "Herbert Baxter Adams and the Study of Local History," *American Historical Review* 89 (December 1984): 1225–1239, and Ross, "American Historical Consciousness in the Nineteenth Century."

6. "Significance of History," 52.

7. Ibid., 52–54. Compare this with Herbert Baxter Adams, *Methods of Historical Study* (Baltimore: Johns Hopkins University Press, 1884).

8. Among the many works on biology, evolution, and historical thought, see Peter J. Bowler, *The Invention of Progress: The Victorians and the Past* (Oxford: Oxford University Press, 1989); Stephen Toulmin and June Goodfield, *The Discovery of Time* (Chicago: University of Chicago Press, 1965), esp. 141–246; Hayden White, *Tropics of Discourse: Essays in Cultural Criticism* (Baltimore: Johns Hopkins University Press, 1978), 121–134; Maurice Mandelbaum, *History, Man, and Reason: A Study in Nineteenth-Century Thought* (Baltimore: Johns Hopkins University Press, 1971); and Ross, "American Historical Consciousness in the Nineteenth Century."

9. On Turner as rhetorician, see Merrill Lewis, "Language, Literature, Rhetoric, and the Shaping of the Historical Imagination of Frederick Jackson Turner," *Pacific Historical Review* 45 (August 1976): 399–424, and Ronald Carpenter, *The Eloquence of Frederick Jackson Turner* (San Marino, Calif.: Huntington Library, 1983).

10. Georg W. F. Hegel, *The Phenomenology of Spirit*, trans. A. V. Miller (orig. ed., 1807; Eng.-lang. ed., Oxford: Oxford University Press, 1977), and *The Philosophy of History*, trans. J. Sibree (Eng.-lang. ed., New York: Dover, 1956). The quote "ritualistic three-step" comes from Walter Kaufmann's *Hegel:*

A Reinterpretation (Garden City, N.Y.: Doubleday, 1966), 158. See also Robert C. Solomon, *In the Spirit of Hegel: A Study of G. W. F. Hegel's Phenomenology of Spirit* (New York, 1983), esp. 22; Charles Taylor's magisterial *Hegel* (Cambridge: Cambridge University Press, 1975), esp. 127–147, 214–224; Josiah Royce, *The Spirit of Modern Philosophy* (Boston: Houghton Mifflin, 1892), 215–216; and Royce, *Lectures on Modern Idealism* (1919; reprint, New Haven: Yale University Press, 1967), 136–160.

11. On Hegelianism in America, see Henry A. Pochmann, *New England Transcendentalism and St. Louis Hegelianism* (Philadelphia: Carl Schurz, 1948), and *German Culture in America: Philosophical and Literary Influences, 1600–1900* (Madison: University of Wisconsin Press, 1957); Jürgen Herbst, *The German Historical School in American Scholarship* (Ithaca: Cornell University Press, 1965); William H. Goetzmann, *The American Hegelians: An Intellectual Episode in the History of Western America* (New York: Alfred Knopf, 1973); Loyd D. Easton, *Hegel's First American Followers* (Athens: Ohio University Press, 1966); Elizabeth Flower and Murray G. Murphey, *A History of Philosophy in America* (New York: Capricorn, 1977), 2: 463–514; and Bruce Kuklick, *Churchmen and Philosophers: From Jonathan Edwards to John Dewey* (New Haven: Yale University Press, 1985), 117–190. On Turner and Hegel see W. Stull Holt, "Hegel, the Turner Hypothesis, and the Safety-Valve Theory," *Agricultural History* 22 (July 1948): 175–176.

12. "Significance of History," 53. The quote is from Droysen's *Grundriss,* 442 (*Outline,* 44). Turner may also, as Holt suggests, have known Hegel in the original or in translation (Sibree's English edition of *The Philosophy of History* came out in 1862). And if he read carefully those works he listed in the bibliography to "Significance of History," he would have encountered Hegel both glossed and quoted in Rudolf Rocholl, *Aufbau einer Philosophie der Geschichte* (1878; reprint, Göttingen: Vandenhök und Ruprecht, 1911). We can imagine a young Turner reading with special interest a passage from p. 465: "Hier entfaltete sich in machtigem Aufstreben 'die neue Welt.'—Hegel sagte: Die Weltgeschichte gebt von Osten nach Westen, denn Europe ist schlechthin das Ende der Weltgeschichte, Asien der Anfang." By the 1890s this idea had reached the status of literary formula, and Turner reached Johns Hopkins with this basic figure, if not its full significance, already in hand. In an 1887 letter to his fiancée, he wrote: "The history of this great country remains to be written. . . . I am placed in a *new* society . . . ready to take its course in universal history. . . . The west looks to the future, the east to the past." Turner to Mae Sherwood, September 5, 1887, cited in Michael C. Steiner, "Frederick Jackson Turner and Western Regionalism," in *Writing Western History,* 107.

13. Droysen, *Grundriss,* 442, 443 (*Outline,* 45–46, 48). Turner used this again in "The Development of American Society" (1908), reprinted in Wilbur Jacobs, ed., *Frederick Jackson Turner's Legacy: Unpublished Writings in American History* (San Marino, Calif.: Huntington Library, 1965), 168–169. Herbert Baxter Adams probably brought this passage to Turner's attention, for Adams quoted it himself, although to very different ends. See *Columbus and the Discovery of America* (Baltimore: Johns Hopkins University Press, 1892), 22. Turner made this aphorism a staple in his seminars and repeated it to various

correspondents. See Jacobs, "Introduction," *Turner's Legacy,* 20–21; Turner to Carl Becker, December 16, 1925, in Billington, *Genesis of the Frontier Thesis,* 243; Turner to Merle Curti, August 8, 1928, in ibid., 257; Carl Becker to Frederick Jackson Turner, May 16, 1910, in *What Is the Good of History? Selected Letters of Carl Becker, 1900–1945,* ed. Michael Kammen (Ithaca: Cornell University Press, 1973), 15–17; and Lewis, "Historical Imagination of Frederick Jackson Turner." Billington, *Genesis of the Frontier Thesis,* 298, finds Turner "over-stressing Droysen's dictum that history was the self-consciousness of humanity." Jacobs, *On Turner's Trail,* 30, reads the use of Droysen as evidence of Turner's devotion to social evolutionism. Turner had encountered a similar aphorism in the work of his mentor at Wisconsin, William F. Allen, whose collaborative work with P. V. N. Myers, *Ancient History for Colleges and Highschools,* Part 1: *The Eastern Nations and Greece* (Boston: Ginn and Company, 1890), opens with the sentence: "History is the narrative of the life of humanity" (p. 1).

14. "Significance of History," 53; Droysen, *Grundriss,* 443: "Das Boese haftet an dem endlichen Geist" (*Outline,* 47); Turner to Carl Becker, Dec. 1, 1925, reprinted in Billington, *Genesis of the Frontier Thesis,* 233.

15. "Significance of History," 56, 57.

16. Ibid., 56, 57. Compare this with the formulation in one of Turner's more traditional sourcebooks, E. Benjamin Andrews, *Brief Institutes of General History,* 5th ed. (Boston: Silver, Burdett, 1897), 1: "The term history has both an objective and subjective signification—events in themselves, and man's apprehension of events." Here and in the preface to Charles K. Adams, *Manual of Historical Literature* (New York: Harper, 1889), history as past events and history as human consciousness were separated much more sharply than in Turner or Droysen.

17. Droysen, *Grundriss,* 422, 442 (*Outline,* 11, 45). See Acton's unflattering reading in "German Historical Schools." A good account of Droysen's place in German historicism can be found in Georg Iggers, *The German Conception of History* (Middletown, Conn.: Wesleyan University Press, 1968). See also Robert Southard, *Droysen and the Prussian School of History* (Lexington: University Press of Kentucky, 1995); Jörn Rüsen, *Begriffene Geschichte: Genesis und Begründung der Geschichtstheorie J. G. Droysens* (Paderborn: Ferdinand Schöningh, 1969); Rüsen, *Studies in Metahistory* (Pretoria: Human Sciences Research Council, 1993), 97–128; Hans-Georg Gadamer, *Truth and Method,* trans. Joel Weinshimer and Donald G. Marshall, rev. ed. (New York, 1992), 212–218; and Hayden White, "Droysen's *Historik:* Historical Writing as a Bourgeois Science" (1980), in *The Content of the Form: Narrative Discourse and Historical Representation* (Baltimore: Johns Hopkins University Press, 1987), 83–103.

18. Whitman, "Sunday Evening Lectures," in *The Collected Writings of Walt Whitman,* ed. Gay Wilson Allen and Sculley Bradley (New York: New York University, 1984), 2011. See also Whitman, "Carlyle from American Points of View," in *Complete Prose Works* (Philadelphia: David McKay, 1897), 170–178.

19. Whitman, "Passage to India" (1870), in *Leaves of Grass,* rev. ed. (Philadelphia: David McKay, 1900), 346; Kenneth Burke, *Attitudes toward History* (1937; reprint, Berkeley: University of California Press, 1984), 1–33. On Whitman's metaphysics and the frontier metaphor, see Edwin Fussell, *Frontier:*

American Literature and the American West (Princeton: Princeton University Press, 1965), 397–442.

20. Emerson, "Journals," December 22, 1839, in *Selected Writings of Ralph Waldo Emerson*, rev. ed., ed. William A. Gilman (New York: New American Library, 1983), 87; Emerson, "The Poet," reprinted in *The Portable Emerson*, rev. ed., eds. Carl Bode and Malcolm Cowley (New York: Viking, 1981), 261, 262. On Turner's use of Emerson, see Billington, *Genesis of the Frontier Thesis*, 68, and Carpenter, *Eloquence of Frederick Jackson Turner*, 6–7. Of the many commentaries on Emerson, I have found the following especially helpful here: Burke, *Attitudes toward History*, 1–33; John Dewey, "Ralph Waldo Emerson" (1929), in Milton Kovnitz and Stephen Whicher, eds., *Emerson: A Collection of Critical Essays* (Englewood Cliffs, N.J.: Prentice-Hall, 1962), 24–30; David Robinson, *Apostle of Culture: Emerson as Preacher and Lecturer* (Philadelphia: University of Pennsylvania Press, 1982); Richard Poirier, *The Renewal of Literature: Emersonian Reflections* (New Haven: Yale University Press, 1987), 67–94; and Cornel West, *The American Evasion of Philosophy: A Genealogy of Pragmatism* (Madison: University of Wisconsin Press, 1989), 9–41.

21. Still insightful is Perry Miller, "Emersonian Genius and the American Democracy" (1953), in Kovnitz and Whicher, *Emerson*, 60–71. On Emerson's reception, see Mary Kupiec Cayton, "The Making of an American Prophet: Emerson, His Audiences, and the Rise of the Culture Industry in Nineteenth-Century America," *American Historical Review* 92 (June 1987): 597–620.

22. Turner, "The Poet of the Future" (1883), reprinted in Carpenter, *Eloquence of Frederick Jackson Turner*, 122, 123. On this essay, see ibid., 22, 23; Cronon, "Turner's First Stand"; Lewis, "Historical Imagination"; and Billington, *Turner*, 23, 24.

23. On Emerson and Hegel, see Rene Wellek, "Emerson and German Philosophy," *New England Quarterly* 16 (March 1943): 41–62; Pochmann, *New England Transcendentalism;* Kuklick, *Churchmen and Philosophers*, 178–183; and Joseph G. Kronick, *American Poetics of History: From Emerson to the Moderns* (Baton Rouge: Louisiana State University Press, 1984), 37–89. The quotes are from Emerson, "History," in *Portable Emerson*, 114, 115; and Hegel, *Philosophy of History*, 201.

24. Emerson, "Journals," August–September 1851, in Gilman, *Selected Writings*, 153.

25. Compare "Nature" with "The Over-Soul." On this point see Kuklick, *Churchmen and Philosophers;* Perry Miller, *Errand into the Wilderness* (1956; reprint, New York: Harper and Row, 1964), 184–203; and Barbara Packer, "Origin and Authority: Emerson and the Higher Criticism," in Sacvan Bercovitch, ed., *Reconstructing American Literary History* (Cambridge: Harvard University Press, 1986), 67–92.

26. Hegel, *Philosophy of History*, 74. Among the countless works on this topic, compare Taylor, *Hegel*, 389–427; Leon J. Goldstein, "Dialectic and Necessity in Hegel's Philosophy of History," in L. Pompa and W. H. Dray, eds., *Substance and Form in History* (Edinburgh: University of Edinburgh Press, 1981), 42–57; and Paul Ricoeur, *Time and Narrative*, trans. Kathleen McLaughlin and David Pellauer (orig. ed., 1983; Eng.-lang. ed., Chicago: University of Chicago Press, 1984), 3:193–206.

27. Turner, "Significance of History," 63, 64.

28. Droysen, *Grundriss,* 444 (*Outline,* 48). Turner, "Significance of History," 58, 65, 66, 67. Turner's essay here parallels Droysen rather strikingly; see esp. *Grundriss,* 48, 449 (*Outline,* 54, 55, 56). Compare with David Hollinger, "Inquiry and Uplift: Late Nineteenth-Century American Academics and the Moral Efficacy of Scientific Practice," in Thomas L. Haskell, ed., *The Authority of Experts: Studies in History and Theory* (Bloomington: Indiana University Press, 1984), 142–156.

29. "Significance of History," 67. Again compare with Droysen, *Grundriss,* 448, 449 (*Outline,* 49, 54, 55). Turner also used this invocation in a 1910 commencement address at the University of Indiana: "Those who investigate and teach within the university walls must respond to the injunction of the church, '*Sursum corda*'—lift up the heart to high thinking and impartial search for the unsullied truth in the interests of all the people; this is the holy grail of the universities." See "Pioneer Ideals and the State University," reprinted in his *The Frontier in American History* (reprint, New York, 1962), 286, 287.

30. Turner, "Poet of the Future," 122. In a letter to Carl Becker, February 13, 1926, Turner closes with this aside: "No there's no science of history. Sometimes I doubt if there is a real science (in the sense that cuts out history) of anything." Reprinted in Billington, *Genesis of the Frontier Thesis,* 246–247. Again, compare Droysen's articulation in *Grundriss* 449 (*Outline,* 57).

31. Turner, "Significance of History," 64; "Problems in American History" (1892), in Mood, *Early Writings,* 72. See also Tiziana Bonazzi, "Frederick Jackson Turner's Frontier Thesis and the Self-Consciousness of America," *Journal of American Studies* 27 (August 1993): 149–172.

32. Turner, "The Significance of the Frontier in American History" (1893), in Turner, *Frontier in American History,* 4; all references will be to this edition unless otherwise noted. For the publication history of this article, as well as a comparison of its slightly different editions, see Fulmer Mood, *Early Writings,* 1–40, 273–294. By emplotting the story as dialectic, Turner distanced himself from his mentor's version of scientific history. Herbert Baxter Adams wrote United States history as the story of the growth of American democracy from the germs of Anglo-Saxon culture transplanted in New World soil. See Herbert Baxter Adams, *The Germanic Origin of New England Towns* (Baltimore: Johns Hopkins University Press, 1882); Dorothy Ross, "American Historical Consciousness in the Nineteenth Century," *American Historical Review* 89 (December 1984): 1225–1239; John Higham, "Herbert Baxter Adams and the Study of Local History," *American Historical Review* (October 1984): 909–928; Billington, *Frederick Jackson Turner,* 63–75, 162–163; Billington, *Genesis of the Frontier Thesis,* 5–7, 27–29, 90–91, 236; and Herbst, *German Historical School,* 125–126.

33. Perhaps the best overview is again in Mandelbaum, *History, Man, and Nature.* On Droysen, see *Outline,* 9: "Nature and History are the widest conceptions under which the human mind apprehends the world of phenomena." See also the essay "Nature and History," appended to this and the 1882 edition, pp. 90–105. The quotation from Whitman is from "Song of the Red-Wood Tree" (1874), in Lawrence Buell, ed., *Leaves of Grass and Selected Prose* (New York: Random House, 1981), 168. Edwin Fussell, *Frontier: American Literature*

and the American West (Princeton: Princeton University Press, 1973), 3–26, 397–442, places Whitman and, more briefly, Turner in this discursive context.

34. Turner, *Frontier in American History,* 111. See Lee Benson's exercise in source criticism, "The Historian as Myth-Maker: Turner and the Closed Frontier," in David M. Ellis, ed., *The Frontier in American Development: Essays in Honor of Paul Wallace Green* (Ithaca: Cornell University Press, 1969), 3–19.

35. Turner, *Frontier in American History,* and "The Children of the Pioneers" (1926), in *The Significance of Sections in American History* (reprint, Gloucester, Mass.: Peter Smith, 1959), 277–278.

36. Turner, *Frontier in American History,* 267. For different readings, see Smith, *Virgin Land: The American West as Symbol and Myth* (Cambridge: Harvard University Press, 1950), 250–262; David Noble, *Historians against History: The Frontier Thesis and the National Covenant in American Historical Writing since 1830* (Minneapolis: University of Minnesota Press, 1965), 37–65; and Noble, *The End of American History: Democracy, Capitalism, and the Metaphor of Two Worlds in Anglo-American Historical Writing, 1880–1980* (Minneapolis: University of Minnesota Press, 1985), 3–40. For histories of "nature," compare the classic account in R. G. Collingwood, *The Idea of Nature* (1945; reprint, New York: Galaxy, 1960), with those in Carolyn Merchant, *The Death of Nature: Women, Ecology, and the Scientific Revolution* (San Francisco: Harper and Row, 1980), and Londa Schiebinger, *Nature's Body: Gender in the Making of Modern Science* (Boston: Beacon Press, 1993).

37. On gender, nature, and frontier literature, see especially Annette Kolodny, *The Lay of the Land* (Chapel Hill: North Carolina University Press, 1975).

38. On the "free land" metaphor, see William Cronon's summary in "Turner's First Stand." On Turner and social evolution, see Rudolf Freund, "Turner's Theory of Social Evolution," *Agricultural History* 19 (April 1945): 78–87; Coleman, "Science and Symbol"; Billington, *Genesis of the Frontier Thesis,* 53, 168; and Cronon, "First Stand." For an overview of the growing literature on the role of the reader in creating textual meaning, see the essays in Jane P. Tompkins, ed., *Reader-Response Criticism: From Formalism to Post-Structuralism* (Baltimore: Johns Hopkins University Press, 1980). Dominick LaCapra, "History, Language, and Reading: Waiting for Crillon," *American Historical Review* 100 (June 1995): 799–828, discusses historiography and reading. On Turner's readership, see the brief but interesting discussions in Carpenter, *Eloquence of Frederick Jackson Turner.*

39. "The Poet of the Future" (1882), in Carpenter, *Eloquence of Frederick Jackson Turner,* 121–124; "Architecture through Oppression" (1884), in Carpenter, *Eloquence,* 125, 126. All references will be to these editions. Among the scholars who have discussed these essays, see Carpenter, *Eloquence of Frederick Jackson Turner,* 22, 23; Cronon, "First Stand"; and Lewis, "Historical Imagination."

40. "Significance of History," 48. On Turner's literary metaphors, see Lewis, "Historical Imagination." On period use of the textual metaphor, see Lionel Gossman, *Between History and Literature* (Cambridge: Harvard University Press, 1990), 257–284.

41. "Significance of History," 47; "Architecture through Oppression," 125. I do not mean to argue that this is an exhaustive understanding, but it does seem to have been Turner's, and it is one that has been widely shared. See Orrin E. Clapp, "Tragedy and the American Climate of Opinion" (1958), in Robert W. Corrigan, ed., *Tragedy: Vision and Form* (San Francisco: Chandler, 1965), 302–314.

42. David Levin, *History as Romantic Art* (Stanford: Stanford University Press, 1960). For Turner's view of Parkman, see his "Francis Parkman and His Work," *The Dial* (December 16, 1898): 451–453. Henry Steele Commager, *The American Mind: An Interpretation of American Thought and Character since the 1880s* (New Haven: Yale University Press, 1950), 277–298, remains insightful.

43. See Northrop Frye's discussion of romance in *Anatomy of Criticism: Four Essays* (Princeton: Princeton University Press, 1957). That Leatherstocking did not achieve heroic status until the last book in the series has been observed by generations of literary critics. Of the countless essays in this tradition, see especially D. H. Lawrence, *Studies in Classic American Literature* (New York: Thomas Seltzer, 1923) and Smith, *Virgin Land,* 59–70.

44. See Frye's comments, in *Anatomy of Criticism,* on proletarian themes in romance; also A. C. Hamilton, *Northrop Frye: Anatomy of His Criticism* (Toronto: University of Toronto Press, 1990), 123–153; Turner, *The Rise of the New West, 1819–1829* (reprint, New York: Collier, 1962), 46.

45. Whether these critics of romance escaped its grasp is another question. For arguments that they did not, see Richard Chase, *The American Novel and Its Tradition* (Garden City, N.Y.: Doubleday, 1957); Lazar Ziff, *Literary Democracy: The Declaration of Literary Independence in America* (New York: Viking, 1981); and Evon Carter, *The Rhetoric of American Romance: Dialectic and Identity in Emerson, Dickinson, Poe, and Hawthorne* (Baltimore: Johns Hopkins University Press, 1985). Turner's preference for social and psychological types rather than "realistic" characters à la Henry James has been often noted. This taste he seems to have developed quite early. See his early unpublished essay "The Hunter Type" (1890), in Jacobs, *Turner's Legacy,* 153–154; Turner, "Some Sociological Aspects of American History," in ibid., 155–168; and Carpenter, *Eloquence of Frederick Jackson Turner.*

46. Turner, "The Middle West" (1901), in his *Frontier in American History,* 153, 154.

47. Turner acquired a number of translations of canto 26 of Dante's *Inferno* and laboriously made his own translation from the Latin typescript he owned. See Carpenter, *Eloquence of Frederick Jackson Turner,* 28. Turner also later quoted Tennyson's reworking of this canto, "Ulysses." See Turner's "The West and American Ideals," in his *Frontier in American History,* 310: "The Western spirit must be invoked for new and nobler achievements. Of that matured Western spirit, Tennyson's Ulysses is a symbol." For Dante's discussion of *The Divine Comedy,* see his "Letter to Can Grande," in Robert S. Haller, ed., *Literary Criticism of Dante Alighieri* (Lincoln: University of Nebraska Press, 1973), 100. For Northrop Frye's discussion of comedy, see *Anatomy of Criticism,* 167.

48. Its kernel is the agon of nature and history, but Turner spun out a series

of additional dialectical moments. On the French and British wars: a "world-historic conflict" over the "mastery of the interior basin of North America" (*Frontier in American History*, 163, 181). On the Revolution: "In nearly every colony prior to the Revolution, struggles had been in progress between the party of privilege, chiefly the Eastern men of property allied with the English authorities, and the democratic classes, strongest in the West and the cities" (ibid., 111). On regional conflict: "The East has always feared the result of an unregulated advance of the frontier, and has tried to check and guide it" (ibid., 33). On slavery: "Even the slavery struggle . . . occupies its important place in American history because of its relation to westward expansion" (ibid., 3).

49. Turner, "Middle Western Pioneer Democracy" (1918), in his *Frontier in American History*, 349. Billington, *Turner*, 372, reads this passage as evidence of Turner's geographic determinism and commitment to the ideal of the melting pot. Jacobs, *On Turner's Trail*, 23, 25, 52, 53, finds in Turner's prose a careerlong commitment to the "melting-pot theory."

50. Turner, "The Significance of the Mississippi Valley in American History" (1909), in his *Frontier in American History*, 204. Although Turner did not emplot this story within a larger Christian master narrative, there was nothing to prevent his readers from understanding it this way.

51. *Frontier in American History*, 336.

52. On Hegel, Droysen, and liberalism, see Iggers, *German Conception of History*. The quote here is from Anne and Henry Paolucci, eds., *Hegel on Tragedy* (Garden City, N.Y.: Doubleday, 1962), 52. On Hegel's emplotment compare Hayden White, *Metahistory: The Historical Imagination in Nineteenth-Century Europe* (Baltimore: Johns Hopkins University Press, 1973), 90–97, 110–111, 117–123, and Josiah Royce, *Lectures on Modern Idealism*, 136–212.

53. Herbst, *German Historical School*, 203–230, discusses the crisis of German historicism in the United States. On Turner and World War I, see Billington, *Turner*, 345–356. For Turner's comments, see "Middle Western Pioneer Democracy"; also the notes and editorial comments in Wilbur R. Jacobs, *The Historical World of Frederick Jackson Turner* (New Haven: Yale University Press, 1968), 143–149. Turner did not grapple with this problem alone. See the discussion by one of his most famous students, Carl Becker, in *The Declaration of Independence: A Study in the History of Political Ideas* (1922; reprint, New York: Vintage, 1970), 224–279.

54. Turner, "Contributions of the West to American Democracy" (1903), in his *Frontier in American History*, 243.

55. Turner, "Middle Western Pioneer Democracy," 354. Since most commentators have read Turner as a materialist, whether environmental or economic, much criticism has addressed what then looks like a vulgar contradiction: the frontier on which democracy was founded was disappearing. See, for instance, the readings by Smith, *Virgin Land*, 250–262, and Gene Wise, *American Historical Explanations: A Strategy for Grounded Inquiry*, rev. ed. (Minneapolis: University of Minnesota Press, 1980), 179–222. But as we have already seen, Turner's idealism imagined civilization and primitivism to be interdependent rather than exclusive concepts. I do not mean to argue, though, that the vision first set forth in "The Significance of History" continued entirely unmodified throughout his career. Turner grew more conservative and naturalistic with age

and professional success. Compare "The Significance of History" with his 1910 Presidential Address to the American Historical Association, "Social Forces in American History," in his *Frontier in American History*, 311–324.

56. Turner, "The West and American Ideals" (1914), in his *Frontier in American History*, 290–310; quotes from p. 305. See also Jacobs, *On Turner's Trail*, 103–136.

57. *Frontier in American History*, 320, 325.

58. Ibid., 309, 310, 336; Turner to Farrand, February 13, 1919, in Jacobs, *Historical World*, 113. Smith, Wise, and Billington see this as a contrived escape from the straits to which social evolutionism had led him. But Turner expounded this vision in "The Significance of History" well before he developed his frontier history. As we have seen, this theme is explicit in Droysen's *Outline*, and it is one that Turner reiterated throughout his career in essays and commencement addresses. See his "The Extension Work of the University of Wisconsin," *University Extension: A Monthly Devoted to the Interests of Popular Education* 1 (April 1892): 311–324; "The Democratic Education of the Middle West," *World's Work* 6 (August 1903): 3754–3759; "Pioneer Ideals and the State University"; "The West and American Ideals"; "The State University," in Jacobs, *Turner's Legacy*, 194–195; "The Idea of Service in the University," in ibid., 196–197; "The University of the Future," in ibid., 197–199; "The High School and the City," in ibid., 200–208; and the notes and editorial comments in Jacobs, *Historical World*, 67–123.

59. Turner, *The Significance of Sections in American History* (reprint, Gloucester, Mass.: Peter Smith, 1959). Turner invoked Royce in a 1901 address before the Ohio Valley Historical Association, "The Ohio Valley in American History," in his *Frontier in American History*, 157, and again in "The Significance of the Section in American History," in his *Sections*, 45. See Josiah Royce, *Race Questions, Provincialism, and Other American Problems*, New York: Macmillan, 1908; Robert V. Hine, "Josiah Royce: The West as Community," in *Writing Western History*, 19–41; and Hine, "The American West as Metaphysics: A Perspective on Josiah Royce," *Pacific Historical Review* 58 (August 1989): 267–291.

60. Turner, "Significance of the Section," in his *Sections*, 38; "Sections and Nation," in ibid., 338, 339. On Turner's sectional thesis, see Gerald D. Nash, *Creating the West: Historical Interpretations, 1890–1990* (Albuquerque: University of New Mexico Press, 1991), 101–158; Michael C. Steiner, "Frederick Jackson Turner's Western Regionalism," in *Writing Western History*, 103–136; Steiner, "The Significance of Turner's Sectional Thesis," *Western Historical Quarterly* 10 (October 1979): 437–466; Donald Worster, "New West, True West: Interpreting the Region's History," *Western Historical Quarterly* 18 (April 1987): 141–156; Richard Jenson, "On Modernizing Frederick Jackson Turner: The Historiography of Regionalism," *Western Historical Quarterly* 11 (July 1980): 307–322; and Billington, *Turner*, 209–232, 444–471.

61. "Significance of the Section," 46. Turner's use of "culture," *Kultur*, is still an Arnoldian usage distant from that in Boasian anthropology.

62. Turner quotes Lord Bryce in *Rise of the New West*, 66. The quote on Parkman comes from "The Ohio Valley in American History," in *Frontier in American History*, 167. See also Turner's earlier review of Parkman in *The Dial*.

63. "Sections and Nation," 326; "The Significance of the Mississippi Valley

in American History, in *Frontier in American History*, 179. In "The Significance of the Frontier" Turner called his home region "the typically American region" (*Frontier in American History*, 28). See also "Some Sociological Aspects of American History," wherein Turner declared the Middle West "a more characteristically democratic region than any of the others" (ibid., 177); and "The Children of the Pioneers," in *Sections*, 256–286.

64. See the original edition in *Wisconsin Magazine of History* 8 (March 1925): 254; Harold Bloom, *A Map of Misreading* (Oxford: Oxford University Press, 1975); Turner to William E. Dodd, October 7, 1919; Billington, in *Genesis of the Frontier Thesis*, 195; also "Children of the Pioneers," where Turner lists himself at the end of a long line of midwestern "pioneer boys" who became historians (including Hubert Howe Bancroft, James Harvey Robinson, Reuben Gold Thwaites, Herbert Eugene Bolton, and Carl Becker):

The list is too long for complete presentation. It shows a common quality on the part of these men, not only in striking out new lines of investigation, but in interest in the common people; in the emphasis upon economic and social, geographical and psychological interpretation; in the attention to social development rather than to the writing of narrative history of the older type, wherein the heroes were glorified. To the children of the pioneers, if not to their fathers, history was not the lengthened shadow of the great man; it was not the romantic tale, nor the mere effort to set forth bald annals [pp. 277, 278].

65. On the Turnerian academic community, see H. Hale Bellot, *American History and American Historians: A Review of Recent Contributions to the Interpretation of the History of the United States* (Norman: University of Oklahoma Press, 1952), 1–40; Billington, *Genesis of the Frontier Thesis*, 260n.; William D. Aeschbacher, "The Mississippi Valley Historical Association, 1907–1965," *Journal of American History* 54 (September 1967): 339–353; Billington, *Turner*, 281–290; and Jacobs, *On Turner's Trail*, 149–202. In the *American Historical Review General Index to Volumes 41–60 (1935–1955)* (New York: Macmillan, 1962), entries under the categories "Discovery and Exploration" (pp. 105–106), "Frontier" (pp. 142–143), and "West" (p. 410) are outpaced only by entries under "World War I." By 1944 professional organizations of American historians were recommending that Turner's frontier narrative be effectively institutionalized in primary education, with frontier drama taught in the younger grades, and its result, democracy, discussed in higher grades: "More difficult topics [democracy, American civilization] are allocated to high school levels, and an effort is made to capitalize on the interests of younger people in dramatic action, in frontier stories, and in customs and ways of living." See Report of the Committee on American History in Schools and Colleges of the American Historical Review, Mississippi Valley Historical Association, and National Council for Social Studies, *American History in Schools and Colleges* (New York: Macmillan, 1944), 70.

66. See Nash, *Creating the West*, 101–158.

67. Webb, *The Great Plains* (Boston: Ginn and Company, 1931). On Webb see Elliott West, "Walter Prescott Webb and the Search for the West," in *Writing Western History*, 167–191; Gregory M. Tobin, *The Making of a History: Walter Prescott Webb and "The Great Plains"* (Austin: University of Texas Press,

1976); and Necah Stewart Furman, *Walter Prescott Webb: His Life and Impact* (Albuquerque: University of New Mexico Press, 1976).

68. Webb, "The Historical Seminar: Its Outer Shell and Its Inner Spirit," reprinted in *An Honest Preface and Other Essays* (Boston: Houghton Mifflin, 1959), 148; *Great Plains,* 454; and *Divided We Stand: The Crisis of a Frontierless Democracy* (New York: Farrar and Rinehart, 1937).

69. Webb, *Great Plains,* 454; Webb, "The American West: Perpetual Mirage," *Harper's Magazine* 214 (May 1957): 25–31; Webb, "History as High Adventure," in *An Honest Preface,* 195. More recently some new western historians have contended that only strictly "regional" versions of western history can be truly rigorous. The claim that only a regionalist western history can tell properly tragic tales is empirically wrong, as we will see below in our history of frontier tragedy. The other claim, that the trans-Mississippi West is the "true" or "natural" referent for the word "West" strikes me as suspect metaphysics. The notion that we may empty "West" of its old history as the key word of Orientalism strikes me as naive. "West," whether we mean a strict region or not, always already invokes the millennia of meanings so neatly summarized in Loren Baritz, "The Idea of the West" (*American Historical Review* 66 [April 1961], 618–640). But since we are concerned with broader sweeps of American history, the historiography of regionalism, however important and worthwhile, will have to be left for other days. See also Kerwin Lee Klein, "Reclaiming the 'F' Word, or Being and Becoming Postwestern," *Pacific Historical Review* 65 (May 1996): 179–216.

70. Aristotle, *Poetics,* trans. Gerald Else (Ann Arbor: University of Michigan Press, 1986); Warren I. Susman, "The Frontier Thesis and the American Intellectual," in *Culture as History: The Transformation of American Society in the Twentieth Century* (New York: Pantheon, 1984), 27–38; quote from p. 36. See also Gerald D. Nash, *Creating the West,* 3–48, and Harold P. Simonson, *The Closed Frontier: Studies in American Literary Tragedy* (New York: Holt, Rinehart, and Winston, 1970). It is significant that few of these writers were professional historians, and those few developed their readings in brief essays rather than lengthy monographs. See, for instance, Henry Steele Commager, "The Literature of the Pioneer West," *Minnesota History* 8 (December 1927): 319–320; Charles A. Beard, "The Frontier in American History," *New Republic* 25 (February 16, 1921): 349–350; and George W. Pierson, "The Frontier and the Frontiersman of Turner's Essays," *Pennsylvania Magazine of Biography and History* 64 (October 1940): 453.

71. On Dewey's life and thought I have found the following especially helpful: Morton White, *The Origins of Dewey's Instrumentalism* (New York: Columbia University Press, 1943); White, *Social Thought in America: The Revolt against Formalism* (1949; reprint, Boston: Beacon, 1957); James Gouinlock, *John Dewey's Philosophy of Value* (New York: Humanities Press, 1972); Neil Coughlan, *Young John Dewey: An Essay in American Intellectual History* (Chicago: University of Chicago Press, 1973); R. W. Sleeper, *The Necessity of Pragmatism: John Dewey's Conception of Philosophy* (New Haven: Yale University Press, 1986); Raymond D. Boisvert, *Dewey's Metaphysics* (New York: Fordham University Press, 1988); Steven C. Rockefeller, *John Dewey: Religious Faith and Democratic*

Humanism (New York: Columbia University Press, 1991); and Robert B. Westbrook, *John Dewey and American Democracy* (Ithaca: Cornell University Press, 1991).

72. Dewey, "The American Intellectual Frontier," *The New Republic* 30 (May 10, 1922): 303.

73. Ibid., 303, 304.

74. Ibid., 304, 305. See West's reading, *American Evasion of Philosophy.* Rockefeller, *John Dewey,* is especially good on Dewey's relation to Christian thought and culture.

75. Dewey, *Liberalism and Social Action: The Page Barbour Lectures* (reprint, New York: Capricorn, 1935), 33, 34, 74. See White, *Social Thought in America;* James T. Kloppenberg, *Uncertain Victory: Social Democracy and Progressivism in European and American Thought, 1870–1920* (Oxford: Oxford University Press, 1986); and Westbrook, *Dewey and American Democracy,* for broader contexts.

76. John Dewey, *Logic: The Theory of Inquiry* (New York: Henry Holt, 1938), 225. See also Dewey's comments in *Experience and Nature* (reprint, New York: Dover, 1958), 147–150; also Kloppenberg, *Uncertain Victory,* 107–114. For Dewey's thought on history in the early 1920s, his exchanges with Arthur O. Lovejoy are also illuminating. See Lovejoy, "Pragmatism *versus* the Pragmatist," in Durant Drake et al., eds., *Essays in Critical Realism: A Co-Operative Study of the Problem of Knowledge* (London, 1920), 35–81; Lovejoy, "Time, Meaning, and Transcendence. I: The Alleged Futurity of Yesterday," *Journal of Philosophy* 19 (September 14, 1922): 505–515; Lovejoy, "Time, Meaning, and Transcendence. II: Professor's Dewey's *Tertium Quid,*" ibid. (September 28, 1922): 533–541; John Dewey, "Realism without Monism or Dualism. I: Knowledge Involving the Past," *Journal of Philosophy* 19 (June 8, 1922): 309–317; and Dewey, "Realism without Monism or Dualism. II," ibid. (June 22, 1922): 351–361. The historicity of Dewey's vision has not always been recognized. See, for instance, T. P. Neill, "Dewey's Ambivalent Attitude toward History," in James Blewitt, ed., *John Dewey: His Thought and Influence* (New York: Fordham University Press, 1960), 144–155; and William H. Dray, "Some Varieties of Presentism," in *On History and Philosophers of History* (Leiden: E. J. Brill, 1989), 164–190. Dray draws a useful distinction between necessitarian and normative pragmatism but then describes (mistakenly, I believe) Dewey's presentism as normative.

77. Dewey, *Logic,* 25, 26, 27; Joseph L. Blau, "John Dewey's Theory of History," *Journal of Philosophy* 57 (1960): 89–100. On *Logic* in Dewey's thought, see H. S. Thayer, *The Logic of Pragmatism: An Examination of John Dewey's Logic* (New York: Humanities Press, 1952); George Dykhuizen, *The Life and Mind of John Dewey* (New York: Humanities Press, 1972), 284–287; Sleeper, *Necessity of Pragmatism,* esp. 134–167; Boisvert, *Dewey's Metaphysics,* esp. 178–193; also Richard Rorty, "Dewey's Metaphysics" (1977), in Rorty, *Consequences of Pragmatism* (Minneapolis: University of Minnesota Press, 1982), 72–89.

78. Dewey, *Logic,* 27; Jack Kaminsky, "Dewey's Concept of *An* Experience," *Philosophy and Phenomenological Research* 17 (1957): 316–330. I find Sleeper's reading, in *Necessity of Pragmatism,* 134–167, largely persuasive, al-

though I suspect that his desire to describe Dewey's narrativism in terms of causality (as in, responses are causally related to their stimuli) is potentially confusing. In *Experience and Nature* Dewey repeatedly described events as historical series, or histories, or stories, and he made it clear that he sees causality as an honorific or instrumentally valuable label applied to the story in its entirety:

> Causality is another name for the sequential order itself; and since this is an order of a history having a beginning and end, there is nothing more absurd than setting causality over against either initiation or finality. . . . The reality is the growth process. . . . The real existence is the history in its entirety, the history as just what it is. The operations of splitting it up into two parts and then having to unite them again by appeal to causative power are equally arbitrary and capricious [pp. 100, 275].

See the lucid treatment in Gouinlock, *Dewey's Philosophy of Value,* 80–85.

79. Dewey, *Logic,* 27, 33, 34; Kaminsky, "Dewey's Concept of *An* Experience."

80. See Dewey, *Reconstruction in Philosophy,* rev. ed. (Boston: Beacon, 1957), 88, 89. On Dewey and frontier tradition, see West, *American Evasion of Philosophy,* 71–111.

81. On selves as events, see *Experience and Nature,* 232. Dewey's account also differs from Turner's in its understanding of temporality. For Turner the present was the developing past, the past the undeveloped present. The relation is dualistic, as past and present remake each other. Where Turner located history at the conjunction of existence and memory, Dewey balanced existence between memory and *anticipation.* See *Logic,* 170, 171.

82. Dewey, *Logic,* 503. The implications of "requalification" have provoked a good deal of scholarly anxiety. See, for instance, Thayer's taming of the concept in his *Logic of Pragmatism,* 161–204. Compare Morton White's treatment of these questions in *Social Thought,* 203–235, with Sleeper, *Necessity of Pragmatism,* 141–149, and Gouinlock, *Dewey's Philosophy of Value.* White's own work, especially "Logic of Historical Narration" and *Foundations of Historical Thought,* exemplified his understanding of Deweyan philosophy of history. On history and the future, see Lovejoy, "Present Standpoints and Past History" (1939), in Hans Meyerhoff, ed., *The Philosophy of History in Our Time* (Garden City, N.Y.: Doubleday, 1959), 173–187; Richard Gale, "Dewey and the Problem of the Alleged Futurity of Yesterday," *Philosophy and Phenomenological Research* 22 (1962): 501–511; Leon J. Goldstein, "Discussion: The 'Alleged' Futurity of Yesterday," *Philosophy and Phenomenological Research* 24 (1964): 417–420; Richard Gale, "Discussion: A Reply on the Alleged Futurity of Yesterday," in ibid., 421–422; and John P. Diggins, *The Promise of Pragmatism: Modernism and the Crisis of Knowledge and Authority* (Chicago: University of Chicago Press, 1991).

83. See his discussion of natural ends in *Experience and Nature,* 104–105.

84. On Dewey in the 1920s, see Dykhuizen, *Life and Mind,* 206–225.

85. Dewey, *Experience and Nature,* 76, 89, 170, 206, 299. The italics are mine. Here Dewey moves much closer to the view attributed to him in Rorty,

Consequences of Pragmatism, and Rorty, "Dewey between Hegel and Darwin," in Dorothy Ross, ed., *Modernist Impulses in the Human Sciences, 1870–1930* (Baltimore: Johns Hopkins University Press, 1994), 54–68.

86. Dewey, *Experience and Nature,* 96, 118. See also Dewey's *Art as Experience* (New York: G. S. Putnam, 1934), passim, and Kaminsky, "Dewey's Concept of *An* Experience."

87. *Experience and Nature,* 45, 98; *Art as Experience.*

88. Ibid., 117. This reading clearly owes something to Aristotle, whose work was at the fore of Dewey's thought during this period. See Sleeper, *Necessity of Pragmatism,* 78–105.

89. Hook, *Pragmatism and the Tragic Sense of Life* (New York: Basic, 1974), 13. Hook would not approve a strongly relativist reading of Dewey's philosophy of history. See Hook's essay "Objectivity and Reconstruction in History," in Hook, ed., *Philosophy and History: A Symposium* (New York: New York University Press, 1963), 250–274. See also West, *American Evasion of Philosophy,* 114–123.

90. Hook, *Pragmatism and the Tragic Sense of Life,* 22. See also Hook, *The Hero in History: A Study in Limitation and Possibility* (reprint, Boston: Beacon Press, 1953); and Hook, *Reason, Social Myths, and Democracy* (New York: The Humanities Press, 1940). Dewey's understanding of tragedy as built out of moral and social, rather than individual, conflicts, has clear affinities with Hegel's reading of tragedy. Hook's emphasis on the personal "judgment" of individual actors obscures this aspect of Dewey's aesthetics.

91. Joseph Wood Krutch, *The Modern Temper* (orig. ed., 1929; reprint, New York: Harcourt Brace Jovanovich, 1957), 81, 82. Some sense of the scope of this debate can be grasped by surveying the essays in Robert W. Corrigan, ed., *Tragedy: Vision and Form* (San Francisco: Chandler, 1963). See also Raymond Williams, *Modern Tragedy* (Stanford: Stanford University Press, 1966), 1–84.

92. Ibid., 88.

93. In *Reconstruction in Philosophy,* xxvi, Dewey rejoins morals and inquiry: "The simple fact of the case is that any inquiry into what is deeply and inclusively human enters perforce into the specific area of morals. It does so whether it intends to and whether it is even aware of it or not." Such qualifications notwithstanding, the separation of morals from inquiry marked for many intellectuals the hallmark of objectivity and methodological purity. Irony, though, extends beyond questions of value into questions of fact, and many commentators saw Dewey's work as dangerously relativistic. Lovejoy, for instance, "Present Standpoints and Past History," reacted strongly against what he saw as Dewey's catachretic view of history. See also Herbert J. Muller, *The Spirit of Tragedy* (reprint, New York: Washington Square Press, 1963), 210.

94. Carl Becker, "Frederick Jackson Turner," in Howard W. Odum, ed., *American Masters of Social Science* (New York: Holt, 1927), 273–318; Merle Curti, "The Sections and the Frontier in American History: The Methodological Concepts of Frederick Jackson Turner," in Stuart Rice, ed., *Methods in Social Science* (Chicago: University of Chicago Press, 1931), 353–367; Richard Hofstadter, *The Progressive Historians: Turner, Beard, Parrington* (New York: Alfred A. Knopf), 3–164, 167–498; Billington, *Turner;* Billington, *Genesis of the*

Frontier Thesis; Billington, *America's Frontier Heritage* (New York: Holt, Rine-hart, and Winston, 1966). For broader contexts, see Mark C. Smith, *Social Science in the Crucible: The American Debate over Objectivity and Purpose, 1918–1941* (Durham: Duke University Press, 1994), and JoAnne Brown and David K. van Keuren, eds., *The Estate of Social Knowledge* (Baltimore: Johns Hopkins University Press, 1991).

95. Turner, "The Significance of the Section in American History," 47; Turner called a section-by-section history of the nation "too big a job for one man." Letter to Charles O. Paulin, Nov. 20, 1908, quoted in Jacobs, *Historical World,* 178. On Turner's research methods and seminars, see ibid.; Billington, *Genesis of the Frontier Thesis,* 108–114, 268–269, 273–274; Billington, *Turner,* 468–469.

96. Stanley M. Elkins and Eric L. McKitrick, "A New Meaning for Turner's Frontier, Part 1: Democracy in the Old Northwest," *Political Science Quarterly* 69 (September 1954): 321–353; Elkins and McKitrick, "A Meaning for Turner's Frontier, Part 2: The Southwest Frontier and New England," in ibid. (December 1954): 562–602; Elkins and McKitrick, "Institutions in Motion," *American Quarterly* 12 (Summer 1960): 188–197; Merle Curti, with assistance from Robert Daniel, Shaw Livermore Jr., Joseph van Hise, and Margaret W. Curti, *The Making of an American Community: A Case Study of Democracy in a Frontier County* (Stanford: Stanford University Press, 1959). For reviews of *The Making of an American Community* see Wilbur R. Jacobs, review, *Arizona and the West* 2 (Autumn 1960): 294–299, and Earl O. Pomeroy and Dorothy O. Johansen, review, *Oregon Historical Quarterly* 61 (September 1960): 343–347. I do not claim that *The Making of an American Community* was widely read or even intellectually influential. It deserves our attention here, first, because it has been regularly cited as the most thorough "test" of the "Turner Thesis" and, second, because it exemplifies a number of features of what is variously called analytic or structural or social history.

97. Curti, "Sections and Frontier in American History: Methodological Concepts," 353; Curti, "Frederick Jackson Turner, 1861–1932" (1949), in Curti, *Probing Our Past* (New York: Harper, 1955), 55.

98. Curti, *The Growth of American Thought* (New York: Harper, 1943), 560–569, 640; Robert Allen Skotheim, *American Intellectual Histories and Historians* (Princeton: Princeton University Press, 1966), 149–172; quote from p. 156.

99. Curti, "Democatic Themes in Historical Literature" (1952), in *Probing Our Past,* 30; Curti, "The Social and Economic Characteristics of the Leaders," in Caroline F. Ware, ed., *The New Cultural Approach to History* (New York: Columbia University Press, 1940), 259–263; Caroline F. Ware, "Introduction," in ibid., 10, 11, 13. On the agon of science and priestcraft, see Skotheim, *American Intellectual Histories,* 149–172. For a social historian's view of Curti, see Allan Bogue, "The Attempt to Write a More Scientific History" (1967), in Robert A. Skotheim, ed., *History and Historiography* (New York: Garland, 1985), 167–188; and Bogue's earlier article on community studies, "Social Theory and the Pioneer," *Agricultural History* 34 (January 1960): 21–34.

100. Curti, *Making of an American Community,* 1.

101. For overviews of rhetoric and social science, see Richard Harvey Brown, *A Poetic for Sociology: Toward a Logic of Discovery for the Human Sciences* (Chicago: University of Chicago Press, 1977); Brown, *Social Science as Civic Discourse: Essays on the Invention, Legitimation, and Uses of Social Theory* (Chicago: University of Chicago Press, 1989); and Allan Megill et al., eds., *Rhetoric of the Human Sciences* (Madison: University of Wisconsin Press, 1990).

102. *Making of an American Community*, 83, 179.

103. Ibid., 183, 184, 186, 187, but see also pp. 77–83, where property distribution in Trempeleau is compared with patterns of property distribution in the study's control communities, in Vermont.

104. Ibid., 196, 197.

105. Ibid., 33, 34, 448.

106. Curti, *Growth of American Thought*, 563, 564; Curti, "Human Nature in American Thought: The Retreat from Reason in the Age of Science" (1953), in his *Probing Our Past*, 171.

107. See Turner's cautionary comments in "Geographical Influences in American Political History" (1914), in *Sections*, 184; also Billington, *Turner*, 468–469.

108. *Making of an American Community* 5, 448. One reviewer, John D. Hicks, in *Pacific Historical Review* 28 (November 1959): 395–396, admired the work's rigor but expressed some frustration with its "tentative" conclusions.

109. Though some readers saw this as the bright future toward which the work pointed. Hicks, in his review for *Pacific Historical Review*, concluded that this was the real value of the study.

110. Stephan Thernstrom, *Poverty and Progress: Social Mobility in a Nineteenth-Century City* (Cambridge: Harvard University Press, 1964), 197–198; Higham, *History*, 212–232; Allan Bogue, "Social Theory and the Pioneer" (1960), in Richard Hofstadter and Seymour Martin Lipset, eds., *Turner and the Sociology of the Frontier* (New York: Basic Books, 1968), 78–99; Barton J. Bernstein, ed., *Towards a New Past: Dissenting Essays in American History* (New York: Pantheon, 1968), v–xiii.

111. See Ellen Fitzpatrick, "Caroline F. Ware and the Cultural Approach to History," *American Quarterly* 43 (June 1961): 173–198, esp. 182, 183.

Book Three: Time Immemorial

1. For Turner's master's thesis see "The Character and Influence of the Fur Trade in Wisconsin," in Wisconsin State Historical Society, *Proceedings* 36 (1889): 52–98. For the published dissertation see *The Character and Influence of the Indian Trade in Wisconsin: A Study of the Trading Post as an Institution* (Baltimore: Johns Hopkins University Press, 1891). This has been reprinted in *The Early Writings of Frederick Jackson Turner*, ed. Fulmer Mood (Madison: University of Wisconsin Press, 1938), 85–182. All references will be to the Mood edition (hereinafter "Indian Trade in Wisconsin" in Mood, *Early Writings*). Mary E. Young, "The Dark and Bloody but Endlessly Inventive Middle Ground

of Indian Frontier Historiography," *Journal of the Early Republic* 13 (Summer 1993): 193–206, provides a useful reading. See also David H. Miller and William W. Savage, eds., *The Character and Influence of the Indian Trade in Wisconsin: A Study of the Trading Post as an Institution* (Norman: University of Oklahoma Press, 1977), vii–xxxiv. Ray Allen Billington, *Frederick Jackson Turner: Historian, Scholar, Teacher* (New York: Oxford University Press, 1973), 58–88, offers a good account of this period in Turner's life and work.

2. Among many other ethnographic works, Turner's dissertation cited Henry Rowe Schoolcraft, *Historical and Statistical Information Respecting the History, Condition, and Prospects of the Indian Tribes of the United States,* 6 vols. (Philadelphia, 1851–1857), and Lewis Henry Morgan, *League of the Ho-de-no-sau-nee, or Iroquois,* vol. 1 (Rochester: Sage, 1851). For Turner's view of Parkman, see his review essay "Francis Parkman and His Work," *The Dial* 25 (December 16, 1898): 451–453.

3. Francis Parkman, *The Conspiracy of Pontiac* (1851; reprint, New York, 1948), 1:xxxi. See also Turner, "Parkman and His Work."

4. The classic study is Roy Harvey Pearce, *The Savages of America: A Study of the Indian and the Idea of Civilization* (Baltimore: Johns Hopkins University Press, 1953). This book was reprinted as *Savagism and Civilization: A Study of the Indian and the American Mind* (Berkeley: University of California Press, 1988). More recently, see Robert F. Berkhofer Jr., *The White Man's Indian: Images of the Indian from Columbus to the Present* (1978; reprint, New York: Vintage, 1978), esp. 3–33. For the etymology see also Hayden White, "The Noble Savage Theme as Fetish" (1976), in his *Tropics of Discourse: Essays in Cultural Criticism* (Baltimore: Johns Hopkins University Press, 1978), 183–196. On the oppositions of antiquity see Reinhart Koselleck, "The Historical-Political Semantics of Asymmetric Counterconcepts" (1975), in *Futures Past: On the Semantics of Historical Time,* trans. Keith Tribe (Cambridge: MIT Press, 1985), 159–196.

5. See ibid. Also Richard Bernheimer, *Wild Men in the Middle Ages: A Study in Art, Sentiment, and Demonology* (Cambridge: Harvard University Press, 1952); Edward Dudley and Maximilian E. Novak, eds., *The Wild Man Within: An Image in Western Thought from the Renaissance to Romanticism* (Pittsburgh: University of Pittsburgh Press, 1972); Hayden White, "The Forms of Wildness: Archaeology of an Idea" (1976), in *Tropics of Discourse,* 150–182. On the etymology of wilderness, see also Roderick Nash, *Wilderness and the American Mind* (1967; reprint, Yale University Press, 1982), 1–22.

6. Koselleck, "Historical-Political Semantics"; Pearce, *Savagism and Civilization;* Ronald L. Meek, *Social Science and the Ignoble Savage* (Cambridge: Cambridge University Press, 1976).

7. Pearce, *Savagism and Civilization;* Berkhofer, *White Man's Indian,* 33–62; George W. Stocking Jr., *Victorian Anthropology* (New York: The Free Press, 1987); Nicholas Thomas, *Out of Time: History and Evolution in Anthropological Discourse* (Cambridge: Cambridge University Press, 1989); Morgan, *League of the Ho-de-no-sau-nee, or Iroquois;* Morgan, *Ancient Society: Researches in the Lines of Human Progress from Savagery, through Barbarism, to Civilization* (New York: Henry Holt, 1877).

8. Turner, "Indian Trade in Wisconsin," in Mood, *Early Works,* 90. This essay should be compared with a later address, "American Colonization" (1893), reprinted in Ronald Carpenter, *The Eloquence of Frederick Jackson Turner* (San Marino, Calif.: Huntington Library, 1983), 176–192.

9. Turner, "The Development of American Society" (1908), reprinted in Wilbur R. Jacobs, ed., *Frederick Jackson Turner's Legacy: Unpublished Writings in American History* (San Marino, Calif.: Huntington Library, 1965), 173; Turner to Mae Sherwood, May 14, 1888, cited in Billington, *Frederick Jackson Turner,* 55.

10. See the classic reading by Leo Marx in his *The Machine in the Garden: Technology and the Pastoral Ideal in America* (London: Oxford University Press, 1964), 34–72.

11. Turner, "Indian Trade in Wisconsin," in Mood, *Early Writings,* 120. Turner offered other reasons for the success of the fur trade. One was the superiority of European technology. Iron and gunpowder were labor-saving devices that made life easier and more hospitable. Others were political and military. Tribes that possessed firearms overran those without, and so in the end all the tribes needed guns to survive. Since the Europeans could more or less pick and choose their favorite trading partners, they disrupted internal tribal politics, elevating some tribes and individuals over others, transforming pre-Columbian society with the politics of commerce. The end result was "economic dependence."

12. Ibid., 104, 172.

13. Ibid., 117, 167, 174, 175.

14. Richard T. Ely, *An Introduction to Political Economy* (New York: Chautauqua Press, 1889). Humans imparted *value* to nature by mixing their labor with some part of it. Natural resources became economic goods, or part of history, when transformed by human labor. Hunting and gathering scarcely counted; these were pursuits common to the beasts of the field, and one could not call the hunter's venison roast or the gatherer's berries "goods" in the economic sense of the word. (For those concerned to elevate it to conscious debate, this was a theoretical justification of the conflation of savagery and nature.) For the relation of the two men, see Billington, *Frederick Jackson Turner,* esp. 76–79. For a broader context, see Dorothy Ross, *The Origins of American Social Science* (Cambridge: Cambridge University Press, 1991).

15. Turner, "Indian Trade in Wisconsin," in Mood, *Early Writings,* 92, 93. Among the secondary sources he invoked were Charles Rau, "Ancient Aboriginal Trade in North America," *Annual Report of the Board of Regents of the Smithsonian Institution, 1872* (Washington, D.C., 1873), 348–394; Daniel Wilson, "Trade and Commerce in the Stone Age," *Transactions of the Royal Society of Canada* 7 (1889): 59; and Gates P. Thruston, *The Antiquities of Tennessee and the Adjacent States, and the State of Aboriginal Society in the Scale of Civilization Represented by Them* (Cincinnati, 1890). Turner directed his critical comments at another source, Martin Külischer, "Der Handel auf den Primitiven Culturstufen," *Zeitschrift für Völkerpsychologie und Sprachwissenschaft* 10 (1878): 791–816. Turner's "Indian Trade in Wisconsin," in Mood, *Early Writings,* 166: "The intertribal trade between Montreal and the Northwest, and between Al-

bany and Illinois and the Ohio country, appears to have been commerce in the proper sense of the term [*Kauf zum Verkauf*] [Turner's n.48: Notwithstanding Külischer's assertion that there is no room for this in primitive society]."

16. Turner most likely knew Morgan's *Ancient Society*. He certainly knew Morgan's earlier study, *League of the . . . Iroquois*, for he cited it in his master's thesis, along with C. N. Starcke's *The Primitive Family: In Its Origin and Development* (New York: D. Appleton, 1889), a work that directly attacked some of *Ancient Society*'s more controversial claims (such as Morgan's argument that all human society originated from a matriarchy characterized by "promiscuous intercourse").

17. Turner, "Indian Trade in Wisconsin," in Mood, *Early Writings,* 166–175.

18. Turner, "The Significance of the Frontier in American History" (1893), in Mood, *Early Writings,* 200, 201, 202.

19. Ibid., 203; Turner, "Contributions of the West to American Democracy" (1903), in his *The Frontier in American History* (1920; reprint, New York: Holt, Rinehart, and Winston, 1962), 266, 267.

20. Turner to his sister, 1887, reprinted in Ray Allen Billington, "Frederick Jackson Turner Visits New England: 1887," *New England Quarterly* 41 (September 1968): 409–436. On Turner's racism see Jacobs, *On Turner's Trail,* 54, 55, 166.

21. James Adair, *The History of the American Indians, Particularly Those Nations Adjoining to the Mississippi, East and West Florida, Georgia, South and North Carolina, and Virginia* (London, 1775); William W. Warren, "History of the Ojibways, Based upon Traditions and Oral Statements," *Minnesota Historical Society Collections* 5 (1883): 21–394.

22. Ibid., esp. 53–60.

23. Fulmer Mood, "A Comparison of Differing Versions of 'The Significance of the Frontier,' " in Mood, *Early Writings,* 276, 277. See also Billington, *Frederick Jackson Turner,* 426–430.

24. Frederic L. Paxson, *History of the American Frontier* (New York, 1924), 1; E. Douglas Branch, *Westward: The Romance of the American Frontier* (New York: D. Appleton, 1930); Ray Allen Billington with James Blaine Hedges, *Westward Expansion: A History of the American Frontier* (New York: Macmillan, 1949). R. David Edmunds, "Native Americans, New Voices: American Indian History, 1895–1995," *American Historical Review* 100 (June 1995): 717–740, surveys Indian historiography in the *AHR*.

25. William Christie MacLeod, *The American Indian Frontier* (New York: Knopf, 1928), vii, viii.

26. Ibid., 369, 363, 366, 369.

27. Ibid., 544.

28. Ruth Benedict, *Patterns of Culture* (1934; reprint, Boston: Houghton Mifflin, 1989). All references will be to the reprint edition. Among the many discussions of the book, see Margaret Mead, *An Anthropologist at Work: Writings of Ruth Benedict* (Boston: Houghton Mifflin, 1959), 201–212; Judith Schachter Modell, *Ruth Benedict: Patterns of a Life* (Philadelphia: University of Pennsylvania Press, 1983), 184–215; Marvin Harris, *The Rise of Anthropological Theory* (New York: Thomas Crowell, 1968), 398–407; Clifford Geertz, *Works*

and Lives: The Anthropologist as Author (Stanford: Stanford University Press, 1988), 102–128; and Margaret M. Caffrey, *Ruth Benedict: Stranger in This Land* (Austin: University of Texas Press, 1989), esp. 206–240.

29. Raymond Williams, *Keywords: A Vocabulary of Culture and Society* (New York: Oxford University Press, 1976), 76. The genealogy here and below relies heavily on Williams and on A. L. Kroeber and Clyde Kluckhohn's unusual and useful study, *Culture: A Critical Review of Concepts and Definitions* (1952; reprint, New York: Random House, 1963).

30. Matthew Arnold, *Culture and Anarchy* (London, 1862); Friedrich Nietzsche, *Untimely Meditations*, trans. R. J. Hollingdale (orig. ed., 1873; Eng.-lang. ed., Cambridge: Cambridge University Press, 1983), 5, 6; Turner, *Frontier and Section: Selected Essays* (Englewood Cliffs, N.J.: Prentice-Hall, 1961), 46, 328. A Turner student, Caroline F. Ware, later edited *The New Cultural Approach to History* (New York: Columbia University Press, 1940), and linked "culture" to Turnerian social history. See Ellen Fitzpatrick, "Caroline F. Ware and the Cultural Approach to History," *American Quarterly* 43 (June 1991): 173–198.

31. Edward B. Tylor, *Primitive Culture* (1871; reprint, New York: Harper, 1958), 1; Robert H. Lowie, *Culture and Ethnology* (1917; reprint, New York: Peter Smith, 1929); Clark Wissler, *Man and Culture* (London: George C. Harrap, 1923); Alfred L. Kroeber, "The Superorganic," *American Anthropologist* 19 (1917): 163–213. Lowie uses "civilization" as a synonym for culture. On these debates see George W. Stocking Jr., *Race, Culture, and Evolution: Essays in the History of Anthropology* (New York: Free Press, 1968); and Stocking, *The Ethnographer's Magic and Other Essays in the History of Anthropology* (Madison: University of Wisconsin Press, 1992), esp. 342–361. More recently, see Frederick M. Barnard, "Culture and Civilization in Modern Times," in *Dictionary of the History of Ideas,* ed. Philip P. Wiener (New York: Charles Scribner's Sons, 1968), 613–621; Milton Singer, "The Concept of Culture," in *International Encyclopedia of the Social Sciences,* ed. David L. Sills (New York: Macmillan and the Free Press, 1968), 3:527–543; Robert H. Winthrop, *Dictionary of Concepts in Cultural Anthropology* (New York: Greenwood Press, 1991), 50–61; Philip Gleason, *Speaking of Diversity: Language and Ethnicity in Twentieth-Century America* (Baltimore: Johns Hopkins University Press, 1992); and John S. Gilkeson Jr., "The Domestication of 'Culture' in Interwar America, 1919–1941," in JoAnne Brown and David K. van Keuren, eds., *The Estate of Social Knowledge* (Baltimore: Johns Hopkins University Press, 1991), 153–174.

32. See Stocking, *Race, Culture, and Evolution;* Stocking, *Victorian Anthropology;* Reginald Horsiman, *Race and Manifest Destiny* (Cambridge: Harvard University Press, 1981); and Roger Bannister, *Social Darwinism: Science and Myth in Anglo-American Social Thought* (Philadelphia: Temple University Press, 1979).

33. On Benedict's life and thought, see Modell, *Ruth Benedict;* Caffrey, *Benedict;* and Barbara A. Babcock, " 'Not in the Absolute Singular': Rereading Ruth Benedict," in Nancy J. Parezo, ed., *Hidden Scholars: Women Anthropologists and the Native American Southwest* (Albuquerque: University of New Mexico Press, 1993), 107–128. On the intellectual atmosphere in anthropology at

Columbia see Rosalind Rosenberg, *Beyond Separate Spheres: Intellectual Roots of Modern Feminism* (New Haven: Yale University Press, 1982), 207–236; and Stocking, *Ethnographer's Magic,* 276–340.

34. The title phrase quickly became one of the book's most remarked features, and "pattern," as both noun and verb, joined "complex whole" and "custom" in the communal vocabulary of culture. There is a debt here to John Dewey's *Human Nature and Conduct: An Introduction to Social Psychology* (New York: Henry Holt, 1922), esp. 75. Benedict studied with Dewey and taught this text. An early article version of *Patterns of Culture* (which may have been written after the relevant chapters in the book) used "configurations" (from *Gestalten*). See Benedict, "Configurations of Culture in North America," *American Anthropologist* 34 (1932): 1–27. By 1927 Edward W. Sapir, a Benedict confidant, was using the term. See his "The Unconscious Patterning of Behavior in Society" (1927), in *Selected Writings of Edward Sapir in Language, Culture, and Personality,* ed. David G. Mandelbaum (Berkeley: University of California Press, 1949), 150–159; and "The Emergence of the Concept of Personality in a Study of Cultures" (1934), in David G. Mandelbaum, ed., *Culture, Language, and Personality* (Berkeley and Los Angeles: University of California Press, 1961), 194–207. Judith Modell, " 'It Is Besides a Pleasant English Word'—Ruth Benedict's Concept of Patterns," *Anthropological Quarterly* 62 (January 1989): 27–40, is a valuable discussion.

35. *Patterns of Culture,* 21, 22.

36. Ibid., 36.

37. Ibid., 22. On salvage ethnography see Stocking, *Ethnographer's Magic,* 276–340, and Jacob W. Gruber, "Ethnographic Salvage and the Shaping of Anthropology," *American Anthropologist* 72 (December 1970): 1289–1299.

38. Benedict, "A Brief Sketch of Serrano Culture," *American Anthropologist* 26 (July–September 1924): 366; William Duncan Strong, *Aboriginal Society in Southern California,* University of California Publications in American Archeology and Ethnology 26 (Berkeley: University of California Press, 1929).

39. Benedict, *Patterns of Culture,* 22, 47. See also her earlier, unpublished essay, "The Sense of Symbolism," in Mead, *Anthropologist at Work,* 113–117. In an undated journal entry (ca. 1920s), she wrote: "The secret of art is a love of the *medium*" (ibid., 153).

40. Ruth Benedict, "Serrano Tales," *The Journal of American Folklore* 39 (January–March 1926): 2–7; quotation from p. 2. The article is a series of translations of Serrano oral narratives for which Benedict (as per period ethnographic convention) offered neither introductory frames nor original language versions. Among the many works that discuss such texts, see David Murray, *Forked Tongues: Speech, Writing, and Representation in North American Indian Texts* (Bloomington: Indiana University Press, 1991); Arnold Krupat, *Ethnocriticism: Ethnography, History, Literature* (Berkeley: University of California Press, 1992); Brian Swann and Arnold Krupat, eds., *Recovering the Word: Essays on Native American Literature* (Berkeley: University of California Press, 1987).

41. As poet Anne Singleton, Benedict also wrote "Price of Paradise," a two-stanza verse framed with this "Persian Tale": "And Adam sold Paradise for two

kernels of grain." We might imagine the Serrano as Adam, who "Not valuing Paradise, he sold spendthrift; / But he had lived in Eden from his birth"; in an unpublished manuscript, "Selected Poems: 1941," in Mead, *Anthropologist at Work,* 478. "This Is My Body" and "Eucharist" are also in ibid., 194–195 and 479.

42. Friedrich Nietzsche, *The Birth of Tragedy,* trans. Walter Kaufman (orig. ed., 1872; Eng.-lang. ed., New York: Random House, 1992), section 5 (p. 52). In *The Gay Science,* trans. Walter Kaufman (orig. ed., 1882; Eng.-lang. ed., New York: Random House, 1974), section 106 (p. 163), he extended the trope: "As an aesthetic phenomenon existence is still *bearable* for us." On Benedict and Nietzsche, see Mead, *Anthropologist at Work,* 206, 548n.; Caffrey, *Benedict,* esp. 50–58.

43. Friedrich Nietzsche, *Thus Spoke Zarathustra: A Book For All and None,* trans. Thomas Common (Eng.-lang. ed., 1909; reprint, New York: Russell and Russell, 1964), 3, 4.

44. *The Gay Science,* section 342 (p. 274).

45. The literature on modernism is vast. Especially relevant here are Daniel J. Singal, ed., *Modernist Culture in America* (Belmont, Calif.: Wadsworth, 1991), and Ricardo J. Quinones, *Mapping Literary Modernism: Time and Development* (Princeton: Princeton University Press, 1985), esp. 3–86. On Benedict and modernism see Caffrey, *Ruth Benedict,* 130–138; and Modell, " 'It Is Besides a Pleasant English Word.' "

46. Benedict, *Patterns of Culture,* 46, 48. See also Modell, " 'It Is Besides a Pleasant English Word.' "

47. Oswald Spengler, *The Decline of the West: Form and Actuality,* vols. 1 and 2 (New York: Knopf, 1926–1928). Benedict cited the German edition, which she apparently read with Edward Sapir. See Sapir to Ruth Benedict, February 7, 1928, in Mead, *Anthropologist at Work,* 187. Harris, *Rise of Anthropological Theory,* stresses Benedict's "neo-Kantianism." I find no evidence to support his view and he does not offer any, beyond Benedict's citation of Wilhelm Dilthey, who was hardly a neo-Kantian. And while Benedict cited Dilthey (on p. 52), she did so at the urging of Boas. See Mead, *Ruth Benedict* (New York: Columbia University Press, 1974), 38–49. For us Spengler is the more important of the two, partly because Benedict devotes more space to him, partly because their vocabularies overlap, and partly because of the contrast in their uses of Nietzsche.

48. Benedict, *Patterns of Culture,* 53, 53, 54, 55, 56.

49. Ibid., 73, 76, 78, 79.

50. Ruth Benedict, *The Concept of the Guardian Spirit in North America,* Memoirs of the American Anthropological Association, no. 29 (Menasha, Wis., 1923); *Patterns of Culture,* 88, 176, 177, 181, 182.

51. William Blake, *Selected Poetry,* ed. W. H. Stevenson (London: Penguin Books, 1988), 66, 74; W. B. Yeats to Lady Gregory, September 26, 1902, in *The Letters of W. B. Yeats,* ed. Allan Wade (New York: Macmillan, 1955), 379; Arthur Symons, *William Blake* (New York: E. P. Dutton, 1907), 1; T. S. Eliot, "Blake," in *The Sacred Wood* (1920; reprint, London: Methuen, 1964), 158. See also Patrick Bridgewater, *Nietzsche in Anglo-Saxony: A Study of Nietzsche's Im-*

pact on English and American Literature (Leicester: University of Leicester, 1972); and Harvey Birnbaum, *Between Blake and Nietzsche: The Reality of Culture* (Lewisburg, Ky.: Bucknell University Press, 1992).

52. Nietzsche himself, looking back on *Birth of Tragedy* in a new preface to the 1886 edition, criticized its youthful earnestness, regretted that the work had spoken where it ought to have sung, and noted its "dialectical ill humour" (p. 20). Of the Pima Benedict wrote to Franz Boas in 1927, "These people have more in common with the Serrano than with the Pueblo. The contrast with the latter is *unbelievable*"; quoted in Mead, *Anthropologist at Work*, 206.

53. Spengler, *Decline of the West*, 1:158. His citation is accurate; it comes from the second essay, section 13, of *Genealogy of Morals*. The nature-history split to which Spengler appeals, though, does not reappear in this form in Nietzsche.

54. Nietzsche, "On the Uses and Disadvantages of History for Life," in *Untimely Meditations*, 63, 83, 120. Having made the point, we should not vulgarize it. Nietzsche did not say history was once and for all escapable. This was a relational matter. The opposition of art and history does appear, though, to be the general interpretation of Nietzsche shared by Yeats and Benedict.

55. Ibid., 135, 136, 137.

56. Benedict, *Patterns of Culture*, 10, 20, 175.

57. Ibid., 21. On Benedict and myth see Caffrey, *Ruth Benedict*, 129–130, 139–143.

58. The citation is from an unpublished poem of Ruth Benedict's, quoted in Edward Sapir to Ruth Benedict, February 7, 1928, in Mead, *Anthropologist at Work*, 187, 188.

59. Ruth Benedict, "Myth," in Edwin R. A. Seligman, ed., *Encyclopedia of the Social Sciences* (1933; reprint, New York: Macmillan, 1950), 2:178–181; Benedict, "Folklore," in ibid., 288–293; Georges Sorel, *Reflections on Violence,* trans. T. E. Hulme (orig. ed., 1906; Eng.-lang. ed., New York: Peter Smith, 1921). See also Irving Louis Horowitz, *Radicalism and the Revolt against Reason*, 2d ed. (orig. ed., 1961; 2d ed., Carbondale: Southern Illinois University Press, 1968), 90–126.

60. Benedict, *Patterns of Culture*, 22.

61. Ibid., 223. Benedict invokes the psychological aesthetics of Wilhelm Worringer. See his *Abstraction and Empathy: A Contribution to the Psychology of Style*, trans. Michael Bullock (orig. ed., 1908; Eng.-lang. ed., London: Routledge, 1953).

62. Benedict, *Patterns of Culture,* 224.

63. Ibid., 225.

64. Ibid., 241, 249. This parallels Dewey's discussion of the will to power in his *Human Nature and Conduct*, 140–148. It is a shallow reading of Nietzsche but common for the period.

65. See especially Marianna Torgovnick, *Gone Primitive: Savage Intellects, Modern Lives* (Chicago: University of Chicago Press, 1990); Clifford, *Predicament of Culture* (Cambridge: Harvard University Press, 1988); and T. J. Jackson Lears, *No Place of Grace: Antimodernism and the Transformation of American Culture, 1880–1920* (New York: Pantheon, 1981).

66. Benedict, *Patterns of Culture*, 223–278; Benedict, "Anthropology and

Cultural Change," *American Scholar* 11 (Spring 1943): 243–248; Benedict, "Science of Custom"; Benedict, "Myth." Compare with John Dewey, "Anthropology and Ethics," in William Fielding Ogburn and Alexander Goldenweiser, eds., *The Social Sciences and Their Interrelations* (Boston: Houghton Mifflin, 1928), 24–36.

67. On the appointment of a successor to Boas at Columbia, see Caffrey, *Ruth Benedict*, 276–281, and Modell, *Ruth Benedict: Patterns of a Life*, 256–259.

68. Anthony F. C. Wallace, *Culture and Personality* (New York: Random House, 1961); Robert Redfield, *The Little Community and Peasant Society and Culture* (1956; reprint, Chicago: University of Chicago Press, 1960), esp. 74–80, 136, 162. On the culture and personality school, see the essays in George W. Stocking Jr., ed., *Malinowski, Rivers, Benedict and Others: Essays on Culture and Personality*, History of Anthropology, vol. 4 (Madison: University of Wisconsin Press, 1986); and Stocking, *Ethnographer's Magic*, 138–139, 288–289.

69. Renato Rosaldo, *Culture and Truth: The Remaking of Social Analysis*, 2d ed. (orig. ed., 1988; 2d ed., Boston: Beacon Press, 1993), 128. On ethnography in these years, see Stocking, *Ethnographer's Magic*, esp. 342–361, and Sherry Ortner, "Theory in Anthropology since the Sixties," *Comparative Studies in Society and History* 26 (1984): 126–166.

70. Robert Redfield, Ralph Linton, and Melville Herskovits, "Memorandum on the Study of Acculturation," *American Anthropologist* 38 (1936): 149–152. See also Stocking, *Ethnographer's Magic*, 142–144, 228–229.

71. Melville J. Herskovits, *Acculturation: The Study of Culture Contact* (New York: J. J. Augustin, 1938), 127; Redfield, Linton, and Herskovits, "A Memorandum on Acculturation." See also the Social Science Research Council Summer Seminar on Acculturation, "Acculturation: An Exploratory Formulation," *American Anthropologist* 56 (December 1954): 974. Although *AA* published its first article on acculturation in 1932, the subject effectively began with the 1936 memorandum. As the editor put it, in the editorial comment to *American Anthropologist* 56 (December 1954), that issue (1936) and this one (1954) "mark off the whole history of a subject" (p. 972). The 1954 piece lists 117 items in its bibliography, virtually all of which were published after 1936. For discussions of assimilation and related words, see Philip Gleason, *Speaking of Diversity: Language and Ethnicity in Twentieth-Century America* (Baltimore: Johns Hopkins University Press, 1992), and Russell A. Kazal, "Revisiting Assimilation: The Rise, Fall, and Reappraisal of a Concept in American Ethnic History," *American Historical Review* 100 (April 1995): 437–471.

72. Ralph Linton, ed., *Acculturation in Seven American Indian Tribes* (1940; reprint, Gloucester, Mass.: Peter Smith, 1963), vii. Such appeals to the needs of government administrators quickly became a rhetorical convention for acculturation articles published in the *American Anthropologist*, the discipline's leading journal in the United States and edited by Linton. See, for instance, Laura Thompsen, "Attitudes and Acculturation," *American Anthropologist* 50 (April–June 1948): 200–225; Florence Hawley, "An Examination of Problems Basic to Acculturation in the Rio Grande Pueblos," ibid. (Oct.–Dec. 1948): 612–624; and Edward M. Bruner, "Primary Group Experience and the Processes of Acculturation," ibid. 58 (August 1956): 602–623.

73. Marian W. Smith, "The Puyallup of Washington," in Linton, *Acculturation in Seven Tribes,* 35, 36.

74. Linton, *Acculturation in Seven Tribes,* 37, 38, 117, 118, 206, 257, 258, 462, 463–482, 483–500, 501–520. Compare with Robert Park, "Race Relations and Certain Frontiers" (1934), reprinted in *Race and Culture* (Glencoe, Ill.: The Free Press, 1950), 117–137, and "Our Racial Frontier on the Pacific" (1948), in ibid., 138–151. On Linton see Adelin Linton and Charles Wagley, *Ralph Linton* (New York: Columbia University Press, 1971), esp. 49–52.

75. Natalie F. Joffe, "The Fox of Iowa," in Linton, *Acculturation in Seven Tribes,* 259, 332. Among other works, Joffe drew from Louise Phelps Kellogg's "The Fox Indians during the French Regime," *Wisconsin State Historical Society Proceedings, 1907* (Madison: Wisconsin State Historical Society, 1908), 142–188, a work completed under Turner's direction.

76. SSRC, "Acculturation: An Exploratory Formulation," 974, 987.

77. Bronislaw Malinowski, "Culture," in *Encyclopedia of the Social Sciences,* ed. Edwin R. A. Seligman (1933; reprint, New York: Macmillan, 1950), 621–646.

78. Leslie White, "History, Evolutionism, and Functionalism: Three Types of Interpretation of Culture," *Southwestern Journal of Anthropology* 1 (Summer 1945): 221, 222, 223; White, " 'Diffusion vs. Evolution': An Anti-Evolutionist Fallacy," *American Anthropologist* 47 (July/September 1945): 339–356; White, "Kroeber's 'Configurations of Culture Growth,' " *American Anthropologist* 48 (January/March 1946): 78–93.

79. Alfred A. Kroeber, "History and Evolution," *Southwestern Journal of Anthropology* 2 (Spring 1946): 1, 2, 4, 11, 13; Robert H. Lowie, "Evolution in Cultural Anthropology: A Reply to Leslie White," *American Anthropologist* 48 (April/June 1946): 223–233; David Bidney, *Theoretical Anthropology* (New York: Columbia University Press, 1953), 250–295. Claude Lévi-Strauss divided things differently. While history and anthropology shared subjects, aims, and some methods, "History organizes its data in relation to conscious expressions of social life, while anthropology proceeds by examining its unconscious foundations." See his *Structural Anthropology,* trans. Claire Jacobson and Brooke Grundfest Schoepf (orig. ed., 1958; Eng.-lang. ed., Garden City, N.Y.: Anchor, 1967), 19.

80. Edward H. Spicer, "Letter to the Editor," in *American Anthropologist* 56 (October 1954): 890; Spicer, ed., *Perspectives in American Indian Culture Change* (Chicago: University of Chicago Press, 1961).

81. Spicer, *Perspectives in American Indian Culture Change,* 532, 533.

82. Edward Spicer, *Cycles of Conquest: The Impact of Spain, Mexico, and the United States on the Indians of the Southwest, 1533–1960* (Tucson: University of Arizona Press, 1962).

83. William N. Fenton, "The Training of Historical Ethnologists in America," *American Anthropologist* 54 (July/September 1952): 330; Helen H. Tanner, "Erminie Wheeler-Voegelin (1903–1988), Founder of the American Society for Ethnohistory," *Ethnohistory* 38 (Winter 1991): 58–72. On the Indian claims commission and ethnohistory, see the articles collected in "Anthropology and Indian Claims Litigation: Papers Presented at a Symposium Held at Detroit in December 1954," in *Ethnohistory* 2 (Fall 1955): 287–375; Bruce G. Trigger, "Eth-

nohistory: Problems and Prospects," *Ethnohistory* 29 (1982): 1–19; Francis Jennings, "A Growing Partnership: Historians, Anthropologists, and American Indian History," in *Ethnohistory* 29 (1982): 21–34; and Imre Sutton, ed., *Irredeemable America: The Indian's Estate and Land Claims* (Albuquerque: University of New Mexico Press, 1985).

84. Erminie W. Voegelin, "An Ethnohistorian's Viewpoint," *Ethnohistory* 1 (1954): 168. Subsequent discussions, though often quite interesting, most commonly repeated this construction. See Stanley Pargellis, "The Problem of American Indian History," *Ethnohistory* 4 (Spring 1957): 113–124; Philip Dark, "Methods of Synthesis in Ethnohistory," ibid. 4 (Summer 1957): 231–278; the "Symposium on the Concept of Ethnohistory," in ibid. 8 (Winter 1961), including Richard M. Dorson, "Ethnohistory and Ethnic Folklore," 5–30; Wilcomb E. Washburn, "Ethnohistory: History 'in the Round,' " 31–48; and Nancy Oestreich Lurie, "Ethnohistory: An Ethnological Point of View," 78–92. Also the "Comment" in the Summer 1961 issue of *Ethnohistory*, vol. 8, including Eleanor Leacock, 256–261; John C. Ewers, 262–270; and Charles A. Valentine, 271–280. In 1966 William C. Sturtevant, "Anthropology, History, and Ethnohistory," ibid. 13 (Winter/Spring 1966): 1–51, claimed that ethnohistory is the "integration of the structural and historical approaches to understanding culture" (p.3).

85. In the first volume (1954) Dwight L. Smith surveyed captivity narratives as potential ethnohistorical sources and reviewed the *Jesuit Relations and Allied Documents,* and J. A. Jones published a key to the Annual Reports of the United States Commissioner of Indian Affairs. The spring 1955 issue reprinted the "Official Report of the Owyhee Reconnaissance," and the summer issue led with Gaston Litton's article "The Resources of the National Archives for the Study of the American Indian." See Dwight L. Smith, "The Problem of the Indian in the Ohio Valley: The Historian's View," *Ethnohistory* 1 (1954), 172–180; Smith, "Shawnee Captivity Ethnography," ibid. 2 (Winter 1955), 11–28; J. A. Jones, "Key to the Annual Reports of the United States Commissioner of Indian Affairs," ibid., 58–64; Gaston Litton, "The Resources of the National Archives for the Study of the American Indian," ibid. 2 (Summer 1955), 191–208. See also Fenton's "Historical Training of Ethnologists" and his later contributions to *Ethnohistory,* "Ethnohistory and Its Problems," ibid. 9 (Winter 1962): 1–23, and "Field Work, Museum Studies, and Ethnohistory," ibid., 71–85.

86. Julian H. Steward, "Theory and Application in a Social Science," *Ethnohistory* 2 (Fall 1955): 293; A. L. Kroeber, "Nature of the Land-Holding Group," ibid., 303–314; J. A. Jones, "Problems, Opportunities, and Recommendations," ibid., 348; Nancy Oestreich Lurie, "Problems, Opportunities, and Recommendations," ibid., 373. For a bigger picture see Wilcomb E. Washburn, *Red Man's Land / White Man's Law: A Study of the Past and Present Status of the American Indian* (New York: Charles Scribner's Sons, 1971).

87. Steward, "Theory and Application," 302; Omer C. Stewart, "Anthropologists as Expert Witnesses for Indians: Claims and Peyote Cases," in *Anthropology and the American Indian: Report of a Symposium* (San Francisco: Indian Historian Press, 1973), 35–42; Sutton, *Irredeemable America.*

88. "Symposium on the Concept of Ethnohistory"; Lurie, "Ethnohistory: An Ethnological Point of View," 80. See also Washburn, "Ethnohistory: History 'in the Round.' "

89. Spicer, *Cycles of Conquest*. On Spicer see Thomas E. Sheridan, "How to Tell the Story of a 'People without History': Narrative versus Ethnohistorical Approaches to the Study of the Yaqui Indians through Time," *Journal of the Southwest* 30 (Summer 1988): 168–189; Evelyn Hu-DeHart, "Edward Spicer," in *Historians of the American Frontier: A Bio-Bibliographical Sourcebook*, ed. John R. Wunder (New York: Greenwood Press, 1988), 636–647; and Art Gallagher Jr., "Edward Holland Spicer (1906–1983)," *American Anthropologist* 86 (April 1984): 381–382.

90. *Cycles of Conquest*, vii.

91. Ibid., 1. Spicer seems to have contemplated publishing the work as several different monographs. See Henry F. Dobyns's review in *American Anthropologist* 65 (October 1963): 1139–1143. Dobyns praised the book but thought that dividing it (and improving its annotation) would have made it stronger. The book was not sufficiently comprehensive for Jack D. Forbes, whose review in *American Historical Review* 69 (October 1963): 157–158 cautiously endorsed the text but denounced its lack of archival data and bibliographic omissions.

92. *Cycles of Conquest*, 2, 15.

93. Ibid., 147, 280.

94. Ibid., 283, 285, 418, 503. Compare this with the language in his earlier piece, "Spanish-Indian Acculturation in the Southwest," *American Anthropologist* 56 (August 1954): 663–678.

95. *Cycles of Conquest*, 567. Dobyns's review, though, argued that the book is "not about cycles."

96. Ibid., 567. Note the transfiguration of Linton's "directed" and "nondirected" acculturation.

97. Carl Russell Fish, "The Frontier, a World Problem," *Wisconsin Magazine of History* 1 (December 1917): 121–141; Owen Lattimore, *Studies in Frontier History: Collected Papers, 1928–1958* (London: Oxford University Press, 1962); Herbert Eugene Bolton, "The Epic of Greater America" (1933), in *Wider Horizons of American History* (New York: D. Appleton, 1939), 1–53; Bolton, *History of the Americas: A Syllabus with Maps* (Boston: Ginn and Company, 1928); John W. Caughey, "Herbert Eugene Bolton," in Wilbur R. Jacobs et al., eds., *Turner, Bolton, and Webb: Three Historians of the American Frontier* (Seattle: University of Washington Press, 1965), 40–73; John Francis Bannon, *Herbert Eugene Bolton: The Historian and the Man* (Tucson: University of Arizona Press, 1978); Lewis Hanke, ed., *Do the Americas Have a Common History? A Critique of the Bolton Theory* (New York: Alfred A. Knopf, 1964).

98. Walter Prescott Webb, *The Great Frontier* (1952; reprint, Austin: University of Texas Press, 1970), 1, 3, 8; Arnold J. Toynbee, "Introduction," in ibid., vii–xi.

99. Webb, *Great Frontier*, 7, 9, 11, 413. See also Toynbee, "Introduction"; Joe B. Frantz, "Walter Prescott Webb," in Jacobs et al., *Turner, Bolton, and Webb*, 75–108.

100. Immanuel Wallerstein, *The Modern World-System I: Capitalist Agricul-

ture and the Origins of the European World-Economy in the Sixteenth Century (San Diego: Harcourt Brace Jovanovich, 1974), 4, 5, 37, 38, 39; on Webb, see pp. 78, 281. Wallerstein also discusses Archibald R. Lewis, "The Closing of the European Frontier," *Speculum* 33 (October 1958): 475–483, and Owen Lattimore, "The Frontier in History," in *Relazioni del X Congresso di Scienze Storiche I: Metodologia-Problemi-Science asiliare delta storia* (Florence: G. C. Sansoni, 1955), 103–138. See also Wallerstein's more recent books, including *The Capitalist World Economy* (Cambridge: Cambridge University Press, 1979); *The Modern World System: Mercantilism and the Consolidation of the European World-Economy, 1600–1750* (New York: Academic Press, 1980); and *The Politics of the World-Economy: The States, the Movements, and the Civilizations* (New York: Cambridge University Press, 1984).

101. *Modern World-System I,* 357. On the spatial *topoi* see Edward W. Soja, *Postmodern Geographies: The Reassertion of Space in Critical Social Theory* (London: Verso, 1989), 94–117.

102. *Modern World-System I,* 346–357. Among the many relevant critiques, see Eric R. Wolf, *Europe and the People without History* (Berkeley: University of California Press, 1982), 22–23, and passim; Thomas D. Hall, "Incorporation in the World System: Towards a Critique," *American Sociological Review* 51 (June 1986): 390–402; and Hall, *Social Changes in the Southwest, 1350–1880* (Lawrence: University Press of Kansas, 1989).

103. Richard White, *The Roots of Dependency: Subsistence, Environment, and Social Change among the Choctaws, Pawnees, and Navajos* (Lincoln: University of Nebraska Press, 1983), vii, xvi, xvii, xix, 315, 317, 319. Compare with his more recent story, *The Middle Ground: Indians, Empires, and Republics in the Great Lakes Region, 1650–1815* (Cambridge: Cambridge University Press, 1991).

104. Edward M. Bruner, "Ethnography as Narrative," in Victor W. Turner and Bruner, eds., *The Anthropology of Experience* (Urbana: University of Illinois Press, 1986), 139–155; the citations are from pp. 140 and 148. Note his conflation of acculturation and assimilation.

105. Bruner, "Ethnography as Narrative," 151, 152. He cites White's *Metahistory.* For White's views on appeals to "world conditions" or "history" as a causal factor in changing textual form, see his "Historical Pluralism," *Critical Inquiry* 12 (Spring 1986): 480–493. The appeal to political history as an explanation of shifts in ethnographic imagination also turns up in George A. Marcus, "Contemporary Problems of Ethnography in the Modern World System," in James Clifford and George E. Marcus, eds., *Writing Culture: The Poetics and Politics of Ethnography* (Berkeley: University of California Press, 1986), 167 n. 3. The unlikeliness of this reading is pointed out by Steven P. Sangren, "Rhetoric and the Authority of Ethnography: 'Postmodernism' and the Social Reproduction of Texts," *Current Anthropology* 29 (June 1988): 408.

106. Anthony F. C. Wallace, "Handsome Lake and the Great Revival in the West," *American Quarterly* (Summer 1952): 149–165; Wallace, "Revitalization Movements: Some Theoretical Considerations for Their Comparative Study," *American Anthropologist* 58 (1956): 264–281; Wallace, *The Death and Rebirth of the Seneca* (New York, 1969); Hallowell, "The Backwash of the Frontier: The Impact of the Indian on American Culture" (1957), in Walker D. Wyman and

Clifton B. Kroeber, eds., *The Frontier in Perspective* (Madison: University of Wisconsin Press, 1965), 229–258; Wyman and Kroeber, "American Indians, White and Black: The Phenomenon of Transculturation," *Current Anthropology* 4 (1963): 519–531.

107. This essay is reprinted in Vine Deloria Jr., *Custer Died for Your Sins* (New York: Avon, 1969), 83–103. See also Deloria's later work, *God Is Red* (New York: Grosset and Dunlap, 1973).

108. Margaret Mead, "The American Indian as a Significant Determinant of Anthropological Style," in *Anthropology and the American Indian: Report of a Symposium* (San Francisco: The Indian Historian Press, 1973), 70; Abbott Sekaquaptewa, in ibid., 19. See also Kerwin L. Klein, "Frontier Tales: The Narrative Construction of Cultural Borders in Twentieth-Century California," *Comparative Studies in Society and History* 34 (July 1990): 464–490.

109. Vine Deloria Jr., "Some Criticisms and a Number of Suggestions," in *Anthropology and the American Indian,* 98, 99. He was citing the Society of Friends, *Uncommon Controversy: Fishing Rights of the Muckleshoot, Puyallup, and Nisqually Indians* (Seattle: University of Washington Press, 1970), 67. The anthropologist/witness is not named in this text, but the authors elsewhere quote ethnographer Marian W. Smith, *The Puyallup-Nisqually,* Columbia University Contributions to Anthropology, no. 32 (Columbia: Columbia University Press, 1940), xi: "Puyallup-Nisqually culture is gone." A federal judge later overturned the ruling. On ethnographic discourse and native agency, see Bruner, "Ethnography as Narrative"; Berkhofer, *White Man's Indian,* esp. 62–69; and Berkhofer, "Cultural Pluralism versus Ethnocentrism in the New Indian History," in Calvin Martin, ed., *The American Indian and the Problem of History* (New York: Oxford University Press, 1987), 35–44.

110. Ray Allen Billington et al., *The Historian's Contribution to Anglo-American Misunderstanding: Report of a Committee on National Bias in Anglo-American History Textbooks* (New York: Hobbs, Dorman, 1966), 7, 11. Billington's appeal to the good intentions of most Americans found a more systematic development in Frederick Merk, *Manifest Destiny and Mission in American History: A Reinterpretation* (1963; reprint, New York: Vintage, 1966).

111. Francis Jennings, *The Invasion of America: Indians, Colonialism, and the Cant of Conquest* (1975; reprint, New York: W. W. Norton, 1976), 1–14. The address appeared as chapter 1, "Crusader Ideology and an Alternative"; the citations are from pp. 8, 11, 13. For less sanguine period views about the objectification of language, see Robert F. Berkhofer, *The White Man's Indian: Images of the American Indian from Columbus to the Present* (New York: Vintage, 1978), 195–197.

112. Jennings, "Virgin Land and Savage People," *American Quarterly* 23 (1973): 541, n. 75. He also recommended the SSRC report, *The Social Sciences in Historical Study* (New York: Social Science Research Council, 1946). Jennings was drawing on a tradition of myth criticism developed in American studies that we will examine in book 4, below.

113. Jennings, *Invasion of America,* 15, 325, 326. See also the interesting appendix "The Formative Period of a Large Society: A Comparative Approach," esp. 330.

114. Neal E. Salisbury, "Conquest of the 'Savage': Puritans, Puritan Missionaries, and Indians, 1620–1680," Ph.D. diss., University of California, Los Angeles, 1972; Salisbury, *Manitou and Providence: Indians, Europeans, and the Making of New England, 1500–1643* (New York: Oxford University Press, 1982), 237, 238, 239. Like Jennings, Salisbury took as his primary historiographic target Alden T. Vaughan's *New England Frontier: Puritans and Indians, 1620–1975* (Boston: Little, Brown, 1965). Ironically, a recent review concludes that "Alden T. Vaughan's *New England Frontier* (1965), which Jennings accuses of justifying the Puritan conquest, offers far more information than Jennings does regarding who was who among native leaders and what they were doing to confront Puritan expansion." See Berkhofer, "Cultural Pluralism versus Ethnocentrism in the New Indian History," 42.

115. Wilcomb Washburn, *The Indian in America* (New York: Harper and Row, 1975), xvii; Henry Steele Commager and Richard Brandon Morris, "Editors' Introduction," in ibid., xi, xii. Compare these texts with older surveys by anthropologists such as Harold E. Driver, *Indians of North America* (Chicago: University of Chicago Press, 1961); Robert F. Spencer, Jesse D. Jennings et al., eds., *The Native Americans: Prehistory and Ethnology of the North American Indians* (New York: Harper and Row, 1965); Edward H. Spicer, *A Short History of the Indians of the United States* (New York: Van Nostrand Reinhold, 1969); and Eleanor B. Leacock and Nancy O. Lurie, eds., *North American Indians in Historical Perspective* (New York: Random House, 1971).

116. William Appleman Williams, "The Frontier Thesis and American Foreign Policy," *Pacific Historical Review* 24 (November 1955): 379–395; Wilbur Jacobs, *Dispossessing the American Indian: Indians and Whites on the Colonial Frontier* (New York: Scribner's, 1972); Robert V. Hine, *The American West: An Interpretive History* (Boston: Little, Brown, 1973); Robert F. Berkhofer Jr., *Salvation and the Savage: An Analysis of Protestant Missions and American Indian Response, 1787–1862* (Lexington: University of Kentucky Press, 1965); Berkhofer, "The Political Context of a New Indian History," *Pacific Historical Review* 40 (August 1971): 357–382. See Daniel J. Singal, "Introduction," in Singal, ed., *Modernist Culture in America* (Belmont, Calif.: Wadsworth, 1991), for a Boasian comedy of cultural pluralism.

117. Clifford, *Predicament of Culture*, 15.

118. See the treatment of experimental modes in Clifford, *Predicament of Culture*, esp. 117–151; Stephen A. Tyler, "Post-Modern Ethnography: From Document of the Occult to Occult Document," in Clifford and Marcus, *Writing Culture*, 122–140; Vincent Crapanzano, *The Fifth World of Enoch Mahoney: Portrait of a Navajo* (New York: Random House, 1969).

119. Herbert Eugene Bolton, "The Mission as a Frontier Institution in the Spanish-American Colonies," *American Historical Review* 23 (1917): 42–61; Bolton, *The Spanish Borderlands: A Chronicle of Old Florida and the Southwest* (New Haven: Yale University Press, 1921); Bolton, "Epic of Greater America"; David J. Weber, "Turner, the Boltonians, and the Borderlands," *American Historical Review* 91 (February 1986): 66–81; John Francis Bannon, *Herbert Eugene Bolton: The Historian and the Man* (Tucson: University of Arizona Press, 1978); Donald Worcester, "Herbert Eugene Bolton: The Making of a Western Historian," in Richard W. Etulain, ed., *Writing Western History: Essays on Ma-*

jor Western Historians (Albuquerque: University of New Mexico Press, 1991), 193–216; and Albert L. Hurtado, "Herbert E. Bolton, Racism, and American History," *Pacific Historical Review* 62 (May 1993): 127–142.

120. Kerwin Lee Klein, "Reclaiming the 'F' Word, or Being and Becoming Postwestern," *Pacific Historical Review* 65 (May 1996): 179–215.

121. Wallace, "Handsome Lake and the Great Revival in the West"; Wallace, "Revitalization Movements"; Wallace, *The Death and Rebirth of the Seneca;* Hallowell, "The Backwash of the Frontier"; Hallowell, "American Indians, White and Black." See also Everett C. Hughes and Helen M. Hughes, *Where Peoples Meet: Racial and Ethnic Frontiers* (Glencoe, Ill.: The Free Press, 1952).

122. Jack D. Forbes, "The Indian in the West: A Challenge for Historians," *Arizona and the West* 1 (1959): 210; Forbes, "Frontiers in American History," *Journal of the West* 1 (July 1962): 64, 65; Forbes, "Frontiers in American History and the Role of the American Historian," *Ethnohistory* 15 (Spring 1968): 203–235.

123. Klein, "Frontier Tales"; Stocking, *Ethnographer's Magic;* Berkhofer, *White Man's Indian;* James A. Clifton, "Alternate Identities and Cultural Frontiers," in Clifton, ed., *Being and Becoming Indian: Biographical Studies of North American Frontiers* (Chicago: Dorsey Press, 1989), 1–37.

124. Fredrik Barth, "Introduction," in *Ethnic Groups and Boundaries: The Social Organization of Culture Difference* (Boston: Little, Brown, 1969), 10, 14, 15. Barth had given a plenary address before the American Anthropological Association in 1966 ("On the Study of Social Change"). For samplings of the vast body of literature on "ethnicity," see G. Carter Bentley, "Theoretical Perspectives on Ethnicity and Nationality, Part 1," *Sage Race Relations Abstracts* 8 (May 1983): 1–53; Bentley, "Theoretical Perspectives on Ethnicity and Nationality, Part 2," in ibid. (August 1983), 1–26; William Boelhower, *Through a Glass Darkly: Ethnic Semiosis in American Literature* (Oxford, 1984); Werner Sollors, *Beyond Ethnicity: Consent and Descent in American Culture* (Oxford, 1986); Sollors, ed., *The Invention of Ethnicity* (Oxford, 1989); Anthony Smith, *The Ethnic Origin of Nations* (Oxford, 1986); William A. Douglass, "A Critique of Recent Trends in the Analysis of Ethnonationalism," *Ethnic and Racial Studies* 11 (April 1988): 192–206; David Hollinger, "Postethnic America," *Contention* 2 (Fall 1992): 79–96; and Hollinger, "How Wide the Circle of the 'We'? American Intellectuals and the Problem of the Ethnos since World War II," *American Historical Review* 98 (April 1993): 317–337.

125. Edward H. Spicer and Raymond H. Thompson, eds., *Plural Society in the Southwest* (New York, 1972); see Spicer's introduction, pp. 1–20, and "Plural Society in the Southwest," pp. 21–75. For the discussion of Barth, see esp. pp. 54–64. For the connection to Spicer's earlier frontier studies, see esp. pp. 10–11. Miguel Leon-Portilla, "The Norteño Variety of Mexican Culture: An Ethnohistorical Approach," 77–114, strongly complemented Spicer's account and usage, but John H. Parry, "Plural Society in the Southwest: A Historical Comment," 299–320, at times verged on the older assimilationist tale that Spicer and most of his coauthors were criticizing. Paul Bohannon, "Introduction," in Bohannon and Fred Plog, *Beyond the Frontier: Social Process and Cultural Change* (Garden City, N.Y.: Natural History Press, 1967), xi.

126. Howard Lamar and Leonard Thompson, "Comparative Frontier His-

tory," in Lamar and Thompson, eds., *The Frontier in History: North American and Southern Africa Compared* (New Haven: Yale University Press, 1981), 3–13; Paul Kutsche, "Borders and Frontiers," in Ellwyn R. Stoddard et al., eds., *Borderlands Sourcebook: A Guide to Literature on Northern Mexico and the American Southwest* (Norman: University of Oklahoma Press, 1983), 16–19; William Cronon, George Miles, and Jay Gitlin, "Becoming West: Toward a New Meaning for Western History," in Cronon et al., eds., *Under an Open Sky: Rethinking America's Western Past* (New York: W. W. Norton, 1993), 3–27; "Frontier," in Charlotte Seymour-Smith, *Dictionary of Anthropology* (Boston: G. K. Hall, 1986), 125; William Cronon, "Revisiting the Vanishing Frontier: The Legacy of Frederick Jackson Turner," *Western Historical Quarterly* 18 (April 1987): 157–176; Annette Kolodny, "Letting Go Our Grand Obsessions: Notes toward a New Literary History of the American Frontiers," *American Literature* 64 (1992): 1–18. See also Clifton, "Alternate Identities and Cultural Frontiers"; Robert F. Berkhofer Jr., "The North American Frontier as Process and Context," in *The Frontier in History*, 43–75; and Peggy Pascoe, "Western Women at the Cultural Crossroads," in *Trails*, 40–58 (one of the few contributions to this collection that uses "frontier" without wincing). And while Lamar and Thompson's definition fairly demands that at least one half of a frontier equation be European or Euro-American, that usage is hardly universal. Forbes, Kutsche, and Kolodny all employ the word for any interethnic or intercultural collision. See also Igor Kopytoff, ed., *The African Frontier: The Reproduction of Traditional African Societies* (Bloomington: Indiana University Press, 1987).

Book Four: Histories of Language

1. Sacvan Bercovitch and Myra Jehlen, eds., *Ideology and Classic American Literature* (Cambridge: Cambridge University Press, 1986); Henry Nash Smith, "Symbol and Idea in *Virgin Land*," in ibid., 21–35 (the editors solicited this essay); Smith, *Virgin Land: The American West as Myth and Symbol* (1950; reprint, Cambridge: Harvard University Press, 1970). For overviews of Smith and American studies, see Cecil F. Tate, *The Search for Method in American Studies* (Minneapolis: University of Minnesota Press, 1973); Richard Bridgeman, "The American Studies of Henry Nash Smith," *American Scholar* 56 (Spring 1987): 259–268; Henry F. May, *The Divided Heart: Essays on Protestantism and the Enlightenment in America* (New York: Oxford University Press, 1991), 33–60; and Lee Clark Mitchell, "Henry Nash Smith," in Richard W. Etulain, ed., *Writing Western History: Essays on Major Western Historians* (Albuquerque: University of New Mexico Press, 1991), 247–276; Gene Wise, " 'Paradigm Dramas' in American Studies: A Cultural and Institutional History of the Movement," *American Quarterly* 31 (1979 bibliography issue): 293–337; Günter Lenz, "American Studies—Beyond the Crisis? Recent Redefinitions and the Meaning of Theory, History, and Practical Criticism," *Prospects* 7 (1982): 53–113; Robert F. Berkhofer Jr., "A New Context for a New American Studies?" *American Quarterly* 41 (December 1989): 588–613; and Allen F. Davis, "The Politics of American Studies," *American Quarterly* 42 (September 1990): 353–374.

2. Vernon L. Parrington, *Main Currents in American Thought*, vol. 1: *The Colonial Mind, 1620–1800* (New York: Harcourt Brace Jovanovich, 1927); Parrington, *Main Currents*, vol. 2: *The Romantic Revolution in America, 1800–1860* (New York: Harcourt Brace Jovanovich, 1927); Parrington, *Main Currents*, vol. 3: *The Beginnings of Critical Realism, 1860–1920* (New York: Harcourt Brace Jovanovich, 1930). Gerald Graff, *Professing Literature: An Institutional History* (Chicago: University of Chicago Press, 1987), offers a useful account of academic English in this period. See also Wise, " 'Paradigm Dramas,' "; Lenz, "American Studies"; and Elizabeth Renker, "Resistance and Change: The Rise of American Literature Studies," *American Literature* 64 (June 1992): 347–365.

3. On Parrington's background and reception see Robert Allen Skotheim, *American Intellectual Histories and Historians* (Princeton: Princeton University Press, 1966), 124–148; and Richard Hofstadter, *The Progressive Historians: Turner, Beard, Parrington* (1968; reprint, New York: Vintage, 1970), 349–434.

4. See, for instance, Parrington, *Main Currents*, vol. 1: *The Colonial Mind*, 133, 134. On Parrington criticism, see Hofstadter, *Progressive Historians*, especially 349–357. Lionel Trilling, *The Liberal Imagination* (1948; reprint, Garden City, N.Y.: Doubleday, 1954), 15–32.

5. Parrington, *Main Currents*, vol. 2: *The Romantic Revolution*, 172; Parrington, *Main Currents*, vol. 3: *Critical Realism*, 260.

6. Perry Miller, "Thomas Hooker and the Democracy of Connecticut" (1931), reprinted in his *Errand into the Wilderness* (1956; reprint, New York: Harper, 1964), 16–47; ibid., 17; Miller, *Orthodoxy in Massachusetts, 1630–1650* (Cambridge: Harvard University Press, 1933); Miller, *The New England Mind: The Seventeenth Century* (Cambridge: Harvard University Press, 1939); Miller, *The New England Mind: From Colony to Province* (Cambridge: Harvard University Press, 1952). Again see Skotheim, *American Intellectual Histories and Historians*, 186–212.

7. Percy Holmes Boynton, *The Rediscovery of the Frontier* (1931; reprint, New York: Greenwood Press, 1968); Miller, *Errand into the Wilderness*, vii.

8. Bernard DeVoto, *Mark Twain's America* (Cambridge, Mass.: Houghton Mifflin, 1931); DeVoto, "The Real Frontier: A Preface to Mark Twain," *Harper's* 163 (June 1931): 60–71; Wallace Stegner, *The Uneasy Chair: A Biography of Bernard DeVoto* (Garden City, N.Y.: Doubleday, 1974).

9. DeVoto, *Mark Twain's America*, 301, 305. DeVoto was capable of much more discriminating descriptions of frontiers. See his "How Not to Write History," *Harper's* 168 (January 1934): 199–208.

10. Henry Steele Commager, *The American Mind: An Interpretation of American Thought and Character since the 1880's* (New Haven: Yale University Press, 1950). On the reception of *Virgin Land*, see Marks, "The Concept of Myth in *Virgin Land*"; Mitchell, "Henry Nash Smith's Myth of the West"; and Bridgeman, "Henry Nash Smith."

11. Smith, *Virgin Land*, 3. See the reviews by Richard Hofstadter, in *American Quarterly* 2 (Fall 1950): 279–282; Marvin Wachman, in *Mississippi Valley Historical Review* 37 (December 1950): 544–545; and Fulmer Mood, in *American Historical Review* 56 (July 1951): 905–907. Curiously, of these reviewers only Mood did not place the book in Turnerian historiography.

12. "What Is the Frontier?" *Southwest Review* 21 (October 1935): 100, 101. See also Smith's earliest article, "Culture," *Southwest Review* 13 (January 1928): 249–255.

13. Henry Nash Smith, "Rain Follows the Plow: The Notion of Increased Rainfall for the Great Plains, 1844–1880," *Huntington Library Quarterly* 10 (February 1947): 169–193; Smith, review of *Year of Decision, New England Quarterly* (Spring 1943); Smith, "The Salzburg Seminar," *American Quarterly* 1 (Spring 1949): 30–37; on Smith at Harvard see Mitchell, "Henry Nash Smith"; May, *Protestant Heart;* and Bridgeman, "Henry Nash Smith."

14. This was the chapter Smith chose to publish in article form: see "The Myth of the Garden and the Turner Hypothesis," *American Quarterly* 2 (Spring 1950): 3–11. An even more pointed statement came a year later in a less well known article, "The West as an Image of the American Past," *University of Kansas City Review* 18 (Autumn 1951): 29–40. In this piece Smith hinted at what would later become a virtual proposition: the West was actually more reactionary than the East.

15. Smith, *Virgin Land,* 253, 254, 296.

16. Ibid., 237, 249.

17. See I. A. Richards, *Practical Criticism: A Study of Literary Judgment* (New York: Harcourt, Brace, 1929); Robert E. Spiller, "Criticism and Literary History: Toward a Methodology for a New History of American Literature," *American Quarterly* 9 (Fall 1957): 367–370; Perry Miller, *Errand into the Wilderness,* 1, 2; Max Lerner, *America as Civilization: Life and Thought in the United States Today* (New York: Simon and Schuster, 1957), 34–39; Edwin Fussell, *Frontier: American Literature and the American West* (Princeton: Princeton University Press, 1965), 435.

18. Among others, Smith invoked Chester E. Eisinger, "The Freehold Concept in Eighteenth-Century American Letters," *William and Mary Quarterly,* 3d ser., 4 (January 1947): 42–59; Paul W. Gates, "The Homestead Law in an Incongruous Land System," *American Historical Review* 61 (July 1936): 670; Hofstadter, "Frontier Myth." Smith, especially in chapter 20, "The Garden as Safety Valve," also drew off the anti-Turnerian histories associated with the so-called "safety-valve controversy." For a period survey of this literature, see Gene Gressley, "The Turner Thesis: A Problem in Historiography," *Agricultural History* 32 (October 1958): 227–249. More recently, see Gerald D. Nash, *Creating the West: Historical Interpretations, 1890–1990* (Albuquerque: University of New Mexico Press, 1991).

19. *Virgin Land,* xi. On American history in the fifties, see Peter Novick, *That Noble Dream: The "Objectivity Question" and the American Historical Profession* (Cambridge: Cambridge University Press, 1988), esp. 281–411.

20. Joseph Campbell, *The Hero with a Thousand Faces,* 2d ed., Bollingen Series 17 (1949; 2d ed., Princeton, 1968), 3, 28, 289; Northrop Frye, "The Archetypes of Literature" (1951), in *Fables of Identity: Studies in Poetic Mythology* (New York: Harcourt, Brace and World, 1963), 7–20; Northrop Frye, *Anatomy of Criticism: Four Essays* (Princeton: Princeton University Press, 1957), 7. The question is whether Frye can be considered a new critic. For our purposes it seems useful to consider him separately while keeping in mind that the new criticism

held power for so long partly by adapting to and assimilating challengers. See the statement on myth and symbol in the touchstone of postwar new criticism, Rene Wellek and Austin Warren, *Theory of Literature* (1942; reprint, New York: Harcourt, Brace, 1956), 175–200. For a broader context compare Gerald Graff, *Professing Literature,* esp. 183–246; and Vincent Leitch, *American Literary Criticism from the '30s to the '80s* (New York: Columbia University Press, 1988), 103–146.

21. Smith nonetheless separated myth as a generic category from other categories, such as history and art. Here he differed from yet another author interested in myth criticism, American studies scholar Richard Chase. Chase's 1949 study *The Quest for Myth* (Baton Rouge: Louisiana State University Press, 1949), 73, discussed "myth" as a concept in Western thought and culture and suggested that myth might be contingently useful for some descriptions but was not a natural kind. Chase later avoided this particular terminological difficulty by discussing popular and high American literature in terms of romance, a specific literary genre. See his *The American Novel and Its Tradition* (Garden City, N.Y.: Doubleday, 1957), especially appendix 2, "Romance, the Folk Imagination, and Myth Criticism," 243–246. More recently, see Marcel Détienne, *The Creation of Mythology,* trans. Margaret Cook (orig. ed., 1981; Eng.-lang. ed., Chicago: University of Chicago Press, 1986).

22. Sir James G. Frazer, *The Golden Bough: A Study in Magic and Religion,* 12 vols., 3d ed. (London: Macmillan, 1907–1915); Lionel Trilling, "On the Teaching of Modern Literature" (1961), in *Beyond Culture: Essays on Literature and Learning* (1965; reprint, New York: Harcourt Brace Jovanovich, 1965), 3–27; John B. Vickery, *The Literary Impact of the Golden Bough* (Princeton: Princeton University Press, 1973). Also relevant here is Joan Shelley Rubin, "Constance Rourke in Context: The Uses of Myth," *American Quarterly* 28 (Winter 1976): 575–587.

23. Merrill Peterson, review of *Virgin Land,* in *New England Quarterly* 24 (December 1951): 558, 559; Marvin Wachman, review, in *Mississippi Valley Historical Review* 37 (December 1950): 544; Fulmer Mood, review, in *American Historical Review* 66 (July 1951): 906; Richard Hofstadter, review, in *American Quarterly* 2 (Fall 1950).

24. Barry Marks, "The Concept of Myth in *Virgin Land,*" *American Quarterly* 5 (Spring 1953): 71–76.

25. R. W. B. Lewis, "The Hero in the New World: William Faulkner's *The Bear,*" *Kenyon Review* 13 (Autumn 1951): 642; Lewis, *The American Adam: Innocence, Tragedy, and Tradition in the Nineteenth Century* (Chicago: University of Chicago Press, 1955); Henry Nash Smith, review of *The American Adam,* in *American Literature* 28 (November 1956): 389–391; Sherman Paul, review, in *New England Quarterly* 29 (June 1956): 256; John William Ward, *Andrew Jackson, Symbol for an Age* (New York: Oxford University Press, 1955), 10.

26. Henry Nash Smith, "Can American Studies Develop a Method?" *American Quarterly* 9 (Summer 1957): 197–208; citation from pp. 201, 206. The piece became a focus of later discussions and was included in Joseph J. Kwiat and Mary C. Turpie, eds., *Studies in American Culture: Dominant Ideas and Images* (Minneapolis: University of Minnesota Press, 1960), 3–15. For other

period discussions compare Ben Halpern, " 'Myth' and 'Ideology' in Modern Usage," *History and Theory* 1 (1961): 129–149, and Peter Munz, "History and Myth," *Philosophical Quarterly* 6 (1956): 1–16.

27. Smith, "Can American Studies Develop a Method?" passim. Compare this with Smith's "Culture," 253, where he initially described culture as the "texture of daily life" but used only high culture for his examples. For period assessments of Smith's usage, see Robert E. Spiller, "American Studies, Past, Present, and Future," in Kwiat and Turpie, *Studies in American Culture*, 207–220, and Robert Merideth, "Introduction: Theory, Method, and American Studies," in Robert Merideth, ed., *American Studies: Essays on Theory and Method* (Columbus, Ohio: Charles E. Merrill, 1968), v–xiv.

28. Richard E. Sykes, "American Studies and the Concept of Culture: A Theory and Method," *American Quarterly* 15 (Summer 1963): 253, 254, 258, 262, 263; Seymour Katz, " 'Culture' and Literature in American Studies," *American Quarterly* 20 (Summer 1968): 318–320.

29. Katz, ibid., 318; Robert F. Berkhofer, "Clio and the Culture Concept: Some Impressions of a Changing Relationship in American Historiography," *Social Science Quarterly* 53 (1972): 297–320. Berkhofer thought that "culture" still had too many aesthetic connotations and predicted "society" would replace it as a term of choice. For a sense of the depth of these debates, see Kwiat and Turpie, *Studies in American Culture;* Merideth, *American Studies: Theory and Methods;* Roy Harvey Pearce, "Art in Culture: Some Points of View," *American Quarterly* 11 (Spring 1959): 78–83; Max Lerner, "Notes on Literature and Civilization," ibid., 212–224; and R. Gordon Kelly, "Literature and the Historian," ibid., 26 (May 1974): 141–159.

30. Vance Packard, *The Hidden Persuaders* (New York: David McKay, 1957); Jacques Ellul, *The Technological Society,* trans. John Wilkinson (orig. ed., 1954; Eng.-lang. ed., New York: Alfred A. Knopf, 1964); C. Wright Mills, *The Sociological Imagination* (Oxford: Oxford University Press, 1959); William H. Whyte Jr., *The Organization Man* (New York: Simon and Schuster, 1956); Arnold J. Toynbee, *A Study of History,* abridgement of vols. 7–10 by D. C. Somervell (New York: Oxford University Press, 1957), 308.

31. Henry Nash Smith, *Mark Twain: The Development of a Writer* (Cambridge: Harvard University Press, 1962); Smith, *Mark Twain's Fable of Progress: Political and Economic Ideas in "A Connecticut Yankee"* (New Brunswick, N.J.: Rutgers University Press, 1964); Smith, *Democracy and the Novel: Popular Resistance to Classic American Writers* (New York: Oxford University Press, 1978); Perry Miller, "The Responsibility of Mind in a Civilization of Machines," *American Scholar* 31 (Winter 1961/1962): 51–69; James Hiner, "On Distinguishing a 'Machine' from Its System," *American Quarterly* 14 (Winter 1962): 612–617. Hiner's article was sufficiently well regarded to be anthologized in Merideth, *American Studies,* 135–142.

32. Leo Marx, "The Machine in the Garden," *New England Quarterly* 29 (March 1956): 28; Leo Marx, Bernard Bowron, and Arnold Rose, "Literature and Covert Culture" (1957), in Kwiat and Turpie, *Studies in American Culture,* 84–95; Leo Marx, *The Machine in the Garden* (Oxford: Oxford University Press, 1964).

33. William Empson, *Some Versions of Pastoral* (1935; reprint, Norfolk, Conn.: New Directions, 1960), 6, 189. See also Marx's recent discussions in "Pastoralism in America," in Bercovitch and Jehlen, *Ideology and Classic American Literature,* 36–69, and *The Pilot and the Passenger: Essays on Literature, Technology, and Culture in the United States* (Oxford: Oxford University Press, 1988), esp. 160–178, 291–314.

34. Marx, *Machine in the Garden,* 341, 345. He is quoting from Trilling's revised edition of "Reality in America" (1940, 1946), in *The Liberal Imagination,* 15–32. Marx's discussion of dialectic here also, though, seems partially indebted to another source he invoked, Raymond Williams, *Culture and Society, 1780–1950* (New York: Oxford University Press, 1960). See also his more recent statement in the introduction to Leo Marx, *The Pilot and the Passenger,* ix–xviii.

35. Marx, *Machine in the Garden,* 71, 72. Marx credited Frank Kermode with some of the inspiration for this reading. See his introduction to William Shakespeare, *The Tempest,* Arden edition, 5th ed., rev. (London, 1954). In his review of the book Alan Trachtenberg gave highest praise to this reading. See "The American Way of Life," *The Nation* 20 (July 19, 1965): 42–45. Compare Marx's reading with that of Octave Mannoni, *Prospero and Caliban: The Psychology of Colonization,* trans. Pamela Powesland (orig. ed., 1959; Eng.-lang. 2d ed., New York: Praeger, 1964). Alden T. Vaughan and Virgina Mason Vaughan, *Shakespeare's Caliban: A Cultural History* (Cambridge: Cambridge University Press, 1991), traces critical interpretations of *The Tempest.*

36. Marx, *Machine in the Garden,* 364, 365.

37. See Charles L. Sanford's brief but discriminating review of the book in *American Quarterly* 17 (1965): 272–276. Kenneth S. Lynn's polemic "The Regressive Historians," *American Scholar* (1978), placed Marx in this context, as did Marx himself, in "American Pastoralism," where he identified Savio's exhortation with the figures of Thoreau and the radical tradition of pastoralism. See also Marx, *The Pilot and the Passenger.*

38. Leo Marx, "American Studies—A Defense of an Unscientific Method," *New Literary History* 1 (October 1969): 75–90. The paper initially was presented at the 1967 symposium "Public Opinion, Foreign Policy, and the Historian" and was included in Marvin Small, ed., *Public Opinion and the Historian: Interdisciplinary Perspectives* (Detroit: Wayne State University Press, 1969). See also Jeffrey Louis Decker, "Dis-Assembling the Machine in the Garden: Antihumanism and the Critique of American Studies," *New Literary History* 23 (Spring 1992): 281–306.

39. Marx, "Defense of an Unscientific Method," 89, 90. The formulation is not immeasurably distant from either Turner or Hegel, and it effectively reconstructed a nineteenth-century understanding of historicism with a new vocabulary. See also the somewhat different reading in Decker, "Dis-Assembling the Machine in the Garden."

40. Berkhofer, "Clio and the Culture Concept." An anonymous author for *Time* magazine also placed Henry Nash Smith and *Virgin Land* (and, by implication, its epigoni) into the conservative consensus school of historiography. We should point out that Collingwoodian conceptions of history were predict-

ably congenial to American studies scholars hoping to keep behaviorism at bay. See John William Ward, *Red, White, and Blue: Men, Books, and Ideas in American Culture* (New York: Oxford University Press, 1969), 3–9.

41. Lynn, "The Regressive Historians"; Marx, "Pastoralism in America"; Marx, "Pastoral Ideals and City Troubles" (1968), in Ian G. Barbour, ed., *Western Man and Environmental Ethics* (Reading, Mass.: Addison-Wesley, 1973), 93–114. More recently, see Merritt Roe Smith and Leo Marx, eds., *Does Technology Drive History? The Dilemma of Technological Determinism* (Cambridge: MIT Press, 1994).

42. Ellul, *Technological Society;* Martin Heidegger, "The Question Concerning Technology" (1953), in David F. Krell, ed., *Martin Heidegger: Basic Writings* (New York: Harper and Row, 1977), 283–318.

43. Smith, "Preface to the Twentieth Anniversary Printing," *Virgin Land,* vi, vii, ix. See Marks, "The Concept of Myth in *Virgin Land*"; Laurence R. Veysey, "Myth and Reality in Approaching American Regionalism," *American Quarterly* 12 (Spring 1960): 31–43; and Trachtenburg, "Myth, History, and Literature in *Virgin Land.*" Whether the construction improves Turner's historicism is another question. For the Victorian, myths, images, and symbols stood *within* history, and the relation of free will and determinism was rather differently worked out. Turner had stressed history's dependence on behavior that was *not* purposive, and the stories of historicists from Hegel and Marx forward had made much of unintended consequences and ironic reversal. Smith, after all, did not purposefully draw an overcrude distinction between fact and myth. In his reformulation, though, *Virgin Land*'s inadvertent reduction of myth is not, strictly speaking, a historical affair but rather a symptom of humanity's inability ever to break completely free of irrationality. Deceived by his own socialization and far more dependent on Turnerian myth than he had realized, Smith too had fallen out of history and into myth.

44. *Virgin Land,* 78, 80. Smith could be quite suspicious of the sublime when treated by other critics. See his scathing review of Muriel Rukeyser's *Willard Gibbs* (Garden City, N.Y.: Doubleday, 1942), in *New England Quarterly* 16 (September 1943): 525–527. Rukeyser's surrender to "cosmic emotions" "tempts her to strain language" past the limits of prose and toward sublimity, and "sublimity has always been notoriously dangerous" (p. 527).

45. On the gendering of such aesthetics see Jane Kneller, "Discipline and Silence: Women and Imagination in Kant's Theory of Taste," in Hilde Hein and Carolyn Korsmeyer, eds., *Aesthetics in Feminist Perspective* (Bloomington: Indiana University Press, 1993), esp. 170–174; and Christine Battersby, *Gender and Genius: Towards a Feminist Aesthetics* (Bloomington: Indiana University Press, 1989). Compare Smith's account with Joan Wallach Scott, *Gender and the Politics of History* (New York: Columbia University Press, 1988), 68–92, where she argues that E. P. Thompson's *The Making of the English Working Class* (1963) valorizes working class politics and Thompson's preferred forms of poesy by gendering both as masculine.

46. Robert Forrey, "Interviews on American Studies: Henry Nash Smith," *Amerikastudien* 22 (1977): 196, 197; Susan Lee Johnson, " 'A memory sweet to soldiers': The Significance of Gender in the History of the 'American West,' "

Western Historical Quarterly 24 (November 1993): 495–518; Renker, "Resistance and Change"; Andreas Huyssen, *After the Great Divide: Modernism, Mass Culture, Postmodernism* (Bloomington: Indiana University Press, 1986), 44–62.

47. Roy Harvey Pearce, *Gesta Humanorum: Studies in the Historicist Mode* (Columbia: University of Missouri Press, 1987), 15.

48. Bruce Kuklick, "Myth and Symbol in American Studies," *American Quarterly* 24 (October 1972): 435–450; quote from p. 436. See also Wise, " 'Paradigm Dramas' "; Lenz, "American Studies"; Decker, "Dis-Assembling the Machine in the Garden"; and Bruce Kuklick, "Reply to Decker," *New Literary History* 23 (Spring 1992): 281–306.

49. John G. Blair, "Structuralism, American Studies, and the Humanities," *American Quarterly* 30 (1978): 261–281; David Pace, "Structuralism in History and the Social Sciences," in ibid., 282–297; John G. Cawelti, *The Six-Gun Mystique* (Bowling Green: Bowling Green University Popular Press, 1971); Will Wright, *Six-Guns and Society: A Structural Study of the Western* (Berkeley: University of California Press, 1978); Cecil F. Tate, *The Search for a Method in American Studies* (Minneapolis: University of Minnesota Press, 1973), 197; Forrey, "Interviews on American Studies"; Wise, " 'Paradigm Dramas' "; Lenz, "American Studies."

50. Annette Kolodny, *The Lay of the Land* (Chapel Hill: University of North Carolina Press, 1974); Richard Slotkin, *Regeneration through Violence: The Mythology of the American Frontier, 1600–1860* (Middletown, Conn.: Wesleyan University Press, 1973). Among the book's many reviews and notices, see Henry Nash Smith, *American Historical Review* 91 (1986), 1188; Leo Marx, *Journal of American History* 61 (1975): 365–366; Roy Harvey Pearce, *Pacific Historical Review* 43 (1974): 111–112; David Grimstead, *William and Mary Quarterly* 31 (1974): 143–146; Mary Young, "Reflections on Violence," *Reviews in American History* 3 (1975): 8–12; and Michael J. Colacurcio, "The Symbolic and the Symptomatic: D. H. Lawrence in Recent American Criticism," *American Quarterly* 27 (1975): 486–501.

51. Smith, "*Virgin Land* Revisited," *Indian Journal of American Studies* 3 (June 1973): 84, 85; Forrey, "Interviews on American Studies: Henry Nash Smith." On Smith in the sixties and seventies, see Mitchell, "Henry Nash Smith's Myth of the West," and Bridgeman, "Henry Nash Smith." Wise, " 'Paradigm Dramas,' " and Davis, "The Politics of American Studies," discuss radicalism and American studies.

52. Roy Harvey Pearce, *The Savages of America: A Study of the Indian and the Idea of Civilization* (Baltimore: Johns Hopkins University Press, 1953), reissued as *Savagism and Civilization: A Study of the Indian and the American Mind* (1967; reprint, Berkeley: University of California Press, 1988) (all page citations will be from this edition); Smith, "*Virgin Land* Revisited"; Smith, "Symbols and Ideas in *Virgin Land*"; Pearce, "Afterword," *Savagism and Civilization,* 253, 254.

53. Arthur O. Lovejoy, *The Great Chain of Being: A Study in the History of an Idea* (Cambridge: Harvard University Press, 1936); Lovejoy and George Boas, *Primitivism and Related Ideas in Antiquity: A Documentary History of Primitivism and Related Ideas* (Baltimore: Johns Hopkins University Press,

1935); Lovejoy, "The Historiography of Ideas" (1938), reprinted in *Essays in the History of Ideas* (1948; reprint, New York: Capricorn, 1960), 9; Pearce, *Savagism and Civilization,* xvii, xix.

54. Pearce, *Savagism and Civilization,* 74, 91, 211.

55. Ibid., 49. Smith, *"Virgin Land* Revisited," invoked this passage. What is especially interesting is the anachronistic anthropological use of "culture" in a work that elsewhere eschews anachronism.

56. Pearce, *Savagism and Civilization,* 189.

57. Ibid., iv, 105, 251. Even Albert Keiser, whose *The American Indian in Literature* (1933; reprint, New York: Octagon–Farrar, Straus, and Giroux, 1970), was probably the closest precursor to *Savages of America,* could say in review: "It is a dark and gloomy picture our author has chosen to paint. . . . In fact, the present book soon becomes a weariness to the flesh, as the same depressing tale is told page after page." Keiser doubted whether the tale was sufficiently important to justify Pearce's "indefatigable" work. See his review in *American Literature* 36 (1954): 276.

58. Pearce, "The Leatherstocking Tales Re-examined," *South Atlantic Quarterly* 46 (October 1947): 524–536; Smith, *Virgin Land,* 269; Pearce, "The Significances of the Captivity Narrative," *American Literature* 19 (1947): 1–20; Pearce, "The Metaphysics of Indian-Hating: Leatherstocking Unmasked" (1957), reprinted in *Historicism Once More: Problems and Occasions for the American Scholar* (Princeton: Princeton University Press, 1969), 109–136.

59. See Pearce, "Art in Culture"; Pearce, "Historicism Once More" (1958), reprinted in *Historicism Once More,* 3–45; Arnold Krupat, *The Voice in the Margin: Native American Literature and the Canon* (Berkeley: University of California Press, 1989), 57–95.

60. Américo Paredes, *"With His Pistol in His Hand": A Border Ballad and Its Hero* (Austin: University of Texas Press, 1958), 20, 21.

61. Ibid., xi. The book was not reviewed by the *American Quarterly* or even the *Hispanic-American Historical Review* but did win a brief glowing notice from Austin E. Fife in the *Journal of American Folklore* 73 (January/March 1960): 78–79. On Paredes see José David Saldívar, "Chicano Border Narratives as Cultural Critique," in Hector Calderón and José David Saldívar, eds., *Criticism in the Borderlands: Studies in Chicano Literature, Culture, and Ideology* (Durham and London: Duke University Press, 1991), 167–187; José Limon, *Dancing with the Devil: Society and Cultural Poetics in Mexican-American South Texas* (Madison: University of Wisconsin Press, 1994), 76–96. See also Limón, *Mexican Ballads, Chicano Poems: History and Influence in Mexican-American Social Poetry* (Berkeley: University of California Press, 1992), and Renato Rosaldo, *Culture and Truth: The Remaking of Social Analysis* (Boston: Beacon Press, 1989), esp. 147–166.

62. Paredes, *"With His Pistol in His Hand,"* 7, 8, 9.

63. Ibid., 15.

64. Walter Prescott Webb, *The Texas Rangers* (Cambridge, Mass.: Houghton Mifflin, 1935); J. Frank Dobie, *The Flavor of Texas* (Dallas: Dealey and Lowe, 1936); Paredes, *"With His Pistol in His Hand,"* 15, 17, 283. Webb, *The Great Plains,* cited in Paredes, *"With His Piston in His Hand,"* 17.

65. Paredes, *"With His Pistol in His Hand,"* 147, 247. See Paredes's review of Merle E. Simmons, *The Mexican Corrido as a Source for the Interpretive Study of Modern Mexico (1870–1950)* (Bloomington: University of Indiana Press, 1957), in *Journal of American Folklore* 71 (October/December 1958): 582–583.

66. Paredes, *"With His Pistol in His Hand,"* 51, 186.

67. Ibid., 125.

68. Ibid., 150. For other readings see J. D. Saldívar, "Chicano Border Narratives"; Teresa McKenna, "On Chicano Poetry and the Political Age: *Corridos* as Social Drama," in Calderón and Saldívar, *Criticism in the Borderlands,* 188–202; Limón, *Mexican Ballads, Chicano Poems;* Ramon Saldívar, *Chicano Narrative: The Dialectics of Difference* (Madison: University of Wisconsin Press, 1990), 26–73; and Rosaldo, *Culture and Truth,* 147–166.

69. Paredes, *"With His Pistol in His Hand,"* 107, 247.

70. Leslie Fiedler, "Come Back to the Raft Ag'in, Huck Honey!" *Partisan Review* 15 (June 1948): 664, 666, 667, 670, 671. On homosexuality and McCarthyism see John D'Emilio, *Sexual Politics, Sexual Communities: The Making of a Homosexual Minority in the United States, 1940–1970* (Chicago: University of Chicago Press, 1974), esp. 40–53. On Fiedler and cold war politics, see Donald E. Pease, "Leslie Fiedler, the Rosenberg Trial, and the Formulation of an American Canon," *boundary 2,* 17 (Summer 1990): 155–198. Fiedler spent the fifties building his early theses on American history into a larger work, *Love and Death in the American Novel* (New York: Criterion, 1960).

71. Leslie A. Fiedler, *The Return of the Vanishing American* (New York: Stein and Day, 1968), 21.

72. Ibid., 14, 50.

73. Ibid., 12, 165, 177. Compare Fiedler's treatment with that in Eve Kosofsky Sedgwick, *Epistemology of the Closet* (Berkeley: University of California Press, 1990).

74. Slotkin, *Regeneration through Violence;* Berkhofer, *The White Man's Indian;* Fredi Chiappelli, ed., *First Images of America: The Impact of the New World on the Old* (Berkeley: University of California Press, 1976); Stephen P. Greenblatt, "Learning to Curse: Linguistic Colonialism in the Sixteenth Century" (1976), reprinted in his *Learning to Curse: Essays in Early Modern Culture* (New York: Routledge, 1990), 32. H. Aram Veeser, ed., *The New Historicism* (New York: Routledge, 1989), collects many of the key theoretical statements. For the impact on American literary history, compare Frederick Crews, "Whose American Renaissance?" *New York Review of Books* 35 (October 27, 1988): 68–69, with Donald E. Pease, "New Americanists: Revisionist Intentions," *boundary 2,* 17 (Spring 1990): 1–37.

75. Leslie Fiedler, "The New Mutants" (1965), reprinted in *The Collected Essays of Leslie Fiedler* (New York: Stein and Day, 1971), 379–400. Again, compare with the essays in Veeser, ed., *The New Historicism.* See also Dominick LaCapra's comments on "weak montage" in *Soundings in Critical Theory* (Ithaca: Cornell University Press, 1989), 182–209.

76. See, for instance, Christopher P. Wilson, "Containing Multitudes: Realism, Historicism, American Studies," *American Quarterly* 41 (September

1989): 466–495; Lawrence Buell, "It's Good, but Is It History?" ibid., 496–500; George Lipsitz, "Listening to Learn and Learning to Listen: Popular Culture, Cultural Theory, and American Studies," *American Quarterly* 42 (December 1990): 615–636; Steven Watts, "The Idiocy of American Studies: Poststructuralism, Language, and Politics in the Age of Self-Fulfillment," *American Quarterly* 43 (December 1991): 625–660; Barry Shank, "A Reply to Steven Watts's 'Idiocy,' " *American Quarterly* 44 (September 1992): 439–448; Nancy Isenberg, "The Personal Is Political: Gender, Feminism, and the Politics of Discourse Theory," ibid., 449–458; Steven Watts, "Reply to the Critics," ibid., 459–462; Decker, "Dis-Assembling the Machine in the Garden"; Kuklick, "Reply to Decker"; T. J. Jackson Lears, "Reply to Jeffrey Decker," *New Literary History* 23 (Spring 1992): 281–306; Jeffrey Louis Decker, "American Studies— Toward and Beyond an Antihumanist Method: A Reply to Bruce Kuklick and T. J. Jackson Lears," ibid., 313–317.

77. Octavio Paz, *The Labyrinth of Solitude*, trans. Lysander Kemp et al. (orig. ed., 1961; Eng.-lang. ed., New York: Grove Weidenfeld, 1985).

78. Herbert Eugene Bolton, "The Mission as a Frontier Institution in the Spanish-American Colonies," *American Historical Review* 23 (1917): 42–61. See also John Francis Bannon, *Herbert Eugene Bolton* (Tucson: University of Arizona Press, 1978); David Weber, "Turner, the Boltonians, and the Borderlands"; Weber, "John Francis Bannon and the Historiography of the Spanish Borderlands: Retrospect and Prospect," *Journal of the Southwest* 29 (Winter 1987): 331–362; and Donald Worcester, "Herbert Eugene Bolton," in *Writing Western History*, 193–214.

79. George I. Sánchez, *Forgotten People: A Study of New Mexicans* (Albuquerque: University of New Mexico Press, 1940); Mario T. García, *Mexican Americans: Leadership, Ideology, and Identity, 1930–1960* (New Haven: Yale University Press, 1989), 252–272; Carey McWilliams, *North from Mexico* (New York, 1947); Robert Redfield, *Tepoztlán, a Mexican Village: A Study of Folk Life* (Chicago: University of Chicago Press, 1930); Redfield, *The Little Community, and Peasant Society and Culture* (1955, 1956; reprint, Chicago: University of Chicago Press, 1961); Oscar Lewis, *Life in a Mexican Village: Tepoztlán Restudied* (Urbana: University of Illinois Press, 1951).

80. Paz, *Labyrinth of Solitude*, 65, 66, 76, 77. The meaning of "otherness" for the book is much debated. In the text Paz repeatedly alludes to various well-known existentialists, notably Kierkegaard, Jose Ortega y Gasset, and Miguel de Unamuno, but in "The Other Mexico" (1970), reprinted in *Labyrinth of Solitude*, 287–290, he attributes Freud and Marx as generic sources as well. See also Claud Fell's interview with Paz, "Return to *The Labyrinth of Solitude*" (1970), reprinted in ibid., 329–353.

81. Paz, *Labyrinth of Solitude*, 86, 87, 128, 194. In "The Other Mexico," 309, Paz read this denial back onto the Aztecs who "wanted to forget their Chicimec (barbarian) past." See also ibid., 291: "To live history as a rite is our way of assuming it: if, for the Spaniards, the Conquest was a *deed,* for the Indians it was a *rite,* a human representation of a cosmic catastrophe. The sensibilities of the Mexican people have always oscillated between these two extremes, the deed and the rite."

82. "El Plan Espíritual de Aztlán," *Aztlán: Chicano Journal for the Social Sciences and the Arts* 1 (Spring 1970): iv, v; Jesus Chavarria, "A Precis and a Tentative Bibliography on Chicano History," ibid., 133–141; Juan Gomez-Quiñones, "Toward a Perspective on Chicano History," ibid. 2 (Fall 1971): 1–50; Gomez-Quiñones and Luis L. Arroyo, "On the State of Chicano History: Observations on Its Development, Interpretations, and Theory, 1970–1974," *Western Historical Quarterly* 7 (April 1976): 155–185; Carlos E. Cortes, "New Chicano Historiography," in Ellwyn R. Stoddard et al., eds., *Borderlands Sourcebook: A Guide to Literature on Northern Mexico and the American Southwest* (Norman: University of Oklahoma Press, 1983), 60–63; Weber, "Turner, the Boltonians, and the Borderlands"; Weber, "John Francis Bannon and the Historiography of the Spanish Borderlands," 331–363; Renato Rosaldo, "Chicano Studies, 1970–1984," *Annual Review of Anthropology* 14 (1985): 405–427; Yves-Charles Grandjeat, "Conflicts and Cohesiveness: The Elusive Quest for a Chicano History," *Aztlán* 18 (Spring 1987): 45–58; Alex Saragoza, "Recent Chicano Historiography: An Interpretive Essay," *Aztlán* 19 (Spring 1988–90): 1–77; Ramón A. Gutíerrez, "Community, Patriarchy and Individualism: The Politics of Chicano History and the Dream of Equality," *American Quarterly* 45 (March 1993): 44–72; David G. Gutierrez, "Significant to Whom? Mexican Americans and the History of the American West," *Western Historical Quarterly* 24 (November 1993): 519–539; Rodolfo Acuña, *Occupied America: A History of Chicanos* (New York, 1974). Of these various works Chavarria, Gomez-Quiñones, Cortes, and Weber all adopt Spanish borderlands history (or even Hubert Howe Bancroft, in the case of Gomez-Quiñones) as a starting point for their historiographies. The Cortes essay, in *Borderlands Sourcebook,* points to yet another development, the creation of a scholarly community devoted to transnational, international, or comparative studies of the United States–Mexico border regions.

83. John R. Chávez, *The Lost Land: Chicano Images of the Southwest* (Albuquerque: University of New Mexico Press, 1984). For critiques see Alex Saragoza, "Recent Chicano Historiography: An Interpretive Essay," *Aztlán* 19 (Spring 1988–90): 1–77. Compare the frontier regionalism of Chávez with that in Richard Nostrand, "A Changing Culture Region," in Stoddard et al., *Borderlands Sourcebook,* 6–15, and Oscar J. Martinez, *Troublesome Border* (Tucson: University of Arizona Press, 1983).

84. Norma Alarcón, "Chicana's Feminist Literature: A Re-Vision through Malintzín / or, Malintzín: Putting Flesh Back on the Object," in Cherrie Moraga and Gloria Anzaldúa, eds., *This Bridge Called My Back: Writings by Radical Women of Color,* 2d ed. (1981; 2d ed., New York: Kitchen Table, 1983), 182–190. See also Alarcón, "Traddutura, Traditora: A Paradigmatic Figure of Chicana Feminism," in Donna Przybylowicz et al., eds., *The Construction of Gender and Modes of Social Division,* special issue of *Cultural Critique* 13 (Fall 1989): 57–87, and Alarcón, "Chicana Feminism: In the Tracks of 'the' Native Woman," in Rosa Linda Fregoso and Angie Chabram, eds., *Chicana/o Cultural Representations: Reframing Alternative Critical Discourse,* special issue of *Cultural Studies* 4 (October 1990): 248–256.

85. Audre Lorde, "An Open Letter to Mary Daly," in Moraga and Anzal-

dúa, *This Bridge*, 96. On the book itself, see Norma Alarcón, "The Theoretical Subject(s) of *This Bridge Called My Back* and Anglo-American Feminism," in *Criticism in the Borderlands*, 28–39, and Sonia Saldivar-Hull, "Feminism on the Border," in ibid., 203–219. Gutierrez, "Significant for Whom?" includes the work in his ʼsurvey of Chicano history. See also Alma García, "The Development of Chicana Feminist Discourse, 1970–1980," *Gender and Society* 3 (1989): 217–238.

86. Gloria Anzaldúa, *Borderlands/ La Frontera: The New Mestiza* (San Francisco: Spinsters/Aunt Lute, 1987). See the discussions in Saldivar-Hull, "Feminism on the Border"; Ramon Saldívar, *Chicano Narrative*, 218; and José David Saldívar, "The Limits of Cultural Studies," *American Literary History* 2 (Summer 1990): 251–266. David Gutierrez, "Significant for Whom?" includes *This Bridge* in the canon of Chicano history and almost raises *Borderlands/ La Frontera* to the surface of his text, but finally leaves it in the footnotes. Ramon Gutierrez, "Community, Patriarchy, and Individualism," notes the questions of genre the book poses. Carla L. Peterson, "*Borderlands* in the Classroom," *American Quarterly* 45 (June 1993): 295–300, situates the text in an instructional context.

87. See, for instance, *Frontiers: A Journal of Women's Studies; boundary 2*; Maria Herrera-Sobek and Helena Maria Viramontes, eds., *Chicana Creativity and Criticism: Charting New Frontiers in American Literature* (Houston, 1988); and Annette Kolodny, "Letting Go Our Grand Obsessions: Notes towards a New Literary History of the American Frontiers," *American Literature* 64 (March 1992): 1–18.

88. Anzaldúa, *Borderlands/ La Frontera*, 3, 11. The quote follows and is partly a prose gloss and exegesis of a versified passage that likewise begins by placing Anzaldúa at the fence separating Tijuana from San Diego ("this thin edge of / barbwire"), identifies the border as a physical trauma, and concludes with "Que la Virgen de Guadalupe me cuide / Ay, ay ay, soy mexicana de este lado." Throughout the book the border is symbolized by metal instruments (chainlink, barbed-wire, fence rods, scalpel) and invasive verbs.

89. Ibid., 63, 64.

90. Ibid., 21, 27–34. Anzaldúa cites June Nash, "The Aztecs and the Ideology of Male Dominance," *Signs* (Winter 1978): 349–362.

91. Gilles Deleuze and Félix Guattari, *Anti-Oedipus: Capitalism and Schizophrenia* (1972; Eng.-lang. ed., Minneapolis: University of Minnesota Press, 1983). They described paranoia and schizophrenia as "two opposite poles" and claim that "oscillation between the poles is a constituent aspect" of "delirium"; see p. 376. See also Fredric Jameson's rendition in his "Postmodernism and Consumer Society," in Hal Foster, ed., *The Anti-Aesthetic: Essays on Postmodern Culture* (Port Townsend, Wash.: Bay Press, 1983), 111–125.

92. Even Hayden White's early essays had pointed in this direction. See his *Tropics of Discourse: Essays in Cultural Criticism* (Baltimore: Johns Hopkins University Press, 1978); *The Content of the Form: Narrative Discourse and Historical Representation* (Baltimore: Johns Hopkins University Press, 1987); and "Historical Emplotment and the Problem of Truth," in Saul Friedlander, ed., *Probing the Limits of Representation: Nazism and the 'Final Solution'* (Cambridge: Harvard University Press, 1992), 37–53.

93. Anzaldúa, *Borderlands/La Frontera*, 67.

94. Ibid., 79, 80.

95. It is not clear if this pattern corresponds to that delineated in Jörn Rüsen, *Lebendige Geschichte. Grundzüge einer Historik III: Formen und Funktionen des historischen wissens* (Göttingen: Vandenhoek and Ruprecht, 1989), 39–61; Rüsen, *Studies in Metahistory* (Pretoria: Human Sciences Research Council, 1993), 3–14. It deviates from White's Vichian cycle of romance, tragedy, comedy, and farce.

96. The quickest of glances at the changing tables of contents in the *American Quarterly* suggests the breadth of this debate. See, for instance, Linda Kerber, "Diversity and the Transformation of American Studies," *American Quarterly* 41 (September 1989): 415–431; Elizabeth Fox-Genovese, "Between Individualism and Fragmentation: American Culture and the New Literary Studies of Race and Gender," *American Quarterly* 42 (March 1990): 7–34; and Gary Kulik, ed., "Special Issue on Multiculturalism," *American Quarterly* 45 (June 1993).

97. Smith, "Symbol and Idea in *Virgin Land*," 22, 33 n.9. Fredric Jameson, *The Political Unconscious: Narrative as a Socially Symbolic Act* (Ithaca: Cornell University Press, 1981); Smith refers especially to p. 87. At roughly the same time, the other doyen of American studies, Leo Marx, similarly linked his work to newer forms of criticism, specifically, that of Bakhtin, in his introduction to *The Pilot and the Passenger,* ix–xvii.

98. Jameson, *Political Unconscious*, 17–101, 19, 20. Compare Hayden White, "Getting Out of History: Jameson's Redemption of Narrative" (1982), in White, *The Content of the Form*, 142–167, with Dominick LaCapra, "Marxism in the Textual Maelstrom: Fredric Jameson's *The Political Unconscious* (1982), in his *Rethinking Intellectual History: Texts, Contexts, Language* (Ithaca: Cornell University Press, 1983), 234–266.

99. Jean-François Lyotard, *La Condition postmoderne: Rapport sur le savoir* (Paris: Les Editions de Minuit, 1979); Lyotard, *The Postmodern Condition: A Report on Knowledge,* trans. Geoff Bennington and Brian Massumi (Eng.-lang. ed., Minneapolis: University of Minnesota Press, 1984); Lyotard, *Instructions païennes* (Paris: Galilee, 1977). This section of his argument is developed more fully in *The Differend: Phrases in Dispute,* trans. George Van den Abeele (orig. ed., 1983; Eng.-lang. ed., Minneapolis: University of Minnesota Press, 1988). See also his refinement in "Histoire universelle et differences culturelles," *Critique* 41 (mai 1985): 559–568. I have treated this at greater length in Kerwin Lee Klein, "In Search of Narrative Mastery: Postmodernism and the Peoples without History," *History and Theory* 34 (1995): 275–298.

100. Lyotard, *Postmodern Condition*, 37, 41. See also David Carroll, "Narrative, Heterogeneity, and the Question of the Political: Bakhtin and Lyotard," in Murray Krieger, ed., *The Aims of Representation* (New York: Columbia University Press, 1987), 69–106; J. M. Bernstein, "Grand Narratives," in David Wood, ed., *On Paul Ricoeur: Narrative and Interpretation* (London, 1991), 102–123; and Alphonso Lingis, "Some Questions about Lyotard's Postmodern Legitimation Narrative," *Philosophy and Social Criticism* 20 (1994): 1–12.

101. Lyotard, *Postmodern Condition*, 19–23, 60; Lyotard, *Le Différend* (Paris: Les Editions de Minuit, 1983); Lyotard, *The Differend,* 151–181; the

citation is from p. 155. The claim, as it is stated here, is highly problematic; again, see Klein, "In Search of Narrative Mastery."

102. Stephen J. Greenblatt, "Towards a Poetics of Culture" (1986), reprinted in his *Learning to Curse,* 151. Greenblatt mentions, without citation, Wolfgang Iser as another source of the trope of "oscillating discourses." See also two more recent works in the same volume, "Introduction," 1–15, and "Resonance and Wonder," 161–183. Compare Greenblatt's gloss with those of Mark Poster, "Postmodernity and the Politics of Multiculturalism: The Lyotard-Habermas Debate over Social Theory," *Modern Fiction Studies* 38 (Autumn 1993): 567–581, and Seyla Benhabib, "Epistemologies of Postmodernism: A Rejoinder to Jean-François Lyotard," *New German Critique* 33 (Fall 1984): 103–126; and Benhabib, "Legitimacy and the Postmodern Condition: The Political Thought of Jean-François Lyotard," *Praxis International* 7 (Winter 1987/88): 286–304.

103. Clifford, *Predicament of Culture,* esp. 13–15. For the "monotonous alternation" of the "bad infinity," see Georg W. F. Hegel, *Science of Logic,* trans. A. V. Miller (Eng.-lang. ed., Atlantic Highlands, N.J.: Humanities Press International, 1989), 137–143, 150–154. For Clifford's comments on Hayden White, see his "Introduction: Partial Truths," in James Clifford and George E. Marcus, eds., *Writing Culture: The Poetics and Politics of Ethnography* (Berkeley: University of California Press, 1986), 1–26. See also Klein, "In Search of Narrative Mastery."

104. Claude Lévi-Strauss, *Tristes Tropiques,* trans. John and Doreen Weightman (orig. ed., 1955; Eng.-lang. ed., New York: Atheneum, 1977); on memory see esp. pp. 27, 28, 33, 34, 39, 49. Among other critical readings see Clifford, *Predicament of Culture,* and Clifford Geertz, *The Interpretation of Cultures* (New York: Basic Books, 1973), 345–359. Micaela di Leonardo, "Malinowski's Nephews," *Nation* 248 (March 13, 1989): 350–352, contrasts Geertz and Clifford.

105. Lévi-Strauss, *Tristes Tropiques,* 52, 285, 286.

106. Ibid., 120, 275, 331, 333, 334, 336, 337, 338.

107. Claude Lévi-Strauss, *The Savage Mind* (1962; Eng.-lang. ed., Chicago: University of Chicago Press, 1966), esp. 1–34, 217–269; quotation from p. 257. For his fullest explication of totemism, see his *Totemism,* trans. Rodney Needham (orig. ed., 1962; Eng.-lang. ed., Boston: Beacon, 1963).

108. Jacques Derrida, *Of Grammatology,* trans. Gayatri Spivak (orig. ed., 1967; Eng.-lang. ed., Baltimore: Johns Hopkins University Press, 1976), 131. See also ibid., 24–27; Derrida, "The Pit and the Pyramid: Introduction to Hegel's Semiology" (1968), in *Margins of Philosophy,* trans. Alan Bass (orig. ed., 1972; Eng.-lang. ed., Chicago: University of Chicago Press, 1982), 69–108. Derrida's brief comment may be counterintuitive, but it does bring out the ambiguities in Lévi-Strauss; though the anthropologist associates writing with enslavement, Derrida's suggestion that this understanding calls forth the possibility of writing as liberation resonates with Lévi-Strauss's hopeful implication that careful research might recover a "historical dimension" for pre-Columbian America.

109. The best reading of Clifford here is *not* an ironic viewpoint. There is irony aplenty in *Predicament of Culture,* but the denunciations (or celebrations)

of his text as a catachretic affirmation of relativism strike me as overwrought. For different readings see P. Steven Sangren, "Rhetoric and the Authority of Ethnography: 'Postmodernism' and the Social Reproduction of Texts," *Current Anthropology* 29 (June 1988): 405–424, and Arnold Krupat, *Ethnocriticism: Ethnography, History, Literature* (Berkeley: University of California Press, 1992), 101–126.

110. Clifford, "Identity in Mashpee," in his *Predicament of Culture,* 277, 289. See the different accounts of the case in Paul Brodeur, *Restitution: The Land Claims of the Mashpee, Passamaquoddy, and Penobscot Indians of New England* (Boston: Northeastern University Press, 1985); Francis G. Hutchins, *Mashpee: The Story of Cape Cod's Indian Town* (West Franklin, N.J.: Amarta Press, 1979); and Jack Campisi, *The Mashpee Indians: Tribe on Trial* (Syracuse: Syracuse University Press, 1991).

111. Ibid., 302, 317.

112. Ibid., 329. For a different reading see Krupat, *Ethnocriticism,* 101–126. On oral literature and legal evidence, see Allogan Slagle, "The Native American Tradition and Legal Status: Tolowa Tales and Tolowa Places," *Cultural Critique* 7 (Fall 1987): 103–118.

113. Clifford, *Predicament of Culture,* 14, 333. See also the account in Campisi, *The Mashpee Indians,* esp. 14–15, 43–45. Brodeur's account, in *Restitution,* 59, 60, of the coverage by the *Wall Street Journal* is also relevant.

114. Clifford, *Predicament of Culture,* 342. In part, the difficulties lie in the different uses of "metanarrative." For Lyotard any narrative winding the names of different groups into a single story is a *grand récit.* For Clifford any big story emplotting a naively unitary subject seems to be a master narrative. On Lyotard's account, both of Clifford's plots would be a metanarrative; on Clifford's operational usage, Lyotard's imagined stories naming a "single name" might qualify for the insidious label. See Klein, "In Search of Narrative Mastery."

115. See also Richard Rorty, "Habermas and Lyotard on Postmodernity" (1984), in *Essays on Heidegger and Others: Philosophical Papers* (Cambridge: Cambridge University Press, 1991), 2:164–175, and "Cosmopolitanism without Emancipation: A Response to Jean-François Lyotard" (1985), in *Objectivity, Relativism, and Truth: Philosophical Papers* (Cambridge: Cambridge University Press, 1991), 1:211–222. Rorty uses "metanarrative" differently from Lyotard, to distinguish those tales that explicitly ground their truth claims in some transcendent, ahistorical order. See their brief exchange in "Discussion entre Jean-François Lyotard et Richard Rorty," *Critique* 41 (mai 1985): 581–584, and Klein, "In Search of Narrative Mastery."

116. Jacques Derrida, "Différance" (1968), in *Margins of Philosophy,* trans. Alan Bass (orig. ed., 1972; Eng.-lang. ed., Chicago: University of Chicago Press, 1982), 11; Derrida, "Structure, Sign, and Play in the Discourse of the Human Sciences" (1966), in *Writing and Difference,* trans. Alan Bass (orig. ed., 1967; Eng.-lang. ed., Chicago: University of Chicago Press, 1978), 293. But see also Paul de Man, "The Rhetoric of Blindness," in *Blindness and Insight: Essays in the Rhetoric of Contemporary Criticism,* 2d ed. (1971; 2d ed., Minneapolis: University of Minnesota Press, 1983), esp. 120–122.

117. Lévi-Strauss, *Savage Mind,* 262.

118. Clifford's treatment of the Mashpee trial subsequently appeared as a key datum in the center of a critical maelstrom over multiculturalism. See Walter Benn Michaels, "Race into Culture: A Critical Genealogy of Cultural Identity," *Critical Inquiry* 18 (Summer 1992): 655–685; Daniel Boyarin and Jonathan Boyarin, "Diaspora: Generation and the Ground of Jewish Identity," ibid., 19 (Summer 1993): 693–725; Avery Gordon and Christopher Newfield, "White Philosophy," ibid. 20 (Summer 1994): 737–757; Walter Benn Michaels, "The No-Drop Rule," ibid., 758–769.

119. Michael S. Roth, "Introduction," in Roth, ed., *Rediscovering History: Culture, Politics, and the Psyche* (Stanford: Stanford University Press, 1994), 3. Such concerns have shadowed the much celebrated return of history to anthropology. James D. Faubion, "History in Anthropology," *Annual Review of Anthropology* 22 (1993): 35–54, offers a good overview of this vast literature. See also Nicholas Thomas, *Out of Time: History and Evolution in Anthropological Discourse* (Cambridge: Cambridge University Press, 1989); William H. Lyon, "Anthropology and History: Can the Two Sister Disciplines Communicate?" *American Indian Culture and Research Journal* 18 (Spring 1994): 159–178; Clifford Geertz, "History and Anthropology," *New Literary History* 21 (Winter 1990): 321–336; Renato Rosaldo, "Response to Geertz," ibid., 337–342; Raymond J. DeMaillie, " 'These Have Ears': Narrative and the Ethnohistorical Method," *Ethnohistory* 40 (Fall 1993): 515–539; John Comaroff and Jean Comaroff, *Ethnography and the Historical Imagination* (Boulder, Colo.: Westview Press, 1992); Jay O'Brian and William Roseberry, eds., *Golden Ages, Dark Ages: Imagining the Past in Anthropology and History* (Berkeley: University of California Press, 1991); and Micaela di Leonardo, "Gender, Culture, and Political Economy: Feminist Anthropology in Historical Perspective," in di Leonardo, ed., *Gender at the Crossroads of Knowledge: Feminist Anthropology in the Postmodern Era* (Berkeley: University of California Press, 1991), 1–50.

120. Calvin Martin, ed., *The American Indian and the Problem of History* (New York: Oxford University Press, 1987), especially "Introduction" (pp. 3–26), "The Metaphysics of Writing Indian-White History" (1979) (pp. 27–34), and "Epilogue" (pp. 192–220); citations from pp. 6, 15, 195. At the time, what Martin had in mind was not entirely clear. His first book, *Keepers of the Game: Indian-Animal Relationships and the Fur Trade* (Berkeley: University of California Press, 1978), offered an imaginative interpretation of the origins and meanings of the fur trade and the Mic Mac Indians but had evoked a torrent of criticism from scholars who questioned its evidentiary base. See Shepard Krech III, ed., *Indians, Animals, and the Fur Trade: A Critique of Keepers of the Game* (Athens: University of Georgia Press, 1981). Martin's *In the Spirit of the Earth* (Baltimore: Johns Hopkins University Press, 1993) mixes cultural ecology with New Age religiosity.

121. Richard Drinnon, "The Metaphysics of Dancing Tribes," in Calvin Martin, *American Indian and the Problem of History*, 106–112; Drinnon, *Facing West: The Metaphysics of Indian-Hating and Empire-Building* (Minneapolis: University of Minnesota Press, 1980); Henry F. Dobyns, "Demographics of Native American History," in Martin, *American Indian and the Problem of History*, 67–73; Neal Salisbury, "American Indians and American History," in ibid.,

46–53; Robert Berkhofer, "Cultural Pluralism versus Ethnocentrism in the New Indian History," in ibid., 35–44; Mary Young, "Pagans, Converts, and Backsliders, All: A Secular View of the Metaphysics of Indian-White Relations," in ibid., 75–82; Michael Dorris, "Indians on the Shelf," in ibid., 98–104.

122. Mircea Eliade, *Cosmos and History: The Myth of the Eternal Return,* trans. Willard R. Trask (Eng.-lang. ed., New York: Harper and Row, 1959). See esp. Martin's appeal to Eliade in his "Epilogue." Martin also invokes Eliot, Huxley, and Jung as well as (more relevant for our inquiry) Lévi-Strauss. The literature on myth is far too grand to survey here. Compare Hans Blumenberg, *Work on Myth,* trans. Robert M. Wallace (orig. ed., 1979; Eng.-lang. ed., Cambridge: MIT Press, 1985), and Détienne, *The Creation of Mythology.* Jonathan D. Hill, ed., *Rethinking Myth and History: Indigenous South American Perspectives on the Past* (Urbana: University of Illinois Press, 1988), anthologizes recent discussions.

123. For Martin's comments on literate natives, see "Epilogue," in Eliade, *Cosmos and History,* 211. In support, he cites Frederick Turner, *Beyond Geography: The Western Spirit against the Wilderness* (New York: Viking, 1980). Susan Hegeman's important essay "History, Ethnography, and Myth," *Social Text* 23 (Fall/Winter 1989): 144–160, makes similar points. For an interesting discussion of linear and cyclic temporal figures in Native American thought, see Michael Harkin, "History, Narrative, and Temporality: Examples from the Northwest Coast," *Ethnohistory* 35 (Spring 1988): 99–130.

124. Thomas Biolsi, "Review Article: *The American Indian and the Problem of History,*" *American Indian Quarterly* 13 (Summer 1989): 262, 263. See also Hegeman, "History, Ethnography, and Myth."

125. Frances E. Mascia-Lees and Patricia Sharpe, "Culture, Power, and Text: Anthropology and Literature Confront Each 'Other,' " *American Literary History* 4 (Winter 1992): 678–696; Richard Rodriguez, *Days of Obligation: An Argument with My Mexican Father* (New York: Penguin, 1992). For very different but important contributions to the recent literature on posthistory, see Francis Fukuyama, *The End of History and the Last Man* (New York: Avon, 1992), and Lutz Niethammer, *Posthistoire: Has History Come to an End?* trans. Patrick Camiller (orig. ed., 1989; Eng.-lang. ed., London: Verso, 1992).

126. Jan Vansina, *Oral Tradition: A Study in Historical Methodology* (Chicago: Aldine, 1961); John Gumperz and Dell Hymes, eds., "The Ethnography of Communication," special issue of *American Anthropologist* 66 (1965); Dennis Tedlock, "Towards an Oral Poetics," *New Literary History* 8 (Spring 1977): 509; Tedlock, "Phonography and the Problem of Time" (1981), in his *The Spoken Word and the Work of Interpretation* (Philadelphia: University of Pennsylvania Press, 1983), 206, 207; Joel Sherzer and Anthony C. Woodbury, eds., *Native American Discourse: Poetics and Rhetoric* (Cambridge: Cambridge University Press, 1987), 9, 10, 11. For an overview of this immense literature, see David Murray, *Forked Tongues: Speech, Writing, and Representation in North American Indian Texts* (Bloomington: Indiana University Press, 1991).

127. For discussions of Native American scholars and historical imagination, see the special issue of *Historical Reflections/Réflexions Historiques* 21 (Spring 1995), especially M. A. Jaimes Guerrero, "Afterword: Shifting Para-

digms for an Anticolonialist Discourse," 385–392. For works that suggest the variety of interpretive approaches we might think of as "source criticism," compare Andrew O. Wiget, "Truth and the Hopi: An Historiographic Study of Documented Oral Tradition Concerning the Coming of the Spanish," *Ethnohistory* 29 (1982): 181–199, and Paula Gunn Allen, "Kochinnenako in Academe: Three Approaches to Interpreting a Keres Indian Tale," in *The Sacred Hoop: Recovering the Feminine in American Indian Traditions* (Boston: Beacon, 1986), 222–244.

128. Keith H. Basso, " 'Stalking with Stories': Names, Places, and Moral Narratives among the Western Apache," in his *Western Apache Language and Culture: Essays in Linguistic Anthropology* (Tucson: University of Arizona Press, 1990), 114. For other works suggesting the complexity of narrative form in storytelling across ethnic boundaries, see Basso, " 'Speaking With Names': Language and Landscape among the Western Apache," *Cultural Anthropology* 3 (May 1988): 99–130, and Ronald Scollon and Suzanne Scollon, *Narrative, Literacy, and Face in Interethnic Communication* (Norwood, N.J.: ABLEX, 1981).

129. Leslie Silko, "Language and Literature from a Pueblo Indian Perspective," in Leslie A. Fiedler and Houston A. Baker, eds., *English Literature: Opening Up the Canon,* selected papers from the English Institute, n.s. 4 (Baltimore: Johns Hopkins University Press, 1979), 54.

130. Silko, "Language and Literature from a Pueblo Indian Perspective," 54, 55.

A Bibliographic Note

Even a selective bibliography of works in history and theory could run to thousands, if not hundreds of thousands of items. Such journals as *History and Theory, History and Memory, Clio, New Literary History, Philosophy of the Social Sciences, Critical Inquiry,* and *Annual Reviews in Anthropology* publish regularly on these topics and are indispensable to keeping abreast of current scholarship. This brief bibliographic note on general works in history and theory may help to indicate some of the recent books important to this study which have not been treated in the body of the text.

We do not have a book-length survey of twentieth-century philosophy of history. Overviews may be pieced together from such anthologies as Patrick Gardiner, ed., *Theories of History* (New York: The Free Press, 1959); Hans Meyerhoff, ed., *The Philosophy of History in Our Time* (Garden City, N.Y.: Doubleday, 1959); Sidney Hook, ed., *Philosophy and History: A Symposium* (New York: New York University Press, 1963); William H. Dray, ed., *Philosophical Analysis and History* (New York: Harper and Row, 1966); W. H. Burston and D. Thompson, eds., *Studies in the Nature and Teaching of History* (London: Routledge, 1967); Hans-Georg Gadamer, ed., *Truth and Historicity* (La Haye: Martinus Nijhoff, 1972); Robert Canary and Henry Kozicki, eds., *The Writing of History: Literary Form and Historical Understanding* (Madison: University of Wisconsin Press, 1978); Yirmiahu Yovel, ed., *Philosophy of History and Action* (Dordrecht: D. Reidel, 1978); Georg Iggers and Harold Parker, eds., *International Handbook of Historical Studies* (Westport, Conn.: Greenwood, 1979); L. Pompa and W. H. Dray, eds., *Substance and Form in History* (Edinburgh: The University of Edinburgh Press, 1981); Richard Rorty, J. B. Schneewind, and Quentin Skinner, eds., *Philosophy in History* (Cambridge: Cambridge University Press, 1984); Bernard P. Dauenhauer, ed., *At the Nexus of Philosophy and History* (Athens: University of Georgia Press, 1987); and Frank Ankersmit and Hans Kellner, eds., *A New Philosophy of History* (Chicago: University of Chicago Press, 1995).

W. H. Walsh, *Philosophy of History: An Introduction* (1951; rev. ed., New York: Harper, 1960), and William H. Dray, *Philosophy of History* (Englewood Cliffs, N.J.: Prentice-Hall, 1964), remain useful introductions to postwar "critical" philosophy of history.

A number of twentieth-century philosophical texts are crucial to historiography even though their authors are not primarily concerned with historical criticism. Benedetto Croce, *History: Its Theory and Practice,* trans. Douglas Ainslie (orig. ed., 1916; Eng.-lang. ed., New York: Russell and Russell, 1960), and *History as the Story of Liberty* (1938; Eng.-lang. ed., New York: Meridian, 1955), are indispensable, as is R. G. Collingwood, *The Idea of History* (Cambridge: Oxford University Press, 1946). Less cited but valuable is *R. G. Collingwood: An Autobiography* (Cambridge: Clarendon Press, 1936). Raymond Aron, *Introduction to the Philosophy of History: An Essay on the Limits of Historical Objectivity,* trans. George Irwin (orig. ed., 1938; Eng.-lang. ed., Boston: Beacon, 1961), is sometimes described as the first "critical" philosophy of history. Michael Oakshott, *Experience and Its Modes* (Cambridge: Cambridge University Press, 1933), in many ways anticipated later discussions about "constructionism." Martin Heidegger's formidable *Being and Time,* trans. John MacQuarrie and Edward Robinson (orig. ed., 1927; Eng.-lang. ed., San Francisco: HarperSanFrancisco, 1993), is crucial for changing notions of historicity. Some of its influence can be seen in the important works of his student Hans-Georg Gadamer, especially his classic *Truth and Method,* trans. Joel Weinsheimer and Donald G. Marshall (orig. ed., 1960; 2d Eng.-lang. ed., New York: Crossroad, 1989), and more recently, *Reason in the Age of Science,* trans. Frederick G. Lawrence (Cambridge: MIT Press, 1981). John Dewey, *Logic: The Theory of Inquiry* (New York: Henry Holt, 1938), especially chapter 12, offers the most explicit, if not the most lucid account of Dewey's pragmatic narrativism. More accessible are his *Reconstruction in Philosophy* (New York: Henry Holt, 1920), and *Experience and Nature* (La Salle, Ill.: Open Court Press, 1929). More recently, the work of Joseph Margolis, especially *The Flux of History and the Flux of Science* (Berkeley: University of California Press, 1993) and *Interpretation Radical but Not Unruly* (Berkeley: University of California Press, 1995), mediates "Anglo-American" analysis and "continental" criticism.

Three books effectively opened the narrativist debates in history and theory. W. B. Gallie, *Philosophy and the Historical Understanding* (New York: Schocken Books, 1964), appeared first but is today the least cited. Arthur C. Danto's *Analytical Philosophy of History* (1965) has been more influential and has been reprinted, with some additional essays, as *Narration and Knowledge* (New York: Columbia University Press, 1985). Morton White's *Foundations of Historical Knowledge* (New York: Harper and Row, 1965), remains useful, but see also his *Toward Reunion in Philosophy* (Cambridge: Harvard University Press, 1956), and *Pragmatism and the American Mind: Essays and Reviews in Philosophy and Intellectual History* (London: Oxford University Press, 1973).

Narrativist accounts of history have proliferated since the mid-sixties. Hayden White's *Metahistory: The Historical Imagination in Nineteenth-Century Europe* (Baltimore: Johns Hopkins University Press, 1973), remains the best known, but his later collections of essays, *The Tropics of Discourse: Essays in Cultural Criticism* (Baltimore: Johns Hopkins University Press, 1978), and *The Content of the Form: Narrative Discourse and Historical Representation* (Baltimore: Johns Hopkins University Press, 1987), should be read for the often surprising changes they reveal in White's thought. The more rigorous (and superbly readable) work of Louis O. Mink deserves more attention from historians. His essays, collected in *Historical Understanding*, ed. Brian Fay et al. (Ithaca: Cornell University Press, 1987), journey comfortably through speculative, analytic, and narrativist philosophy of history. Sande Cohen, *Historical Culture: On the Recoding of an Academic Discipline* (Berkeley: University of California Press, 1986), offers the sort of skeptical critique of historical narrative that is often attributed to White. In sharp contrast to Cohen's work is David Carr's *Time, Narrative, and History* (Indianapolis: Indiana University Press, 1986), a phenomenological defense of historical narrative. More idiosyncratic, but provocative, is F. R. Ankersmit, *Narrative Logic: A Semantic Analysis of the Historian's Language* (The Hague: Martinus Nijhoff, 1983). The work of Paul Ricoeur is essential, especially his *History and Truth* (1964; Eng.-lang. ed. Evanston, Ill.: Northwestern University Press, 1965) and *Time and Narrative*, vols. 1–3, trans. David Pellauer and Kathleen Blamey (orig. ed., 1980–1983; Eng.-lang. ed., Chicago: University of Chicago Press, 1983–1985).

A variety of other historiographic works draw from linguistics and literary criticism without foregrounding narrativity. Among the most important are the works of Dominick LaCapra: *Rethinking Intellectual History: Texts, Contexts, Language* (Ithaca: Cornell University Press, 1978), *History and Criticism* (Ithaca: Cornell University Press, 1987), and *Soundings in Critical Theory* (Ithaca: Cornell University Press, 1989). Of the many writers on historical discourse, Hans Kellner, *Language and Historical Representation: Getting the Story Crooked* (Madison: University of Wisconsin Press, 1989), and Stephen Bann, *The Inventions of History: Essays on the Representation of the Past* (Manchester: Manchester University Press, 1990), are perhaps the closest to Hayden White in terms of interests and vocabularies. Still, there is nothing like a "Whitean" school.

Michel Foucault's histories have probably had a greater impact on recent Anglo-American historiography. One could list virtually all of his works, but *The Archeology of Knowledge* (1971; Eng.-lang. ed., New York: Pantheon, 1972) is especially valuable for its thematization of Foucault's early approach to intellectual history. Michel de Certeau, *The Writing of History*, trans. Tom Conley (orig. ed., 1975; Eng.-lang. ed., New York: Columbia University Press, 1988), offers a structuralist analysis of historical discourse attentive to ethnography and psychoanalysis. Joan Wallach Scott, *Gender and the Politics of History* (New York: Columbia University Press, 1988), is a pioneering work in gender analysis, poststructuralism, and historiography. The essays of Lionel Gossman, *Between History and Literature* (Cambridge: Harvard University Press, 1990), and Reinhart Koselleck, *Futures Past: On the Semantics of Historical Time*, trans. Keith Tribe (orig. ed., 1979; Eng.-lang. ed., Cambridge: MIT Press, 1985), deserve special attention. Koselleck's work, in particular, is an exemplary exploration of the historicity of historical language. Jörn Rüsen, *Grundzüge einer Historik*, vols. 1–3 (Göttingen: Vandenhoeck 7 Ruprecht, 1983–1989), is one of the more impressive studies by a professional historian. Some of his work is available in English as *Studies in Metahistory*, ed. Pieter Duvenage (Pretoria: Human Sciences Research Council, 1993). Hans Ulrich Gumbrecht, *Making Sense in Life and Literature*, trans. Glen Burns (Minneapolis: University of Minnesota Press, 1992), develops a phenomenology of historiographic reading. Robert F. Berkhofer Jr., *Beyond the Great Story* (Cambridge: Harvard University Press, 1995), is a postmodern sequel to the same author's classic methods text, *A Behavioral Approach to Historical Analysis* (New York: The Free Press, 1968). Somewhat less rewarding are Jack Hexter, *Doing History* (Bloomington: Indiana University Press, 1971), and Jacques Rancière, *The Names of History*, trans. Hassan Melehy (orig. ed., 1992; Eng.-lang. ed., Minneapolis: University of Minnesota Press, 1994). H. Aram Veeser, ed., *The New Historicism* (New York: Routledge, 1989), offers a quick introduction to the recent enthusiasms for historicist literary criticism and includes many theoretical essays by principals in those debates. Lynn Hunt, ed., *The New Cultural History* (Berkeley: University of California Press, 1989), aims to make such studies accessible to nonspecialists.

Analytic or critical philosophy of history did not end with the rise of narratology, and a number of works demonstrate the continuing vitality of this interdisciplinary field even as it moves away from its earlier focus on the covering law battles. Christopher Lloyd, *Explanation in Social History* (Oxford: Basil Blackwell, 1986) and *Structures in History* (Oxford: Basil Blackwell, 1993), explore a variety of topics in philosophy of social science while focusing on theory building in social history. A similar focus, but somewhat different approach, can be found in Murray G. Murphey, *Our Knowledge of the Historical Past* (Indianapolis: Bobbs-Merrill, 1973) and *Philosophical Foundations of Historical Knowledge* (Albany: SUNY Press, 1993). Geoffrey Hawthorn, *Plausible Worlds: Possibility and Understanding in History and the Social Sciences* (Cambridge: Cambridge University Press, 1991), centers on counterfactuals but opens out onto much broader topics. Paul A. Roth's *Meaning and Method in the Social Sciences: A Case for Methodological Pluralism* (Ithaca: Cornell University Press, 1987); Jürgen Habermas, *On the Logic of the Social Sciences*, trans. Shierry W. Nicholsen and Jerry A. Stark (orig. ed., 1967; Eng.-lang. ed., Cambridge: MIT Press, 1988); and Hilary Putnam, *Reason, Truth, and History* (Cambridge: Cambridge University Press, 1981), cover many of these same issues and relate them to history. Readers searching for a less abstract, but still rigorous account may find it in Raymond Martin, *The Past Within Us: An Empirical Approach to Philosophy of History* (Princeton: Princeton University Press, 1989), which is remarkable both for its lucidity and its attention to historical texts. Peter McClelland, *Causal Explanation and Model Building in History, Economics, and the New Economic History* (Ithaca: Cornell University Press, 1975), is similarly accessible. Donald McCloskey, *If You're So Smart: The Narrative of Expertise in Economics* (Chicago: University of Chicago Press, 1990), is an engaging account of narrative in economics aimed at the general reader.

For a more technical contribution to recent discussions of causality, see G. H. von Wright's *Explanation and Understanding* (Ithaca: Cornell University Press, 1971). Wright's book rehabilitated teleological causation and provoked a volume of responses: Juha Manninen and Raimo Tuomela, eds., *Essays on Explanation and Understanding* (Dordrecht: D. Reidel, 1976). For one rendition of teleological causation, see Rex Martin, *Historical Explanations: Reenactment and Practical Inference* (Ithaca: Cornell University Press, 1977). C. Beham McCullagh, *Justifying Causal Descriptions* (Cambridge: Cambridge University Press, 1984), offers an intriguing look at the interaction of logic and evidence. J. L. Gorman, *The Expression of Historical Knowledge* (Edinburgh: Edinburgh University Press, 1982), suggests that poetic conceptions of history may not be incompatible with historical science. Readers should also compare Leon J. Goldstein, *Historical Knowing* (Austin: University of Texas Press, 1976), with Maurice Mandelbaum's *The Problem of Historical Knowledge: An Answer to Relativism* (New York: Liveright, 1938), *The Anatomy of Historical Knowledge* (Baltimore: Johns Hopkins University Press, 1977), and *Philosophy, History, and the Sciences: Selected Critical Essays* (Baltimore: Johns Hopkins University Press, 1984). Goldstein is frequently denounced for his skeptical "constructionist" take on historical discourse, but see the more radical argument in Jack W. Meiland, *Scepticism and Historical Knowledge* (New York: Random House, 1965). William H. Dray, *On History and Philosophers of History* (Leiden and New York: E. J. Brill, 1989), collects recent essays by the famous "intentionalist." Haskell Fain's *Between Philosophy and History: The Resurrection of Speculative Philosophy within the Analytic Tradition* (Princeton: Princeton University Press, 1970) has not received the attention it deserves, especially given its exposition of themes later developed by Hayden White.

Finally, the "end of history" and "posthistory" have been among the more intriguing metaphors in recent historiographic discourse. This debate now bids to replace the old disputes over the relations of liberalism and history found in such classic texts as Reinhold Niebuhr, *Faith and History: A Comparison of Christian and Modern Views of History* (New York: Charles Scribner's Sons, 1949); Roderick Seidenberg, *Posthistoric Man: An Inquiry* (orig. ed., 1950; reprint, Boston: Beacon, 1957); Isaiah Berlin, *Historical Inevitability* (London: Oxford University Press, 1954); Charles Frankel, *The Case for Modern Man* (New York: Harper and Brothers, 1955); and Karl Popper, *The Poverty of Historicism* (London: Routledge and Kegan Paul, 1957). Francis Fukuyama, *The End of History and the Last Man* (New York: Avon, 1992), is the most influential of the recent works claiming that history has finally come to an end. Of the many commentaries on Fukuyama, some of the best are found in Arthur M. Melzer et al., eds., *History and the Idea of Progress* (Ithaca: Cornell University Press, 1995). Lutz Niethammer, *Posthistoire: Has History Come to an End?* trans. Patrick Camiller (orig. ed., 1989; Eng.-lang. ed., London: Verso, 1992), traces "posthistoire" in recent German thought. Perry Anderson, *A Zone of Engagement* (London: Verso, 1992), offers an intriguing comparison of Fukuyama and "posthistoire" thinkers.

Index